BLOWBACK

How the Feud Between the CIA & FBI Let 9-11 Happen

Peter Kross

Adventures Unlimited Press

Dedication:

To Beth and Joe, New Beginnings.

Books by Peter Kross:

The JFK Files
The Vatican Conspiracy
American Conspiracy Files
Tales From Langley
The Secret History of the United States
JFK: The French Connection
Spies, Traitors and Moles
The Encyclopedia of World War II Spies
Oswald, the CIA and the Warren Commission

BLOWBACK

How the Feud Between the CIA & FBI Let 9-11 Happen

Peter Kross

Blowback: How the Feud Between the CIA & the FBI Let 9-11 Happen

by Peter Kross

ISBN: 978-1-939149-20-6

Published by:
Adventures Unlimited Press
One Adventure Place
Kempton, Illinois 60946 USA
auphq@frontiernet.net

Printed in the United States of America

Cover by Joe Boyer

AdventuresUnlimitedPress.com

TABLE OF CONTENTS

"It takes a thousand voices to tell one story"

—Native American proverb.

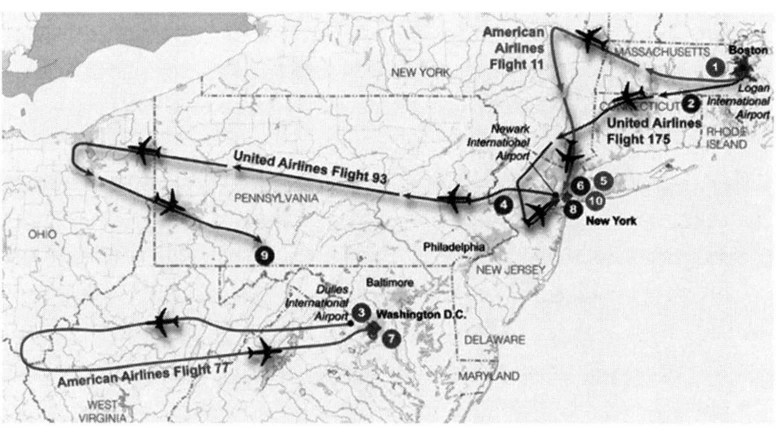

Flight paths of the highjacked planes on September 11, 2001.

Introduction

There are certain events in American history that stand out starkly in the mind. The assassination of President John F. Kennedy on November 22, 1963 is indelibly etched in the American psyche, as was the destruction of the *Challenger* space craft. For an older generation, the defining moment was the December 7, 1941 attack by Japan on our fleet in Pearl Harbor, Hawaii, which set off World War II. The events of September 11, 2001 was another dagger sent into the heart of the American nation, one that was entirely unanticipated. The 9-11 attacks also led directly to the U.S. invasion of Iraq in thousands of American soldiers died, in what some would say was an unnecessary war, the consequences we are still dealing with as of this writing. For over two hundred years the United States believed it was protected by two oceans, and that any catastrophic events would take place elsewhere. In our innocent minds we believed that we could control any threat to our national sovereignty. After all, with the collapse of the Soviet Union, the United States was the only remaining super-power in the world. No nation could face us militarily, and our economic strength was the envy of the world.

What Americans did not understand, that bright, clear September morning, was the rise of global terrorism across the world, run by men whose names were unknown to the majority of the American public, men who hated our very existence, our core values and beliefs, and most of all, our freedom.

If he American public at large did not know the name of Osama bin Laden, the son of a wealthy Saudi Arabian construction magnate, the intelligence services of the United States surely did. But that was before the carnage and death of 9-11. After the events, things would change in America. A highly controversial war was fought in Iraq, one that many people thought we should never have begun. Like Vietnam, Iraq caused the country.

In *Blowback: How the feud between the FBI and CIA Let 9-11 Happen,* I will endeavor to put all the pieces of that horrible event in historical perspective. This is not a conspiracy book, but a true account of the events and people who perpetrated one of the most horrific events in our history.

The book contains information on the rise of Osama bin Laden, from his origins in Saudi Arabia to his founding of Al Qaeda, and his pledge to destroy America. I will tell the story of the historical events in what I call the Terror Time Line, a series of events like the fall of the Shah of Iran, the USS Cole bombing, the two Embassy bombings in East Africa, Middle Eastern hijackings of planes, the destruction of Pam Am flight 103 over Lockerbie, Scotland, and much more.

Chapter 2 covers the FBI's long road to 9-11, its probe of Al Qaeda's cell in New York City, the killing of Rabbi Meyer Kahane, the first World Trade Center bombing in 1991 and the search for the men responsible, including the mastermind, Kalid Sheik Mohammed.

Chapter 3 is about the CIA's hunt for bin Laden, the secret CIA station that took over that investigation, US foreign policy towards Afghanistan, the relationship between the CIA and the Pakistani ISI, the 1979 Russian invasion of Afghanistan and its unforeseen blowback as far as the US was concerned.

The Able Danger Program is covered in detail, as well as the large number of warning signs in the months leading up to 9-11 in which the failure of both the FBI and CIA is clearly detailed. The most striking detail in the book is the failure of the CIA and FBI to share intelligence with each other, one whose origins dated back to the World War II era.

The last chapter details the activities of 9-11 mastermind Mohamed Atta in Florida and his American contacts.

This is the story, warts and all, and is a cautionary tale of just how unprepared as a nation we were to the events that we never saw coming.

Peter Kross
North Brunswick, NJ

Preface

The planes that hit the World Trade Center and the Pentagon on 9-11-2001, came as a total shock at the time. But, in reality, it shouldn't have. When writing fiction, novelists invent many ways in which terrorists or other nasty people wreak havoc against their targets of opportunity. But could it be done in real life, against real targets?

In the time frame between 1993 and 1994, such a scenario was being debated among certain segments of the United States government. A panel of experts was commissioned by the Pentagon in 1993 that postulates that a plane or series of planes, could be used as a missile to bomb national landmarks. This study was commissioned by a company called Forecasting International, whose president at the time was Marvin Cetron. He later told the panel that, "Coming down the Potomac, you could make a left turn at the Washington Monument and take out the White House, or you could make a right turn and take out the Pentagon."

When the report by Forecasting International was in its final stages, someone from the State Department took out that quote. In reaction to that deletion, Mr. Cetron said, "We were told by the Department of Defense not to put it in... and I said, "It's unclassified, everything is available. In addition, they said, "We don't want it released, because you can't handle a crisis before it becomes a crisis. And no one is going to believe you."

Air Force Colonel Doug Menarchik, who organized the study for the Pentagon, later said regarding this report, "It was considered radical thinking, a little too scary for the times. After I left, it met with a quiet death."

In 1994, Mr. Cetron wrote an article in *Futurist* magazine regarding the Pentagon study. "Targets such as the World Trade Center not only provide the requisite causalities but, because of their symbolic nature, provide more bang for the buck. In order to maximize their odds for success, terrorists groups will likely consider mounting multiple, simultaneous operations with the aim of overtaxing a government's ability to respond, as well as demonstrating their professionalism and reach."

Another study that was detailed by the Pentagon came in June 1994 called Terror 2000. It' goal was to prepare the American people for threats of new terrorism that might be in the future. The person in charge of the study was Peter Probst in the Pentagon's Office of the Assistant Secretary of Defense for Special Operations and Low-Intensity Conflict. The panel consisted of 40 people from different fields of knowledge, including a top Russian intelligence official and a senior Israeli intelligence official. The report concluded that the world is witnessing the dawn of a new age of "super terrorism." It predicts that terrorists will soon use chemical and biological attacks and continues to say that terrorists will soon try to conduct simultaneous bombings and attacks.

The study will also predict what actually happened with Al Qaeda and its religious attacks against the West and our beliefs. "Also, in contrast to the state-sponsored terrorism familiar to most Americans at the time, the report says tomorrow's most dangerous terrorists would be motivated not by political ideology but by fierce ethnic and religious hatreds. Their goal will not be political control but utter destruction of their chosen enemies." It also postulates the use of planes as weapons, but this was not put in the report, partly for fear of giving potential terrorists ideas.

The Terror 2000 report was given to the following government agencies; the Congress, FEMA, the CIA, FBI, NSA, DIA, Justice Department, State Department, and other important people in the federal government.

It was at first decided to release the report to the public, but cooler heads prevailed and it never saw the light of day.[1] Sadly, none of these warnings were ever given credence by the American government.

1 History Commons: Context of 1993-1994 Expert Panel Predicts Terrorists Will Use Planes as Weapons on Symbolic US Targets.

Chapter 1

The Terror Timeline

The attacks on 9-11 did not happen overnight. Since the late 1970s, America and her citizens had been the target of terrorists, mainly operating out of the Middle East. Unlike bin Laden's al Qaeda, these terrorists were state sponsored, mainly with the backing of Iran and Libya. These terrorist attack incidents against Americans and other Western targets grew out of the Israeli-Palestinian conflict, especially American support for Israel.

Until 9-11, the United States proper had not been the target of a terrorist attack. The last time that American soil was invaded by a foreign power was during the War of 1812 when the British set fire to Washington, burning down the White House and setting ablaze other government buildings.

The Atlantic and Pacific Oceans were a natural barrier that prevented the United States from an external invasion. Even during World War II, the U.S. escaped German or Japanese attacks, despite a few, unremarkable attacks by Japan against sites. 9-11 changed all that. Using tools of modern communications, and utilizing the basic tradecraft of espionage, and the right amount of luck, nineteen hijackers, armed with only box cutters, managed to foil the very nerve center of airline security that resulted in the deaths of 3,000 of our fellow citizens.

In order to get a better view of the events that culminated in 9-11, we must put the entire story of international terrorism at the time in perspective, as far as the United States was concerned. The tale is one of death and destruction on a massive scale, of assassinations, bombings, and brazen airplane hijackings on the hot tarmacs of the world's airports.

On November 4, 1979, 52 Americans were taken hostage when militant "students," with the backing of Iran, stormed the

U.S. Embassy in Tehran, Iran. Iran had once been a staunch ally of the United States during the Cold War days, when the Shah of Iran worked with various American presidents to seek stability in the Middle East. Iran was the beneficiary of U.S. largesse when in 1953, the CIA, working with the British, overthrew the government of Prime Minister Mohammed Mossadegh, which resulted in the return to the throne of the Shah of Iran, Muhammad Reza Pahlavi.

After the Shah fell during the Iranian revolution in the late 1970s, a radical, religious, anti-U.S. government took its place.

During the early part of the hostage ordeal, 13 prisoners were freed, some taken out of the country by clandestine means. For 444 brutal days, the remaining 52 hostages suffered the brutal treatment of their captives. In response to the embassy takeover, President Jimmy Carter placed a total trade and military embargo on Iran, and cut off all diplomatic relations.

When the government of Iran failed to release the hostages, President Carter ordered a covert mission to release them from captivity. In April 1980, Operation Eagle Claw was put into motion. Members of the elite Delta Force commandos, and other specially trained U.S. paramilitary Special Forces, took off from positions outside of Iran and landed in the desert outside of Tehran. From there, these men were to saddle up and mount a hostage rescue mission that would storm the compound where the prisoners were being held.

As the commandos prepared for their mission from their location called "Desert One," a fatal incident took place. On April 25, 1980, just as the helicopters were about to take off, one of the choppers collided with a refueling tanker and burst into flames. Eight U.S. soldiers were killed and the president canceled the escape attempt.

On January 20, 1981, a few hours after Ronald Reagan was sworn in as the new president, the 52 hostages were released from their 444-day captivity.

In the wake of the failed hostage rescue incident, the military began a new effort to train and equip elite commandos for such high profile missions. Their efforts resulted, years later, in the elite SEAL, Ranger, and Delta Force troops which worked so well in the invasion of Afghanistan after 9-11.

In 1983, U.S. Marines entered the shell-shocked city of Beirut, Lebanon in order to implement a cease fire between Israeli and Palestinian forces that had battered the city for months. The Reagan administration sent the unprepared Marines to take up positions near the Beirut airport where they were sitting ducks for snipers.

At the U.S. Embassy in Beirut, diplomats tried desperately to facilitate an Israeli pullout from Lebanon. On April 8, 1983, a suicide bomber drove a pick-up truck loaded with bombs that crashed into the Embassy with devastating force. In the aftermath of the attack, sixty-three people were killed, including 17 Americans. Among the dead were eight members of the CIA, including Station Chief Kenneth Haas, and Robert Ames, the agency's chief Middle East Analyst.

In the wake of the attack, CIA analysts said that the bombers belonged to the radical Middle Eastern Islamic terrorist group Hezbollah, which carried out many attacks against Israeli targets. Further investigation revealed that Hezbollah received training and financial help from Iran and Syria.

The Reagan administration decided not to retaliate against Hezbollah, despite the overwhelming body of evidence pointing in their direction.

Six months after the embassy bombing in Beirut, another act of terrorism against U.S. military forces in that city took place.

On October 23, 1983, a suicide bomber driving a hijacked truck filled with 400-pounds of explosives rammed the U.S. Marine barracks which was located near the Beirut airport. The powerful blast killed 241 Marines and wounded more than 100 others. The truck contained between 15,000 and 21,000 tons of TNT. Doors on apartment buildings over 250 feet away were ripped from their hinges, and trees at a distance of 370 feet were uprooted. A huge crater up to eight feet deep was chiseled into the ground.

The driver of the truck was later identified as Ismalal Ascari, an Iranian. He drove the truck past a high wire fence that surrounded the Marine compound, and two guard posts whose occupants had no time to react.

At the White House, President Reagan assembled his national security team to ponder what reaction the U.S. should take. Defense Secretary Casper Weinberger said at the time that the

U.S. "Lacks the actual knowledge of who did the bombing." All evidence however, pointed once again at Hezbollah. A military strike was planned to destroy the Sheik Abdullah barracks in Baalbek, Lebanon that was one of the locations of the Iranian Revolutionary Guards (in 2019, the Trump administration declared the Guards a terrorist organization). Both Secretary Weinberger and General John Vessey Jr. the chairman of the Joint Chiefs of Staff, counseled the president against any retaliatory strike because it might inflame America's allies in the region. Instead, the USS *New Jersey*, which was stationed off the coast of Lebanon as a show of force in the region, lobbed off a few ineffective shells into the hills near Beirut.

Four months after the Marine barracks were attacked, the remaining U.S. Marines were pulled out of Lebanon.

The investigation by U.S. authorities into the tragedy was led by U.S. District Court Judge Royce Lamberth. In his findings, Judge Lamberth wrote, "It is beyond question that Hezbollah and its agents received massive material and technical support from the Iranian government."

U.S. intelligence also received important information from the Israelis regarding the Marine barracks attack. Among the items the CIA received was the fact that $50,000 was paid to a Lebanese man named Hassan Hamiz, and that the money was sent from the Iranian Embassy in Damascus, Syria. The person whom U.S. intelligence held primarily responsible for the attack was a prominent Shiite leader, Sheik Mohammed Hussein Fadlallah.

Despite this information, the top men in the CIA's Near East Division believed that there was no "smoking gun" and no American action was taken. Once again, the United States took no action against the deaths of innocent Americans.

The next act of terror against Americans in the Middle East took place on June 14, 1985, when two Lebanese men hijacked TWA Flight 847 as it was taking off from Athens, Greece to Rome, Italy. A total of 145 passengers and 8 crewmembers were aboard the jumbo jet, including thirty-nine Americans. The hijackers held the plane and its occupants hostage for 17 long and grueling days, as the plane traveled to Beirut and then to Algiers.

Viewers around the world watched as the hijackers held press conferences with the pilot, a gun pointing at his head. During the ordeal, a young U.S. Navy diver named Robert Stehmen, twenty-three, was killed by the hijackers. Eventually, the aircraft and its hostages were freed when the United States exerted force on Israel to release 435 Lebanese and Palestinian prisoners held in their jails.

At the CIA, Director William Casey and his top aides were certain that the hijacking was the work of Libya's Muammar Qaddafi. The NSA (National Security agency) was able to intercept numerous messages between Libyan intelligence operatives and were convinced that their leader was behind the hijacking. From 1985 to 86, the CIA and the Reagan White House put out a full court press to blunt Libya's terrorist attacks. CIA analysts were able to learn that Libya's intelligence services were supplying known Middle Eastern terrorists groups with training, money, weapons, and bases of operations in which to carry out their deadly attacks. It would be later in the Reagan administration that the White House would order American military attacks against Libyan targets after a Berlin disco was attacked in which a number of Americans were killed. In the aftermath of the TWA 847 hijacking, no American response was offered.

In 1987, Inmd Mughniyah, a top-ranking member of Hezbollah, was indicted for his participation in the TWA 847 hijacking. Another man indicted in the affair, Mohammad Ali Hamadei, was arrested in Frankfurt, Germany. He was convicted by a German court and was sentenced to life in prison.

The next incident involving Americans took place on October 7, 1985 when the Italian ship *Achille Lauro,* which was steaming off the coast of Egypt, was hijacked by four Palestinian gunmen. The hijackers called for the release of Palestinian prisoners being held in jails in Egypt and Italy. Of the 700 people on board the ship, the terrorists picked out an American Jew named Leon Klinghoffer, 69, a disabled man who was wheelchair bound. The hijackers deliberately murdered the defenseless man by throwing him off the ship into the Mediterranean.

After three days of fruitless negotiations, the Egyptian government agreed to let the ship dock in Egypt, and agreed to let the hijackers go free.

The U.S. intelligence services were closely monitoring the situation and were able to intercept two-way talks between Egyptian President Hosni Mubarak and his foreign minister. The NSA intercepted a conversation in which it was learned that the hijackers were in Egypt. President Mubarak was also heard saying that it would be "crazy" if Egypt would agree to hand over the hijackers to the U.S.

The much-needed break came when U.S. intercepts overheard Mubarak telling his associates the exact time and location when the four hijackers would fly out of the country. The airplane carrying the men was to take off from the al-Maza Air Base in Cairo, it was an Egyptian Boeing 737.

President Reagan's National Security Council, which included a little known Marine officer named Oliver North and Admiral John Poindexter, the National Security Advisor, devised an ingenious plan to intercept the plane in mid-air and take the hostages to a U.S. base.

Four F-14 jets on board the USS *Saratoga,* took off on an intercept course with the hijackers' aircraft. The Navy jets were successful in forcing the plane down and diverted it to Sicily, Italy.

After a trial that ended in 1986, the four hijackers were found guilty by an Italian court. Unfortunately, two of the men managed to escape from jail. Authorities were able to apprehend Magid-al-Molgi, who admitted to killing Mr. Klinghoffer.

The mastermind of the *Achille Lauro* attack, Abu Abbas, escaped. In April 2003, just after the U.S. invasion of Iraq took place, it was announced by U.S. authorities that Mr. Abbas was captured in Iraq. It seems that he had been living there as a guest of Saddam Hussein for 17 years. He briefly took up residence in the Gaza Strip in Israel during the 1990s when Israel no longer showed any interest in him. It has been alleged that while in Iraq, Abbas trained Palestinian guerillas in their attacks against Israel.

The *Achille Lauro* affair was the first time that U.S. military action was taken in response to the hijacking or killing of an American citizen.

Besides such high profile targets as the *Achille Lauro* and Flight 847, individual Americans were also marked for death. One such person was CIA officer Richard Welsh. On December 23,

1975, two days before Christmas, Richard Welsh, who was the CIA Station Chief in Athens, Greece, was returning home from a holiday party when he was ambushed and killed. A group called the "Revolutionary Organization of November 17th" took credit for the assassination. Welsh's death was a clear-cut murder but the circumstances surrounding his demise are linked to the renegade CIA agent Philip Agee.

In order to embarrass the CIA, rogue agent Philip Agee published a book that listed the names and addresses of then current CIA agents worldwide. One of the names listed was that of Richard Welsh. By the time Agee's damaging information was published, Welsh was working as the CIA Station Chief in Athens. His cover was blown again, this time when an English-language newspaper in Greece called *Athens News* reported his true identity. Now, any radical who had a beef with the CIA, or with Richard Welsh in particular, knew just where he was.

On the night of December 23, 1975, three unidentified hit men staked out Welsh's home and killed him in cold blood. His body was returned to the United States. The funeral took place in Arlington National Cemetery with President Gerald Ford in attendance.

After the death of Richard Welsh, the editors of *Counterspy,* the book that named him, quickly put the blame for the assassination not on those directly responsible, but on the CIA.

Another American who was targeted by Islamic radicals in the Middle East was CIA officer William Buckley.

During the Reagan administration the United States found itself involved in an arms for hostage scandal called Iran-Contra. Numerous civilians were captured in Lebanon and held, sometimes for years, by militant terrorists who wanted to show their disapproval of the United States. One of the men who fell into their deadly trap was William Buckley who was the CIA Station Chief in Beirut, Lebanon.

Buckley covertly joined the CIA while still in the army. He kept this secret, and only a few of his most trusted officers and colleagues knew of his agency ties. During the Cold War years, Buckley served in Berlin and worked on the secret CIA led Berlin tunnel operation. After a stint back at CIA headquarters, Buckley served in various international hot spots over the following decades, including Egypt, Vietnam, Syria, Pakistan, and Lebanon.

In the early 1980s, Buckley came to the attention of then CIA Director William Casey. Casey was given the job of combating Middle Eastern terrorism centered on the U.S. He asked Buckley to head back to Lebanon even though he was known to our enemies in that part of the world. Part of his job was to oversee American counterterrorist polices in Lebanon after the U.S. embassy in West Beirut was attacked on April 18, 1983, in which sixty-seven people were killed, including a number of CIA personnel.

On March 6, 1981, Buckley was captured in Beirut by members of the radical group called Islamic Jihad. In the wake of the Buckley kidnapping, Director Casey set up an interagency task force to plan Buckley's rescue; members included assets from the FBI, CIA, and NSC. One plan called for the ransoming of Buckley to the tune of one million dollars, some of which would be supplied by Texas millionaire Ross Perot. However, the design was scrubbed as being too impractical to succeed.

Another operation called for the U.S. to kidnap Imad Mugniyed, a powerful Lebanese Shiite leader who was in charge of Islamic Jihad, while he was on a trip to France. It was decided to cancel the plan because of the likelihood of French displeasure that the operation was to be conducted on French soil.

Buckley was tortured by his kidnappers who knew just whom they had in custody. He eventually died of pneumonia, which he caught after his captivity. Hezbollah (Party of God) sent a video of Buckley's torture to CIA headquarters in a show of utter disrespect. Before he died, Buckley was forced to admit to "crimes" he carried out against the Islamic people.

His body was eventually returned to the United States and he was buried in Arlington National Cemetery.

The next assault against American military personnel took place in the early morning of April 5, 1986, when a bomb was set off at the La Belle Discotheque in Berlin. The club was a popular spot for off-duty American soldiers. The bomb killed three U.S. servicemen, including Sgt. Kenneth Ford, 21, Nermin Hannay, 29, and Sgt. James Goins, 25. Another 229 people were injured in the blast, including 79 Americans.

Even before the attack, U.S. eavesdroppers picked up the vital clue that linked Libya to the attack. On April 4, the NSA intercepted a conversation from Libyan intelligence operatives in East Berlin to their headquarters in Tripoli that said, "Tripoli will be happy when you see the headlines tomorrow."

Another communication was intercepted just hours after the attack from East Berlin to Tripoli which said that things were "happening now." The so-called "smoking gun" was now centered at the door of Libya's dictator Qaddafi, and the Reagan administration held hurried meetings on how to respond.

This time the United States took direct action against Libya when, on April 14, 30 Air Force and Navy planes took off from their bases in England for the nearly 3,000 mile flight to Libya. The bombers attacked Qaddafi's headquarters and ordnance was dropped directly on Qaddafi's personal living quarters, killing his adoptive daughter and wounding two of his sons. The Libyans said that the attack had killed 37 people. If Qaddafi was a target of the attack, he somehow survived (he would later be killed by his own people years later when a revolution took place in Libya).

More information on the La Belle disco attack came in 2000 with the release of a number of once secret files from the dreaded East German intelligence service, STASI. The files put the blame for the attack on a number of people, including Ali Chanaa, a German of Palestinian origin. Chanaa worked for the STASI and had direct links to Qaddaffi's regime. Mr. Chanaa's wife, Verena, was the one responsible for the planting of the bomb. Other members of the attack team were Musbah Eter, a Libyan diplomat, and Yasir Chraidi, a Palestinian who was arrested by Lebanese authorities.

Their trial began in November 1997, but it wasn't until four years later that the verdicts were handed down. Verena Channaa was found guilty of murder, Chraidi was sentenced to a 14-year term in jail, and Eter, and Ali Chanaa were given 12 year jail terms. Andrea Haeusler, Verena Channa's sister, was the only one found innocent of the charges.

Only days after the U.S. attack on Qaddafi's headquarters, three people who worked for the University of Beirut—American Peter Kilburn and two Britons, John Douglas and Phillip Padfield—

were found dead in a Beirut street. It was believed that these men were killed in response to the U.S. attack.

In the decade of the 1980s, Libya was not the only nation that the United States would confront in the Persian Gulf. Since the 444-day hostage standoff with Iran in 1979-80, tensions between the nations continued. In order to contain Iran from causing further trouble in the Persian Gulf, the Unites States Navy began escorting Kuwaiti oil tankers carrying their cargo to oil installations throughout the region. Hostilities also broke out between the U.S. and Iraq when the Navy ship USS *Stark* was fired upon by an Iraqi plane on May 17, 1987, resulting in the deaths of 37 sailors.

On July 3, 1988, in circumstances that are still being debated today, the U.S. Navy ship USS *Vincennes,* a sophisticated Aegis controlled vessel, shot out of the sky a civilian Iranian passenger plane carrying 290 people. Radar controllers on board the ship mistook the Airbus A300, which had just taken off from the city of Bandar Abbas enroute to Dubai in the UAE, for an Iranian F-14 jet.

While the shoot down of the Iranian Airbus took place in a split second, other military incidents between the two nations were taking place around the same time. Earlier in the day, three Iranian patrol boats fired on a helicopter that had taken off from the *Vincennes.* The chopper was unharmed and returned to the ship. At around the same time as the chopper incident, the USS *Elmer Montgomery* attacked the same patrol boats, sinking two and crippling the third.

How and why the *Vincennes,* which was equipped with the most sophisticated electronic and radar detection devices, failed to see that the Airbus was a civilian passenger plane rather than a military jet is hard to imagine.

In an investigation that followed, electronic devices on board the navy ship recorded the Airbus coming on a downward vector toward the *Vincennes.* The navy ship also sent an IFF (the identification code for friend or foe) to the Airbus without any reply. When the airliner did not respond, the crew of the *Vincennes* sent out a number of warnings over the civilian emergency channel, as well as four on the military band.

When the radars aboard the *Vincennes* spotted the Airbus

speeding up toward the ship, as well as veering off course, the American ship opened fire with two heat seeking missiles, striking the plane which was then nine miles away.

In Washington, U.S. naval authorities including Admiral William Crowe Jr., the chairman of the Joint Chiefs of Staff, defended the actions of the *Vincennes.* While he regretted the loss of life, he supported the navy's actions to the hilt by saying, "The number one obligation of the commanding officer was to protect his ship and his people. We've made that clear throughout the Persian Gulf mission." Over time, the tragedy of the *Vincennes* faded from memory as other, more horrific terrorists attacks were perpetrated against American targets.

On December 21, 1988, four days before the Christmas holidays, Pan Am Flight 103 took off from Frankfurt, Germany en route to New York via London. The 747 called "The Maid of the Seas" was cruising uneventfully over Lockerbie, Scotland when a powerful bomb exploded, killing all 259 people aboard, as well as 11 unlucky people on the ground.

As U.S. and British investigators arrived at the scene of the carnage and began sifting through the debris, it was evident that Pan Am 103 had been destroyed by a bomb. The explosive device was planted in the forward baggage comparment. The explosion was so terrific that it blew the plane into five pieces at an altitude of 30,000 feet.

As soon as word reached the White House, the administration of George Bush sent a number of FBI agents to Lockerbie to take part in the crime scene investigation. At CIA headquarters, Director William Webster put the new counterterrorism center on alert and they also took part in the probe. Webster gave the job of overseeing the crash investigation to a 25-year veteran of the clandestine service, and the person who was now in charge of the CTC, Fred Turco. Turco had access to a new CIA database called DESIST, which linked all known terrorists as well as their modus operandi. During the investigation, the CIA received the full cooperation of not only the FBI, but foreign intelligence services as well, including the Germans, French, and the British. Turco's two main assistants were Vincent Cannistraro who had experience in counterterrorism affairs, and Walter Korsgaard who was an expert in bombs of all types.

As the probe began, the CIA looked toward the two countries that had the means, motive, and opportunity to take down Pan Am 103, Libya and Iran.

As the team began sniffing out clues, it became obvious that a new, unexpected wrinkle had now been thrown into the mix. On board Flight 103 were two highly placed agency employees, 34-year-old Matthew Gannon, an expert in Middle Eastern affairs, and Charles McKee who was on assignment by the Pentagon to Lebanon to help with the rebuilding of the Lebanese military. For his part, Gannon was a highly trained CIA officer who began his agency career in 1977. He was stationed in North Africa and worked to capture the notorious terrorist Abu Nidal. To investigators, the problem came down to this—were the two CIA agents the targets of the bombing because of their work in Lebanon (the U.S. was then in the process of trying to win the release of a number of kidnapped Americans being held in the region), or was the bombing in retaliation for U.S. actions taken against Libya or Iran? Also on board were two State Department employees, Daniel O'Connor and Ronald Lariviere. Lariviere had been stationed in Beirut as a security officer starting in June of 1988. Daniel O'Connor was posted to Nicosia, Cyprus and was also a security team member.

Charles McKee, too, had an interesting covert life. As noted, the time, McKee was on loan to the CIA from the Pentagon. He was a graduate of the Army's Airborne and Ranger schools and also served in the Green Berets. He worked at the American embassy in Lebanon as the U.S. Defense Intelligence agency's liaison officer. It has been reported that McKee's real job was to covertly work to release the Americans being held hostage in Beirut as part of the ongoing Iran-Contra dealings. At the time of the crash, investigators found amid the rubble strewn over the Scottish highlands over a half a million dollars in bundled travelers checks. More importantly, searchers found amid the wreckage a map of a building in Beirut that could possibly be the layout of the location in which the missing American hostages were being held.

Days later the CIA said that they believed that a pro-Qaddafi unit called the 15 May Group was responsible for the downing of Pan Am 103. Another man on the CIA's most wanted list, Mohammed Hussein Rashid who ran terror-supported groups, was also now the prime suspect.

As the probe went on, investigators were able to locate the exact place where the bomb was secreted, and that it was concealed in a Toshiba Bombeat radio.

Suspect Mohammed Hussein Rashid worked closely with Abu Ibrahim whose terrorist groups operated throughout the Middle East, especially in Syria, Lebanon, and Libya. Abu Ibrahim also had close ties to Libya's Qaddafi.

Another man who attracted the CIA's spotlight in the bombing case was Ahmed Jabril, the head of the dangerous Palestinian terror group PFLP—Popular Front for the Liberation of Palestine. Western intelligence agents in Europe were reporting that Jabril's groups were planning a spectacular attack against U.S. interests somewhere in the world during 1988.

A top man in Jabril's network, Marwan Kreeshat, an expert bombmaker, was taken into custody by German police and then, unexpectedly, was set free. The CIA believed that the Germans had made a major mistake in releasing Kreeshat because U.S. officials thought he knew more about the incident than he revealed.

Despite the tantalizing leads that came from the Middle East, by 1991, the trail led U.S. and British authorities back to Libya. On November 14, 1991, Scottish investigators issued an arrest for two Libyans associated with their intelligence services, Lamen Khalifa Fhimad and Abel Baset Ali Mohammed al-Megrahi. Al-Megrahi was educated in the United States and spoke fluent English. He worked as chief of airline security for the Libyan Arab Airlines in Malta at the time of the downing of Pam Am 103. He was also the director for the Center for Strategic Studies in Libya, and more importantly, served as a Libyan intelligence agent.

In April 1992, the United Nations imposed economic sanctions on Libya over its refusal to turn over the two men for trial. In April 1998, Libyan leader Qaddafi said that he would hand over the two accused men to a Scottish court in a neutral nation. In August 1998, the U.S. and Great Britain changed their position and agreed to a trial of the two suspects in The Netherlands. The trial was held on the grounds of a former air force base at Camp

Zeist near the city of Utrecht.

At the trial of Al-Megrahi and Al-Amin Khalifa, conflicting testimony was heard. Two CIA officers testified that the bomb-making material that was seized in West Africa linked the two men to the disaster. The owner of a Swiss electronics company called MEBO said that in the weeks before the crash, his company was given an accelerated order for timers from the Libyan Army that they were unable to make. The person who made the timer said to have been used in the blast testified that he believed he was making them for the East German secret police. A Maltese shopkeeper said that he sold Al-Megrahi a batch of clothing that was found wrapped around the bomb. Other witnesses disputed that claim. Maltese immigration officials said that both defendants entered Malta on December 20, 1988, and left on December 21, the exact day that Pan Am 103 went down. Two employees of the Toshiba Company said that a Libyan company accepted 20,000 stereo cassette recorders in 1988. An identical Toshiba cassette recorder held the bomb in place.

In a trial that seemed to last forever, both men were convicted of their participation in the downing of Pan Am 103 and were sentenced to life in prison in 2001. Sanctions imposed by the U.N. against Libya were suspended—but not lifted—in May 2001, when the government of Libya made a $2.7 billion settlement offer to the relatives of the victims of the crash. Each family would get up to $10 million.

In an interesting twist not reported in the major media of the time, an investigation was begun on orders from Pan Am using the services of an ex-Israeli counterintelligence specialist named Juval Aviv and his firm Interfor. The Interfor report was full of conspiracy theories linking not one, but two separate CIA teams—CIA-1 and CIA-2—trying to free the hostages in Lebanon.

The Interfor report said that U.S. intelligence agents had zeroed in on a Syrian drug smuggler name Monzar Al-Kassar in connection with the bombing. It seems that Al-Kassar had been a middleman in the shipment of arms to the Contra guerillas then fighting the Sandinista's in Nicaragua. Two of the top names in the Iran-Contra scandal, Richard Secord and Albert Hakim, were used by Al-Kassar in the shipment of these arms. The Interfor investigation said that agent McKee learned of Al-Kassar's covert relationship with another group of rogue CIA agents (CIA-1), based in Germany who were also running drugs and guns on the side. This conspiracy theory postulates that once McKee learned about CIA-2, the "bad guys" couldn't allow them to return home. Hence, they planted a bomb on board Pan Am 103 to silence them—along with the other 270 innocent people who happened to be in the wrong place at the wrong time.

On November 5, 1990, the first shot against America took place in a crowded ballroom at Manhattan's Marriot East Side Hotel and no one realized it.

Giving a fiery speech against the Arab Peoples was the militant founder of the Jewish Defense League, and a member of Israeli's parliament, the Knesset, Rabbi Meir Kahane. Rabbi Meir Kahane was so disliked even by members of his own legislative body that he was barred from occupying his seat, and derisively called all Arabs '"jackals."

One of the people in the audience that night was El Sayyid Nosair, a follower of the militant blind Sheik Omar Abdel Rahman who was spouting poisonous language against Americans and Jews in New York City. Nosair had ben stalking Kahane for some time and tonight he would kill his hated enemy. As Rabbi Kahane began his exit from the hotel, Nosair pulled out his hidden. 357 Magnum and shot Rabbi Kahane twice, mortally wounding him. In the commotion that followed, Nosair hightailed it out of the hotel and looked frantically for a waiting car that was supposed to act as his getaway car. The driver was a friend, Mahmoud Abouhalima, a fellow Egyptian.

Unfortunately for Nosair, he got into the wrong cab, and exited the auto quickly. An off-duty U.S. Postal Police Officer named Carlos Acosta spotted the gun toting Nosair, and a short firefight ensued. Acosta was hit but was saved by his bulletproof vest. He was able to shoot Nosair and the assassin was quickly arrested.

Immediately after the assassination of Rabbi Kahane, NYPD detectives went to the home of Nosair in Cliffside Park, New Jersey. Inside Nosair's home, the police found his two accomplices, Mahmoud Abouhalima and Mohammad Salameh, and took them in for or questioning. What else the detectives found in Nosair's home was astonishing. They discovered bombmaking formulas, 1,400 rounds of ammunition, and more interesting, texts belonging to the John F. Kennedy Special Warfare Center at Fort Bragg, marked "Top Secret for training." They also found maps of landmarks in New York City, among them, the Statue of Liberty, the Lincoln Tunnel and the World Trade Center. In all, 47 boxes of evidence were taken back to New York.

When the FBI was notified of the findings in Nosair's home, they went through their files and came up with some very startling information. Abouhalima, Salameh, and El Sayydi Nosair were among a number of Arab men trailed by the FBI to a shooting range in Calverton, Long Island where, on numerous occasions, they spent hours taking target practice. The FBI did nothing regarding these men as no law had been violated.

During his stay in the New York-New Jersey area, Nosair got a full time job at a religious center in Brooklyn called the al-Kifah Refugee Services Center that was the American headquarters of the Pakistani based Office of Services, the predecessor of Osama bin Laden's al Qaeda. It was from the halls of al-Kifah that Muslim Americans and others would be recruited and sent to Afghanistan to fight the Russians.

During his time at the Brooklyn mosque, Nosair was in touch with Sheik Rahman who took him under his wing. In Nosair, Sheik Rahman had a willing and eager soldier to the cause of militant Islam. The FBI soon learned of the Nosair-Rahman connection and kept a number of men under surveillance as they made their way across the city and onto Long Island.

Hours after the Kahane murder, New York legal authorities came to the conclusion that Nosair had acted alone and that there were no other lurking accomplices anywhere else. A defense fund was created to help pay Nosair's legal bills. In an interesting twist, Nosair's cousin, Ibrahim el Gabeowny, went to Saudi Arabia where he was given $25,000 for Nosair's legal fund. The man who gave him the money was a little known Saudi financier, Osama bin Laden.

Nosair was represented by the flamboyant lawyer William Kuntsler who wanted to plead insanity for his client. Nosair put a monkey wrench in Kuntsler's plans when he refused to plead insanity and had the moxie to say he hadn't shot Rabbi Kahane, despite many eyewitnesses.

In a verdict that is hard to fathom, the jury acquitted Nosair of the murder. The same jury found him guilty of other charges that resulted in a sentence of 22 years in jail.

Because the FBI did not have sufficient Arabic speaking translators, the 42 boxes of materials seized from Nosair's home were not gone over until after the first WTC bombing in 1993. Part of the unread material that was in Nosair's files was a formula for the construction of a fuel oil and urea nitrate bomb, the same type used by Ramai Yousef in the 1993 WTC attack.

What the FBI and NYPD did not realize at the time of the Kahane assassination was that Mohammed Salameh, Nidal Ayyad, Ibraham Elgabrowney, and Sayyid Nosair, were all associated with the radical blind Shiek Abdul Rahman, and more importantly, would later take part in the 1993 WTC attack. How much history might have been changed if federal and local authorities had the manpower to translate the boxes found in Nosair's Jersey home at that time.

The al-Kifah mosque had a strange and covert relationship that was not visible to the untrained eye. In the mid-1980s, Osama bin Laden and his close associate Abdullah Azzam founded a charity which was based in Pakistan called Maktab al-Khidaamat or MAK, or service office. A number of branches were launched in the United States, including one in Tucson, Arizona and the one in Brooklyn. One of the interesting men who worked in the Brooklyn mosque was Jamal al-Fadl, a founding member of al Qaeda and a man who would one day work for the FBI as an undercover informant. According to History Commons:

> The Brooklyn office recruited Arab immigrants and Arab-Americans to go fight in Afghanistan, even after the Soviets withdrew in early 1989. As many as 200 were sent there from the office. Before they go, the office arranges training in the use of rifles, assault weapons, and handguns, and then helps them with visas, plane tickets, and contacts. They are generally sent to the MAK/Al-Kifah office in Peshawar, Pakistan, and then connected to either the radical Afghan faction led by Abdul Rasul Sayyaf, or

the equally radical one led by Gulbuddin Hekmatyar. The CIA has some murky connection to Al-Kafah that has yet to be fully explained. Newsweek will later say that the Brooklyn office doubled as a recruiting post for the CIA seeking to steer fresh troops to the mujaheddin, fighting in Afghanistan. At the same time, the Brooklyn office is where veterans of the Afghan war arrived in the United States—many with passports arranged by the CIA.[1]

The Brooklyn mosque was also used by important members of bin Laden's associates to give lectures to those who wanted to hear the message.

The more popular lectures were held upstairs in the roomier Al-Faroqu Mosque, such as was the case in 1990 when Sheik Omar Rabdul-Rahman, traveling on a CIA supported visa, came to town. One frequent instructor was double agent Ali Mohammed, who was in the U.S. Special Forces at the time. Bin Laden's mentor Azzam frequently visits and lectures in the area. Ayman Al-Zawahiri, future al Qaeda second in command, makes a recruiting trip to the office in 1989. The Brooklyn office also raises a considerable amount of money for MAK/Al-Kifah back in Pakistan. Abdul Rahman, better known as the "Blind Sheik," is closely linked to bin Laden. In 1990, he moves to New York on another CIA supported visa and soon dominates the Al-Kifah Refugee Center. [2]

The Al-Kifah center also owns a safe house in Pakistan where a number of bin Laden's associates stay when they are in that country. Among those who frequent the safe house are two men, a Houston, Texas pizza deliveryman named Ahmad Ajaj and San Antonio cabdriver Ibraham Ahmad Suleiman. Suleiman is a Texas contact of the Al-Kifah Refugee Center, based in Brooklyn, and has been raising funds for the Afghan war in Texas in the late 1980s. When they arrive in Pakistan, they stay at a hotel

1 History Commons: 1986-1993, CIA and Bin Laden both closely tied to Recruiting and Fund-Raising Office for Afghanistan.

2 Ibid.

in Peshawar, near the Afghanistan border, known as the Abdullah Azzam House which is named after bin Laden's mentor, Abdullah Azzam. For the next several months, Suleiman and Ajaj will make the Azzam center their home. Both men are rumored to have taken arms training while they are in residence.

On September 1, 1992, Ajaj and Ramzi Yousef, the mastermind of the 1993 WTC bombing, arrive in New York from Pakistan. In his possession, Ajaj is carrying some bomb manuals. Later, police will find the fingerprints of Ajaj, Yousef, and Suleimann on them.[3]

In December 1992, in a humanitarian effort that ultimately led to disaster, the administration of George H.W. Bush sent American troops to Somalia to try to end the famine in that war-torn country. The mandate of the United Nations was to send in an international force which would set the conditions for the massive relief assistance that would follow.

Disagreements emerged among the highest levels of the new Clinton administration, including Defense Secretary Les Aspin who told reporters that he did not think U.S. troops should remain in Somalia for more than 18 months.

Like the Marines stationed in Beirut in the 1980s, the Army Rangers and other troops were sitting ducks for any sniper who wanted to take a potshot at them. Also, the mandate of the troops was ambiguous at best. Where they there for a peacekeeping mission or to help with relief efforts for the starving people of Somalia? As time went on, that answer would be felt in a bloody attack against American troops which would lead to their withdrawing in humiliating fashion.

The U.S. troops in Somalia were not the only ones targeted for death. In June 1993, armed militants killed 24 Pakistani troops that were part of the U.N. peacekeeping force. U.S. intelligence believed that the attacks had been perpetrated by the Somali warlord General Muhammad Aidid. After an August 22, 1993, attack by Somali forces led by Aidid which wounded six Americans riding in a truck in the city of Mogadishu, Somalia, the Clinton

3 History Commons: April 24-September 1, 1992: WTC Bombers have numerous links to Al-Kifah Charity Front.

administration decided it was time to get rid of Aidid, in any way possible. Aidid's forces were also believed to be responsible for an attack on August 8, 1993, which killed four U.S. Army M.P.s

Shortly after the August 22 attack, the president ordered that a large group of elite Delta Force commandos located at Fort Bragg, N.C., be sent to Somalia. Also ordered to Somalia were detachments from Ft. Campbell, Kentucky, and Army Rangers stationed at Fort Benning, Georgia.

Their orders were to link up with a specially trained group of CIA agents who were already on the ground. Their mission was to "snatch" General Aidid and take him into custody. What began as a purely humanitarian effort had now morphed into a dangerous military operation.

In Washington, the president gave the orders to snatch General Aidid to Joint Chiefs of Staff General Colin Powell who relayed the order to General Joseph Hoar, the head of Central Command whose purview covered Somalia. Hoar did not believe the mission was militarily feasible but put it in motion despite his objections.

A major American military operation to capture Aidid began on October 4, 1993, led by a number of highly mobile, and heavily armed, Black Hawk helicopters. The mission planners believed the operation would only last a few hours. Instead, when the helicopters landed in the middle of Mogadishu all hell broke loose. Heavily armed militias on the ground wielding rocket-propelled grenades knocked down two Black Hawks. In the ensuing, bloody battle in the heavily fortified streets of Mogadishu, 18 U.S. soldiers were killed and at least 75 wounded. In the 16-hour firefight an estimated 500 Somalis died. This incident would later be the basis of a major motion picture called *Black Hawk Down.*

In the wake of the attacks, two American soldiers who were taken captive were released on October 14.

In March 1994, the final American troops were pulled out of Somalia with their main objective—the capture of General Aidid—still not achieved.

Years later, after an intensive investigation by U.S. intelligence agencies, a direct link between Osama's bin Laden's al Qaeda and the Somali operation was made.

In February 1994, Indian police arrested a Pakistani national with ties to al Qaeda named Maulana Mashood Azhar. Azhar was determined to have been responsible for the deaths of a number of Americans in India and Pakistan in the 1990s. Azhar was the leader of a militant Islamic group called Jaish-e-Mohammed. During his interrogation, he told Indian authorities that he traveled to Nairobi, Kenya in 1993 where he met with members of the Somalian group, al-Ittihad, who the U.S. said was trained by al Qaeda. Azhar was arrested in Kashmir after his arrival from Karachi, Pakistan using a fake Portuguese passport.

The American FBI, it seems, also had a go at interrogating Azhar. FBI agents met with him on July 4, 1995, when he was being held in an Indian jail. A second session was also held in 1998. The U.S. could not get any more information from Azhar after he was released by the Indian police in December 1999. After the 9-11 attacks, Azhar was taken into custody and then released.

When the case against Osama bin Laden was presented after 9-11, additional information linking to the Somalian attack with al Qaeda were found. Mohammed Atef, bin Laden's military commander, traveled to Somalia and met with members of bin Laden's supporters there. By 1993, Atef and Saif Adel, another top al Qaeda member, began training like-minded Somalis against the U.N. peacekeeping forces in that country. These same men took part in the brutal events of October 3 and 4 that resulted in the deaths of 18 U.S. soldiers.

In another part of the Arabian Peninsula, American Marines were sent to the hot, dusty country of Yemen, and its capital of Aden, in a mission that made no military sense. In December 1992, in his last days as President, George H.W. Bush sent a large contingent of Marines and Army Rangers to Somalia to help in the relief efforts in the famine-ravished nation. A small contingent of the Marine Corps Aerial Relief/Transport Squadron 352 which flew the large KC-130 Hercules transports from Aden to Somalia, was on the ground in Aden. The flight crews had little to do except for the once-a-day trip to Somalia. For the most part, this mission was purely R&R, a chance to live in a good hotel, with air conditioning to control the stifling heat outside, and take a good swim in the pool.

But to others in Aden, the Marines were a target of opportunity—

one that could not be missed. On December 29, 1992 a small band of terrorists made their final plans to attack the Americans whom they believed were still in two hotels, the Aden and the Goldmore.

Standing near the entrance to the Aden Hotel, a security guard saw two men approach his position carrying a suitcase. Before the guard could react, the suitcase—which contained a powerful bomb—exploded, wounding all three. Police were called to the scene and they soon found another, unexploded bomb which was placed under a nearby car. Fortunately, the bomb was diffused.

While this was going on, another bomb had been placed inside the Goldmore Hotel by an unknown person. At 9 o'clock that night the bomb went off inside the hotel, sending shrapnel in all directions, wounding many guests.

As the police made their inquiries at the scene of the Aden Hotel blast, they found a large stockpile of weapons and explosives inside the car that belonged to the terrorists.

Two of the surviving terrorists told Yemeni authorities that they had been trained in camps in Afghanistan headed by bin Laden. Police also found incriminating documents inside their home that further linked them to bin Laden.

What the terrorists did not know was that the large contingent of U.S. soldiers that were staying at the Goldmore Hotel had left two days previously. The remaining one hundred Americans stationed at the Aden Hotel were unharmed when the bomb destined for their quarters was disarmed outside.

The Aden attack was supposed to be the first blow by Osama bin Laden against the United States. This time it failed. Others, however, would be more successful.

All was calm at the entrance to CIA headquarters in the early morning of January 25, 1993. agency employees were lining up in their cars waiting to clear security at Langley headquarters, a routine that went on every day. Suddenly, the early morning stillness was shattered as a man carrying an AK-47 rifle left his car and began shooting randomly at the people sitting in their cars. The shooting spree lasted only a few seconds, but when it was over, two CIA employees were dead. The victims were Frank Darling, 28 years old, an employee of the Directorate of Operations, and Lansing Bennett, sixty-six, a doctor.

In the furious commotion that followed the shooting, the gunman was able to elude his pursuers and flee the scene. What followed was one of the most intensive manhunts in CIA history, a path that would lead American intelligence agents to Pakistan where, four years later, they would nab the assassin and bring him back to face justice.

In the months following the incident, the CIA focused its attention on a 33-year-old Pakistani citizen named Mir Aimal Kasi who came to the United States in 1991. Mr. Kasi lived with his roommate Zahed Mir in an apartment in nearby Reston, Va. Shortly after the attacks Mir notified police that Kasi was missing. When the police came to investigate, they found the smoking gun that would link Kasi to the killings at the CIA. an AK-47, 600 rounds of ammunition, and a bulletproof vest. Mr. Mir told the police that he helped Kasi purchase the items by allowing him to use his credit card.

While the police were starting their probe, Mr. Kasi fled the United States and returned to his home in Pakistan. Kasi's family lived in the province of Quetta in southwest Pakistan where they owned a building contracting company. Kasi grew up in Quetta and received a master's degree in English literature from Baluchistan University. Once in Quetta, Kasi was in familiar hands and was protected by a local network of fellow Muslims who shared his anti-American views.

At CIA headquarters, the hunt for Kasi took shape at the newly created Counterterrorism Center. In a well-coordinated and detailed plan the CIA recruited a number of Afghans from one family who lived in the city of Kandahar. They were given the cryptonym FD/TRODPINT, and were supplied with all-terrain vehicles for use in the rugged Afghan mountains. The focal point in the search for Kasi was Karachi, Pakistan where the CIA had its on-site forces ready to pounce if and when the need arose. A detailed plan to capture Kasi was developed whereby a unit of American Special Forces would be infiltrated upon the capture of Kasi by the FD/TRODPINT team. A secure landing strip was located and a special U.S. plane would fly the fugitive back to U.S. soil.

It was an open secret along the streets of Quetta that the United States had placed a two-million reward on Kasi's head and soon, legitimate tips were coming in concerning his whereabouts. In May 1997, a man entered the U.S. Consulate in Karachi, and said he had information regarding Kasi. In further talks with CIA men in the embassy, the informer gave them an application for a Pakistani driver's license that had been requested by Kasi using a phony name. The person also had a real picture of Kasi. With irrefutable proof now in their hands, American authorities began their final plans to capture America's most wanted man.

Since the abduction of Kasi was to be a covert operation, it needed the approval of the Clinton administration's National Security Council. The president was persuaded to sign a National Intelligence Finding in order to carry out the mission.

CIA and FBI teams were covertly sent into Pakistan, and working with the Pakistani intelligence service, ISI, were able to locate Kasi at the Shalimar Hotel in Der Ghazi Kahn. On June 15, 1997, agents swarmed down on Kasi's room and took him to a safe location. He was swiftly taken out of Pakistan and returned to the United States for trial. On November 10, 1997, a jury in Fairfax County convicted Mir Kasi of murder and sentenced him to death. On November 14, 2002, Mir Kasi was executed in Virginia for the brutal murders of Frank Darling and Lansing Bennett.

This was the first attack on American soil by foreign terrorists. As time and events were later to prove, it would not be the last.

On February 26, 1993, shortly after noon, a large explosion took place in the underground parking deck of a hotel located beneath the World Trade Center in New York. The explosion was so powerful that it could be heard one mile away. New York City police, EMS workers, and FBI agents quickly arrived on the scene and began the job of rescuing the thousands of people who worked in the twin towers. As a light snow began to fall, rescue workers began the arduous task of removing the scared, and sometimes bloody victims of this yet unknown case. In the aftermath of the blast, six people lay dead and over a thousand were wounded. What took place next was a full court press by members of the U.S. intelligence community and local police to find the perpetrators of this act of terrorism on American soil. The irony of the first WTC attack was that the FBI and the NYPD, had they connected the dots before the event, may have stopped it before it took place.

What the CIA and FBI did not know at the time was that the bombing of the WTC was linked to a mysterious Saudi financier whose family owned one of the largest construction companies in the Middle East, Osama bin Laden. Not many people in the intelligence community at the time knew of Osama bin Laden and the organization that he would call his own: "al Qaeda," the base. The immediate trail led federal investigators to a number of Arabs living in the New York-New Jersey area. As the initial hunt for the suspected bombers got active, the main player in the event, Ramzi Yousef, boarded a plane just a few miles from the smoke-filled Twin Towers and made his way to Pakistan and his allics in bin Laden's al Qaeda. Over the next few years, Yousef would find sanctuary in the familiar surroundings of Pakistan and other parts of Asia, where he would continue his lethal plots to sow terror inside the United States. Eight years later, U.S. intelligence would learn that the uncle of Ramzi Yousef, Kalid Shaikh Mohammed, was one of the high level participants in the 1993 WTC bombing, and also a co-conspirator with bin Laden on 9-11. What the world also didn't know, that cold February day in 1993, was that the heir of Ramzi Yousef, Osama bin Laden, would finish the job he began with the total destruction of the World Trade Center on September 11, 2001.

Within a week of the blast, a number of Arabs living in the New York area were arrested and later tried for their roles in the WTC bombing. They would subsequently be found guilty and sentenced to long prison terms. Later investigations would lead U.S. authorities to learn that a number of these men and their cohorts were planning to bomb New York landmarks and infrastructure, such as the Holland and Lincoln Tunnels, and other federal buildings. They would also learn that the ringleader of the plots to destroy New York's prominent landmarks, the blind Egyptian radical cleric named Sheik Omar Abdel Rahman discussed above, was recruiting and training gullible Muslim youths in New York and New Jersey to carry out terror plots against the United States. If U.S. intelligence had looked more carefully into Sheik Omar Abdel Rahman's background, they would have been surprised to learn that his name had been placed on a State Department "watchlist" of potential terrorists who had no business being in the U.S. His name was also known to certain members of the CIA, those who funneled millions of dollars into the pockets of the Afghan freedom fighters who were battling the Russians in Afghanistan after the Soviet invasion of 1979. Rahman was one of the recipients of CIA largesse.

In the intervening years between the first and last World Trade Center bombings, a plethora of new information concerning the events leading up to and following the 1993 WTC attack would focus on a number of factors: who was "Ramzi Yousef;" was he using an identity of another person; was Iraq somehow involved in both events; was the November 5, 1990 murder of Rabbi Kahane by El Sayyid Nosair a prelude to the events of February 26, 1993?

If any members of the U.S. intelligence community were really paying attention in the months leading up to WTC-1, they should have been listening to an undercover FBI informant by the name of Mamdouh Zaki Zakhary who had been keeping tabs on a number of radicals attending religious services at the El Salaam mosque in Jersey City, New Jersey. It was from this location that a number of the WTC-1 plotters hatched their plans to destroy the Twin Towers. Zakhary lived in Jersey City, owned an import-export company, and kept a close watch on three members of the mosque in particular: Mohammed Salameh, Ibraham Elgabrowney, and the fiery spiritual leader, Sheik Rahman. While Zakhary knew that the three men held violently anti-American views, he was not able to get close enough to them to learn what they were up to. Another member of the El Salaam Mosque was El Sayyid Nosair, who assassinated Rabbi Kahane. Unknown to Zakhary was that all of these people (with the exception of Sheik Rahman) would be co-conspirators in the WTC-1 plot.

Within days of the WTC-1 attack, bureau agents had captured all of the conspirators with the exception of Ramzi Yousef who fled to Pakistan. Among them were:

Mohammed Salameh. He was a 25-year-old Pakistani who came to the United States and settled in Jersey City, New Jersey. Salameh met Sheik Rahman at the El Salaam Mosque and rented the Ryder truck that was used to transport the bomb to the WTC. After the blast, he went back to the rental agency to have his deposit refunded, stating that it was stolen. Not known by Salameh, a sharp-eyed investigator digging through the rubble of the underground parking garage found the distinctive VIN number of the van and traced it back to the rental company. Salameh was arrested by FBI agents waiting for him when he tried to get his money back. When the FBI arrived at Salameh's apartment, they found evidence linking him to another conspirator, Nidal Ayyad. They also questioned Salameh's roommate, Ahmed Yassin. Through the efforts of Yassin, FBI agents located the apartment where the bomb used in the WTC-1 attack was made.

Nidal Ayyad. A friend of Salameh's who worked as a chemical engineer for Allied Signal Company. Ayyad bought the ingredients that were used to put the bomb together.

Ibraham Elgabrowney. He was the cousin of El Sayyid Nosair, the man who shot Rabbi Khahane. Elgbrowney would oftentimes travel to Attica prison where Nosair was being held to plan a possible jailbreak for his cousin. Elgabrowney lived in Brooklyn and his home was a central meeting place where the conspirators would gather and talk strategy.

Mahmoud Abouhalima. He was a driver for Sheik Rahman, and would later be found guilty in the bombings of the U.S. Embassies in East Africa in 1998. He was also supposed to be the driver for Nosair after he shot Rabbi Kahane. He fled the United States to Saud Arabia and then to Egypt. Egyptian police captured him and relayed the information to the FBI, where agents arrived and took him back to the U.S. on board an Air Force plane. On the return trip to the United States, Abouhalima all but confessed that Ramzi Yousef had masterminded the WTC-1 attack.

Sheik Omar Abdul Rahman. A blind, Egyptian cleric, he was implicated, and stood trial in the assassination attempt on the life of the late Egyptian President Anwar Sadat on October 6, 1981. After the Sadat murder, he was picked up but was eventually acquitted in the crime. He soon left Egypt and arrived in the United States despite his name having been placed on a State Department "watchlist" of potential terrorists. Once in the United States, Sheik Rahman brought his fiery, anti-American harangues to the El Salaam Mosque in Jersey City, and the El Farouq Mosque in Brooklyn. The Sheik used these two religious institutions to recruit like-minded revolutionaries to his cause. It was from these two mosques that Rahman would recruit a number of men involved in the WTC-1 plot.

From his perch at the El Farouq mosque, Sheik Rahman came into conflict with Mustafa Shalabi who was in charge of the Al Kifah Center. While these two men worked together to use the mosque as a center for Islamic endeavors in New York, Shiek Rahman decided that he wanted to take over, making it clear that Mustafa Shalabi was no longer wanted. Shalabi began to worry about his safety. His suspicions proved correct on February 26, 1991, when he was murdered in his Brooklyn home. Mahmoud Abouhalima, a giant of a man with red hair, told police that he was the dead man's brother, identified Shalabi's body. On his body, police found a number of red hairs.

During the investigation of Mustafa Shalabi's murder, Abouhalima was never charged in any way with his death. With the demise of his main adversary, Sheik Rahman effectively took control over the mosque and continued making his secret plans to destroy New York landmarks, as well as using the mosque for clandestine meetings with the men who would eventually attack the WTC on February 26, 1993.

Sheik Rahman had direct ties with the Mujahideen fighters who were equipped and trained by the CIA during the Afghan war. He also directly aided the Islamic terrorist group in Egypt, and founded a militant, anti-Egyptian organization called Al Gamaat al Islamia. During the Afghan war, Sheik Raman traveled to Pakistan where he held meetings with the leader of the Mujahideen, It is not inconceivable that the CIA, which had a direct hand in supplying the Mujahideen fighters, came across Sheik Rahman at one time or another. Over the years, CIA officials made it abundantly clear that the United States knew of Sheik Rahman's terrorist past, yet decided to play ball with him in order to defeat the Russians.

If Sheik Rahman's first goal was the overthrow of the Egyptian government, his next, unstated objective was to bring the holy war, or jihad, to American shores.

Once safely in America, Sheik Rahman moved his headquarters to the El Salaam Mosque in Jersey City, New Jersey. The mosque's founder was Sultan Ibraham El Gawli, an Egyptian who was convicted in July 1986 by a federal grand jury for conniving to export 150 pounds of C-4 explosives to Israel for use by the PLO. Mahmoud Zaki Zakhary, the man who infiltrated the Brooklyn and Jersey City mosques, was directly responsible for fingering El Gawli.

Sheik Rahman was convicted for his alleged role in plans to blow up the Lincoln and Holland Tunnels in New York, as well as other high profile targets.

The congressional investigation into the 9-11 attacks reported that in May 2001, al Qaeda sympathizers were planning a possible hijacking of an American airliner, or the storming of an undisclosed American embassy abroad in order to obtain the release of Sheik Rahman.

The one man who was at the heart of the WTC-1 plot was an elusive figure from the province of Baluchistan in Pakistan, a master bombmaker, Ramzi Yousef. Yousef grew up in Kuwait, and as a young man, went to the Swansea Institute in England, and graduated in 1989 with a master's degree in electronic engineering. During and after his college years, Yousef traveled frequently to Pakistan where he lent his support to Osama bin Laden's al Qaeda. New information coming to light after the 9-11 tragedy was the fact that Ramzi Yousef's uncle was Khalid Sheikh Mohammed, one of bin Laden's most powerful henchmen. After he fled the United States following the February WTC-1 attack, Yousef found his way to Pakistan and received shelter from Khalid Sheikh Mohammed. We now have proof that Ramzi Yousef, through his uncle KSM, was in lockstep behind bin Laden's al Qaeda years before the 9-11 attacks.

Yousef came to the United States on September 1, 1992 on a bogus Iraqi passport and since his name wasn't on any "watchlist," he was allowed entry into the country. Immediately upon entering the U.S., Yousef asked for asylum and without any paperwork being done at the airport, was allowed to proceed to his new destination and told to report for a formal hearing at a later date. A debate has been raging about the true identity of Ramzi Yousef. Investigators believed that his real name is Abdul Basit Karim. Some writers have postulated that the name Abdul Basit Karim is also a fake. Some interested parties say that the government of Iraq purposely forged his records, including his fingerprint files, in order to create a "legend" for him. These writers also postulate that Yousef/Basit Karim was really an Iraqi intelligence officer sent by the government of Iraq to blow up the World Trade Center. The February 1993 attack coincidently took place on the second anniversary of the liberation of Kuwait by coalition forces following the first Gulf War.

Traveling with Yousef to the U.S. was his friend Ahmad Ajaj, a Palestinian. While Yousef successfully entered the country, Ajaj was not so lucky. He was detained by passport control officers at Kennedy airport while carrying a false Swedish passport.

Yousef observed Ajaj's arrest and saw his traveling partner being taken in for questioning. When he was later interrogated by federal authorities, Ajaj had on his person papers containing formulas for bombmaking purposes which prosecutors said were to be used to destroy bridges and tunnels in NYC. While Ajaj was in a New York jail cell, Yousef met Mohammed Salameh and the other members of the WTC-1 plot. Besides teaming up with Salameh, Yousef ingratiated himself with Sheik Rahman in obtaining and mixing the ingredients that would be placed inside the bomb that would detonate at the World Trade Center.

In the confusing immediately after the bombing, Yousef fled the United States and relocated to Pakistan. He began a new round of terrorist attacks and took part in a botched assassination plot against President Benazir Bhutto of Pakistan.

With Yousef out of the country, the FBI's New York field office, as well as its Joint Terrorism Task Force (JTTF) led by Neil Herman, began the biggest manhunt in history. They called their investigation of the WTC-1 attack, TRADEBOM. Soon after the WTC-1 attack, the CIA and FBI were at each other's throats laying the blame for the blast on each other. Neil Herman told author Gerald Posner in an interview for his book *Why American Slept: The Failure to Prevent 9-11,* that "Back then, I don't think they [CIA] could have found the bathroom. They didn't have any information." In the aftermath of the WTC-1 bombing, President Clinton fired FBI Director William Sessions. The president chose as his successor, Louis Freeh, a former bureau agent, and assistant U.S. Attorney. Director Freeh would later find himself embroiled in such scandals as the shootout at Ruby Ridge, the massacre of the people at the Branch Davidian compound in Waco, Texas, as well as the death of White House aid Vincent Foster.

Months after the WTC-1 attack, Director Freeh, to show his anger over the lack of cooperation between the two agencies, closed the FBI's post at the CIA's Counterintelligence Center.

In 1995, U.S. authorities got a tip that they hoped would lead to Ramzi Yousef's arrest. The clue led them to Manila, Philippines where Yousef was visited by his uncle, Khalid Sheik Mohammed, or KSM, and two other co-conspirators in the jihad, Abdul Hakim Murad and Wali Khan Amin Shah.

Since November 1994, the men had been living at the Dona Josefa Apartments in Manila which was financed by the bin Laden affiliate, the Abu Sayyaf Group, as well as a cutout organization called Konsonjaya, which was bankrolled by Mohammed Jamal Kalifa, bin Laden's brother-in-law.

The small apartment was turned into a bombmaking facility where the men planned a nightmare scenario whereby they would blow up eleven American airplanes as they were flying across the Pacific Ocean beginning on January 21, 1995. The secret plan became known as the Bojinka plot, a Croatian word meaning "explosion." They planned to place the bombs in carry-on bags which would be left under the seats. These bombs would be scheduled to go off on the exact leg of the flight over the Pacific Ocean. One of these devices was successfully tested when a bomb blew up on December 11, 1995 on a plane from Cebu in the Philippines headed for Japan. In this successful "wet test," a bomb was placed under seat 26K on PAL Flight 434, and killed a Japanese tourist. The plane failed to go down and made a successful emergency landing in Okinawa. Prior to the explosion, Yousef disembarked at Cebu City.

After Yousef's arrest, U.S. intelligence authorities found more incriminating evidence against him, detailing a more sinister plot.

Part of the plan was to hijack an airliner and crash it into a power plant inside the United States. Another scheme called for the hijacking of airliners and using them as arial bombs which would be flown into such high profile targets as the WTC, the Pentagon, and CIA headquarters. This was the exact scenario that would go down on 9-11.

As the investigation into the Bojinka plot unraveled, U.S. intelligence was apprised of the fact that Murad had taken flight training in schools in the United States in places such as Texas, California, and New York. This was the same scenario that many of the hijackers used prior to 9-11. A separate part of their deadly diagram was the assassinations of Pope John Paul II and President Bill Clinton when they made their trips to the Philippines.

On the night of January 6, 1995, while the men were mixing chemicals needed to make their bombs, a fire erupted in their room, number 603 at the Dona Josefa apartments. Police and firemen were called, and arrested Murad who went back to retrieve computer equipment. Walid Kahn Amin Shah was arrested but managed to bribe his way out of jail. He was re-arrested in Malaysia. Ramzi Yousef's uncle, Khalid Sheikh Mohammed, KSM, escaped, along with his nephew.

Before Murad was brought back to the United States for questioning, he told Col. Rodolfo Mendoza of the Philippine National Police that Yousef and his uncle, KSM, had selected six high-profile targets inside the United States for attack, among them, the WTC, CIA headquarters, the Pentagon, an unnamed nuclear facility, the Sears Tower in Chicago, and the Transamerica Tower. This information was given to the U.S. Justice Department but no further action was taken.

Less than one week after Yousef fled Manila, the FBI got a tip that would finally seal his fate. Yousef had checked into a guesthouse in Islamabad, Pakistan. A multi-million dollar reward was posted for Yousef's arrest and the man who stepped up to collect the prize was Yousef's sometime friend, Istiaque Parker. On February 3, 1995, Parker made contact with the U.S. Embassy in Pakistan and gave up Yousef's whereabouts. Four days later, a joint U.S.-Pakistani army military unit burst down the door of Yousef's apartment and took him into custody.

After a marathon flight back to the United States, a heavily guarded helicopter carrying Yousef back to New York for trial passed the still standing twin towers. One of his guards said something to the effect that the mammoth buildings were still standing. Answering in a smug way, Yousef replied that, "They wouldn't be if I'd gotten a little more money."

In 1996, Yousef and Shah stood trial in New York in a Federal District Court for trying to blow up U.S. airliners (the Bojinka plot) and were convicted on September 6, 1996. Also indicted was Uncle Khalid who fled the country.

The what-ifs in the case of the Bojinka plot are a poor man's fantasy. What if Philippine National Police had nabbed KSM in 1995 instead of after the 9-11 attacks? Would they then have been able to connect the dots between him, bin Laden, Ramzi Yousef, and Murad's tale of attacks on high-profile targets in the U.S.—the Pentagon, WTC—as far back as 1995? If, as PNP Col. Mendoza said, he sent Murad's information to the U.S. Justice Department, then why didn't both the CIIA and the FBI look into the matter? And why wasn't KSM put on the FBI's radar when they knew he was a co-conspirator in the Bojinka plot, nor did they know of his blood relationship with Ramzi Yousef?

According to author Peter Lance in his book called *Cover-Up,* FBI agent Frank Pellegrino debriefed Murad during his flight back to the U.S. In an FBI 302 memo, Agent Pellegrino said Murad told him that Ramzi wanted to return to the U.S. in the future to bomb the World Trade Center a second time.

Ramzi Yousef is now residing in a federal maximum security prison out west with no hope for parole (more about the FBI and Ramzi Yousef in a later chapter).

In 1991, two years before the WTC-1 attack, a man entered the United States in unremarkable fashion. At that time, no one knew who he was, just another traveler from a foreign nation coming to our shores. The man's name was Hani Hanjour, who was one of the hijackers on 9-11. Other accounts in the press said he had entered the county back in 1990, but that is in dispute. Hani Honjour was a busy man when he arrived in the States, taking English lessons in Tucson, Arizona until early 1992. While Hanjour was in Arizona, there were a number of other al Qaeda operatives living in the city but it is not known if he had any contact with these elusive people. He was on no federal watchlist, so the feds had no reason to keep him under surveillance. In testimony from his brother, Abulrahman, Hani stayed in Arizona for three months before returning to Saudi Arabia, where he spent the next five years managing his family's lemon and date farm.

It was later learned that FBI Director Robert Mueller reported that he too believed that Hani Hanjour had stayed in the United States for three months. This was disputed by an unnamed FBI source who said that Hanjour stayed in the U.S. for as long as 15 months.[4]

The story of Hani Hanjour does not end with his leaving the United States. That was just the beginning. After going back to Saudi Arabia, Hanjour returned to the United States for a second time. After arriving back in the country, he moved to Miramar, Florida with a number of friends. A person who knew him while he was in Miramar said of him, "Of all my husband's colorful friends, he was probably the most nondescript. He would blend into a wall." The *Washington Post* would write about him saying,"Hanjour's meek, introverted manner fits a recurrent pattern of the al Qaeda network of unsophisticated young men being recruited as helpers in terrorist attacks." FBI agents said people they have interviewed about Hanjour said that he "fit the personality to be manipulated and brainwashed."

Hanjour left the warmth of Florida around April 30, 1996 and moved to San Francisco, California where he stayed with an unidentified family. He stayed with his family from April to September of that year. While in San Francisco, he took English lessons at rate of 30 hours per week at a college in Oakland.

After finishing up his English courses, Hanjour took on a different route in his life. He enrolled in a rigorous one-year flight training program at the Sierra Academy of Aeronautics in Oakland, even though his English was not that proficient. For whatever reason, Hanjour only attended the 30-minute orientation class on September 6 and never came back.

But Hanjour was still not done with his flight training sessions. He moved to Scottsdale, Arizona in late 1996 where he enrolled

4 October 3, 1991 to February 1992: Hanjour is First 9-11 Hijacker to enter US-History Commons.

in the CRM Training Center for three months. Once again, he had to drop out. The owner of the training center where Hanjour took lessons later said of him that he was a "weak student" who was "wasting our resources." The man who spoke these words was Duncan Hastle who later added this comment regarding Hanjour, "He was not able to fly solo in a small plane, which is equivalent to getting out of a parking space [in a car] and stopping." In an interesting move on his part, he returned to the CRM School with two friends: Bandar Al Hazmi, a fellow Saudi, and Rayed Abdullah of Qatar. Hanjour took an additional three lessons, but still failed to make the grade and was not able to complete the coursework necessary to get a license to fly a single-engine plane. After dropping out, he had the nerve to call the school back, asking for more flying lessons. Mr. Hastle, the manager said to him, "We don't want you back at our school."[5]

At the same time that Hani Hanjour was having trouble learning how to fly small engine planes in the United States, another interesting development regarding one of the 9-11 hijackers was also playing out in the States.

The man in question is named Abdulaziz Alomari who was then living in Denver, Colorado. It was 1995 and it seemed that his passport has been stolen. He had been taking studies at the University of Colorado from 1993 to 2000. What makes this event more interesting is the fact that Alomari had the first and last name of one of the 9-11 hijackers. His passport was stolen when a robber entered his apartment, and he reported the theft to the police. In the aftermath of the 9-11 attacks, the FBI reported that its investigation recorded two birthdates for Alomari. One of them, May 28, 1979, would be used by the hijacker, for example on his U.S. visa application. The other birthdate, December 24, 1972, belonged to the former Denver student, who worked as a telecommunications engineer in Riyadh, Saudi Arabia. When the Alomari who lived in Denver heard of the fact that someone associated with 9-11 had used his birthdate he remarked, "I couldn't believe it when the FBI put me on their list. They gave my name and my birth date, but I am not a suicide bomber. I am here, I am alive. I have no idea how to fly a plane. I had nothing to do with this." What all this meant

5 History Commons: October-1996-December 1997: Hani Hanjour Twice Attends Scottsdale Flight School.

in the long run of interesting events leading up to 9-11 is still an open mystery, but it raises more questions than answers about the number of al Qaeda personnel living in the United States in the six years prior to the September 11, 2001 attacks, and what the purpose of these men in the country really was.[6]

We can add one more name to the list of suspects in the WTC bombing case who, like Hani Honjour and Abdulaziz Alomari, was up to no good in the years preceding 9-11. It is a well-known name in this narrative, Ramzi Yousef.

From late 1993 up to December of 1995, the FBI learned from a foreign source, WTC bomber Ramzi Yousef used a mosque in Milan, Italy called the Islamic Cultural Institute, which served as a base of operations for al Qaeda. Soon, Italian authorities began investigating the Center and found out that it was indeed the main European headquarters for a terrorist group called al-Gama'a al Islamiyya, a radical Egyptian militant group. From there, recruits were sent to fight in Bosnia, among other places. The center was run by a man named Anwar Shaaban, who was a close associate of the blind Sheik Abdul Rahman. On June 25, 1995, Italian police raided the center and arrested over 70 people in other parts of the country. After the raid, Shaaban escaped arrest but was killed in Croatia a short time later. Later, the center would re-open and continue to carry out anti-Western activities.

Another person with al Qaeda ties who infiltrated into the United States during the late 1990s (1997-1998) was Raed Hijazi, who was convicted in Jordan for attempting to blow up hotels there; he took up residence in Boston. Over time, Mr. Hijazi was contacted by the FBI who were investigating a drug trafficking ring bringing in white heroin from Afghanistan to the United States. Hjazi would later become an informant for the FBI and provide valuable information regarding supposed terrorists inside the United States. However, for whatever reason, the FBI was more interested in what he had to say regarding the heroin network than any information regarding potential al Qaeda or other terrorists living in the U.S.

There is another interesting connection regarding Raed Hijazi and al Qaeda. One of his friends in Boston at that time was Nabil

6 History Commons: 1995: Passport of 9/11 Hijacker's Namesake Stolen in Denver.

Al-Marabh who transferred and deposited large sums of money that a bank in Boston flagged as suspicious. It was ascertained later that Al-Marabh sent certain funds to his friend Raed Hijazi while he was living in Boston. Investigators never could accurately figure out where the money came from.

While all these myriad events were taking place in the United States and across the world involving some of the players in what would become the 9-11 attacks, an event that took place in late 1969 and early 1970 would soon resonate in the halls of the Pentagon that only a select few military officers knew about.

The person who was at the center of this very interesting story was a man named Dan Hill, a U.S. Army Ranger who was then taking officer candidate training. He came up with a hypothetical plan in which the Soviet Union could start a war with the United States, a part of which called for a suicide pilot to fly a plane into the U.S. Capitol building in Washington, D.C.

How Dan Hill was chosen for developing this rather unusual plan began as part of his training when he was at Fort Benning, GA.. One of the courses he was taking was in nuclear weapons deployment. One of the parts of the course that he was assigned to was yo imagine that he is a Soviet Premier who wants to start World War III against the United States. Hill and the other members of his class were asked to develop a plan to effect this. The plan that Dan Hill came up with was called "State of the Union." The gist of the plan was that a military C-47 plane, filled with explosives, would fly into the U.S. Capitol during the State of the Union address by the president of the Unite States. The suicide plane would crash into the Capitol, killing all the representatives and senators, the cabinet, and the president and vice president. At the same moment as the crash in Washington, the Soviet Union would initiate its attack on the United States. (This scenario is similar to the plot of a TV show called *Designated Survivor* starring Kiefer Sutherland, who played a cabinet member who was asked to stay behind in case of an attack such as theone described in the Hill scenario, thus, the "Designated Survivor").

Now, things begin to get weirder for Dan Hill. After his plan was submitted to his superiors at the Pentagon, he was asked to meet with Major General John Carley, the assistant commander of the infantry school for an undisclosed talk. Along with General Corley were six other men who were wearing civilian clothing. Major General Carley asked Hill the following question, "How did you come up with this?"

Hill replied, "This is my area of expertise." He told the men in the room that he was well versed in unconventional warfare, counterterrorism, and the use of explosives. After talking with the men in the room for almost an hour, he is told by General Carly, "We'd prefer you forget you ever heard this." Hill followed orders and forgot about the matter as instructed.

Later, Dan Hill would tell a friend, Rick Rescoria, an army veteran, about the incident. Mr. Rescoria told Hill the following. "You evil-minded b-stard. When you have these thoughts, don't publicize them to anyone. The plan is a tactically and technically proficient; it makes sense, but only to people like you and me. To the rest of the world, it looks like the workings of a deviant mind. This kind of thing terrifies people."[7]

In the wake of that fateful meeting, Hill would later learn that the government ordered an increase in the air defense around Washington, D.C.

One last interesting tidbit of information regarding al Qaeda operatives in the United States prior to 9-11 concerns the activities of a con man named Randy Glass and the story he told to the FBI. This event took place in July 1999, when Glass, a sometime U.S. government informant, met for dinner with other men in a restaurant overlooking the World Trade Center. Among those at the dinner besides Glass were an illegal arms dealer named Diaa Moshen, Mohammed Malik, a former Egyptian judge named Shireen Shawky, and Pakistani ISI (intelligence service) agent Rajas Gulum Abbas. Unknown to the rest of the men in attendance was the fact that Glass was recording their conversation.

FBI agents posing as customers were also in attendance and watched the entire proceedings go down. Mr. Abbas said that he wanted to purchase a shipload of weapons from the United States military to give to Osama bin Laden. This was two years before the attack on 9-11, a time in which the United States government had bin Laden in its sights due to the numerus attacks al Qaeda

7 History Commons: Trainee Army Officer Imagines Scenario of Suicide pilot crashing plane into U.S. Capitol.

had been perpetrating around the globe. During their conversation, Abbas pointed to the looming tower of the WTC and remarked to his dinner companions, "Those towers are coming down." Abbas continued his tirade against the United States saying, "Americans are the enemy. We would have no problem with blowing up this entire restaurant because it is full of Americans." Mr. Glass's recording was reviewed by the leadership of the FBI, but no action was taken.

In August 1999, the same group of men who attended the meeting with Randy Glass met again in a West Palm Beach, Florida warehouse. A Stinger missile was shown to the men which was part of a U.S. government sting operation. It was soon learned by U.S. intelligence of the connection between two of the men in the meeting (Mr. Abbas and Mohammed Malik) and the Islamic radical groups in Kashmir, India, and the Taliban. Malik suggested that the missiles would be used in Kashmir or Afghanistan. During the Afghan-Soviet war, Stinger missiles were used successfully by the fighters to down a number of Soviet planes and helicopters which eventually turned the tide of the war.

History Commons reported:

> According to Dick Stoltz, a federal undercover agent posing as a black market arms dealer, one of the Pakistanis at the warehouse claims he is working for A.Q. Kahn. A Pakistani nuclear scientist, Khan is considered the father of Pakistan's nuclear weapons program and also the head of an illegal network exporting nuclear technology to rogue nations. Government informant Randy Glass passes these warnings before 9-11, but he claims, "The complaints were ordered sanitized by the highest levels of government.[8]

Two years after the bombing of the World Trade Center, another destructive act of homegrown terrorism took place in the heartland of America. On April 19, 1995, a massive bomb destroyed the Alfred Murrah Federal Building in Oklahoma City, killing 168 and wounding hundreds more. Within days of the attack, two men were arrested in connection with the bombing, Timothy McVeigh and Terry Nichols. Both men served in the army together and had

8 History Commons: August 17, 1999-Arms merchants seek nuclear materials in U.S. Report is sanitized.

no previous criminal record.

Tim McVeigh grew up in the small town of Pendelton in upstate New York where he graduated in 1986. After high school, he got a job as a security guard with an armored car company near Buffalo called Burke Armor Inc. Not liking the job, he joined the Army in 1989 and was sent to basic training at Fort Benning, GA. McVeigh proved to be a perfect soldier, and despite keeping to himself, was well liked by his fellow soldiers. One of the men whom McVeigh befriended was the oldest man in his unit, Terry Lynn Nichols. This odd pair would soon begin a deep friendship which would take them far beyond their small world of military action to being the centerpiece of one of the greatest acts of terrorism on American soil. While in the Army, McVeigh tried to enlist in the elite Army Special Forces but failed to make the grade. After his enlistment was up, he mustered out and began a round of endless trips across the country. He stayed for a while with Terry Nichols at the latter's Michigan farm. In the rural area surrounding the Nichols farmhouse, the men would build bombs made out of fertilizer. It was a mammoth fertilizer bomb that would be used in the Oklahoma City attack. While staying at the Nichols home, McVeigh would attend meetings of the underground, and oftentimes violent, Michigan Militia whose verbal attacks against the federal government were legendary. It was their absolute hatred of the United States, federal authorities said, that led the two men to destroy the Murrah Building and take 168 innocent lives.

After the bombing, and with McVeigh and Nichols in custody, federal officials were able to track down the trail that led them to the Alfred P. Murrah Federal Building. In the months prior to the bombing, both McVeigh and Nichols focused their activities on the lonely stretch of highway along U.S. 77 in Kansas. Their route took them from Fort Riley to Junction City where they made preparations for the attack.

The FBI believed that Nichols and McVeigh financed their operation by robbing a number of banks in Kansas City, Missouri and other parts of the Midwest from January 30, 1994 to March of 1995. In September 1994, they were seen in the small Kansas town of Herrington where at the same time, someone stole 299 sticks of dynamite and 500 blasting caps from a rock quarry nearby. On

April 6, 1995, Nichols drove McVeigh from Oklahoma City to Junction City where McVeigh said that "something big" qas going to happen. On April 17, McVeigh and an as yet unidentified man (called "John Doe 2"), rented a Ryder truck from Elliot's Body Shop. The men were in Herrington, Kansas, the home of Terry Nichols, when McVeigh drove the Ryder truck to a rental shed where unidentified materials were probably taken and placed into the truck. At that point in time McVeigh is said to have told Nichols, "If I don't come back in a while, you'll clear out the storage shed." Clearly, from McVeigh's perspective, something was about to happen.

On April 19, 1995, according to federal authorities, McVeigh and other unnamed co-conspirators drove to Oklahoma City where they set off a huge explosion which destroyed the Murrah Federal Building (the same type of Ryder truck used in the OK City bombing was also used in the WTC-1 attack).

However, that may not be the end of the story. New evidence in the years since the event show the possible, sinister connection of a number of Middle Eastern men to the events in Oklahoma City, and interesting clues that possibly tie Terry Nichols to Ramzi Yousef.

This information was discovered by a journalist named Jayna Davis who was a broadcast reporter for KFOR-TV in Oklahoma City at the time of the attack. (Her book, *The Third Terrorist,* tells this most interesting story in detail.) Right after the explosion took place, the FBI and the Oklahoma State Police began an intensive search for the unidentified Middle Easterner who was seen fleeing the Murrah Building. Police were originally looking for a brown Chevrolet pickup "occupied by Middle Eastern subjects." When queried by local police if "this was good information or do we really not know, they were told, "authorization FBI." Soon, this all-points bulletin was canceled.

Ninety minutes after the bombing of the Murrah Building, an alert Oklahoma State trooper pulled Tim McVeigh over along an isolated stretch of highway in Perry, OK for speeding. The arresting officer found a .9 millimeter pistol in his possession and took McVeigh in for questioning. While McVeigh spent the night in jail, a composite sketch of the prime suspect in the bombing was flashed to all police departments across the nation. As the Perry police were about to release McVeigh, the photograph came crackling over their teletype. Much to their astonishment, the man in custody matched the description of the person wanted in the federal building attack. McVeigh led them to Nichols as being part of the conspiracy.

According to information gathered by Jayna Davis, employees of a propertymanagement company located in Oklahoma City saw a brown Chevy truck near their office a few days before the bombing. She says that the original "John Doe 2" was really an Iraqi man named Hussain al-Hussaini. This person came from Saudi Arabia to the U.S. in 1994 and worked in Oklahoma City in a restaurant. Mr. al-Hussaini sued Davis for libel but the charge was thrown out of court.

After the Oklahoma City bombing, Mr. al-Hussaini relocated to Boston but soon left for another location.

In the course of the Murrah investigation, other onsite witnesses described Middle Eastern looking men driving away at high speed immediately after the blast. Ms. Davis also said she uncovered information that put eight Iraqi men in close association with both Nichols and McVeigh prior to the attack.

When a federal grand jury indicted both McVeigh and Nichols in 1995, part of the language of the indictment said that both men acted with "others unknown" in the destruction of the Murrah Building. For whatever reasons, federal prosecutors did not pick up this possible foreign conspiracy angle, concentrating their focus on Nichols and McVeigh.

The "others unknown" in the indictment just might have been WTC-1 bomber, Ramzi Yousef. At the same time that Yousef was in the Philippines for the Bojinka plot, Terry Nichols and his mail-order Philippine wife were there too. Why Nichols was in Cebu, in the Philippines is open to dispute but writers believe that he might have been in touch with members of the Abu Sayyaf terrorist group based in that nation. How an almost destitute Nichols had the funds to travel to the Philippines is not known, unless he was being supported financially by "others unknown."

Another link between Ramzi Yousef and Nichols was given by Edward Angeles, a leader of Abu Sayyaf. Under questioning by

Philippine police, he told them that the men met in the Philippines, although he did not know their exact relationship. Angeles was killed in 1999 in a shootout.

Stephen Jones, McVeigh's lawyer, was a firm believer in the "others unknown" theory and even wrote a book by that title. Talking to a magazine, Jones remarked about McVeigh saying, "Tim couldn't blow up a rock. Then Terry goes to the Philippines and they now are able to make a highly dangerous bomb that brought down the Murrah Federal Building."

In 2006, the Oklahoma City bombing case took on a new emphasis when the U.S. Congress began its own investigation. The committee that had jurisdiction was the House International Relations Oversight Committee headed by Congressman Dana Rhorabacher. Their report was called "The Oklahoma City Bombing: A Foreign Connection?" Their chief investigator was named Phaedra Dugan who turned up new information on a possible Ramzi Yousef-Terry Nichols connection. Here are the highlights of the House report.

•A tour guide name Daisy Gelaspie told police that on a trip to the Philippines in 1990, Nichols asked if she knew anyone who could build bombs.

•Nichols made additional trips to the Philippines during the early 90s, and was even in Cebu at the same time as Ramzi Yousef in December 1994. Within days of Yousef's Manila bomb factory being raided by police, on January 6, 1995, Nichols beat a hasty retreat from the Philippines.

•Ramzi Yousef had been training members of the Abu Sayyaf, the al Qaeda splinter group in the early 90s near the Southern Philippine town of Davao City.

•In a sworn deposition, Edwin Angeles said that he was in Davao City in a hotel room with Terry Nichols, Yousef, Abdul Hakim Murad, and Wali Khan Amin Shah where they discussed bombmaking and handling.

•Before the OKC bombing, McVeigh only attempted to explode an ammonium-nitrate bomb that failed, according to key government witness Michael Fortier. But after Nichols and Yousef were in the Philippines at the same time in Cebu, McVeigh and

Nichols took down the federal building.

•On the day of the OK City bombing, Yousef's oldest friend, a pilot trained in four U.S. flight schools, took credit for the blast while in a cell at the Metropolitan Correctional Center in lower Manhattan. The FBI wrote this all down in a 302 memo.[9]

The report also goes into the activities of a man named Samir Khalil, a Palestinian who had hired a number of Middle Eastern men to work on his properties in OKC prior to the bombing, Khalil's ex-wife, Carole See Khalil, was killed in the fifth floor of the Murrah Building when the explosion took place. According to his former bookkeeper, Khalil was at the Circus Circus Hotel in Las Vegas two days later at a time that Terry Nichols' phone records show that two calls came to his home in Herrington, Kansas from the Circus Circus. The same Samir Khalil is on a list of 172 unindicted co-conspirators in the "Day of Terror" case which was co-prosecuted by Assistant U.S. Attorney Patrick Fitzgerald and Andrew McCarthy. Other names on the list were bin Laden, and his brother-in-law, Mohammed Jamil Khalifa and Ali Mohammed (more about him later in the book).

Congressman Rohrabacher, who ran the investigation, asked the Dept. of Justice to determine if this was the "Samir Khalil" relating to the OK City bombing, but he was stonewalled. Rep. Rohrabacher asked the DOJ to determine if the man's name on the unindicted conspirators in the WTC bombing list was the same man in Oklahoma City. A letter responding to his request stated that such a task would be too "burdensome."[10]

On August 10, 1995, Timothy McVeigh and Terry Nichols were indicted by a federal grand jury in Oklahoma City on charges that they blew up the Murrah Federal Building.

McVeigh has subsequently been executed for his crime.

Terry Nichols has been convicted on both federal and state charges and is serving a life term in prison.

On June 25, 1996, three men drove a fuel-laden tanker truck to the outskirts of the Khobar Towers apartment complex in Dhahram, Saudi Arabia. Members of the U.S. Air Force's 440th

9 Peter Lance.com. Vindication on the Ramzi Yousef-Terry Nichols connection.

10 Ibid.

Fighter Wing were living in the large apartment complex as part of the force that was flying reconnaissance missions over Iraq after the Gulf War. The approximately 3,000-5,000 pounds of fuel were brought in from Lebanon purposely for the attack.

The men parked the gasoline truck next to a fence and after giving the go-ahead signal, quickly left the scene. Near the compound, an American Air Force sentry named Staff Sgt. Alfredo Guerrero, saw the mysterious activity near his station and realized something was wrong. He was able to quickly alert the security team near the Khobar Towers and his quick work enabled the men living on the top floors to evacuate the building.

The rest of the people living in the building were not so lucky. The truck exploded in a huge fireball which destroyed the six-story structure. The blast left an 85-foot-wide crater, with the blast being felt as far away as Bahrain which was located some 20 miles away. The explosion left 19 U.S. servicemen killed and over 300 wounded.

Saudi authorities captured a number of suspects, and summarily executed them before American FBI agents arrived to speak to them. The Khobar Towers attack was originally blamed on the Middle Eastern terrorist group Hezbollah, which had been responsible for past killings of American citizens. In 1998, Osama bin Laden said that he and his al Qaeda were responsible for the planning of the attack. In June 2001, a U.S. District Court in Virginia indicted 13 people, mostly Saudis, in the Khobar Tower attack. In an ironic twist, the bin Laden construction company was given the job of rebuilding the apartment complex.

The next act of international terrorism sponsored by bin Laden took place on August 7, 1998 when two powerful bombs went off almost simultaneously at two U.S. Embassies in Nairobi, Kenya and one in Dar es Salaam, Tanzania. The Nairobi blast leveled the building and killed 213 people, including two Americans. The Tanzania blow killed 11 and wounded 85. These two deadly attacks were blamed on al Qaeda and showed just how potent bin Laden's terrorist network really was.

On August 4, 1998, both al Qaeda and the Egyptian Islamic Jihad released a statement threatening Americans for the capture of three Islamic fighters who were taking part in operations in Albania. Three days later the East Africa Embassies were attacked.

What was not known at the time of the East Africa bombings, and would only come out in subsequent investigations, was that a man named Ali Mohammed, an ex-Egyptian army officer and sometime FBI informant—a well as being a double agent for al Qaeda—took pictures of the East Africa embassies on behalf of bin Laden. His photographs were instrumental in the planning of the bombs. Ali Mohammed was also linked to the Muslim men whom the FBI watched take target practice over a two week period at a Calverton, Long Island shooting range. After the police raided El Sayyid Noasir's Jersey home, they found top secret Army documents that belonged to Ali Mohammed (although at the time they did not realize the documents belonged to him).

Following the embassy attacks, bin Laden and 22 of his cohorts were indicted for their roles in these attacks. Of these, only four were apprehended and convicted at trial.

On August 20, 1998, in retaliation for the East Africa attacks, President Bill Clinton ordered an American military strike against suspected bin Laden training camps in Afghanistan. From U.S. warships in the Persian Gulf, a number of cruise missiles rained down on bin Landen's camps in the mountains of Afghanistan. It is believed that bin Laden was possibly warned by his informers inside the Pakistani intelligence service, ISI, and left hours before the strikes occurred. A number of bin Laden's followers were killed, but if the U.S. was aiming at bin Laden personally, they missed him.

Another target was a pharmaceutical plant located in the Sudan where, it was believed, VX gas agents were being produced. The plant was destroyed and over the decades since, there was no conclusive proof that any deadly agents were being manufactured at that facility.

In his memoirs, President Clinton defended these attacks on bin Laden, noting that he didn't expend millions of dollars worth of American military ordinance just to redistribute some dirt in the Afghan mountains.

On January 3, 2000, bin Laden's al Qaeda mounted an attack against an American warship, the USS *The Sullivans* which was docked in the harbor of Aden, Yemen. A small boat laden with explosives headed from shore with a raiding party in tow. Unknown to the American sailors on board, the dingy was supposed to be on a kamikaze mission designed to sink the huge warship. Before the small boat could get near *The Sullivans* she sank from the heavy load she was carrying. American naval authorities knew nothing about the proposed attack. On that day a terrorist strike against an American warship was averted. Their second try would turn out much differently.

Nine months later, the USS *Cole* was taking on fuel and supplies in the same port of Aden, Yemen that the USS *Sullivans* had visited. Learning from their mistakes in October, a group of bin Laden associates steered a rubber boat into the warm waters in search of a new target. Their prey was an American destroyer, the USS *Cole*. Sailors aboard the *Cole* saw the approaching boat but paid no mind to it. Seconds later, the bomb-carrying boat slammed into the destroyer, leaving a huge gash in the middle of the ship. In all, 17 U.S. sailors were killed and 40 injured, but thankfully, the destroyer did not sink.

The *Cole* attack came during the last months of the 2000 presidential election in the United States and the Clinton administration did not respond militarily to the incident. Instead, teams of CIA and FBI agents converged to Aden to conduct their own investigation (along with the Yemeni government).

As the weeks went on, no conclusive proof that al Qaeda was responsible for the *Cole* incident could be found. However, National Security Advisor Sandy Berger asked General Hugh Shelton to formulate military plans against bin Laden, whom the administration believed was ultimately responsible. The Pentagon developed a multi-faceted military plan called "Phased Campaign Concept." which included strikes against Taliban targets in Afghanistan, although no coordinated plan to invade Afghanistan was included.

A contingent of 100 FBI agents were sent to Yemen's capital, San'a, led by the brash, opinionated lead investigator from the New York office, John O'Neill. Once on the ground in San'a, O'Neill began an intensive FBI investigation into the events leading up to the *Cole* attack. O'Neill began to butt heads not only with the government of Yemen, but with the U.S. Ambassador, Barbara Bodine. Bodine did not like O'Neill's lectures, nor the fact that his agents were determined to run the investigation no matter whose shoes they were going to step on. Ambassador Bodine disapproved of the fact that the FBI agents were allowed to carry guns. Another point of contention was the fact that the State Department did not believe that the U.S. embassy faced any lingering terrorist threat, despite O'Neill's warnings to the contrary. Ambassador Bodine also rankled O'Neill when she told him bluntly that she believed that the FBI presence in Yemen was too large. Ambassador Bodine further inflamed O'Neill when she openly berated two of his women agents over the way they were dressed.

At one point in the investigation, all but 50 FBI agents left Yemen amid hard feelings on both sides. Barry Mawn who was a lead investigator in the *Cole* affair said of the situation on the ground in Yemen, "It became clear that (Bodine) simply hated his (O'Neill's) guts." Mawn would later say after spending ten days on the ground in Yemen that O"Neill was doing a fine job with his FBI team. Despite what Mawn had to say regarding O'Neill, Ambassador Bodine refused to allow the FBI team to return to Yemen to finish up its investigation.

Later, the prime minister of Yemen said that one of the 9-11 hijackers, Khalid Almihdar was one of the *Cole* perpetrators who was involved in preparations for the attack. He was in Yemen at the time of the attack and stayed after the ship was struck. He subsequently left the country. Writing of the *Cole* attack, the *Sunday Times of London* wrote the following of the incident, "The failure in Yemen may have blocked off lines of investigation that could have led directly to the terrorists operating September 11."

It would later be found out that there was a bin Laden connection to the *Cole* attack. Bin Laden's brother-in-law, Mohammed Jamal Khalifa, helped fund a militant group in Yemen that would later take credit for the bombing of the ship. The name of the group in question was the Islamic Army of Aden, which was formed in 1996 or 1997, but was not officially heard from until May 1998. The groups carried out the kidnappings of 16 mainly British tourists in December 1998 and four of the tourists were killed during a shootout with police. It was also alleged that Jamal Khalifa was linked to Ramzi Yousef's Bojinka plot but he denied that allegation.

Vincent Cannistraro, a member of the CIA's Counterterrorist Center would later say that not only did Khalifa fund the Islamic Army of Aden, but that 9-11 hijacker Khalid Almihdar had ties to the group as well. Cannistraro also said that Khalifa went on to form the group after being deported from the U.S. in 1995. He should have never been allowed to leave U.S. custody. It was also reported that bin Laden gave permission for the Aden group to use a training base in Yemen that was under his control.[11]

In late October, Yemeni police announced the arrest of a number of foreign operatives and nationals in connection with the *Cole* bombing, including the Egyptian suicide bomber, a number of Yemenis, and Algerians. President Saleh of Yemen said that the perpetrators were part of militant Egyptian Islamic Jihad, headed by bin Laden's second in command, Dr. Ayman al-Zawahri.

Jack O'Neill left Aden in late November 2000, along with the rest of the FBI team, after seven weeks of battling not only al Qaeda but a U.S. ambassador who gave him as much grief as those who attacked the *Cole.*

If Jack O'Neill felt he had dodged a bullet escaping his time in Yemen, things were now to go from bad to worse upon his arrival in the United States. On August 19, 2001, there appeared an article in the *New York Times* reporting that the FBI had started an internal investigation into the activities of O'Neill for losing his briefcase, which contained various intelligence papers. O'Neill was then the head of the FBI's national security division in New York.He had misplaced his briefcase as he attended a meeting in Orlando, Florida. Lucky for the FBI, and also for O'Neill, the briefcase was found a few hours later with nothing missing. In the wake of the incident, the FBI's Office of Professional Responsibility started an investigation to look into all the details of the incident. When all was said and done, it was determine by the investigating office that no crime had been committed and prosecution of O'Neill was not recommended. One part of the internal investigation said, "FBI officials were alarmed, in part, because of the sensitivity of the documents involved, including the details about the bureau's counterterrorism and counterintelligence operations. One document contained highly sensitive information about an FBI source."

11 1996-1997 and After-Bin Laden's Brother-in-law Khalifa said to Found al Qaeda linked group in Yemen.

It seemed that there was more to the story regarding O'Neill and his lost briefcase. In an article in the *New Yorker* magazine, the author wrote that the leaking of the details of the FBI probe to the *Times,* "seemed to be timed to destroy ONeill's chance of being confirmed for a National Security Council job." The leaker was portrayed as "somebody being pretty vicious to John." John O'Neill later thought that the person responsible for the leak was Thomas Pickard, who was the acting FBI Director at that time. Valerie James, who was O'Neill's girlfriend at the time, said Pickard was "out to get John for a long time and John never really knew why." Pickard denied he was the leaker of the news story. Other possible leakers were supposed to have been Dale Watson, the assistant director of the bureau's counterterrorism division, Ambassador Bodine who clashed with O'Neill in Yemen, and possibly Richard Clarke, who served as the White House counterterrorism chief. For the one man who was so determined to hunt down Osama bin Laden, his undoing was partly his own responsibility, as well as the many enemies he made over a lifetime working in the FBI.

In one of his last acts as an FBI official, O'Neill signed papers ordering FBI agents back to Yemen after Ambassador Barbara Bodine left her position. The agents arrived in Yemen only a few days before the 9-11 attacks.

Once back in New York, O'Neill pressured his bosses and the State Department to allow him to return to Yemen to make further inquiries into the *Cole* incident. He was turned down. In August 2001, John O'Neill left the FBI and took on a new, higher paying job—that of head of security at the World Trade Center. He died on September 11, 2001 and his body was found days later amid the rubble.

In Yemen, the trial of the conspirators took shape. Eight men were charged with orchestrating and carrying out the attack. In September 2004, two men were sentenced to death and four others were given prison terms. Sentenced to death were Abd Rahim Nashri, a Saudi citizen who was the al Qaeda operations chef in the Persian Gulf, and Jamal Badawi, a Yemeni national who was the top al Qaeda agent in Yemen. Fehd Quso, the man who was supposed to film the attack but was not there, got a ten year sentence. Jamal Badawi's assistant in passing the money from bin Laden to the operatives, Maamoun Msouh, got eight years in jail. Two others, Ali Mohammed Saleh and Morad Sirouri, who provided false identification papers, both got five years. Besides being tried for the *Cole* attack, both Quso and Badawi were also indicted for their participation in the abortive plot against the USS *The Sullivans.*

Despite the military preparations and procedures that the Pentagon put in place after the attack on the *Cole*, the Clinton administration decided not to retaliate. Bin Laden believed that an American response would be coming and from his base in Kandahar he dispersed his most trusted aids, including Mohammed Atef and his deputy, Ayman al Zawahri, to other parts of Afghanistan. Following the attack, bin Laden's propaganda machine went into gear and al Qaeda developed a propaganda film which included a reenactment of the attack. The film was a great aid to the recruitment of more followers to bin Laden's growing anti-U.S. jihad movement.

From the time of the *Cole* attack to December 2000, the CIA and the president's top national security officials were at loggerheads as to who was responsible for the incident. It wasn't until December 21, 2000 that the CIA presented its findings to the Small Group of Principles. The CIA briefer said that it was their "preliminary judgment" that bin Laden's al Qaeda "supported the attack." The CIA report hedged in the end by saying, "intelligence gave some ambiguous indicators on an al Qaeda direction of the attack." Only a few weeks into his term, President Clinton decided not to respond to the attack because "he did not think it would be responsible for a president to launch an invasion of another country just based on a preliminary judgement."

When the new Bush administration came into power they took up the *Cole* response, and, like the Clinton administration before, decided not to take any retaliatory action. The consensus among the Bush national security team, including National Security Advisor Condoleeza Rice, Sec. of State Colin Powell, and Defense Sec. Donald Rumsfeld, was that an American response that was "tit-for-tat" would be counterproductive. Rumsfeld's deputy, Paul Wolfowitz, said that the *Cole* incident was "stale." In the end, no U.S. response was taken. With one more attack unanswered by the

United States, bin Laden set forth for what he hoped would be a spectacular attack on U.S. soil at the dawn of the new century.

At the approach of the new millennium, the United States intelligence community began to fear that a new wave of terrorist attacks would take place. Heightened security was taken to ensure that the millions of people taking part in the New Year‘s celebrations would be safe. The U.S. intelligence community did have something to fear. Unknown to them, an Algerian national was plotting to set off a powerful bomb at LAX—Los Angeles International Airport—on January 1, 2000.

In December 1999, the Jordanian government uncovered a terrorist plot to attack a number of hotels in that country, including the Raddison. Working closely with the Jordanians, the CIA was able to link certain members of the Jordanian cell to people living in Boston and Los Angeles.

In the United States, the FBI mounted a full court press to unravel any terrorist plot inside the United States and mobilized all of its field offices nationwide in its effort. They asked for, and received, a number of FISA (Foreign Intelligence Surveillance Act) warrants to investigate potential suspects.

While these undercover efforts were going on an Algerian named Ahmed Ressam, who trained in Afghanistan with al Qaeda, prepared to attack LAX airport at the time of the millennium celebrations.

Ahmed Ressam was born on May 19, 1967 to a large family in Algiers. He moved to France in 1984 for medical treatment but soon returned to Algiers. During the protracted civil war that broke out in Algeria in 1992, Ressam one again moved to France where he lived as an illegal alien. In February 1994, using a false passport, he traveled to Canada and asked for political asylum.

He settled in Montreal for four years and lived in an apartment building that catered to members of the radical Algerian terrorist group called the Armed Islamic Group GIA, which had close ties to bin Laden’s al Qaeda. In Montreal, Ressam was a petty thief, robbing tourists. Despite his record, he was convicted only four times, and unexpectedly, never served any jail time. He also met up with another Algerian named Mokhtar Harouari. Together, the two men sold bogus drivers licenses, credit cards, and other forms of identification.

In 1995, Ressam failed to show up at his court hearing regarding his application for political asylum and an arrest warrant was put out. He also began using an alias from a stolen baptismal certificate with the name “Bennie Antoine Norris.” He was thus able to obtain a credible Canadian passport using the Norris identity. Unknown to Ressam, the Canadian Security Service was conducting an investigation of GIA members then living in Canada. Since Ressam was going by the name of “Bennie Norris,” the Canadian police were never able to get him in their sights.

In March 1998, Ressam left Canada for the wilds of Afghanistan. He was met in the Pakistani city of Peshawar, a lawless, no man’s land of spies and terrorists, a place where someone could lose themselves if they had the right connections. Ressam was met by bin Laden’s trusted advisor Abu Zubaida. Zabaida took Ressam under his wings and the Afghan underwent intensive training in al Qaeda camps. His job upon leaving Afghanistan was to become part of al Qaeda’s European cell which was tasked with the job of conducting operations in Canada and the United States.

Over the next few months, Ressam traveled from Canada to Seoul, South Korea, to Los Angeles where he made a surveillance trip to LAX to see the layout of the airport and test it security. He then went back to Montreal where he began to gather the chemicals needed for his bomb. It was at this rime that Ressam renewed his relationship with Mokhtar Haouari who gave Ressam a contact in New York.

On November 17, 1999 Ressam left for Vancouver, British Columbia for the final preparations for his LAX plot. In Vancouver, Ressam met another Algerian named Abdelmajid Dahoumane. Collectively, they put the final pieces of the explosive together.

On December 14, 1999, Ressam boarded the ferry from Victoria, British Columbia en-route to Port Angeles, Washington. Inside the trunk of his car were 100 pounds of explosives which he hid in the wheel bed of his trunk.

Using his fake passport in the name of Bennie Norris, Ressam was questioned at the Canadian side but was allowed to board, despite the suspicion of the Canadian guards.

Once the boat docked at Port Angeles, Ressam was stopped

at the immigration station by Customs Agent Diana Dean. Miss Dean asked Ressam to open his trunk and saw what looked like drugs stored in plastic bags. When asked to step out of the car, Ressam bolted, and was arrested.

In the wake of Ressam's arrest, Canadian and FBI agents nabbed both Mokhtar Haorari and Ressam's supposed New York contact, Abdelghani Mwskini. The arrests of all three men led FBI agents to other cells inside the United States, as well as overseas.

Ressam was found guilty on April 6, 2001 on nine counts of conspiracy to perform an international terrorist act. He was given a sentence of 130 years in jail. His accomplice, Abdelmajid Dahoumane, fled to Afghanistan and a five million dollar bounty was placed on his head. He was later apprehended by Algerian police.

In a twist, Ressam testified in court in July of 2001 against his fellow co-conspirator in the LAX plot, Mr. Haouari. The testimony took place in the Federal District Court in Manhattan on charges that Ressam withheld information from investigators who questioned him as part of his agreement to cooperate with the government.

In his court testimony, Ressam told the jurors that he withheld certain information in order to protect his friends. Under questioning from Joseph Bianco, the United States attorney, Ressam said that he hid certain information from the government, but that he didn't lie to them.

When questioned by Mr. Haouari's lawyer, Daniel Oilen, about why he was not originally forthcoming during the 14 interviews he gave to the Feds, he wasasked following question, "The reason you weren't upfront with the government about your friends in Canada was because you were trying to protect them from prosecution, correct?"

Ressam answered as follows, "For two reasons, actually. I was concerned about them being prosecuted and also I was afraid about my family." Ressam also admitted that he never told Mr. Haouari about his original target—LAX—or his plans to carry out an "act of jihad" or holy war in the United States. [12]

At his trail, Ressam said that his al Qaeda network was going

12 Mansnerus, Laura, "Witness in Bombing trial says he withheld names of Friends." *New York Times*, July 7, 2001.

to carry out major attacks against U.S. targets. "If one is to carry out an operation, it would be better to hit the biggest enemy. I mean America."

The United States had caught another break. Credit has to go to the alert border crossing guard, Diana Dean, who suspected there was something untoward with Ahmed Ressam.

One last story in the terror timeline concerns the terrorist network headed by Abu Nidal that sowed terror amidst the hot sands of the Middle East and elsewhere around the globe.

The Abu Nidal group was also called the Fatah Revolutionary Council and was established in Baghdad by a radical Palestinian named Sabri al-Banna who was born in Jaffa in 1937. After the 1948 Arab-Israeli war, his family was forced to move to the West Bank where he became radicalized against Israel. He took on the nom de guerre of Abu Nidal and soon his name would be recognized across the Middle East as terrorist number one on Western intelligence lists. Beginning in the 1970s, his organization began terror attacks against Israeli targets across the region. Over time, they would conduct such brazen attacks as on El Al ticket counters in the Vienna and Rome airports, which killed eighteen and wounded forty others.

By 1979, Abu Nidal had opened secret cells in Western Europe whose targets would become active upon orders from the top. One of their most brazen attacks was an attempted assassination attempt on the life of Israeli's ambassador to London, Shlomo Argov, on June 3, 1982. The attempt failed and the assassins were put on trial in March 1983 in a British court.

On September 11, 2001, America's luck finally ran out. The plot that Ramzi Yousef and his uncle KSM hatched in Manila in 1994 at long last succeeded.

Ahmed Ressam.

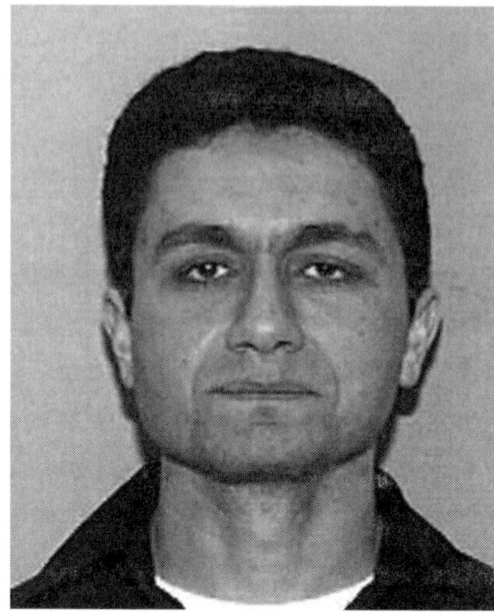

Mohamed Attta.

The north face of the South Tower of the World Trade Center, September 11, 2001.

Chapter 2

The Law of Unintended Consequences

The years 1996, 1997, and 1998 were pivotal in the United States' war on bin Laden and the Taliban regime that was harboring him in Afghanistan. President Clinton began to take certain, concrete steps in order to beef up our national security in ways that were unheard of in previous years. Some of these worked, and some didn't, but at the time it seemed necessary that something be done to try and stop to war of terror that bin Laden and his followers were unleashing around the world.

In May 1998, President Clinton made one of his first appointments in the covert war against bin Laden and his followers. He created a new top-level governmental position called the National Coordinator for Security Infrastructure, Protection, and Counterterrorism. The peron in this position would be dubbed the "tsar," like the ruthless men who ran Russia for generations. The man he named to be the "tsar" was Richard Clarke. This new position was created under the guise of a new presidential directive on counterterrorism, Presidential Directive 62 or (PDD-62), which also outlined the nation's developing strategy for combating international terrorism. Richard Clarke had been working quietly in the White House on certain terrorism issues, outside of the public eye. It would be the same Richard Clarke who, only a few year later, would come before the 9-11 Commission and apologize for the United States' failure to foresee the events that led up to the New York and Washington attacks.

If Clarke's job as terrorism tsar had any appreciable meaning, his job didn't start out so well. He had a staff of only 12, which was nothing compared to other governmental agencies that had similar responsibilities. Among the many restrictions that Clarke had to deal with was the fact that he was not allowed to have jurisdiction over law enforcement agents in the United States, spies, or active military personnel which was necessary if he was to conduct his covert assignment. The only saving grace for Clarke was the fact that he was able to attend cabinet meetings where he was able to tell the president and his fellow cabinet members what he was doing.

Richard Clarke was not a novice when it came to government service; his career began in 1973 when he was a nuclear weapons analyst in the Office of the Secretary of Defense. He stayed on in the Reagan administration and served as the deputy assistant secretary of state for intelligence from 1985 to 1989. (After his stint in government service, Clarke would write spy novels). He left the State Department in 1992 and worked for six years on the National Security Council Staff.

However, there were many people inside the Clinton administration who had different thoughts about Clarke than did the president. Some people believed he was a war hawk, a charge that would later taint many of the people in the George W. Bush administration after 9-11, especially those who wanted a war against Iraq which had nothing to do with the attacks. One of Clarke's critics was Robert Gelbard, who worked with him at the State Department, who said of him that he "is no liberal. He is very hawkish." Another critic of Clarke was CIA officer Vince Cannistraro who worked with Clarke in the decade of the 1980s. He said of Clarke, "You can't accuse him of being passive or too liberal on foreign policy."

Clarke was a Republican in the Democratic Clinton administration, but that fact didn't stop him from gaining the confidence of the president. Clarke fitted the agenda that Clinton wanted and they worked in sync for their mutual purposes.

One person who knew Clarke from Boston was Larry DiCara, the former president of the Boston City Council who was a friend of Clarke' s when both were younger. DiCara said of his old friend, "He was fiercely conservative at a time when just about everyone in Boston was a Democrat. I'm amazed he worked for President

Clinton."

Another influential person who had strong things to say about Richard Clarke was Daniel Benjamin, who served as a counterterrorism official in the Clinton administration. He said of his time with Clark, "But that was one of the things that made him valuable to his masters and to the political leadership. He broke a lot of crockery, but Dick's mastery of the bureaucracy was almost unrivaled in the 1990s."

Sandy Berger, who served at one time as Clarke's boss and was the national security advisor for Bill Clinton said that "he regularly had to turn down demands from colleagues that Clarke be fired."

Another person who had strong ideas on Clarke was Phyllis Oakely, who ran the Intelligence and Research bureau at the State Department during the Clinton administration. She described Clarke as "someone who could get things done on peacekeeping, organizing the military because he knew where to go in the Pentagon." She further said that Clinton's two national security advisers, Sandy Berger and Anthony Lake, didn't know how to line up the troops.[13]

However, it was after he left government service that Clarke made a name for himself when he published a best-selling book called *Against All Enemies,* which caused a sensation around the country. The book was a scathing indictment against both the Clinton and Bush administrations regarding the so-called war on terror. The book criticized George W. Bush and his top advisors including Secretary of Defense Donald Rumsfeld and his deputy, Paul Wolfowitz, regarding the events after the 9-11 attacks. Clarke wrote that the Bush crowd was not interested in the rise of al Qaeda, yet were obsessed with Iraq and Saddam Hussein and tried to persuade Bush that Saddam Hussein had something to do with the 9-11 attacks.

Clarke wrote in his book that he was upset with the actions of George H. W. Bush when the president failed to take any concrete action in 1991 after Hussein put down a Shiite uprising in Iraq. He also said he believed that the Clinton administration should have undertaken a large bombing campaign in response to the attempted

13 Eggan, Dan and Walter, Pincus, "The Book on Richard Clarke," *Washington Post*, March 23, 2004.

assassination of the late President George H.W. Bush by Iraq. In the wake of the attempted assassination of Bush the first, Clarke helped formulate a plan of retaliation against Iraq. The Clinton administration made a strike against Iraqi intelligence headquarters in Baghdad, but Clarke said he was "initially disappointed that the retaliation had been so small, that targets had been taken off the list, and that the raid was scheduled in the middle of the night when few Iraq intelligence officers would be present."

Clarke was also involved in a 1996 incident regarding a noted terrorist with ties to bin Laden named Imad Mugniyah who was wanted by the government of Saudi Arabia. Mugniyah was the leader of a Hezbollah group that killed U.S. soldiers in Lebanon from April 18 to October 23, 1983. The CIA found out about Mugniyah and that Saudi Arabia would not aid the U.S. in his capture. Clarke would later say about this incident that "in 1996 the CIA learned that Mugniyah had boarded a commercial airliner in Khartoum, Sudan, that would make a stopover in Riyadh, Saudi Arabia. U.S. authorities pleaded with the Saudis to hand him over but they refused. Clarke would say about this event, "We raised the level of appeals all the way through Bill Clinton who was on the phone at three in the morning to Saudi Crown Prince Abdullah to grab him. Instead, the Saudis refused to let the plane land and it continued on to Damascus." Mugniyah was finally arrested in 2008.

After the disputed 2000 presidential election between George W. Bush and Vice President Al Gore was settled by the U.S. Supreme Court, the new Bush administration, in the person of National Security Advisor Rice, kept Clarke on in the White House to work on counterterrorism matters, but on a lesser scale. While keeping his job, Clarke now found himself downgraded in the power he had under Bill Clinton but decided to stay on nevertheless. He was now limited as to whom he could speak to inside the White House and what his everyday duties were. Before his departure from the Bush administration, Clarke never had a one-on-one meeting with the president to discuss matters involving al Qaeda.

Clarke would later recall what he was thinking at the beginning of the Bush administration regarding his lesser position in the White House pecking order.

> I asked for a meeting with the president several times beginning, if fact, before Condoleezza Rice even took office in the transition briefing. I said I have given this briefing to the vice president, I've given it to the secretary of state, I've given it now to you, I would like to give it to the president. And what I was told was I could brief the president on terrorism after the policy development process had been completed.

Clarke did indeed have one meeting with the president before 9-11, but only to talk about cyber security issues. During that meeting, neither the president nor Clarke talked about al Qaeda or bin Laden, a missed opportunity if there ever was one. When later asked why the subject did not come up, Clarke said, "Because I had been told by Dr. Rice and her deputy that this was a briefing on countering the cyber threats and not on al Qaeda and that I would have my opportunity on al Qaeda if I just held on, eventually they would get to it, probably in September."

In the summer of 1995, the CIA began the genesis of a program called rendition that would, in later years, cause a storm of controversy that would have its nadir in the Bush administration when it came to the war against Saddam Hussein. The proposal, which the Clinton administration signed off on, called for abducting Islamic Jihad members and sending them to Egypt for detention and interrogation. The policy of rendition was new in the lexicon of the war on terror and in later years, many of the top members of the CIA, including some of its prior directors, said the use of rendition in breaking terrorists was not necessary and sometimes illegal.

The rendition program did not go at a fast pace at first, as many countries wanted nothing to do with it. Michael Scheuer, the head of the CIA's bin Laden office, was one of the men who originated the use of rendition in Egypt. He wrote of the decision, "It was begun in desperation. We were turning into voyeurs. We knew where these people were, but we couldn't capture them because we had nowhere to take them, due to legal and diplomatic complications. The CIA had to come up with a third party."

The Egyptian secret police force, called the Mukhabarat, was one of the most brutal organizations when it came to interrogation, and when they did their dirty work, American officers were never in the room to watch what was going on. The first person to have the dubious distinction of being renditioned in Egypt was Talaat Fouad Qassem. Unfortunately, he would not be the last.

Michael Scheuer of the CIA said that the agency lawyers were all over the beginnings of the rendition program and followed every step along the way. He said of the legal maneuvering,

> There is a large legal department within the CIA, and there is a section of the Department of Justice that is involved in legal interpretations for intelligence work, and there is a team of lawyers at the National Security Council, and on all of these things those lawyers are involved in one way or another and have signed off on the procedure. The idea that somehow this was a rogue operation that someone has dreamed up is just absurd.

Michael Scheuer told Congress that he ran the CIA's rendition program against al Qaeda and other Sunni militants from August 1995 until June 1999. The CIA set up an official Renditions Branch at Langley headquarters beginning in 1997, but it is not known just what role Mr. Scheuer played in it.

In October of 1995, the Clinton administration took the first, tentative steps against the bin Laden network that would consume the next administration too. At that time, the president signed a presidential order directing the Departments of State, Justice, and Treasury, the National Security Council, the CIA, and other departments of the federal government to combat the rising tide of terrorist money-laundering and other nefarious activities. When this information came to light, it got attention in the nation's press and it was reported thusly. The *New York Times* wrote of the new Clinton plan saying, "They failed." If the government had any idea that they would be successful in tracking bin Laden' secret funds, they were mistaken. A person knowledgeable about these matters, William Wechsler who worked on the National Security Council staff under Bill Clinton, said that "the government agencies given the task suffered from a lack of institutional knowledge, a lack of expertise. We could have been doing much more earlier. It didn't happen."

Let's step back a bit and see how bin Laden and al Qaeda got on the official radar.

In January 1992, Operation Desert Storm/Desert Shield commenced with a fierce air and land attack. Allied armies liberated Kuwait and drove the Iraqi's back to their own country. Despite the Saudis' promise that American forces would soon leave Saudi Arabia, a large contingent would remain in place for many years to come. In 2003, when the United States attacked Iraq, Saudi Arabia refused to allow the U.S. to use its territory as a staging base for the attack.

After Operation Desert Storm, bin Laden continued to harangue the royal family, attacking them politically for their pro-Western stance. In response, the Saudi regime put bin Laden under house arrest to keep him quiet.

In 1991, bin Laden fooled the government into letting him travel to Pakistan and then went on to Afghanistan. From there, he moved his entourage to the Sudan where he was to make his new home. Jamal al Fadl, his brother-in-law, made a trip to Sudan where he paid off that country's ruler, al-Turabi. He bought a farm near the capital of Khartoum for $250,000 as well as a salt farm for $180,000 near Port Sudan.

In Sudan, bin Laden's construction company developed roads and built other infrastructure in that poor country. In return, he was allowed free reign and brought a large number of al Qaeda followers with him. Sudan would now become his new Afghanistan, and he commenced to turn Sudan into jumping off point in his crusade against the West.

The CIA was following bin Laden's progress in Sudan, especially tracing his money that was well disbursed to buy everything from medicine to construction equipment, and guns and ammunition for people in Egypt. The agency saw bin Laden as an up-and-comer in radical Islamic circles, a main financier of the jihad, not the operational player he would later become.

Despite his standing with the government, not all those in Sudan liked him. In 1994, a botched assassination attempt on his life took place. Believing that he was in a particular Khartoum mosque, four men sprayed the place with machine gun fire but bin Laden was not present. A number of people died and a few of the assailants were themselves killed.

From Sudan, bin Laden continued his anti-Saudi diatribe, and despite their wish that bin Laden cease and desist, he refused. In retaliation, the Saudi royal family stripped him of his citizenship. He was now a man without a country.

While all this was going on, the CIA station in Khartoum was compiling a large dossier on bin Laden's secret operations. They traced his whereabouts to a number of training camps in Sudan, investigated his contacts with Sudanese intelligence, and found out that he had brought to Sudan hundreds of false passports that he gave to his al Qaeda followers. Men from Algeria, Tunisia, Egypt, and other places took training in these camps, all under bin Laden's care. When the government of Pakistan expelled large numbers of Afghan men for anti-governmental activity, bin Laden paid for three hundred of these men to come to Sudan. According to author Steve Coll in his book *Ghost Wars,* a number of bin Laden's followers in Sudan put out an assassination attempt on CIA officer Cofer Black. When the U.S. ambassador found out about the plot he confronted the Sudan government who reluctantly put an end to the secret plan.

The Clinton administration described bin Laden as the "Ford Foundation of Sunni Islamic terrorism," and the agency elevated him from being just a terrorist financier to a player in the game, a person to be watched. (It was also from Sudan that the blind Sheik, Abdul Rahman, would, in 1990, be given an entry visas to travel to the United States).

During the late 1990s, the agency had a number of on going operations in Sudan and elsewhere regarding the actions of bin Laden. One of the undercover operatives in Sudan was a man named Billy Waugh who was a trainer for various al Qaeda operatives around the world. He wrote about his time in that region in his autobiography, "I worked right there with these al Qaeda operatives and heard these arguments [about the badness of U.S. policy] firsthand many times, especially during an assignment in Yemen." Mr. Waugh reflected about his attitudes towards the extremists he met saying, "I have spoken to some of those terrorists and they consider terror attacks against the public their only outlet to hurt and destroy the infidels who have wrongly ousted them from their homes so many years in the past."

In February of 1991-92, Billy Waugh was in Khartoum, Sudan, conducting surveillance on bin Laden. He drafted a plan to assassinate bin Laden for the CIA and would say that it was one of "hundreds" of such proposals he prepared for the agency. It was prepared as a routine part of his job, he said, and "it isn't anything special, but is just written in case someone decide that was the necessary course of action." The assassination plan, such as it was, was to kill bin Laden while he was on the move because he would not be as well protected as if he were in a stationary position. One CIA car would follow bin Laden on one of his regular trips out of town, and another would approach bin Laden from the opposite direction and ram into his car. The driver of the trailing car would then get out and shoot bin Laden. All of this planning came to naught as it was cancelled due to the fact that American government would not assassinate of a foreign leader as a matter of policy. Billy Waugh had the thought of killing bin Laden himself but decided not to go through with the plan (good idea on his part).[14]

Billy Waugh and the CIA would take part in another covert operation regarding bin Laden, this time regarding his finances. Waugh took part in a surveillance operation against the bank that bin Laden used to finance his operations. He said regarding this operation, "bin Laden went to the bank every day, and you might figure that if the CIA knew which bank he used, it would recruit someone within the bank to provide information. Well, by God, they did." Waugh also said that the agency had information on bin Laden's personal bank account, although no more information regarding the account was made public. The name of the bank that Waugh is probably referring to is the Al-Shamal Islamic Bank (located in the Sudan).

When Billy Waugh arrived in the Sudan around February 1991, the CIA Station Chief took him aside and told him what the agency knew about bin Laden's activities in that nation, but said that "we don't know what he's up to, but we know he's a wealthy

14 1991-1992: CIA Contractor Drafts plan to assassinate bin Laden but it is not implemented-History Commons.

financier and we think he's harboring some of these outfits called al Qaeda. See what you can find out." Waugh said, "I was familiar with bin Laden from CIA traffic but this was the first time I had heard the term al Qaeda." If agent Waugh was aware of al Qaeda at that time, it seems that the rest of the American government was one step behind. For example, the U.S. State Department did not officially use the term al Qaeda until 1996, two years prior to the North African embassy bombings. The magazine *U.S. News and World Repor,* wrote, "So limited was the CIA's knowledge that it began using al Qaeda's real name only in 1998—ten years after bin Laden founded the organization."[15]

Besides the military and the CIA running covert and overt military operations against al Qaeda, we can now add another shadowy, paramilitary organization that conducted secret, off the books missions in the so-called war on terror. The name of the organization in question is Blackwater Worldwide which was run at the time by a former Navy Seal named Erik Prince. Blackwater's mission during that time was a covert program of "snatch and grab" operations against Taliban forces in Afghanistan and in Iraq. At the beginning of Blackwater's operations, there was little difference between the private contractor and the members of the CIA. A number of Blackwater operatives had once worked for the agency and both organizations kept a close watch on what the other was doing. Part of Blackwater's job was to serve as protection for agency officers and the lines between the groups soon became muddy. Oftentimes, Blackwater employees became intermingled with the CIA on operations to capture or kill enemy operatives.

In the investigation that followed the actions taken by Blackwater during the Iraq/Afghanistan conflict, it was learned that certain Blackwater employees took part in a secret mission to kill top leaders of al Qaeda. This certainly crossed the line between military and contract workers doing the job that professional military soldiers were supposed to do. "What is not clear is if the CIA had planned to use the contractors to capture or kill al Qaeda operatives, or just to help with training and surveillance." It was also reported that certain Blackwater employees helped to provide security on a number of CIA flights which were transporting detainees to certain parts of the world for interrogation.

15 History Commons: February 1991-CIA Already Aware of al Qaeda.

In reporting by the *New York Times,* "the CIA did not have a formal contract with Blackwater for this program but instead had individual agreements with top company officials, including the founder, Erik Prince, a politically connected former member of the Navy Seals and the heir to a family fortune (Prince's sister, Betsy DeVoss, was in the cabinet of President Trump).

The press reported that "a retired intelligence officer told the *Washington Post,* that outsourcing gave the agency more protection in case something went wrong." The *Post* wrote that Blackwater, "was given operational responsibility for targeting terrorist commanders and was awarded millions of dollars for training and weaponry, but the program was canceled before any missions were conducted."[16]

Blackwater was paid more than $5 million to send a small team of men inside Afghanistan during the early part of U.S. operations beginning in 2002, one year after 9-11. In the early stages of its work, Erik Prince arrived in Afghanistan as part of the original twenty-man team. Blackwater personnel worked for the CIA at its station in Kabul as well as in Shkin, which was located along the border between Pakistan and Afghanistan.

There was not unanimity among those in the intelligence community regarding the actions of Blackwater during this time. One unnamed CIA official said, "There was a feeling that Blackwater eventually became an extension of the agency." Former New Jersey congressman Rush Holt was a frequent critic of Blackwater's operations and he said at one point, "the use of contractors in intelligence and paramilitary operations is a scandal waiting to be examined."

Jack Rice, a former CIA agent said regarding the actions of Blackwater, "When the agency actually cedes all oversight and power to a private organization, an organization like Blackwater, most importantly they lose control and don t understand what's going on. What makes it worse is that you can turn around and have deniability. They can say, it wasn't us, we weren't the ones making the decisions."[17]

If the covert paramilitary missions undertaken by Blackwater

---

16 Risen, James and Mazzetti, "Blackwater guards ties to secret CIA raids," *New York Times*, December 10, 2009.

17 Scahill, Jeremy, "Blackwater: CIA Assassins?" *The Nation*, August 20, 2009.

weren't controversial enough, the company lost its million dollar plus contract with the State Department to provide diplomatic security for the United States Embassy in Baghdad after a 2007 shooting that left 17 Iraqi civilians dead, and made headlines in the papers across the United States.

There seemed to be a revolving door between the employees of the CIA and Blackwater as many former high-ranking agency officials went to work at Erik Prince's company. Among those former CIA officers who went to work for Blackwater were Cofer Black, the former head of the CIA's Counterterrorism Center, Robert Richer, former No. 2 for operations, Alvin "Buzzy" Krongard, former executive, and Enrique Prado, the military chief of the Counterterrorism Center. There was some pushback among certain high ranking CIA officials regarding the exodus of its employees to Blackwater. Former CIA Director Michael Hayden tried to reverse this trend by refusing to allow security clearances to contract employees until at least 12 months after they had left the CIA. Hayden said regarding the use of contractors, "We go to contractors because they possess certain experiences or certain knowledge that we don't have inherently inside our workforce. We generally use the best athlete available in the draft."

Blackwater was founded in June 1997 by Erik Prince shortly after he was discharged from the SEAL program. The name of his facility was the Blackwater Training Center which was located on more than 400 acres in North Carolina, bought for a price of $756,000. Another facility was located in Camden County, and went for a selling price of $616,000. The facility was built in an out-of-the-way location near the Great Dismal Swamp. The idea of Blackwater was to "fulfill the anticipated demand for government outsourcing of firearms and related security training." It began official operations in May 1998 and was mostly staffed by a legion of former military men who had special warfare skills. In 2002, Erick Prince opened up a new part of Blackwater called Blackwater Security Consulting with a former CIA operative named Janie Smith. The aforementioned Alvin Krongard provided Blackwater with one of its first government contracts (since many of Blackwater's contracts were secret, little is known just what they were hired to do). Mr. Krongard said about his deal with

Erick Prince's company, "Blackwater got a contract because they were the first people that could get people on the ground. The only concern we had was getting the best security for our people. If we thought Martians could provide it, I guess we would have gone after them." In 2007, Mr. Krongard joined Blackwater as a member of its board of directors.

In the end, the proposed Blackwater assassination program targeting certain al Qaeda leaders was never put into action, although the CIA spent millions of dollars on the program. The details of the program were finally released to the public by CIA Director Leon Panetta in 2009 among much fanfare in the press. The *New York Times* did a story on the assassination operation and wrote "paramilitary hit teams to kill al Qaeda operatives ran into logistical, legal, and diplomatic hurdles almost from the outset." The *Times* also wrote of the program that, "government officials said that bringing outsiders into a program with lethal authority raised deep concerns about accountability in covert operations."

Robert Baer, a former CIA officer who worked covertly in Afghanistan and who would later appear on several news shows had a scathing indictment of Blackwater's conduct. "Panetta must have been horrified that the CIA turned to mercenaries to play a part in its dirty work. It's one thing, albeit often misguided, for the agency to outsource certain tasks to contractors. It's quite another to involve a company like Blackwater in even the planning and training of targeted killings, akin to the CIA going to the mafia to draw up a plan to kill Castro." Baer also believed that the operations to kill al Qaeda leaders "were more about bilking the U.S. taxpayer than killing Osama bin Laden or other al Qaeda leaders."[18]

An interesting, and as yet unexplained, event that tied Blackwater to the so-called "20th" hijacker, Zacarias Moussaoui, has come to light. Moussaoui was taking flight training lessons in Minnesota and had gotten the attention of the FBI. It seems that authorities later looking into the Moussaoui case found out that the name and telephone number of Blackwater was found in his notebook. There is no concrete reason why the phone number was listed in his personal papers, but it is just another intriguing

18 History Commons: 2008-CIA program to Assassinate and capture al Qaeda leaders terminated, then revealed and outsourced to Blackwater.

question that never had a real answer.

In recent years, Erik Prince came back into the national spotlight during the lead up to the Trump administration. He was interviewed by Special Counsel Robert Mueller who was looking into Russian interference in the 2016 presidential election. He was part of the Trump transition team and came to know a number of leading figures during that time period, including Steve Bannon who has subsequently left the Trump administration. Robert Mueller was looking into any possible ties that Prince had with Russian officials and anything that he might have talked with them about.

The incident in question came in January 2017 when Prince met with a Russian named Krill Dmitriev, the chief executive officer of Russia's sovereign wealth fund in the Seychelles Islands which are located in the Indian Ocean. In interviews Prince gave to various media outlets after the meeting took place, he said that he just happened to be in the Seychelles on a business trip when he met Mr. Dmitriev. He said the meeting was of no importance and said that he could not even remember Mr. Dmitriev's name.

But now the story of the Prince/Dmitriev meeting takes on a new character. According to the Mueller report, before going to the Seychelles, Prince met with an emissary of the United Arab Emirates, George Nader, many times in New York where both men talked about Mr. Dmitriev. Nader told Prince that the Russians were interested in making contact with the Trump campaign and wondered if Prince could help them out? Prince said that he was not representing the Trump campaign in any way when he met with the Russian. The Mueller Report said of this incident that Prince told Dmitriev that he would relay information to Trump's campaign chief executive Steve Bannon. The Mueller report said of this meeting that "Nader told Prince to meet with Dmitriev in light of Prince's relationship with the Trump Transition Team in order to discuss issues of mutual concern."

In the meeting between Nader and Dmitriev, the Russian told Nader, "We want to start rebuilding the relationship in whatever is comfortable place for them. We understand all of the sensitivities and are not in a rush."

When he met with Dmitriev in the Seychelles, Prince told

Dmitriev that he wanted a new relationship with the Russians, and Dmitriev, who had good contacts with Russian President Vladimir Putin, agreed. The Mueller report said that "Dmitriev was disappointed with his meeting with Prince for two reasons. First, he had hoped to speak with someone with closer ties to the administration. Second, he had hoped to have outlined a strategic road map for the U.S. and Russia." Prince then met with Steve Bannon to report on the meeting, and got the impression he was relatively uninterested in what had transpired."

For George Nader, things did not go so well. In 2019, he was arrested when he arrived in New York and had in his possession a batch of child pornography.

The event that impacted the fate of bin Laden and his anti-Western jihad, took place on November 20, 1995. On that day, Islamic militants in Islamabad, Pakistan, conducted a high-profile truck bomb attack against the Egyptian embassy. Fifteen were killed and eighty were injured. A number of al Qaeda members took part in the attack. The Pakistani government arrested 150 Arabs, including a high bin Laden associate, Mohammed Yussuf Abbas, the director of the MAK office.

By February 1996, certain members of the Sudanese government approached members of the American government about what to do with bin Laden. He was now becoming a liability, rather than an asset. Sudan opened talks with the Saudis and offered him back if they would pardon him. They refused. On May 9, 1996, Sudan expelled bin Laden to Afghanistan. Back in the familiar territory, bin Laden and his al Qaeda began planning their war against America which would culminate on 9-11.

By 1998, the Clinton administration was made aware of the links between the notorious Pakistani intelligence services, ISI (more about ISI later in the book), the Taliban and bin Laden's al Qaeda. Over the decades since 9-11, President Clinton had been criticized over his handling of al Qaeda prior to the attacks on New York and Washington. Whether the criticism was warranted or not,is open for debate, but when he wrote his autobiography in 2005, the former president had a lot to say on the matter of telling the Pakistani government of the U.S. missile strike against the Taliban in order to kill bin Laden. He wrote,

> Although we were trying to work with Pakistan to defuse tensions on the Indian subcontinent, and our two nations had been allies during the Cold War, Pakistan supported the Taliban and, by extension, al Qaeda. The Pakistani intelligence service used some of the same camps that bin Laden and al Qaeda did to train the Taliban and insurgents who fought in Kashmir. If Pakistan had found out about our planned attacks in advance, it was likely that Pakistani intelligence would warn the Taliban or even al Qaeda.

Most people who have studied this part of the bin Laden saga came to the conclusion that Pakistan somehow warned bin Laden prior to the U.S. launching its missile strike against him. ISI was riddled with spies who were ideologically close to bin Laden and his political philosophy and would have had no compunction to inform him of U.S. intentions.

The years 1997 to 1998 were important in the development of the U.S. response to the rise of al Qaeda and bin Laden, but 1997 took on new meaning as the Clinton administration made war on bin Landen and the Taliban regime that was harboring him. It was decided by President Clinton to re-enter Afghanistan in a covert way and unleash the CIA in an effort to kill or capture bin Laden. Rather than keeping quiet, bin Laden continued to urge his followers to attack Western targets across the globe. Three years previously, the Taliban received its biggest boost when the Pakistani ISI all but created the new Afghan government, giving all necessary aid in its creation. For the United States, the recognition by its erstwhile ally in the hunt for international terrorists was a blow that could not be left standing.

A further blow to U.S. interests vis-a-vis the Taliban regime came on May 26, 1997 when Saudi Arabia officially recognized the Taliban. It should also be remembered that 18 of the 9-11 hijackers came from Saudi Arabia. Soon, the United Arab Emirates would join Pakistan and the Saudis as one of only three nations in the world to give its nod.

The United States decided it was time for an unofficial plan to get bin Laden, and in 1998, in a secret move, allied itself with the government of Uzbekistan, once a former Soviet republic. A covert plan was developed in which U.S.soldiers and troops from Uzbekistan conducted joint military operations against the Taliban.

At Langley headquarters, the CIA was working the midnight fires in order to capture or kill bin Laden. While he was still in the Sudan, the CIA instituted an "Issue Station" which would exclusively track every movement he made. The CIA named their bin Laden watch the "TFL," or terrorist financial links. With bin Laden now back in Afghanistan, the agency put him in another category—that of a main terror suspect, not just a financier as he had originally been seen. In secret, the CIA began to try to cultivate new assets inside Afghanistan to monitor bin Laden's every move.

With CIA Director George Tenet's approval, the OBL (Osama bin Laden) station developed a detailed plan to capture bin Laden from his Afghan hideout. The plan, which was first developed in 1998, called for an assault by a number of Afghan rebels who were allied with the CIA on a terrorist training base where bin Laden was staying. The plan called for the unit to capture him and bring him back to an undisclosed area, where he would be flown out of the country and taken back to the United States. In heated discussions at CIA headquarters, it was decided by Tenet and his top policymakers that the plan was unlikely to succeed and it was called off.

A new plan to get bin Laden took shape after the 1998 East Africa bombings which killed hundreds of people, among them, Americans. The White House and the CIA tasked the agency with recruiting varied Afghan tribesmen who wanted to work for the United States in an effort to capture bin Laden. On a number of occasions, these informants gave the CIA details of where bin Laden would be on a particular day. However, no attack took place as bin Laden was so well protected that it would have been foolish to attempt a strike. Another time, bin Laden suddenly changed his route and when the attack team got to the location, he was already gone.

By the summer of 1999, it was obvious that a new plan was needed to disrupt bin Laden. At CIA HQ, Cofer Black, a veteran of the CIA-Afghan wars, took control of the Counterterrorism Center. He developed a new plan which relied less on their Afghan assets and included more trained CIA agents who would be able to infiltrate Afghanistan. The plan also called for a new alliance with the North Alliance which had been allowed to fade after the U.S. pulled out after the Soviet-Afghan war ended.

For men like Cofer Black, the war against bin Laden and his followers was an ongoing obsession. It wasn't until 2001, after the 9-11 attacks, that Black and others would describe just what was going on during that time. Black said in an interview, "It was very evident that we were going to be struck, we were gonna be struck hard and lots of Americans were going to die. There were real plots being manifested." Black's boss at the time, Director George Tenet, said in an interview, "The world felt like it was on the edge of eruption. In this time period of June and July, the threat continues to rise. Terrorists were disappearing [as if in hiding in preparation for an attack]. Camps were closing. Threat reportings on the rise."

The covert war hatched by Cofer Black and George Tenet took on a new name, "the Blue Sky paper," which took shape in the spring of 2001. It called for a covert CIA and military campaign to: end the al Qaeda threat getting into the Afghan sanctuary; launch a paramilitary operation; and create a bridge with Uzbekistan. "And the word back," says Tenet, "was we're not quite ready to consider this. We don't want the clock to start ticking." Black would later say of the early Bush administration's thinking about bin Laden, "I think they were mentally stuck back eight years before. They were used to terrorists being European lefties—they drink champagne by night, blow things up during the day, how bad can this be? And it was a very difficult sell to communicate the urgency to this." [19]

With the lights now burning brightly in the CIA, DCI Tenet made a call to Bush's National Security Advisor, Condoleeza Rice, asking for an urgent meeting. Richard Blee, one of the members of the group that was at the meeting said, "There will be significant terrorist attacks against the United Sates in the coming weeks or months. The attacks will be spectacular. They may be multiple. al Qaeda's intention is the destruction of the United States." What do you think we need to do, asked Rice? "We need to go on a wartime footing now," replied Black.

Black further elaborated on his meeting with Rice and

19 Wipple, Chris, "What the CIA knew before 9/11: New details," *Politico*, 11/14/15.

the other principals in the room that day. "To me it remains incomprehensible still. I mean, how is it that you could warn senior people so many times and nothing actually happened? It's kind of like "The Twilight Zone." Condi Rice had her own recollections of the meeting and this is what she said. "My recollection of the meeting is not very crisp because we were discussing the threat every day. I thought we were doing what needed to be done."

In an interview with *Politico* years later regarding the events leading up to 9-ll, Director George Tenet explained his position at the time. He said he was in a meeting at CIA headquarters with his staff, talking about the threat level then going on in the country.

> We were just thinking about all of this and trying to figure out how this attack might occur. And I'll never forget this until the day I die. Rich Blee looked at everybody and said, "They're coming here." And the silence in the room that followed was deafening. You could feel the oxygen come out of the room. They're coming here. When asked by a reporter about what responsibility he personally had before the attacks, Tenet said, "I can only tell you what we did and what we said. There was never a moment in all the time when you blamed yourself, asked again, Tenet said, "Well, look, there… I still look at the ceiling at night about a lot of things. And I'll keep them to myself forever. But we're all human beings."

To show just how serious the Clinton administration was in getting bin Laden, the president, in August 1998, signed a Memorandum of Notification which gave the CIA permission to capture bin Laden or better yet, kill him. A basic lack of intelligence forced the CIA to abandon its initial plan. Those CIA officers who took part in the covert plan to get bin Laden said the administration accepted the policy of "risk avoidance" when it came to killing bin Laden (the SEAL team that finally killed him had no such reluctance).

After the 1998 embassy bombings, the U.S. ordered the Navy to station two submarines in positions off the Indian Ocean equipped with cruise missiles in a plan to kill bin Laden. Once intelligence agents on the ground pinpointed bin Laden's position, it would take up to ten hours to program the missiles, more than enough time for him to get away. On a few occasions, the CIA had bin Laden in their sights and were ready to unleash the missiles. At the last minute, DCI Tenet decided that there was not enough corroborative information to authorize such a strike and it was not carried out.

One such strike did take place after the 1998 embassy bombings but bin Laden apparently was tipped off (possibly by the ISI), and while a number of his followers were killed, the main target eluded his pursuers once again. After the 1998 attack, Richard Clarke, the president's counterterrorism tsar, said that if the ISI had wanted to fully cooperate with the CIA about bin Laden's location, they could have easily picked up the phone. Unfortunately, no call ever came.

In the wake of the U.S. retaliation for the embassy bombings, the Clinton administration decided on a full pronged strategy to target bin Laden. The president asked Richard Clarke to develop such a plan. Clarke came up with a far-ranging structure called "Delenda," which derived from the Latin "to destroy." It was Clarke's job to lay out the potential strategy and report to the higher ups in the White House who would accept or reject his proposals. The goal of the plan was the elimination of any threat from the bin Laden organization. Other pertinent parts of the plan were to prevent al Qaeda from acquiring weapons of mass destruction and eliminating any further threat from al Qaeda against Americans, worldwide.

The strategy for "Delenda" was the following:

•Diplomacy to eliminate the sanctuary in Afghanistan and bring terrorists to justice.

•Covert action to disrupt terrorist cells and prevent attacks. The highest priority was to target the enemy in Afghanistan.

•Financial measures, beginning with the just-adopted executive order to freeze the funds of bin Laden-related businesses.

•Military action to attack targets as they were developed. This would be an ongoing campaign, not a series of responses; and retaliations to particular provocations.

Despite Clarke's extensive work on Delenda, the powers that be in the Clinton administration decided not to implement the plan.

Actionable intelligence was put to the test in December 1998 when the U.S. located bin Laden at a location in Afghanistan and was preparing to take him out in a missile strike. The attack was not recommended because of worries about collateral damage to civilians in the immediate area. While the use of cruise missiles was nixed, another proposal to use precision guided bombs fired from aircraft over the target area was also rejected by General Anthony Zini who was the chief of the U.S. Central Command. General Zini did not want to use U.S. war planes over Afghanistan.

While the story so far has been about CIA reluctance to strike bin Laden, an incident that took place in October 1998 sheds light on how "actionable intelligence" was ignored by various agencies of the U.S. government in relation to bin Laden.

At around that time, an analyst for the Defense Intelligence agency, a brave agent named Julie Sirrs, made a covert trip to Afghanistan to see for herself the conditions on the ground. Sirrs met with Ahmed Shah Massoud who pleaded for more money to carry the fight to the Taliban. Massoud told Sirrs that bin Laden was the prime financier of the Taliban and if it weren't for his aid, they would not be able to stay in power. She also reported that an Afghan airline called Ariana Airlines was the principal facilitator of exporting drugs and importing arms to the Taliban from other countries.

Upon her return to Washington, her reports were met with downright hostility and skepticism on the part of the State Department. Sirrs said, "The State Department didn't want to have anything to do with Afghan resistance, or even, politically, to reveal that there was any viable option to the Taliban."

In another affront to her character, all of the material she brought back from her trip was taken away and her security clearance was yanked. In the end, she was exonerated of any wrongdoing but eventually quit the DIA. The fact that the State Department and the CIA refused to cooperate on Julie Sirrs' dangerous trip to Afghanistan, with her life potentially on the line, is outrageous.

In April 1998, while the capture/assassination plans were being implemented against bin Laden, the Clinton administration sent U.N Ambassador Bill Richardson on a fact-finding trip to South Asia which included a stop in Afghanistan. Richardson was the first official of the U.S. government to travel to Afghanistan in years, and more to the point, while bin Laden was given sanctuary by the Taliban. In a tense meeting with Taliban leaders, Ambassador Richardson asked that bin Laden be expelled (which was denied) and asked that the civil war between the various Afghan factions be stopped (another failure). Why Richardson went to talk with the Taliban to begin with is questionable, as the journey was a failure.

In another attempt to kill bin Laden, the CIA's Counterterrorist Center came up with a daring plan that called for the capture of bin Laden at his main headquarters called Tarnak Farms located near the city of Kandahar. The CIA was able to lay out with precision all the main buildings at Tarnak Farms, and by 1997, were training with local allies in the region to implement the attack.

DCI George Tenet briefed National Security Advisor Sandy Berger about the plan and the CIA was given permission to put the operation in motion. The operation called for a group of Afghan allies to snatch bin Laden from Tarnak Farms and take him to a location near Kandahar where he would be turned over to another group. From that location, bin Laden was to be flown to the U.S. When discussing the plan, it was noted by the men involved that if anything went wrong, innocent people, or the men directly involved in the mission, might be killed. One of the principals involved in the decision justified the job saying, "Sooner or later, bin Laden will attack U.S. interests, perhaps using WMD." That's weapons of mass destruction—the same WMD that were NOT found in Iraq prior to the 2003 war against Saddam Hussein.

In recent years, a number of previously classified documents on bin Laden and the Taliban have been declassified; they give historians a better picture of what was going on during that time. These documents can be found at the National Security Archive site and can be accessed free of charge.

One memo outlined possible steps to be taken:

> One option would be to revitalize [Blank] effort by providing more direct tasking which would allow them to directly assault his quarters. This option would be much less complicated than a capture attempt of a road convoy and would perhaps be more in line with the type of raids [Blank] conducted during the war. It might require

modification of the existing MON covering this operation. Given the threat posed by UBL to the United States, this is an option worth considering.

A second option would be to enlist the support of Afghan warlord Ahmed Shah Masood. Masood is currently in Northern Afghanistan fighting Taliban forces who are attacking him. It is thought that he will be able to successfully withstand the Taliban attacks and will be a force to consider in Afghanistan for many years to come. Masood is a soldier and accomplished guerilla fighter. He has demonstrated an ability to plan and execute difficult operations. Many of these options are not in and of themselves a clear best choice. The more options we pursue, the greater the likelihood that one will succeed.[20]

Another document, most of which is redacted, concerns an attempt on bin Laden's life. It is sent to Michael Scheuer from a person unidentified. It reads in part,

Mike, [Blank] planning for ubl rendition is going very well. [Blank] have come up with a very good plan—it fits the military model and is detailed, thoughtful, realistic, and keeps the risks up front and clearly addressed. The team really is enthusiastic about the effort and quality of work presented. Still, the odds of success are iffy—as in any special ops raid of this type—hundreds of variables which can be anticipated but not really planned for—and the thing could blow up at any point along the way. Still, a much better plan than I anticipated. Odds the op will get the green light-—50-50; odds it will succeed 40-60 (if we define success as ubl either in custody or dead. (Sent May 5, 1998).[21]

20 Subject: Further Options Available Against Usama Bin Laden, 18 November 1998.

21 Reference Number C05411935.

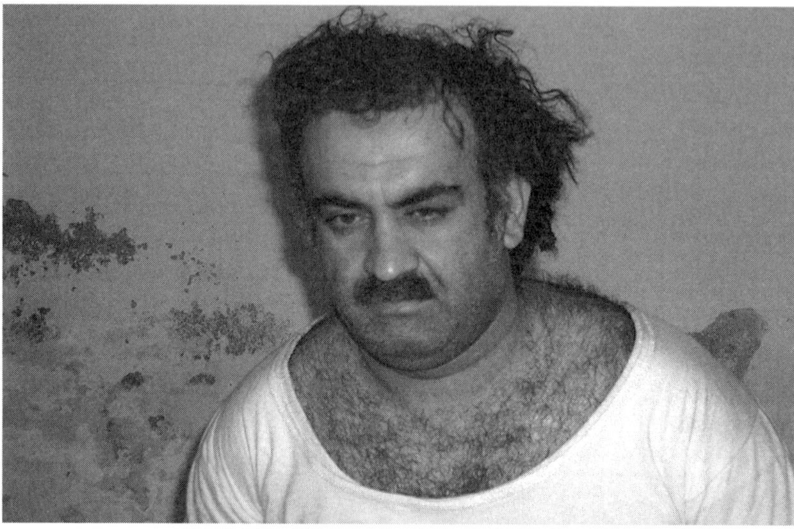

Khalid Shaikh Mohammed after his capture

Osama bin Laden.

Chapter 3:

Blowback: The CIA, Afghanistan, and the Rise of bin Laden

"The match is about to begin. Tomorrow is zero hour."
—An intercept from the NSA (National Security agency) that was picked up from an Arabic broadcast on September 10, 2001, but not translated until September 12, 2001.

For centuries, Afghanistan was the pivotal point of competition between the West and the Islamic republics for control over Central Asia. Over its long history, Afghanistan was strategically situated at the crossroads of Central Asia, bordered by Persian Iran, the old Soviet empire, Muslim Pakistan, and Hindu India. In the 19th century, two of the major players in international relations, the British Empire and Russia, vied with each other for hegemony in this vital region. This is what Rudyard Kipling called the Great Game of high-powered, international politics to see who could dominate Afghanistan. In the end, the rugged, clan people of Afghanistan would be the winners.

Over the centuries, the rulers of Afghanistan were the Parthians, the Hazara, the Tajiks, and the Uzbeks. These fiercely independent peoples banded together against encroachment by the Western powers.

In 1839, forces from the British East India Company arrived in Kabul, Afghanistan in order to stop Russian influence in that region. In 1841, Sir William Macnaughten, the British representative to Afghanistan, was shot by a relative of a tribal ruler whom he forced out of power. It was decided by the authorities in London to withdraw the remaining 4,500 soldiers and the other 12,000 noncombatants, having them exit over the rugged mountains through the Khyber Pass to modern-day Pakistan. In a military disaster of the first magnitude, all but one lucky person was killed.

Undaunted by this horrific military disaster, the British returned thirty years later and defeated the Afghan tribes. At this juncture, the British now had a secure border between British-controlled India and Afghanistan.

Over one hundred years later, the Soviet Union would enter the Afghan fray, just as the British did years before. In 1973, King Zahir Shah of Afghanistan was overthrown by Mohammad Daoud, a relative. Daoud sent the backers of the Soviet Union in the government packing and refused to take orders from Moscow. In 1978, on orders from Soviet Premier Leonid Brezhnev, the Daoud regime was ousted from power. The new rulers in Kabul were a pro-Soviet faction headed by Nur Mohammad Taraki. Taraki lasted only one year before he was overthrown by forces backed by Hafizullah Amin. With Amin in power, Daoud was killed in the ensuing melee.

The country was now ruled by the People's Democratic Party of Afghanistan with Amin and Babark Karmal named as deputy prime ministers. The once deposed Mohammad Taraki was named President. In December 1978, the PDP and the Soviet Union signed a friendship treaty with each other, and behind the scenes talks were held regarding the possible removal of Taraki.

On February 15, 1979, U.S. Ambassador to Afghanistan Adolph Dubs was kidnapped by bandits and later killed when Amin's forces tried to rescue him. The death of Ambassador Dubs was the end of official U.S. representation in Kabul for years to come.

Events took a turn for the worse when, on March 10, 1979, a large Afghan military force located in Herat mutinied with the resulting deaths of 350 Soviet soldiers. In the wake of the killings, a massive Soviet military buildup began in Afghanistan with thousands of Russian soldiers deployed under the command of General Ivan Pavloskiy.

By the fall of 1979, under circumstances that are not clear,

Taraki was killed or died of natural causes and a Communist sympathizer, Babark Karmal, was installed as president under the watchful eye of the Soviets. By December 1979, a total of three Soviet divisions, complete with heavy armor and airborne units took up positions at Bagram air base. The Russians proceeded to arrest any opposition leaders and their troops fanned out across the country. Fifty thousand Soviet troops now occupied Afghanistan. For the next decade, Soviet forces would fight a drawn out, hit-and-run war with thousands of Afghan guerillas (called Mujahideen) in the rugged mountains and valleys of Afghanistan. Soon, the Mujahideen would be joined by other like-minded Muslims from across the globe, mostly from the Middle East, fighting to rid their country of the godless Soviet interlopers.

Among those who would come to aid the Afghan guerillas was the United States, under the guise of the CIA who would run their largest covert operation of all time. Backing the CIA were intelligence units from Pakistan and Saudi Arabia who funneled huge amounts of sophisticated military hardware to the Mujahideen. Another person who made his presence felt amid the Mujahideen fighters was a wealthy Saudi businessman named Osama bin Laden.

By the middle of the 1980s, a relationship between bin Laden, Pakistan and supposedly the CIA, began. In 1986, bin Laden, and Pakistan's intelligence service, ISI, helped by the CIA, built the Khost tunnel complex in Afghanistan. This area would later be a target when the United States attacked Afghanistan after 9-11. Information provided by UPI in June 2001 reported that "bin Laden worked closely with Saudi, Pakistani, and U.S. intelligence services to recruit Mujahideen from many Muslim countries." It was also reported over the years that the CIA helped fund the Maktab al-Khidamat (MAK) a.k.a. "Al Kifah, a bin Laden charity established in the 1980s. The CIA would later say, "For the record, you should know that the CIA never employed, or maintained any relationship whatsoever with bin Laden."

The real reason why the Soviets invaded Afghanistan is open to question but most of the answers lay in Kipling's notion of the Great Game of international relations. At the time of the 1979 invasion, the rise of Muslim fundamentalism in Central Asia was at a high point. At that time the Soviet Union was still one country, with all its ethnic minorities, especially those in regions bordering Afghanistan, bristling for independence. The Soviet Republics of Turkmenistan and Uzbekistan had large Muslim populations and were growing restive of Soviet domination.

Iran, Afghanistan's neighbor, was in the throes of its own revolution, having overthrown the Shah who was replaced by a hardline religious government. The Soviets might have been fearful that Iran might export its religious revolution to the wavering Soviet republics, thus creating more problems for Moscow.

Another factor was the so-called "Brezhnev Doctrine," which said that Moscow had the legitimate right to intervene if any of its allies in the socialist bloc were indanger of being conquered by any other nation.

For whatever reason, the Russian invasion of Afghanistan was, by 1979, a moot point. How the West would react would be the key. As described before, the CIA began a large, covert assistance program to aid the rebels. The United States brought on board both China and Egypt who served as weapons intermediaries to the rebels.

The purported story of the American response to the Soviet intervention was that once major Russian forces arrived in Afghanistan in 1979, the U.S. decided to up the ante and face the Russians down. However, that scenario is now open to new facts. In a 1988 interview with the late Zbigniew Brzezinski, President Carter's National Security Advisor, it seems that U.S. intervention on the side of the Mujahideen took place at least six months earlier.

In an interview with the French newspaper *Le Nouvel Observateur* in Paris, he admitted that President Carter gave the orders to intervene in Afghanistan months before. In an answer to a question regarding the allegations by former CIA Director Robert Gates concerning earlier U.S. intervention, Brzezinski said, "Yes." According to the official version of history, the CIA's aid to the Mujahideen began during 1980, that is to say, after the Soviet army invaded Afghanistan, 24 December 1979. But the reality, secretly guarded all these years, is completely otherwise. Indeed, it was July 3, 1979 that President Carter signed the first directive for secret aid to the opponents of the pro-Soviet regime in Kabul. Said Brzezinski, "And that very day, I wrote a note to the president in which I explained to him that in my opinion, this aid was going to induce the Soviet military intervention."

Brzezinski further stated that despite the risk, "we didn't push the Russians to intervene, but we knowingly increased the probability that they would."

The National Security Adviser stated flatly that he had no regrets about his suggestion to the president to aid the Afghan rebels:

> Regret what? That secret operation was an excellent idea. It had the effect of drawing the Russians into the Afghan trap and you want me to regret it? The day that the Soviets officially crossed the border, I wrote to President Carter. We now have the opportunity of giving the USSR its Vietnam War. Indeed, for almost 10 years, Moscow had to carry on a war unsupportable by the government, a conflict that brought about the demoralization and finally the breakup of the Soviet empire.

When asked by the reporter if he regretted the unsuspecting rise of Islamic fundamentalism and its terrorist consequences, he said, "What is most important to the history of the world? The Taliban or the collapse of the Soviet empire? Some stirred up Moslems or the liberation of Central Europe and the end of the Cold War?"

Brzezinski's words are now seen in a new light. In his defense, he could not have foreseen that the rise of the Taliban in Afghanistan would lead to the rise of Osama bin Laden who was on hardly anyone's radar at that time, and his jihad against the West. Nor could he have envisioned the 9-11 attacks back when he gave that interview.

What he also could not have pictured was the collapse of the Soviet Union and the rise of a new American enemy, the Taliban. His reference to "some stirred up Moslems" was probably not the best phrase to use at that time, but it was said in a different worldwide context when the main enemy was the Soviet Union.

In the end, over 90,000 Afghan fighters were killed in the ten year struggle. Almost 22,000 Soviet soldiers died and 75, 000 were wounded. The most important aftereffect of the Soviet defeat in Afghanistan was the collapse of the Soviet Union and the rise of international terrorism as America's new enemy.

But the story does not end there. In order to understand the rise of bin Laden in the 1990s, we have to get a better understanding of just how vast the covert war led by the CIA and its allies in the Middle East was, and how that "blowback" from America's departure after the Russian defeat led up to the events that culminated on 9-11.

The nexus lining up against the Soviet Union at the time of the Afghan invasion was an unlikely trio of nations, each with their own separate political and military objectives: the United States, Pakistan, and Saudi Arabia. Each would arm, train, and finance the Mujahideen rebels for their own means and objectives.

Politically, the three allies were as different as day and night. The United States was a longstanding democracy, where the rule of the people prevailed. Pakistan was once part of the British Empire but after separation from India it was ruled by a series of military dictatorships, interspersed by periods of democracy. Saudi Arabia was ruled by tribal clans overseen by the House of Saud and used its vast oil wealth and religious zealotry to rule by decree. What the three countries had in common a the dislike of the Soviet Union and its communist system. With the Soviet invasion of Afghanistan, this alliance of convenience was born.

In the United States, the Carter administration took both covert and overt steps in reaction to the invasion. The United States pulled out of the Olympic Games, and in an address to the Congress, Carter called Pakistan "a front line state" in the struggle against communism. The Carter administration changed its mind about giving military aid to Pakistan, which had been stopped in reaction to its decision to acquire nuclear weapons. What the administration did not want to see was the Indian subcontinent, where both Pakistan and India are located, being the scene where foes could wipe each other in a single strike. Carter made this offer of renewed aid to Pakistan's President Zia al-Haq in return for Pakistan's help as a conduit of American aid to the Afghan rebels. Zia refused, but when the Reagan administration took over, changed his mind. On the covert side, Carter began the large scale supply of weapons to the Mujahideen with few strings attached.

On the diplomatic side, the Soviets faced worldwide condemnation. The foreign ministers of the Organization of the Islamic Conference condemned their action and called for the removal of their forces from Afghanistan. The United Nations did not have any luck as far as diplomatic action was concerned. The Security Council was not able to pass a resolution of censure against the Russians as they had veto power over any potential proposal they didn't like.

While the Saudis were deeply angered at the Soviet invasion of Afghanistan, they could do little on the military front except to act as a conduit for the flow of fighters and military supplies to the Mujahadeen. As time went on, one of its most important business families, the bin Ladens, would play a behind-the-scenes role in aiding the Afghan rebels, from building tunnel complexes in the rugged mountains and paving roads, to supplying fighters from across the Muslim world. Osama bin Laden would act early in the war as a main financier of the cause and even took part in a battle against the Russians.

The major participant behind the Afghan rebels was Pakistan. Pakistan used its religious schools, or madrassas, to recruit like-minded Afghani's to fight the Soviet Union. In time, these madrassas would be the linchpin for the rise of the Taliban after the Soviet withdrawal.

The Pakistanis had their own internal reasons for defeating the Soviet Union in Afghanistan. Living in both Pakistan and Afghanistan were the Pashtun, a religious ethnic group whom the Pakistanis wanted to control. During the 1970s, calls for the Pashtuns to create their own homeland called "Pashtunistan" created a high degree of tension in Pakistan. What the Paks did not need was a Pashtun revolt in Pakistan and Afghanistan.

Pakistan was an Islamic state then ruled by Zulfikar ali-Bhutto. In order to cement relations with the Pashtuns living Afghanistan, Bhutto created a policy of militant and fundamentalist Islam with these people. In return for their help in the creation of an Islamic state in Afghanistan, Bhutto gave them military support after the Soviet invasion.

However, Bhutto was seen as an obstacle to many of Pakistan's military officers and he was forced from power by General Mohammed Zia-ul-Haq in July 1977. Two years later, in spite of a worldwide outcry from other nations, General Zia had Bhutto executed in April 1979. Zia took control over Pakistan, ordered a nuclear capability be started, and canceled elections. At home, he called for an Islamic country and instituted Islamic laws such as amputations and floggings for adulterers.

As the Afghan war heated up, Zia cemented covert relations with both the CIA and the Saudi intelligence services. Pakistan would be the way station for the millions of dollars that came pouring in from around the world. In 1980, Prince Turki al-Faisal, the chief of Saudi intelligence, sent an emissary by the name of Ahmed Badeeb to Pakistan to meet with President Zia. Badeeb told Zia that Saudi Arabia was prepared to send millions of dollars' worth of military aid to the rebels, including RPG (Rocket Propelled Grenades), and other weaponry supplied by China. The recipient of all this cash, and the organization that would take control of the day-to-day covert operations against the Russians, was the notorious Pakistani intelligence service, the ISI, or Inter-Service Intelligence. As the ten-year struggle against the Soviets mounted, the ISI would even supplant the CIA as the main organizer for the covert war in Afghanistan.

Oftentimes in its long history, the CIA had to make alliances of convenience with disreputable individuals or groups in order to further its own ends. During the decades of the 1970s and 1980s, the CIA worked closely with the Pakistani ISI, a group not noted for its democratic tendencies, having links to both the heroin trade in Central Asia as well as radical, terrorist groups throughout the region.

The foundation of the ISI goes back to its creation by a British army officer, Major General R. Cawthome, who was the Deputy Chief of Staff in the Pakistani Army. After the partition of India and Pakistan into two distinct countries, the then President of Pakistan, Ayub Khan, expanded the role of the ISI to cover internal espionage and the monitoring of Khan's potential enemies. The modern-day duties of the ISI expanded into both foreign and internal intelligence collection, the coordination of intelligence gathering among the various military departments, and the use of its agents to keep whatever military strongman of the time in power. Critics of the ISI called it "a state within a state," or "the invisible government." Since its inception, the ISI has been linked to drug smuggling, the assassination of political opponents of the ruling government, and being instrumental in the founding of the Taliban regime in Afghanistan after the departure of the Soviet Union.

The headquarters of the ISI is located in Islamabad, and its members total in the thousands. The ISI has many different offices but its most important is the Joint Intelligence bureau which is trusted for the surveillance of Pakistani diplomats abroad, the collection of intelligence in the Middle East, South Asia, China, and most importantly for this story, Afghanistan.

During the decades long running engagements between India and Pakistan over the sovereignty of Kashmir, the ISI had provided insurgents battling the Indian army with training and equipment. It has been estimated by Indian government officials that by 1995, the ISI had trained over 5,000 men to battle its forces in Kashmir.

Over the years, the ISI was granted as much power and influence as the various prime ministers would allow. The most influential ISI director, as far as this narrative is concerned, was Lt. General Hamud Gul who worked closely with Western intelligence agencies in ousting the Soviet Union from Afghanistan. During the height of the Soviet-Afghan war, Gul functioned hand-in-glove with not only the CIA but the Saudi Arabian intelligence service, the General Intelligence Department or GID. Gul's power was so deep inside the Pakistani intelligence and political establishment that he was able to install taps on the phone of Prime Minister Bhutto.

Gul later got his marching orders from Pakistan's President Mohammed Zia-al-Haq, who took control over Pakistan's government in July 1977 when he deposed the government of Zulfikar ali-Bhutto, the father of a latter day Prime Minister, Benazir Bhutto.

In time, Zia canceled national elections, and was instrumental in the development of the radical political movement called Jamaat-e-Islamia, which shunned modern dress and politics and called for an absolute Islamic government in Pakistan.

As the rebels managed to tie down the Soviet troops into a bloody stalemate, Gul and the ISI took steps to insure that a new, pro-Pakistani government was installed in Kabul. Using a large portion of the $25 million supplied by the Saudis, Gul arranged for a figurehead to be installed when the time came.

Despite his pro-Islamic penchants, the new Reagan administration in the United States saw President Zia as an ally of convenience in Central Asia, especially after Russian tanks rolled into Afghanistan in 1979. Without Zia's permission, the United States would not be able to funnel military aid to the Afghan rebels via the CIA. In the end, the Reagan administration (as well as the Carter administration in 1979-80), made a deal with the devil whereby Zia was fundamentally in charge of all covert, CIA/U.S. military aid to the rebels. Zia forbade the CIA to meet on a regular basis with its Afghan rebel allies, but the agency did so anyway.

In order to better facilitate the covert side of the new US-Pakistani relationship, Zia tasked the ISI chief, Akhtar Abdul Rahman, to keep the CIA at arm's length, yet, at the same time, get as much out of them as possible. Rahman, who served as ISI chief from 1980 to 1987, created the Afghan Division and tried to keep the CI

a from infiltrating his new creation. As the Afghan Division's membership swelled to over thrre hundred men, Rahman would send Pashto-speaking officers into Afghanistan where they made contact with local tribesmen allied to their cause.

The CIA agent who had the most contact with Akhtar Rahman was Howard Hart. The ISI chief forcefully told Hart that no CIA officer would be allowed to enter Afghanistan to set up shop or meet with any potential assets. All weapons shipments to the rebels would pass through ISI hands, the CIA would be forbidden to train the Mujahideen, and all training would be held in Pakistani camps.

When he was a very young man, Howard Hart and is family spent many years trapped in Japanese-held Manila during World War II. After being liberated, he moved to India and then back to Manila. During the middle 1960s, he joined the CIA and was posted to the Persian Gulf area, and Iran. In 1981, he was given the job running the agency's Islamabad station. Besides running the

CIA side of the war, Hart was tasked by the CIA to gather as much information as possible on Pakistan's nuclear program.

By 1983, the Saudi-American-Pakistani covert aid had made Afghanistan a killing ground for Soviet troops. In the United States, the Reagan administration got Congress to supply $30 million in covert aid to the rebels. At CIA headquarters, the covert war in Afghanistan was the number one priority for Director William Casey and he pulled out all stops to defeat the Russians.

Casey had an unexpected ally in the secret war in Afghanistan. Texas Congressman Charlie Wilson had made the war against the Russians his number one priority even though he did not sit on any of the intelligence committees in congress. Wilson, oftentimes accompanied by his beautiful girlfriends, went to Afghanistan where he met and took on the cause of the rebels. Returning to Washington, Wilson, a member of the House Appropriations Committee, finagled his fellow members to appropriate an additional $40 million in covert aid to the rebels. However, Casey diverted some of the money to other covert operations that the CIA was running.

With a windfall at his disposal, Casey had more than enough money to send to the CIA station in Pakistan where Hart used it at his discretion. Going against orders not to travel to Afghanistan, Hart, traveling with Abdul Haq, a commander of the anti-Soviet forces and an ally of the CIA, crossed the border where he saw how the rebels were using Uncle Sam's money. He met with various rebel leaders and came away impressed with the determination of the fighters to rid their land of the Soviets (more about Abdul Haq in a later chapter).

As the war against the Soviet Union grew fiercer in the 1980s, the ISI took over more control of both internal and external functions. Its headquarters was in Rawalpindi where it did President Zia's bidding with a heavy-armed rule. ISI troops enforced the martial law decree imposed by Zia, funded guerilla operations against Indian troops in Kashmir, and by 1983, were the backbone of the day-to-day fight against the Soviets in Afghanistan.

While the Reagan administration knew all about the illegal activities of the ISI, they turned a blind eye toward its transgressions. CIA Director Casey made a number of clandestine trips to Pakistan where he assessed the military situation, met with Akhtar, and planned strategy. Casey said of Akhtar, "[He] is completely involved in this war and certainly knows better than anyone else about his requirements. We simply have to support him."

Boosted by the millions of dollars in covert aid provided by the CIA, a new, lethal ingredient was added to the rebels' arsenal. The most effective part in the agency's new stockpile that was provided to the Mujahideen fighters was the highly effective Stinger missile which brought down dozens of Russian helicopters, resulting in the deaths of hundreds of soldiers. The use of the Stinger helped level the playing field and made the rebels a force to be reckoned with.

Another rebel commander who was taken under the wing of the CIA was Ahmed Shah Massoud, who was allied with the United States as well as the ISI (to a certain degree). It is believed that the CIA paid Massoud up to $20,000 a month to supply it with intelligence and other military necessities in the Afghan war.

A rift soon opened up between the CIA and ISI over the agency's relationship with Massoud. The ISI did not trust him and did everything in their power to undermine his authority among the anti-Soviet groups. They even went so far as to intercept CIA arms shipments to Massoud.

In what is now believed to be a prelude to the 9-11 attacks, Massoud was killed on September 9, 2001 by assassins posing as journalists sent to his mountain headquarters by Osama bin Laden. In 2001, Massoud was the leader of the anti-Taliban Northern Alliance, a bitter enemy of bin Laden. With Massoud dead, the United States would have one less important partner to use in its expanded retaliation against the Taliban for the 9-11 attacks which were only days away. There have been unverified reports that the ISI had a hand in the Massoud assassination, even if they did not actually pull the trigger.

By 1992, the Afghan rebels had managed to do the impossible —outlast the might Soviet army and force them to leave Afghanistan. For the United States, the main objective had been accomplished, and by that same year, the CIA had all but closed up shop in Pakistan. The CIA and the United States, in effect, washed their hands of the entire mess and left Afghanistan to sort out its own affairs.

What they left behind was a cauldron of deep seething hatred against the United States, a breeding ground for anti-American, anti-Western, anti-Jewish, Islamic fundamentalists who would use Afghanistan as a station for a new organization called al Qaeda. Al Qaeda, or "the base," was led by a rich Saudi financier named Osama bin Laden. It was from the rugged hills of Afghanistan that bin Laden would unleash his well-trained, true believers into a new enemy of the West.

With the defeat of the Soviets, the CIA, through its Afghan surrogates, targeted the regime of President Muhammad Najibullah, the Soviet-installed puppet who was placed in power in Afghanistan. The other CIA base camp in Pakistan besides Islamabad was in the town of Peshawar where the agency had a large contingent. From Peshawar, CIA agents entered Afghanistan, making contact with the respective guerilla groups, many of them anti-U.S. Islamic fundamentalists who only wanted the U.S. for the military equipment and training they could provide. These radical groups would remain extremely bitter against the United Sates after the conflict ended. With the pullout of CIA forces from the region, a new radical government called the Taliban took power in Kabul. The Taliban gave safe haven to al Qaeda, under the direction of Osama bin Laden.

In April 1992, Ahmed Shah Massoud and his forces triumphantly entered Kabul, the capital of Afghanistan. For a period of four years, Massoud tried to cement the country under his leadership but was frustrated in his efforts by the other independent factions who wanted Afghanistan for themselves. In September 1996, a disheartened Massoud left Kabul and was replaced by the anti-Western, radical leaning Taliban.

During the 1990s, with the United States now the direct target of bin Laden's terror, a new relationship with Massoud was arranged. The relationship would tragically end with his death on September 9, 2001.

Over the past several years, new documents have been declassified regarding the Taliban, bin Laden, and the United States. These documents are interesting in their scope and add new details to the historical record. These documents come via the National Security Archive which is located in Washington, D.C. The NSA has been a wellspring of new material on all sorts of national security and historical endeavors for some time and the Taliban Project is no exception.

The first document I will refer to is titled "Afghanistan Taliban said to loosen grip on bin Laden as they increasingly turn to him for financial support and advice." Following is the summary.

> According to various sources, the Taliban have increasingly turned to Saudi terrorist financier Osama bin Laden for financial support in the past several months. While there is widespread agreement that his influence should not be overstated, there is also speculation that some Taliban leaders seek out bin Laden for advice. In light of bin Laden's May 26 press conference and recent ABC interview, there is a feeling among sources that the Taliban may be loosening their grip on bin Laden. Perhaps as part of a quid pro quo for continued financial support. Other observers speculate that bin Laden's key supporters in the Taliban movement have become more influential in recent months, and have successfully made the case to other Taliban that bin Laden should be given more freedom to operate.

A second part of the document adds goes farther regarding bin Laden and the Taliban. It reads in part:

> A number of sources report that they believe that the Taliban movement is increasingly turning to Saudi terrorist Osama bin Laden for financial support. In a June 12 meeting [Blank], told Poloff that he has heard numerous reports that the Taliban, in preparation for the 1998 warm weather fighting season, made numerous requests to bin Laden to provide funds to purchase arms and ammunition from international gray arms market sources. Bin Laden was also asked to help pay the salaries of Taliban military forces. Bin Laden reportedly obliged and provided the

> Taliban with an unspecified amount of funds for these purposes. [Blank] told Poloff that his sources believe that the amount of funds provided to the Taliban so far in 1998 was considerably larger than the amount he provided the movement during the 1996-97 period.
>
> [Blank] operative who maintains close links with the Taliban, repeated many of [Blank] points about bin Laden in a June 11 meeting with Poloff. [Blank] added that he has heard that the Taliban, facing severe economic constraints, also asked for funds from bin Laden for the purchase of communications equipment, including satellite phones and radios. This equipment, which bin Laden agreed to purchase, is being used by the Taliban for military purposes and to link Taliban movement officers around the country with Kandahar, which serves as the Taliban movement's headquarters.

The documents reveal that Taliban officials met quite often with bin Laden over a long period of time to discuss various topics.

> For example, [Blank], who maintains close links to the Pashton tribes which form the Taliban's main base of support, told Poloff June 11, that he has had many reports that Taliban leaders spend a large amount of time meeting with bin Laden when bin Laden is in Kandahar. Kandahar is a very small town and Taliban leaders are in constant contact with bin Laden. High-level Taliban officials, including Kandahar regional governor Mullah Hassan and "Deputy Foreign Minister" Jalil, purportedly use these meetings to ask bin Laden for advice on how to deal with the UN and the West.[22]

The documents also tell the story of divisions within the ranks of the Taliban leaders as they tried to wrestle with their ongoing attempts to spread jihad around the globe.

> Summary: [Blank] says divisions within the Taliban

22 Subject: Afghanistan: Taliban said to loosen grip on bin Laden as they increasingly turn to him for financial support and advice. Declassified 6/12/08.

are growing as a result of disagreements over goals. He claimed Taliban leader Mohammad Omar wants to become ruler of Afghanistan and is not interested in compromise with the U.N. plan for an interim council. The hard-liners are strengthened by support from Pakistan and Afghan traders, while the moderates are denied aid. (Bank) predicts heavy fighting will start in western Afghanistan before Kabul, and claims the Taliban are ready to defend themselves against Iran, through cross-border operations if necessary. End summary.

[Blank] said there were two main causes of division within Taliban ranks, first, the ambition of leader Mohammed Omar and, second, disagreement over negotiating with other factions. On the first issue, [Blank] complained that Mohammed Omar's principle goal seemed to become the leader of all Afghanistan, and he deeply believes this is his destiny. Poloff said some Taliban had commented that Omar lacked charisma and asked how he maintained his influence. [Blank] responded that it was precisely Omar's lack of education and his low status which gave him cachet as a mystic/visionary. He is from the Khotak tribe, which is not very important. By rejecting the U.N. proposal, Omar had decided to pit the Taliban 'against the world,' he complained.

The deputy governor claimed that the problem facing the moderates within the Taliban movement was that they did not receive much outside support, while the more controllable nobodies were given every facility. Support for the movement mostly came from the government of Pakistan and wealthy Afghan traders, [Blank] averred.

The documents now go into the role played by Pakistan vis a vis the Taliban.

Pakistan, consistent reporting indicates Pakistan provides both military and financial assistance to the Taliban. Islamabad's primary goals are to achieve strategic depth with regard to India, and securing access to Central Asian trade routes. Cultural ties also exist between the Taliban leadership and Pakistan where several Taliban leaders lived for many years following the 1970 Soviet invasion. Pakistan fears a complete Taliban victory may incite irredentist aspirations with its own Pashton population, and will likely attempt to pressure the Taliban into moderating some of its policies.

> Russia: Russia is concerned about the spillover of Islamic militancy into Central Asia and views the Taliban as a significant threat. Moscow defines its near-abroad borders as those of its former Central Asian Republics, and has pledged to use military force should the Taliban push into northern Afghanistan.[23]

The documents also reveal a secret backchannel between the U.S. and the Taliban leader Omar in which the two sides discussed mutual areas of interest. Part of the document reads as follows:

> August 22, Taliban Supreme leader Mullah Omar told a State Department official in Washington that the Taliban was open to the suggestion of establishing a vehicle for secure communications with USG officials, possibly through the embassy in Islamabad. While Omar parroted some of bin Laden's hardline views, he listened to U.S. arguments on the reasons for the U.S. attacks in Afghanistan and Sudan and the reasons why bin Laden's continued activities were not in the interest of the Afghan people. Omar warned that the U.S. strikes would prove counter-productive and arose anti-American feelings in the Islamic world. While he was in no way threatening, he claimed that the strikes could spark more terrorist attacks. He asked for evidence of bin Laden's involvement in terrorist actions. End summary.[24]

The documents also tell of a call between the Taliban leader

23 Subject: Afghanistan: Taliban official says divisions within movement growing, predicts fight with Iran. Declassified 2/9/06.

24 Subject: Afghanistan: Taliban's Mullah Omar's 8/22 contact with State Department.Declassified 8/22/08.

and an American official named Malinowski.

> [Blank] who is a supporter of Afghanistan's Taliban movement approached SA.PAB Director Malinowski August 21 to see if he was willing to communicate with one of the Taliban's top leaders. Malinowski told [Blank] that he was always open to such communications if it were serious. In the early morning hours of August 22, Malinowski was called at home and hooked into a conference call on an open line with [Blank] and Taliban headquarters in Kandahar. [Blank] served as translator. After conversation began with a Taliban aide, Mullah Omar surprisingly came on the line and engaged with Malinowski. This is the first contact that we know of between the reclusive Mullah Omar and a USG official. Omar asked for the bona fides of Malinowski, which the translator provided. The translator, familiar with Omar's voice from previous conversations, vouched that it was Omar.
>
> Malinowski noted that we had much to speak about, especially the continued pressure of Osama bin Laden in Afghanistan and the threat that bin Laden posed to Americans. Omar related that, while he had no particular message for us, he was open to dialogue. Malinowski suggested that open telephone lines were inappropriate for that serious dialogue and suggested that it be best conducted in person with officials of our embassy in Islamabad. Omar countered by saying that we could engage with the Taliban's representatives in Islamabad.
>
> Omar said that while he had no specific message he did have some advice. He said that in order to rebuild U.S. popularity in the Islamic world and because of his current domestic political difficulties congress should force President Clinton to resign. He said he was aware of no evidence that bin Laden had engaged in or planned terrorist acts while on Afghan soil. Parroting much of bin Laden's usual rhetoric, Omar said that the U.S. should remove its forces from the Gulf and he warned that the U.S. was seen as a threat to Islam's holiest sites, including the Kabbah.

He added that eventually the people of Saudi Arabia would force the Saudi government to expel the Americans.

On bin Laden, Omar said that getting rid of one individual would not end the problems to the U.S. by the Islamic world. He again said that he had seen no hard evidence against bin Laden. Malinowski replied that there seemed to be considerable evidence against bin Laden and that the evidence was solid. He noted that Omar and the Taliban should be well aware of what bin Laden had been up to in Afghanistan. He said that the U.S. solely had acted out of self-defense, the President had acted as a father who had to protect his children from jeopardy. Our strikes in no way were directed against the Afghan people or the Taliban. Omar should know that the U.S. had been a friend to the Afghans and wanted only the best for Afghanistan. Picking up on Omar's observation that Afghanistan needed reconstruction assistance, Malinowski observed that reconstruction could not be expected to start as long as Afghanistan remained in turmoil and as long as bin Laden was posing a threat from its soil. Using public statements, Malinowski urged Omar to place bin Laden and other terrorists in custody or expel them from Afghanistan.

Omar conducted himself in a careful and controlled manner. At no time did he bluster or threaten. Comment: Omar's contact with a USG official is rather remarkable. Given his reclusive nature and his past avoidance of contact with all things American, it is indicative of the seriousness of how the Taliban view the U.S. strikes and our anger over bin Laden. The Taliban, despite implying that we should initiate the contact, are interested in a dialogue with us on bin Laden and other issues. This is a long way, however, from the Taliban doing the right thing on bin Laden.[25]

The fact that the American government was in covert contact with Mullah Omar is something that hasn't been talked about much in the writings about the Taliban and the United States. It's too bad that these secret meeting could not have made more progress

25 Summary: In a telephone call on an open line early confidential, classified by Michael Malinowski, Director SA/PAB.

than they did. Note that with these documents we now have two more names of USG officials who were in contact with the Taliban during these times: a man named Poloff and Michael Malinowski. What researches need is more information on just who these two people were and more about their background.

Mullah Omar was not the only high-level person whom the USG was covertly talking with during this time. The aforementioned Mr. Poloff had a meeting with a ranking member of the Taliban called Jalaluddin Haqqani, of the so-called "Haqqani network," whose members controlled the Khost region of Afghanistan. A reporter named Kathy Gannon said about Haqqani, "Had he wanted to, he could have handed the United States the entire al Qaeda network." Haqqani was a powerful figure among the Afghan tribesmen as well as having ties with the Pakistani ISI; there were even rumors that he served as a CIA asset in the 1980s.

Another journalist who wrote about Haqqani was Steve Coll who wrote a best-selling book on Afghanistan and bin Laden called *Ghost Wars*. Coll had this to say regarding Haqqani, "there was always a question about whether Haqqani was really Taliban, because he hadn't come out of Kandahar, he wasn't part of the core group, and it was quite reasonable to believe after 9/11 that maybe he could be flipped. U.S. officials summoned him to Pakistan, and they had a series of meetings with him, the content of which is unknown."

Whether or not Haqqani was working with the CIA, it seems that by April of 2002, seven months after 9-11, both Pakistan and the United States mounted an operation to locate him. Forces from both countries searched for him in Waziristan, in Pakistan's tribal region, but were unable to find him. A mosque that was linked to Haqqani was raided by up to 200 Pakistani soldiers but he wasn't there. In the ensuing years, Haqqani opened up his own network and took the fight against United States forces in Afghanistan. If there was any doubt of his intentions during this time period, his actions spoke louder than his words.

Sometime in 2006, an unnamed ISI official said that Haqqani was a Pakistani intelligence asset, which was later corroborated by a CIA official.

It seems that the United States had an ongoing relationship

with Haqqani in the years after 9-11, even while his forces were doing battle with the United States. In order for the U.S. to find out what the Haqqani network was doing, a surveillance program was set up to find out what help the ISI was giving him. The CIA found out that General Ashfaq Kayani, the head of Pakistan's military, said that Haqqani was a "strategic asset," and this was passed up the chain of command to the Director of National Intelligence, Mike McConnell. U.S. intelligence, at one point, intercepted a call from Pakistani military units to Haqqani, warning him of an imminent Pakistani military operation in the tribal region designed to make it appear to the U.S. that Pakistan was taking action against militant groups. An unnamed source would later explain, "It was something like, 'Hey, we're going to hit your place in a few days, so if anyone important is there, you might want to tell them to scram.'" U.S. intercepts also found out of a plot between the ISI and Haqqani to bomb the Indian embassy in Kabul, Afghanistan.[26]

Here is a summary of the aforementioned Mr. Poloff's meeting with Haqqani, as described in the newly released transcripts.

> In Embassy's first meeting with him in over three years, Poloff met May 22 with high-level Taliban official, Jalaluddin Haqqani, who is known to have close ties with Arab militants. Reiterating U.S. points, Poloff urged that the Taliban expel bin Laden to a place where he can be brought to justice; Haqqani's remarks toed the Taliban line; he asserted that bin Laden was under control and that this solution may be best for all concerned. On the other hand, Haqqani gave voice to a number of concerns, including a recognition that the Taliban's policy on bin Laden was isolating them from the U.S. and Saudi Arabia. He urged continued talks on the issue.

This meeting was also attended by Naqoshbandi Sufi, Amin Mojaddehi, and a number of Haqqani's bodyguards. "Haqqani began the meeting by darkly joking that it was good to meet someone from the country which had destroyed my base, my Madrassah, and killed 25 of my holy warriors. Hearing this,

26 History C ommons: May 2008: U.S. Intelligence allegedly hears head of Pakistani military call Taliban leader a "strategic asset."

Haqqani's assistants glared sullenly at Poloff. (Note: Haqqani was referring to the August 20 cruise missile strike on Osama bin Laden's facilities in Khost Province. Haqqani had close links with a number of the facilities that were hit, including those linked with bin Laden's group, Kashmiri militants, and other extremists."[27]

Big changes also took place in Pakistan when, in October 1999, General Pervez Musharraf, took power in a coup. The Clinton and Bush administrations decided to overlook the anti-democratic way Musharraf came to power and threw their lot in with him. From 1990 until September 11, 2001, Musharraf began reining in the power of the ISI, but it still had considerable power in his government.

In the 1990s, Afghanistan resembled nothing less than Central Asia's version of the wild, wild west. The emboldened Mujahideen fighters, flush from their improbable victory over the Russians and deeply resentful at the way the United States abandoned them, turned their attention inward. From across the Muslim world, like-minded jihadists flocked to Afghanistan where they would export their latest wars to new areas of the globe. Gun-running and opium production flourished in the mountain regions, and plans to fight the new enemy were hatched. From Afghanistan, these Islamic warriors took their fight across the world to Pakistan, Yemen, Bosnia, Egypt, India, the old republics of the Soviet Union, and most importantly, the United States.

A number of terrorists who took their crusade to the United States returned to Afghanistan after carrying out their vengeance. Mir Amin Kasi, the man who killed two CIA employees at agency headquarters, returned to Afghanistan for safe haven. Ramzi Yousef fled New York after the 1993 WTC bombing and returned to Afghanistan. Others who spent time in Afghanistan were a number of men associated with the blind Sheik Omar Abdul Rahman, including Mahmud Abolhalima, Ali Mohammed, the al Qaeda sleeper inside the U.S. Army, Khalid Sheik Mohammed, Yousef's uncle and the prime planner on 9-11, all of the hijack team, as well as Yousef's traveling companion, Ahmad Ajah.

In spy parlance, the term "blowback," meaning an operation that has gone wrong, fits the scenario of Afghanistan after the end

27 Subject: Osama bin Laden: Pressing High-Level Taliban official Haqqani on bin Laden.

of the Soviet invasion to a tee. Armed to the teeth with hundreds of U.S. Stinger missiles, as well as countless rounds of ammunition and arms, rebel fighters now turned their attention to radical Islam, and against the West. In the U.S. intelligence community during the early to middle 1990s, no one expected the scenario that eventually unfolded.

Near the town of Peshawar, the site of the one-time CIA listening post, a radical school of Islamic learning called the University of Dawa and Jihad opened its doors to all comers. It was founded in 1985 by Professor Abdurrab Rasaul Sayyaf, a powerful Afghan military leader. Ramzi Yosef was a one time student at the university. A large percentage of the funds supporting the university came from Saudi Arabia, rom the profits from CIA largess during the Afghan war. The school was the training and recruiting center for those Mujhadeen fighters who decided to stay in Afghanistan, as well as others from places across the globe who shared their political beliefs.

Despite the efforts of the United States to aid the various rebel factions, the bottom line was the majority of these men opposed the United States politically, especially our relationship with Israel, and our perceived anti-Palestinian stand. They also opposed the worldly Middle Eastern countries such as Egypt, and especially Saudi Arabia, who matched dollar for dollar the amount of money spent by the CIA on the rebels.

The most radical of the ex-Mujhadeen, led by bin Laden, who had, by the late 1990s, become the father figure to many of these men, made their headquarters in Peshawar where they began their jihad against America and the West. An amalgam of radical, Islamic, anti-Western groups flocked to Peshawar to take guerilla training. Among the factions who sent men to this most unlikely university were the Palestinian splinter group Hamas, Gama-al-Islamiya from Egypt (Sheik Rahman was the leading figure of this organization), the Philippine Moro Liberation Front, as well as groups from Algeria and other places around the world.

Adding to their hatred of the United States was the presence of hundreds of thousands of foreigners (American troops) among the holy sites in the Middle East, in the wake of the 1991 Persian Gulf War against Iraq. When American troops failed to leave after the conflict was over, another notch against the United States was put in the collective belts of the jihadists. As long as one American (i.e., Infidel) was still on Muslim soil, any means would be taken to oust them.

As preparations for the looming Islamic jihad took shape in Pakistan and Afghanistan, the CIA had closed up shop and abandoned the region, looking for other targets of opportunity. But there were none. In 1989, the Cold War ended with the collapse of the Soviet Union. The CIA had no one to prepare for, and the lack of a clear enemy left many at Langley headquarters in doubt as to their future purpose as the premier national intelligence agency. Soon though, a charismatic wealthy Saudi citizen named Osama bin Laden would take center stage as the agency's number one antagonist.

In the wake of the 9-11 attacks, a cottage industry has grown up trying to link bin Laden to the CIA. No matter how much conspiracy theorists and anti-CIA detractors would love to obtain proof positive of a secret relationship between the world's most wanted man and the CIA, the evidence of any official relationship between the agency and bin Laden is nonexistent.

That is not to say that the agency did not have bin Laden on their radarscopes during the 1980s and early 1990s. What is known during that time period is that bin Laden was more in league with the Saudi intelligence service, the GID, than the CIA. There is no official record of any CIA-bin Laden relationship as the Afghan war heated up, but the agency knew who the GID was using as conduits to move money and men to the Mujahideen. If the GID knew who bin Laden was, the CIA also knew. Writing in his book *Ghost Wars,* author Steve Coll states that certain CIA officers said that bin Laden was working as an unofficial channel of communication between the Saudi GID and the rebels. Another account by a leading Saudi GID officer, Ahmed Badeeb, points to a close relationship between bin Laden and both Saudi Arabia and Pakistan. Badeeb, a top GID officer with close ties to Prince Turki al-Faisal, the chief of Saudi intelligence, said that the bin Laden family construction company got contracts by the early 1980s to build roads and other construction projects for GID purposes.

Badeeb relates that during those years, bin Laden was not the radical he would become. However, he describes meetings between bin Laden, Prince Turki and Prince Naif, the interior minister, and says that bin Laden also attended diplomatic receptions at the Saudi embassy in Islamabad, Pakistan. Badeeb said that, "The Pakistanis saw in him one who was helping them do what they wanted done there." According to author Coll, the Saudis said of bin Laden, "We were happy with him. He was our man. He was doing all of what we asked him."

In Peshawar, bin Laden had connections with an entity called the Islamic Salvation Foundation whose object was to recruit Arab men for the war against the Soviets. Bin Laden was financing these new recruits along the Afghan-Pakistani border region. The CIA's Counterterrorist Center was apprised of bin Laden's work but little more was known about him except that he was a wealthy Saudi who was willing and able to help the rebels.

In the early 1980s, bin Laden's most important task in aiding the rebels was heading up the vast construction projects that his family-owned company could provide. Bin Laden filled the void when he brought in to Pakistan and Afghanistan large earthmoving equipment, including bulldozers which flattened roads which would carry men and military supplies up the mountains. The two areas where the bin Laden construction company were most efficient were the Parrot's Beak region near Peshawar, and the town of Khost in Afghanistan. Large caves were dug out of the mountains where the rebels hid both men and equipment from the Russians.

Wanting to be more of a player in the Afghan war, bin Laden created a military-style camp which opened in 1986. He named the base, "The Lion's Den," which became the home of many new recruits who took military training there.

More importantly in the story of bin Laden's early role in the Afghan war was his relationship with Abdulah Azzam, a powerful cleric from the Palestinian Brotherhood. In the late 1980s, Azzam traveled across Afghanistan, meeting with Massoud and the important warlord Gulbuddin Hekmatyar in order to bring the warring factions together.

On November 24, 1980, Azzam was killed in Peshawar by a car bomb. Bin Laden filled the void left by Azzam's death by creating the Office of Services (Makhtab al-Khidmat) or MAK. He now had control over the large number of men who came to the cause.

In August 1988, bin Laden turned his new military group into what would become the "base" or al Qaeda. No press release or television announcement was put out by bin Laden announcing al Qaeda, and neither the CIA nor the American government knew it existed until many years later.

As al Qaeda grew in scope, it established many components including an intelligence unit' military, financial, and political committees; as well as media and propaganda outlets.

Osama bin Laden was born on March 10, 1957 in Riyadh, Saudi Arabia, the seventeenth child of Mohammed and his young Syrian wife. Mohammed bin Laden's roots were in the Hadramawt region of Yemen where Osama would travel in later years on his long journey to jihad. Hadramawt dates back to the first stories of the Bible. The bin Laden clan came from the village of al-Rubat where the tenets of Islam were revered, and still are today.

Mohammed bin Laden, along with a brother named Abdullah, left Yemen bound for a new life in Saudi Arabia in 1930. His first job upon arriving in Jeddah, was that of a porter. As time went on, Mohammed bin Laden would become one of the wealthiest and most influential men in the Saudi kingdom, making friends with the ruling family, and aiding the country immensely with his far-flung construction company.

In 1964, King Faisal appointed Mohammed bin Laden as minister of public works, and his construction company became known as "the King's private contractors."

As a young man, Osama and his family moved to Medina and the family traveled between Jeddah and the holy cities of Mecca and Medina. In time, Mohammed divorced his wife. As the years passed, Mohammed became such a valued friend at the Saudi court that he was given the job of rebuilding the al-Aqsa mosque in Jerusalem (the mosque was torched by an Australian who was mentally sick). The bin Laden construction company was also given the job of redesigning the holy sites of Mecca and Medina. Among their projects was a highway that linked Jeddah to Taif.

Osama grew up learning the family construction business and

also was taught the tenets of Islamic beliefs.

In 1967, when Osama was ten, his father died in a plane crash. King Faisal intervened on the family's behalf and saw to it that the bin Laden construction company would not falter. In time, his older brother, Salem, was put in charge of the company. Salem would expand the business into other areas like mining, power facilities, and oil exploration. In 1975, Salem bin Laden came to the United States where he met airplane broker James Bath of Houston, and became business partners. Bath was also an investor in George W. Bush's first company, Arbusto Energy. By the late 1990s, the bin Laden fortune was estimated at $5 billion. Its main company, called SBG, had up to 40,000 workers by the turn of the century. A sampling of the work they did across the Middle East includes work on Cairo's airport runways, the construction of a seaside resort in Syria, the rebuilding of the Aden airport in Yemen, the building of a Hyatt Hotel in Amman, Jordan, construction of a mosque in Malaysia, among many other projects.

Like his brother, Salem bin Laden had a shady past and it was believed by some people that he was some sort of an intelligence operative on the side. He was described by an unnamed French intelligence officer as being a very close friend to the then king of Saudi Arabia, King Fahd, as well as possibly doing undercover work for the regime. It was believed that in 1980, Salem bin Laden was involved in secret negotiations in Paris between U.S. and Iranian representatives, although these rumors were never confirmed. These meetings between the U.S. and Iran, and possibly Salem bin Landen, had something to do with the so-called "October Surprise" in which it was alleged that U.S. hostages were delayed in getting their freedom, thus allowing Ronald Reagan to win the 1980 U.S. presidential election. These allegations were never substantiated, but if they were to be determined to be correct, then conspiracy theorists would have solid proof of a connection between the Bush and bin Laden families.

In early 1985, Salem bin Laden is alleged to have told one of his employees, a man named George Harrington, that his brother Osama, "is the liaison between the US, the Saudi government, and the Afghan rebels." Salem also said that he went to the Pakistani city of Peshawar for an anti-Soviet meeting regarding the rebels who were fighting the Soviets at that time. Salem was supposed to have gone with a man named Bengt Johansson to see Osama bin Laden. Osama then gave his brother and Johansson a tour of the base, including rebel training camps in the area.

News reports concerning Salem bin Laden's activities were covered by various U.S. outlets including the PBS *Frontline* television show. A French intelligence official told the *New Yorker* that during the 1980s, when the Reagan administration diverted money to the Contra guerillas operating in Nicaragua using the Saudis as a conduit, that Salem bin Laden "aided this cause."[28]

There is more to the story of Salem bin Laden to be told. Unlike Osama, Salem was on no terror watchlist and he was free to travel as he wished. Around February 1985, Salem bin Laden was in Washington, D.C., to attend a summit between President Ronald Reagan and King Fahd of Saudi Arabia. It is not known just what part he took in these meetings, but the role of the United States in funding the anti-Soviet rebels was probably on the agenda. There were press reports of a picture of both Salem and President Reagan being taken but if it were true, it never made the light of day. Author Steve Coll wrote about the meeting mentioned above saying, "It seems probable that when Salem reached Washington that winter, he would have passed to King Fahd, if not directly to the White House, the video evidence he had just gathered documenting Osama's humanitarian work on the Afghan frontier." How much, if any, information President Regan got regarding the role of bin Laden in reference to the aid the U.S. was giving to the rebels is not known, but it stands to reason that he must have been briefed at some point on who Osama was and what he was doing.

Salem bin Laden was still playing a covert role during these times. Around April 1986 or later, both Osama and Salem met a number of times with South African arms dealers to discuss supplies for the anti-Soviet Mujahidin in Afghanistan. One of these secret meetings was held at the Pearl Continental Hotel in Peshawar, Pakistan, and someone familiar with the meeting later told the lawyer for the victims of 9-11 of this fact. Attending the meeting, according to persons in the know, were Osama bin Laden, an Afghan commander called Abdul Rasul Sayyaf, and two other,

28 History Commons: Mid 1980s—Osama bin Laden's brother is Allegedly involved in the Iran-Contra Affair.

unidentified South Africans. Later, Salem would also meet with arms dealers in Jeddah, Saudi Arabia, and it was said that the government of Saudi Arabia may have aided in the purchase of these weapons. [29]

There is also in interesting connection between George W. Bush and the bin Laden family, in the person of Salem bin Laden. In 1988, a young George W. Bush, whose father was now president of the United States, was trying to get a foothold in the Texas oil market. He was having little luck and had to be bailed out three times by his investors (his company was called Harken, which was located in Texas). In 1988, Harken won a contract to do work in the Persian Gulf and had a financial turnaround. Two of the major investors in Bush Harken Oil were Salem bin Laden and Khalid bin Mahfouz who is a Saudi banker. Tragically for Salem bin Laden, he would be killed in a plane crash in Texas in 1988.

The secret arms dealings that Salem bin Laden had takes us to another well-known arms dealer of the day, a man whose worldwide network spanned anyone who had the money to pay for the much-needed arms that were the backbone of any successful revolution, Victor Bout. Victor Bout was a Russian national who supplied a range of arms and ammunition to tinhorn dictators across the globe, most notably in Africa, making a fortune for himself while unleashing his murderous cargo of death and destruction. Among the leaders with whom Bout dealt were Charles Taylor of Liberia, Mubuto Sese Seko in Zaire, Paul Kagame in Rwanda, and rebel leader Jonas Savimbi in Angola. Bout also armed the leader of the Northern Alliance in Afghanistan, Ahmad Shah Massoud, but when it served his devious purposes, switched sides and armed the Taliban.

In the early 1990s, Bout moved his far-flung enterprise to the United Arab Emirates (UAE) and began to sell his weapons to all comers. He worked out of the airport at Sharjah, where the government turned a blind eye to his dealings. There were little to no restrictions on Bout's business dealings and he soon partnered with an America named Richard Chickakli who was to become the commercial manager of a new free trade zone which was being used by Bout. When talking to a journalsit about Bout's alleged

29 History Commons: (After April 1986). Bin Laden Brothers negotiate with South Africa to buy weapons for Arab Afghans.

illegal activities, Chickakli said of his friend, "He doesn't want to be God. He just wanted to retire to Africa, near the rainforest, to raise his daughter. They didn't get the man, but they sure killed his dream." Chickakli said that he knew Osama bin Laden at one point while he was in Saudi Arabia in the early 1980s, and that they, "sat around eating sandwiches and singing songs, when bin Laden was OK." In 1986, he moved to Texas, joined the Army until 1993 and worked in aviation and intelligence. U.S. authorities had been taking a great deal of interest in his dealings with Victor Bout and in August 2006, the FBI raided his Texas home where they seized computers, documents, and over $1 million in assets. However, it was decided by the feds not to arrest him and he soon moved to Syria where he and Bout were suspected of selling guns to the Middle Eastern terror group Hezbollah. The airport at Sharjah would be a shipping point for arms and ammunition flying to and from Afghanistan on a daily basis, and was used by al Qaeda during that time. There were reports that in mid-October 1998, the mastermind of the WTC attack, Kalid Sheik Mohammad, lived in Sharjah and that the place was also be a landing spot where a number of the 9-11 hijackers met with him while passing through.

Over time, the Sharjah airport was the hub of all sorts of nefarious goings on relating to the Taliban and their allies in Afghanistan. All sorts of merchandise flowed to and from its hangars, including weapons to the Taliban, gold shipments which were converted into cash, along with a large amount of drugs—Afghanistan grew huge crops of poppies which would be converted into heroin and then shipped worldwide.

All sorts of Russian and Arab men worked as loaders at the airport and could be seen daily, loading Victor Bout's planes for destinations far away. One person said of these daily activities, "The only reason to be in Sharjah was smuggling. In Sharjah, it was anything goes."

By 1996, al Qaeda had taken control over Ariana Airlines, which was Afghanistan's national airline. Instead of passengers, Ariana now flew arms, money, gold shipments, and anything else that could be used for battle. Al Qaeda members staffed the planes, using false papers saying they were legitimate workers of Ariana. In Washington, the CIA knew exactly what Victor Bout was doing in Sharjah but decided to leave well enough alone when it came to his illegal activities.

However, that is not to say that the U.S. government did nothing regarding Bout's illegal activities. One man who took notice of Bout was Lee Wolosky who was a staffer on the White House National Security Council and who was also an expert on Russian organized crime. CIA officials tracked Bout's plane shipments across the globe, trying desperately to ask other nations to stop his activities (nothing happed on that score). They also scoured his phone and banking records, looking for any irregularities with which they could make a solid case against him. Lee Wolosky would later say about the CIA's hunt for Bout, "We couldn't directly link him to al Qaeda at that point, but there were red flags that concerned us. He was dancing around the edges. Bout's global reach gave him a capability that no other private air force rivaled. They could almost run certain airports and essentially did. They carried men around on their aircraft with guns. They moved armed helicopter gunships, and they did this as an organization. That is not the thing you see every day."[30]

There was an obsession in the Clinton White House to get Victor Bout and a special task force was established to follow his every move. As his planes ferried their lethal cargo across West Africa and into the Middle East, especially in Afghanistan agents intercepted his calls and had their sources worldwide keeping a close eye on him. Some people in the administration felt that too many resources were being tasked into tracking Bout down, but the endeavor went on steadily. Lee Wolosky had this to say regarding the hunt for Bout, "There were people who said, why are you obsessed with this guy? If you take him out, there are other people who will fill his shoes. My response was that I'm not obsessed with the guy, we were in charge of implementing a presidential directive, and Victor Bout is the first guy on the agenda."

Since 1992, Bout had been selling weapons to the Northern Alliance in Afghanistan but late in the decade he decide to switch sides and began selling his wares to the Taliban and al Qaeda. The

30 Farrah, Douglas and Stephen Braun, *Merchant of Death: Money, Guns, and the Man who Makes War Possible*, John Wiley and Sons, New York, 2007, Page 173.

deal started after the Taliban captured the city of Kabul in late October 1996. In one of his deals, Bout sold 40 tons of weapons to the Taliban for an estimated $50 million. Two unnamed intelligence agencies said that the weapons shipment was made on the behalf of Pakistan. Bout would later sell tanks to the Taliban which was supposedly arranged by the Pakistani intelligence service, ISI. From Washington, the Clinton administration did everything in its power to pressure the United Arab Emirates to close down Bout's enterprise but were rebuffed at every turn. Bout would be called the Merchant of Death by the world's press and his reputation grew in spades.

Victor Bout also had covert relations with some of the members of the ruling Saudi royal family and oftentimes his planes were used to transport some of them to Afghanistan where they would go bird hunting. The CIA was keeping a close watch on these flights and it was rumored at agency headquarters that the Saudis were using these flights to export heroin out of the country. Michael Scheuer of the CIA would say regarding the Saudi flights, "They [the counter-narcotics unit] were very interested about the patterns between Bout's flights and the bustard-hunting season." The British were also watching Bout's endeavors very closely and "at one point they approached the UAE officials for permission to sneak a team of agents aboard one of Bout's flights to search for Afghan heroin. However, they were unable to get permission, and the CIA also did not act on these suspicions."

Bout's end came when he was arrested in Thailand in March 2008 and was charged with a number of crimes including conspiracy to kill U.S. nationals, and conspiracy to provide material support to terrorist groups. He was extradited to the United States where he faced a court date. A movie was made based on his life called *Lord of War* starring Nicholas Cage who played the part of Victor Orlov, an arms merchant based on Victor Bout.

Osama attended Jeddah's King Abdulaziz University and obtained a degree in economics and administration in 1981. He would marry a Syrian woman, and over time, would take on three more wives.

While studying at Abdulaziz University, bin Laden came under the influence of two men who would shape his political thinking for the rest of his life: Abdullah Azzam and Mohammad Qutb. He also began to associate with members of the Muslim Brotherhood. Azzam and Osama would work together in Afghanistan where they would recruit thousands of Islamic followers to their anti-Western crusade. Mohammad Qutb was a distinguished Muslim writer and thinker who preached jihad against the West. Bin Laden absorbed these two men's ideas and would incorporate them as his basic philosophy in the years ahead.

Another man of importance in his life was Ayman al-Zawahiri, an Egyptian who had served a three year jail sentence for his participation in the assassination of Egyptian President Anwar Sadat. The two men became friends during the Afghan-Soviet war and it was al-Zawahiri's preaching that shifted Osama's worldview. Under al-Zawahiri's teachings, bin Laden accepted the idea that it was to be the cause of all principled Muslims to overthrow the Western leaning rulers in the Middle East, and oust any influence of Jews and Christians anywhere in the region.

The decisive event that put Osama bin Laden on the long road against the United States and his native land of Saudi Arabia was the 1991 Persian Gulf War.

When Iraq invaded Kuwait in August 1990 bin Laden was incensed. For the past several months, he and the remnants of his Mujahideen army had begun a small military campaign against the government of South Yemen. The effort was thwarted when the Yemeni government arrested a number of his followers and bin Laden returned to Saudi Arabia. He now turned his attention to ousting Saddam Hussein from Kuwait and spoke out at different schools and other meeting places to get his point across. He offered the Saudi government the use of his vast Mujahideen force that had been flown out from the Afghan campaign. He was more incensed when the Saudi regime invited thousands of American troops to be situated at Saudi bases in response to the Kuwait invasion.

While the American buildup was beginning, a number of Saudi officials, including an Islamic priest named Khalil Khalil, met with bin Laden to hear his complaints. He told Khalil that he wanted to use his forces to rid Kuwait of Iraqi troops and insisted on a private meeting with King Fahd. Instead, he met with Prince Sultan, the Saudi defense minister. Prince Sultan told bin Laden that the Americans were invited by the ruling family and that they would not stay permanently on Saudi soil. In return, bin Laden called the Americans infidels who would cause Saudi Arabia great harm.

In the end, the coalition of forces that responded to the Kuwait invasion, led by the United States, forced Iraq out of Kuwait and ended the battle with little cost of life on all sides. Since the first Persian Gulf war ended without the removal of Saddam Hussein, there has been a longstanding debate among historians as to whether the collation should have gone into Iraq at that time and overthrown Hussein while we had him on the ropes. The thinking was that if we had taken care of Hussein then, the United States invasion of that nation in 2003 would not have been necessary, with all the resulting death and destruction that ensued.

The other part of the equation is that right after 9-11, the Bush administration executed a full court press to put the blame for the attacks on Hussein's Iraq, despite all the evidence to the contrary. President George W. Bush wanted a war with Iraq from the minuteafter the hijacked planes hit the WTC and the Pentagon, and he began the long process that led the United States to invade that nation. Bush tried to peddle the story that Iraq had WMD—Weapons of Mass Destruction—that were hidden somewhere in Iraq, ready to be used against the United States. A huge propaganda campaign was mounted by the United States to convince the public of the great threat posed by Saddam Hussein, even using Secretary of State Colin Powell to appear before the United Nations with easels showing the sites where the WMD were stored and other bogus intelligence. In the end, there was no evidence found of any Iraqi WMD and the war was fought under false pretenses, with consequences we are still living with today (More about the Hussein/9-11 connection later in the book).

For Osama bin Laden, his hopes of driving out the infidels, i.e., the United States, from the Middle East had come to naught. His homeland of Saudi Arabia had now abandoned him for the last time and he left for greener pastures where his revolutionary brand of Islam would be welcome. All of his planning during these heady years would culminate on 9-11, with consequences no one at the time could have comprehended.

In the late 1990s, with the political/military situation in Afghanistan ever changing, the United States decided to make a second alignment with Ahmad Shah Massoud, who gladly accepted the offer. At first, the CIA paid Massoud to supply them with whatever intelligence he could provide on the Taliban and the whereabouts of bin Laden. Soon, they would work together to kill or capture the elusive Saudi.

The CIA ran its covert program with Massoud from the CTC at Langley headquarters. Its first overt help came in October 1999 when a number of its operatives code named JAWBREAKER-5 arrived in Dushanbe, Tajikistan, headed by a man named "Rich" who was head of the agency's bin Laden unit. Flying in a captured Russian MI-17 transport, the CIA team arrived in Afghanistan and renewed their relationship with Massoud. A number of highly placed national security advisors in the Clinton administration were wary of working with Massoud but that did not stop the CIA, who saw Massoud as being the last hope in their efforts to get rid of bin Laden.

The JAWBREAKER-5 team wanted the leader of the Northern Alliance to kidnap bin Laden and hand him over to the United States. They wanted Massoud to at least provide much-needed intelligence on his activities in Jalalabad or Kabul, where the Northern Alliance had many agents in place.

Massoud was willing to go along with the CIA but he challenged them to look at the larger picture rather than just going after bin Laden. In words that would grow more obvious in later years, Massoud told them that, "Even if we succeed in what you are asking for, that will not solve this bigger problem that is growing." Massoud also wanted the U.S. to set up its military relay station, the so-called "Kabul Station," in neighboring Pakistan in the city of Islamabad. Islamabad had the reputation of being the "Wild West" of the Near East, with spies and soldiers of fortune from across the globe inhabiting its teeming streets. It was from here that the CIA would resume its clandestine involvement with Massoud. Intelligence sources reveal that the CIA paid Massoud up to $200,000 a month to supply it with information and other military necessities in the war against the Russians. Massoud was also in the pay of the Pakistani ISI.

In April 1992, Massoud and his forces triumphantly entered Kabul, the capital of Afghanistan. For a period of four years, as previously noted, Massoud tried to cement the country under his leadership but was frustrated in his efforts by the other independent factions who wanted Afghanistan for themselves. In September 1996, a disheartened Massoud left Kabul and was replaced by the anti-Western, Taliban government.

While the CIA decided to work with Massoud, the Pakistani ISI did not like or trust him. During the Afghan-Soviet war, Massoud's enemy was Gulbuddin Hekmatyar, the Soviet backed warlord. The ISI felt some compunction to aid Massoud but did little to help him after the conflict ended.

In his book called *Ghost Wars,* author Steve Coll gives the identity of the main CIA contact during that time, Gary Schroen. During the 1990s, Schroen went to Massoud's headquarters in Afghanistan and gave him a half a million dollars in exchange for a promise from him that his forces would attack Afghan troops at a certain location. Massoud's men never undertook the mission and for a time the US-Massoud ties were put on hold. However, that arrangement soon returned to normal.

By 1997, with the Taliban in control of Kabul, Schroen came to see Massoud in the Panjshir Valley and brought with him $250,000, as well as electronic intercept equipment.

Gary Schroen was the head of the CIA's Pakistan office during the late 1990s and had this to say regarding his dealings with Massoud: "We had connections to the Northern Alliance, sending teams into Northern Afghanistan from 97 up until about 2000 to meet with Massoud's people, to try to get them involved."

The Near East would not be the only place the CIA and Massoud would break bread during this time. In early April 2001, Gary Schroen and his colleague, Richard Blee, met Massoud in a safe house in Paris, France when he was in Europe on a speaking tour. During their meeting, Massoud told the men "that his own intelligence had learned of al Qaeda's intention to perform a terrorist act against the United States that would be vastly greater than the bombings of the American embassies in East Africa." During the meeting, it was reported that the two CIA officers gave cash to Massoud to use as he saw fit. "Blee and Schroen assured Massoud that, although he has been visited less by the CIA recently, we are still interested in working with you, and will continue to make regular payments of several hundred thousand dollars each month."

On September 11, 2001, just as the planes hit New York and Washington, Gary Schroen who was then at work in the CIA's Near East Division, was watching live television as the event took place. Later on he would say of that moment, "We were getting calls from the CTC [the CIA's Counterterrorist Center], friends of the CTC in and around the building, that the World Trade Center, one of the towers had been struck. There were like, 30 of us standing around, and as soon as the second aircraft smashed into the second tower, everyone said, bin Laden. It was bin Laden. This is the attack that bin Laden's been promising."

Earlier, the Clinton administration, via certain agency assets in place in Afghanistan, learned of a plan by Massoud to kill bin Laden. While Massoud had one plan in mind, to kill bin Laden and ask no questions, the White House had a different approach. As far as the United States was concerned, the rules of engagement did not call for Massoud to kill bin Laden, only supply intelligence on his whereabouts. The CIA informed Massoud to stop the planned attack, and a chance to kill bin Laden was wasted.

In September 2001, events on the ground in Afghanistan would deal a death blow to Massoud. On September 9, 2001, two men posing as Arab journalists were given permission to interview Massoud at his home at Khoja Bahauddin in the Panjshir Valley. The men said they were affiliated with a London-based organization called the Islamic Observation Center. The two men entered Massoud's home and set up their camera on a tripod. Then the interview began. The journalists began asking Massoud questions about Osama bin Laden. Before Massoud could answer, a powerful bomb that was hidden inside the camera exploded, mortally wounding Massoud. A number of other men inside the room were killed, along with the so-called journalists. The surviving assassin fled the scene and was later killed. Massoud, badly wounded, was helicoptered over the border to Tajikistan and taken to a hospital where he died of his wounds. News of Massoud's death was not made public for two days, but his murder was soon telegraphed to the CIA's Counterterrorist Center. Also killed in the blast was Mohammed Dashti and Massoud Khalil was badly wounded.

The two men who killed Massoud were Moroccans and carried altered Belgian passports which had been stolen from the Belgian Consulate in Strasbourg, France and The Hague in 1999. The assassins who killed Massoud entered Islamabad, Pakistan on July 25, 2001 and were given passports to enter Afghanistan by the Taliban embassy. From there, they made their way to Kabul. The person who unknowingly helped the two men into Massoud's lair was Northern Alliance leader Abdul Rasul Sayyaf. The two Arabs were treated kindly by their Afghan hosts who never bothered to make routine checks of the equipment they carried.

Speculation of who was behind the murder of Massoud spread quickly among the intelligence services around the globe. The number one culprit was the Taliban who saw in Massoud an enemy who could best them on the field of battle. With the leader of the Northern Alliance out of the way, they could divide the anti-Taliban forces to their own advantage.

Other groups who were blamed for the assassination were the many Afghan warlords who held a grudge against Massoud and saw in him a rival for power.

Pakistani's infamous ISI was also targeted as a possible culprit in Massoud's death. For years, Pakistani governments backed the Taliban and went so far as to give them diplomatic recognition. It is not too bold a statement to say that many high ranking members of both the Pakistani government and the ISI would lose no sleep if Massoud were to be eliminated.

Shortly before his death, Massoud took his crusade for Afghan freedom to Strasbourg, France to speak to the European Parliament. He spoke to the delegates in a manner befitting a statesman and called on the world to view al Qaeda for the dangerous organization it was. He also traveled to Brussels and made an impression there too.

One of the recent documents to be released on the attacks on 9-11 is a highly redacted, one page note on the Massoud assassination and the Taliban. Here is what is says:

> Warning, This is an important report, not finally evaluated intelligence. Report classified.
>
> The relationship between the assassination of the late Northern Alliance commander Massoud and the terrorist incident of 11 September 2001, including al Qaeda involvement. Text-Background. In the early 1990s, the Taliban began as a group of religious students who rejected the Mujahadin takeover of Afghanistan. Due to the Pakistani government support to Taliban forces, the Taliban became militarily powerful and their forces controlled approximately 90 percent of Afghanistan. Many Afghan opposition forces were outnumbered and outgunned by Taliban forces and could not fight the Taliban forces directly. The former commander, Ahmed Shah Massoud, managed to form the Northern Alliance forces and continued his fight against Taliban forces in Northern Afghanistan. On 9 September 2001, Commander Massoud was assassinated in Northern Afghanistan. Warning: Through Northern Alliance intelligence efforts, the late Commander Massoud gained limited knowledge regarding the intentions of the Saudi millionaire, Osama bin Laden and his terrorist organization, al Qaeda, to perform a terrorist act against the U.S.[31]

In the intervening years, the dominant theory of who was responsible for the Massoud assassination was bin Laden. He had the means, motive, and opportunity to eliminate his most formidable rival. With Massoud's death, the CIA lost its most trusted ally in Afghanistan. Two days later, on September 11, 2001, al Qaeda had accomplished two of its most important objectives: the death of Ahmed Shah Massoud, and its successful attack upon the United States.

---

31 The Assassination of Massoud Related to 11 September 2001 Attack. Department of Defense.

Chapter 4:

The US-Saudi 9-11 Connection

Almost twenty years after the attack on the World Trade Center and the Pentagon, there are many unanswered questions as to just what happened that beautiful September morning. Among the points of contention are the possible connections between the hijackers and the government of Saudi Arabia. Of the nineteen men who hijacked the planes that hit the WTC and the Pentagon, fifteen were Saudi nationals. There has been a long connection between al Qaeda and Saudi Arabia dating back to the 1990s, when the Russians invaded Afghanistan and the Taliban morphed into a position of strength in that country. Saudi Arabia was one of a few nations who had diplomatic relations with the Taliban. In the months leading up to the attacks on 9-11, there were a number of covert meetings between two of the hijackers, Khalid al-Midhar and Nawaf al-Hazmi, and persons connected to the government of Saudi Arabia. This is a convoluted story that has many parts, including meetings with Saudi agents in the United States and some of the highest ranking Saudi diplomats then in residence in Washington, as well as a confession by the "20th hijacker," Zacarius Moussaoui, who implicated certain members of the Saudi royal family in the 9-11 attacks.

In 2002, a joint House Senate panel investigated the 9-11 attacks and came up with a number of interesting facts that were later further looked into by the National Commission on Terrorist Attacks Upon the United States, the 9-11 Commission, among which were a reference to a missing 28-page section on al Qaeda's "specific source of foreign support," much of which was then classified (the 28 pages are now declassified and will be talked about in this chapter). In its final report, the 9-11 Commission members said that it "found no evidence that the Saudi government as in institution or senior Saudi officials individually funded the organization," meaning al Qaeda.

The 9-11 Commission described the lapse of intelligence sharing between the CIA and the FBI which might have prevented the attacks from taking place, as well as telling the story of the activities of the above-mentioned two men in the San Diego area that were carried out without the knowledge of either the FBI or the CIA.

This story revolves around two of the 9-11 hijackers, Khalid al-Midhar and Nawaf al-Hazmi, who arrived in the United States in January 2000. Both men settled in San Diego and in April 2000, al Hamzi took flying lessons at the National Air College in San Diego. One week later he received $5,000 from an unnamed person located in the United Arab Emirates. In May 2000, both men enrolled in flight training in San Diego. Later in May, al-Midhar went to Oman and didn't return to the U.S. until July 2001.

al-Hazmi stayed in the San Diego area until December 2000, and then moved to Arizona with another 9-11 hijacker, Hani Hamjour.

At the time that al-Hazmi and al Midhar lived in San Diego, they were in constant contact with an unnamed FBI informant who provided the bureau with information on them. This unnamed informer only knew the first names of both men and relayed that information to his FBI controller. The informant told his FBI handler that they were "good Muslim Saudi youths" who were in America to attend flight schools.

In an intelligence blunder on the parts of the FBI and the CIA, the agency did not inform the FBI that the two men had previously attended an al Qaeda summit in Malaysia in which planning for the 9-11 plot was hatched. Adding to the CIA's sins, it wasn't until August 2001 that the CIA asked that the two men be placed on a watchlist in order to prevent their entry into the United States.

According to the Senate/House report, "During a debriefing in the summer of 2000, the informant told me [his FBI handler] that the informant met two individuals described as good Muslim Saudi youths who were legally in the United States to visit and attend school. According to the informant, they were religious and not involved in criminal or political activities. At some point, but before September 11, the informant told me their names were Nawaf and Khalid. The informant did not tell me their last names prior to September 11, 2001."

The FBI report said they had problems with the informant's bona fides and tried to block his appearance as a witness to give his testimony. The FBI objected when the committee tried to interview the person and he never did attend any of the committee's sessions.

After 9-11, FBI agents had numerous interrogation sessions with the unnamed source and he repeatedly told them that he was kept in the dark about 9-11 and did not know the real reason why the two men were in the United States. The informant also told the FBI in the days after 9-11 the identities of a number of men who al-Midhar and al-Hazmi had been in communication with in San Diego. Four of these people were of operational interest to the FBI.

In his congressional testimony, the FBI handler said that the informant did not mention that al-Hazmi was taking training until after the attacks. "The handling agent said that none of the information provided by the informant about the hijackers before September 11 raised concerns. The fact that the two individuals were Saudi was not a concern before September 11 because Saudi Arabia was considered an ally."

The FBI, according to the joint congressional account, did not believe the informant when he said he did not recognize the other 9-11 hijacker, Hani Hanjour, when he visited al Hamzi in San Diego.

The failure of the CIA to inform the FBI that it was aware that al-Midhar had obtained a U.S. visa and was seen in California in March 2000 was an intelligence offense of the first order. If both agencies had been able to track al-Midhar and al-Hazmi in August 2001, they might have been able to break up the 9-11 plot.

However, the story of how al-Hazmi and al-Midhar were associated once they entered the U.S. grew murkier as events unfolded. It was originally believed that the men had little contact once they entered the United States. That assumption is now in doubt thanks to information that has become public since 9-11.

Prince Turki al-Faisal, the Saudi intelligence minister, reported that in the month before 9-11, Saudi external intelligence told the CIA that Nawaf al-Hazmi and Khalid al-Midhar, were placed on a Saudi terror watchlist. Another person they were tracking was Nawal's brother, Salem. Two other Saudi officials, Saeed Badeeb, Prince Turki's chief analyst, and Nawal Obaid, a security consultant to the Saudi government, backed up Turki's claims regarding the two men, however Turki reneged on his claim about the two hijackers when he became the Saudi ambassador to the U.S.[32]

One of the men they made contact with was a murky Saudi named Omar al-Bayoumi. Al-Bayoumi, who lived in San Diego, is said to have had links with Saudi intelligence, and was possibly keeping track of the large Saudi contingent of college students in the area. While in Saudi Arabia, he worked for the large Saudi Ministry of Defense and Aviation. His "cover," while living in San Diego, was that of a "pilot" or "student."

Al-Bayoumi became a target of interest to the FBI office in San Diego, which began compiling a large dossier on him. While the FBI did not find any illegal activity being carried out by him, they noted that he had "access to seemingly unlimited funding from Saudi Arabia." One FBI report said al-Bayoumi paid $500,000 in cash given him by the Saudi government to buy a mosque in 1998. Despite his shadowy life style, the FBI stopped its investigation of him in 1999. In his book called *The Terror Timeline,* author Paul Thompson says that a classified section of the 9-11 report notes that payments to al-Bayoumi increased dramatically just after he made contact with al-Hazmi and al-Midhar in early 2000.

But the al-Bayoumi story does not end there. When al-Hazmi and al-Midhar arrived in Los Angeles, they met with al-Bayoumi in a restaurant. Shortly after their lunch date, both of the future 9-11 hijackers moved to San Diego, possibly on the recommendation of al-Bayoumi. He helped the men move into an apartment near where he and his family were living, and he even co-signed the lease on their apartment, putting down $1,500 for their initial month's rent and their security deposit.

Al-Bayoumi also introduced another of the 9-11 hijackers,

32 History Commons: Complete 9-11 Timeline "CIA Hiding Knowledge of al-Hazmi and Al-Midhar."

Hani Honjour, to al-Hazmi and all three would soon live together

Instead of living covertly in San Diego, the men blended in with American society. They used their real names when conducting business, were listed in the 2000-01 phone book, had bank accounts and valid driver's licenses.

In the summer of 2000, while living in San Diego, Kalid al-Midhar made a phone call to an al Qaeda safe house in Yemen, which belonged to his father-in-law. The NSA monitored this call, however, the NSA did not realize that the person known as "Khalid" was calling from the United States.

If the FBI bungled in not knowing that al-Hazmi and al-Midhar were living openly in the U.S. they were to face another lost opportunity when it was revealed that the men were living in the same apartment with an FBI "asset" named Abdussattar Shaikh. Shaikh only told the FBI the first names of his roommates, never revealing their last names. If he had told the bureau their full names, they both would have popped up on the watchlist, which now had them in its database.

Abdussattar Shaikh's FBI handler was Steven Butler. Butler's informant gave him the first names, but nothing more. He further told Agent Butler that the men were no menace to society, were in the U.S. for school, and were not associating with any known radicals. Nor did he mention the fact that the men were taking flying lessons.

The 9-11 Commission disbelieved Shaikh's story that he had no prior knowledge of the 9-11 attack, and wrote in its final report that if the FBI had been more proactive in its relation with Shaikh, "It would have given the San Diego FBI field office perhaps the Intelligence Community's best chance to unravel the September 11 plot."

By the spring and summer of 2001, the hijackers moved about the country without being noticed. In March 2001, both Hani Hanjour and Nawaf al-Hazmi moved to Falls Church, Virginia from Phoenix. Others would settle for a time in New Jersey and other places along the east coast. In a bit of bad luck for U.S. intelligence, Nawaf al-Hazmi was issued a speeding ticket in Oklahoma on April 1, 2001, however, his name did not come up on any criminal list. He was given a ticket and the matter was closed.

On the day that al-Midhar and al-Hazmi were put on the government's watchlist (August 24-25, 20001), they purchased their 9-11 tickets by credit card. The FAA and the domestic airline carriers were not told of the men being added to the watchlist, and their ticket purchases were not looked up.

Another person associated with the Saudis was Osama Basnan who was living in California (1998) at the same time as al-Midhar and al-Hazmi and befriended both of them. Osama Basnan wrote a letter to Saudi Prince Bandar bin Sultan and his wife, asking for financial help because his wife was in need of money for a thyroid operation. Prince Bandar's wife, Haifa, sent upwards of $73,000 over a period of three years to Basnan for his wife's medical treatment. Medical records state however that Basnan's wife was treated for her condition in April 2000, two years after the money was first sent. Basnan, it is alleged, funneled some of this money to al-Midhar and al-Hazmi but the FBI could not positively say this happened.[33]

If there was one U.S. Senator who believed that the government of Saudi Arabia was responsible in the 9-11 attacks, it was Florida's Robert Graham. Graham, a Democrat, served on the Senate Intelligence Committee investigating the 9-11 attacks and said he believed there was a "direct line between the terrorists and the government of Saudi Arabia." Senator Graham was one of the panel members who read the secret 28-page report that the Bush administration refused to release to the public, and as he sat in a secure part of the capital beneath the visitor's center in a soundproof room, he was very determined to get to the truth of what happened that day. The secret 28-page report contained classified material revealing the relationship between the Saudi "spies," as Graham called them and the terrorists who hit the WTC. While there was no direct link between the members of the Saudi Royal family and 9-11, Senator Graham, and other members of the panel, believed that a number of lower level Saudi diplomats were associated with al Qaeda, possibly members of the Islamic Affairs Ministry who were in touch with the 9-11 hijackers.

Senator Graham (now out of office), was a maverick as far

33 Thompson, Paul, *The Terror Timeline*, Regan Books, New York, 2004, Page 158. P

as his allegation that the Saudis were involved, as well as his belief that the Bush administration was trying to cover up Saudi involvement in the attack because of their close ties to the Saudi regime, as well as the continuing need for Saudi oil. He was also a harsh critic of the way the FBI conducted its investigation, putting blame directly on the new FBI Director, Robert Mueller. The same Robert Mueller would be in the nation's headlines years later when he carried out an investigation of President Donald Trump's links to the Russian government during the 2016 U.S. presidential election.

In July 2016, the once secret 28-page report was finally declassified and it had some very interesting things to say. Here is a redacted part of the Executive Summary that was dated September 1, 2005 and written by both the FBI and the CIA:

> Since the 11 September attacks, the United States Intelligence Community has been working to assess Saudi Arabia's ties to terrorism, including the 2001 terrorist acts, in order to address questions arising about the country's support for organizations that may have provided support for previous al Qaeda attacks.
>
> Our assessment is as follows:
>
> There is no evidence that either the Saudi Government or members of the Saudi Royal family knowingly provided support for the attacks of 11 September 2001 or that they had foreknowledge of terrorist operations in the Kingdom or elsewhere.
>
> There is evidence that official Saudi entities [Blank] and associated governmental organizations (NGOs) provide financial and logistical support to individuals in the United States and around the world, some of whom are associated with terrorism-related activity.
>
> The Saudi government and many of its agencies have been infiltrated and exploited by individuals associated with or sympathetic to al Qaeda.
>
> [Blank portions] Saudi-funded clerics have been found to be [Blank] Saudi-Americans and other communities in the United States.

> [Blank portions] in the United States, including diplomats, are engaged in a campaign to influence public perception and policy.
>
> The Saudi government and private Saudi individuals support the propagation of the conservative Wahabi-Salafi sect of Sunni Islam in the United States. Jihadists adhere to and interpret this sect's beliefs to justify their actions.
>
> There is no information that either Omar al-Bayoumi or Osama Basnan materially supported the hijackers wittingly, were intelligence officers of the Saudi government or provided material support for the 11 September attacks, contrary to media speculation.
>
> Recent cooperation between Saudi intelligence and the USIC is largely driven by the Saudi royal family's recognition of the domestic threat posed to it by al Qaeda following several bombings by the group inside Saudi Arabia, starting in May 2003.
>
> In the past, the Saudi government found itself in a precarious position, on the one hand it was denouncing al Qaeda as a threat, yet on the other hand was underestimating al Qaeda's vitality within the Kingdom and treating the group with special consideration. Raids by the General Directorate for Investigations following the attacks in May 2003, which have resulted in the death or arrest of al Qaeda members in Saudi Arabia, demonstrate how this policy has changed.[34]

"While in the United States," the report says, "some of the September 11 hijackers were in contact with, and received support or assistance from, individuals who may be connected to the Saudi government."

Upon the release of the 28 pages, the Saudi government was quick to respond. A statement was released by the Saudi Ambassador to the United States which said,

> Several government agencies, including the CIA and the FBI have investigated the contents of the 28-Pages

34 Letter to Senator Pat Roberts from Robert Mueller and Porter Goss, 9-1-2005.

> and have confirmed that neither the Saudi government, nor Saudi officials, nor any person acting on behalf of the Saudi government provided any support or encouragement for these attacks. We hope the release of these pages will clear up, once and for all, any lingering questions about Saudi Arabia's actions, intentions, or long-term friendship with the United States. It should be clear that this Joint inquiry has made no final determination as to the reliability or sufficiency of the information.

The release of the 28 pages gives a detailed analysis of what happened regarding the Saudi government and the 9-11 story.

> Prior to September 11, the FBI apparently did not focus investigative resources on [deleted] Saudi nationals in the United States due to Saudi Arabia's status as an American ally. A number of FBI agents and CIA officers complained to the Joint Inquiry about a lack of Saudi cooperation in terrorism investigations both before and after the September 11 attacks.

The report cites one New York FBI agent who said,

> The Saudis have been useless and obstructionist for years.
>
> Preliminary readings show that there may well have been Saudi involvement in the terror of 9/11 in the Saudi government and within the Saudi country, with Saudi Arabia.

The above statement was issued at the time by New York Senator Charles Schumer who is currently the Senate Minority leader.

Upon the release of the document, Senator Graham, who had long tried to link the Saudi government to the attacks, said this, "The information in the 28-pages reinforces the belief that the 19 hijackers, most of whom spoke little English, had limited education and had never before visited the United States, did not act alone in perpetrating the sophisticated 9-11 plot. It suggests a strong linkage between those terrorists and the Kingdom of Saudi Arabia, Saudi charities, and other Saudi stakeholders. The American people should be concerned about these links."

Two of the commission's staffers who were most involved in digging up the information regarding the Saudi connection to 9-11 were Eleanor Hill, the commission's staff director, and Michael Jacobson, a former FBI lawyer and expert on counterterrorism matters. Jacobson found damming material concerning al-Hazmi and al-Midhar in the files of the FBI's office in San Diego, as well as in the FBI's Washington office. Jacobson learned of their relationship with Omar al-Bayoumi and his association with the Saudi regime. The more Senator Graham read of the classified material, the more he came to believe that the Saudis were connected to al Qaeda prior to the 9-11 attacks and that the Bush administration did not want that information to come to light.

Members of the committee were investigated by the FBI in June of 2002 when CNN received information, possibly coming from the committee, about a message which was exchanged by al Qaeda members referring to the upcoming attacks: "Tomorrow is zero day. The match is tomorrow." This message was intercepted by the NSA but not translated from Arabic until after the attacks took place. At the urging of the Bush administration, the FBI began interviewing members of the Senate panel as well as their staff to find out who the leak was from. Senator Graham was furious at the Bush administration's hard tactics toward his colleagues and believed that the actions taken against them were done in order to stifle any further investigations of the 9-11 attacks.

It was Michael Jacobson who wrote the 28-page summary revealing the possible Saudi relationship to the 9-11 hijackers, which the Bush administration refused to release. It took the Obama administration to finally make the decision to reveal to the American public and the world the contents of these important pages.

Another 9-11 committee staffer who was not intimidated by the bright lights was Dana Lesmann who joined Jacobson on the staff. Lesmann had previously worked for the Justice Department before coming to the committee and took a skeptical view of the FBI and its practices regarding its investigation of the events before 9-11. Lesmann asked Philip Zelikow, the 9-11 Commission's executive director for permission to interview 20 people, including some FBI agents, but he only allowed her to see ten. She also requested to see a copy of the secret 28-page report but that demand was refused. Nevertheless Lesmann acquired a copy of the report, but Zelikow got the last word and fired Lesmann on the spot over her possession of the 28-page report. After her firing, the top members of the 9-11 staff did not leak the firing of Dana Lesmann or why she was let go the press, thus covering up a matter that would have put mud on their faces.

Throughout the investigative process regarding the attacks on 9-11 and the contents of the once-secret 28 pages, Philip Zelikow had his own agenda to play. One doesn't know whether he was covering up the facts before him or he was just being cautious. In an interview with the *New York Times,* he concluded that in the 28 pages, "there was no evidence that the Saudi government and its top officials helped finance al Qaeda." He further opined, "Those involved in the preparation of the famous 28 pages joined the staff of the 9-11 Commission and participated in the follow-up investigation of all the leads that had been developed earlier. I doing so, they were aided by a larger team with more members, more powers and for the first time actually conducted interviews of relevant people both in this country and in Saudi Arabia." He added, "and what we found is reflected in the commission report."

Philip Zelikow was a controversial figure among the group who made up the 9-11 Commission. Condoleezaa Rice and Philip Zelikow co-wrote a book about the implications of German reunification. They had worked together at the National Security Council in the 1980s and early 1990s. Before becoming a member of the 9-11Commisson, Zelikow had been a professor at the Kennedy School of Government at Harvard University, while Rice worked as the provost at Stanford. The name of their book was *Germany Unified and Europe Transformed: A Study in Statecraft.*

Rice and Zelikow would work together in a joint effort between the faculties of Harvard, Stanford, MIT, and the University of Virginia, on a project called the Catastrophic Terrorism Study Group. The director of the project was Zelikow. Also working on the project were Jamie Gorlick and Ernest May, both of whom were to later be members of the Commission. The end result of the study was a report written by Zelikow and its two co-chairs, former Assistant Secretary of Defense Ashton Carter and former CIA Director John Deutch. They wrote, "Long part of the Hollywood and Tom Clancy repertory of nightmarish scenarios, catastrophic terrorism has moved from far-fetched horror to a contingency that could happen next month. Although the United States still takes conventional terrorism seriously, it is not yet prepared for the new threat of catastrophic terrorism." They also wrote that,

> An act of catastrophic terrorism that killed thousands or tens of thousands of people and/or disrupted the necessities of life for hundreds of thousands, or even millions, would be a watershed event in American history. It could involve loss of life and property unprecedented for peacetime and undermine America's fundamental sense of security within our own borders in a manner akin to the 1949 Soviet bomb test, or perhaps even worse, protect itself from further attacks by pressing against allowable limits in surveillance or citizens, detention of suspects, and the use of deadly force.

Some of this scenario played itself out after the 9-11 attacks.

In 1997, Zelikow and Ernest May wrote a book called *The Kennedy Tapes: Inside the White House During the Cuban Missile Crisis*. The book told the story of the 13-day crisis during which the Soviet Union placed intermediate-range nuclear missiles in Cuba and the Kennedy administration's effort to end the crisis. The book was based on transcriptions of recorded meetings, conferences, telephone conversations, and interviews with people who took part in the crisis. After the publication of the book, an historian named Sheldon Stern, then a professor at the John F. Kennedy Library, reviewed the book and gave its less than stellar ratings. After going over the recordings on which the book was based, Professor Stern said that there were hundreds of errors in the book, many quite large in scope. Stern concluded by saying, "Readers deserve to know that even now *The Kennedy Tapes* cannot be relied on as an accurate historical document." He pointed out that in the book, the authors said that Robert Kennedy, then Attorney General, talked about a planned "invasion" of Russian ships heading for Cuba, when the tapes actually showed the man taking a less than hostile attitude toward the approaching ships.[35]

In January 2001, after George W. Bush took over as president after the disputed presidential election, Zelikow was not offered a job in the new administration, and returned to teach at the Miller Center of Public Affairs at the University of Virginia. He had worked as part of the Bush transition team after the election but was not appointed to any post.

Condoleezza Rice fared better. She was appointed as Bush's National Security Advisor and later was appointed Secretary of State. After the 9-11 attacks, Zelikow would find himself back in the national spotlight as a high-ranking member of the 9-11 Commission.

In recent years, two other congressmen who read the 28-page report also put the onus on the government of Saudi Arabia. Walter Jones, a Republican from North Carolina said, "It's about the Bush administration and its relationship with the Saudis." Stephen Lynch, a Massachusetts Democrat told author Lawrence Wright that the document was "stunning in its clarity and that if offers direct evidence of complicity on the part of certain Saudi individuals and entities in al Qaeda's attack on America. Those 28 pages tell a story that has been completely removed from the 9-11 report." Another unnamed congressman who read the evidence of Saudi government also backed up both Jones and Lynch. This lawmaker said the evidence against the Saudi government support for the 9-11 hijacking is "very disturbing, and that the real question is whether it was sanctioned at the royal family level or beneath that, and whether these leads were followed through."[36]

In 2004, a lawsuit was brought forth on behalf of the victims of the attacks, along with some insurers who paid claims to beneficiaries of those who died in the strikes. The suit alleges that some Saudi charities, banks and certain persons were involved in

35 History Commons: May 2000: Future Authors of 9/11 Report Produce John F. Kennedy Book riddled with Errors.

36 Wright, Lawrence, "The Twenty-Eight Pages," *The New Yorker*, September 9, 2014.

the attacks. In 2005, the government of Saudi Arabia was dismissed from the suit on the ground of sovereign immunity, but the U.S. Supreme Court reinstated the Saudis as a defendant. In a statement by the families of those lost on 9-11, they said, "The redaction of the 28 pages has become a cover-up by two Presidents, and cover-up implies complicity."

Philip Zelikow, the man who fired Dana Lesmann, called the 28 pages "an agglomeration of preliminary, unvetted reports" concerning the Saudi regime. "There are wild accusations that need to be checked out," he said.

The members of the 9-11 Commission were never able to make a direct connection between the Saudi government and the hijackers. One person who worked on the commission warned that if the pages were released it would set back US-Saudi relations in the extreme (it seems that things have not really changed in this regard as events in 2019 would show).

In an interview with journalist Lawrence Wright, the 9-11 Chairman, Thomas Keane, the former Governor of New Jersey, had much to say about the 28 pages. He said that while reading the pages in the basement of the capital, he had someone standing over his shoulder. He said that most of the material he read "should never have been kept secret." He also said in relation to the pages that, "a ton of stuff, [documents] is still classified, including the Commission's interviews with George Bush, Bill Clinton, and Dick Cheney. I don't know of a single thing in our report that should not be made public after ten years."

The single most important person involved in 9-11 who accused the Saudis of being complicit in the attacks is Zacarias Moussaoui, a 9-11 co-conspirator who took flight training courses in the U.S. in 2001 and was arrested by federal authorities that year. Moussaoui said that members of the Saudi royal family helped finance al Qaeda prior to 9-11. In a court deposition, Moussaoui said that he was told by al Qaeda officials in Afghanistan in either 1998 or 1999 to create a digital database of donors to his group. Some of these donors were Prince Turki al-Faisal, then the Saudi intelligence chief, Prince Bandar bin Sultan, the ambassador to the U.S., Prince al-Waleed bin Talal, a prominent billionaire investor, and others. He said that Osama bin Laden wanted to keep a record of who donated to al Qaeda. He also said that he was a courier from bin Laden to important Saudi leaders, taking them important messages. [37]

Naturally, the Saudi government refuted Moussaoui's allegations, calling him a "deranged criminal whose own lawyers presented evidence that he was mentally incompetent. His words have no credibility. His goal in making these statements only serves to get attention for himself and try to do what he could do through acts of terrorism—to undermine U.S-Saudi relations." For all of Moussaoui's allegations, he was sentenced to life in prison for his participation in the 9-11 plot.

Other important information coming from the 9-11 Commission pertaining to al Qaeda was that the organization had an operating budget of $30 million a year, and the 9-11 attacks cost between $400,000 and $500,000, and that certain entities in Saudi Arabia provided money for the operation. The 9-11 Commission further wrote, "The staff report also said that prior to the terrorist attacks the U.S. sought the help of Saudi Arabia and the United Arab Emirates to stop the flow of money to al Qaeda entities. But Saudi officials were ambivalent and selectively cooperative in assisting the Unite States, and the U.S. didn't make it a priority."

As written in the 9-11 Commission report dated August 21, 2004,

> The U.S. government approached the Saudis on some narrow issues, such as locating bin Laden's supposed personal wealth and gaining access to a senior al Qaeda financial figure in Saudi custody, with mixed results. The Saudis generally resisted cooperating more broadly against al Qaeda financing, although the U.S. government did not make this issue a priority in its bilateral relations with the Saudis or provide the Saudis with actionable intelligence about al Qaeda fundraising in the Kingdom. Other issues, such as Iraq, the Middle East peace process, economic arrangements, the oil supply, and cutting off Saudi support for the Taliban, took primacy on the U.S.-Saudi agenda.[38]

---

37 No author. "Saudi Arabia and the 9-11 Terrorist Attacks." *The Wire*, February 6, 2015.

38 Kiely, "Eugene, Saudi Arabia and the 9-11 Terrorist Attacks," FactCheck.

While the names of a number a highly placed Saudi princes have been mentioned in this work in conjunction with the lead-up to the 9-11 attacks, the 9-11 Commission took a different tack regarding them. The staff report did not mention by name any of the three princes singled out by Moussaoui, but it did clear, Saudi Princess Haifa al-Faisal of any wrongdoing. "Despite persistent public speculation, there is no evidence Saudi Princess Haifa al-Faisal provided any funds to the hijackers either directly or indirectly."

After the 9-11 attacks, it seems there was a change of heart in the Kingdom as the Saudi government, "Dramatically improved cooperation with the United States on the financing of terrorist activities. Managing this nuanced and complicated relationship will play a critical part in determining the success of U.S. counterterrorism policy for the foreseeable future."

While the 9-11 Commission found no credible link to the Saudi regime in the attacks, they did say that al Qaeda had fertile fundraising ground in Saudi Arabia, including from corrupt fund raising charities and wealthy individuals.

The information provided in this chapter gives a lot of circumstantial evidence that links the government in Riyadh to the 9-11 attacks. Sometimes in a court of law, circumstantial evidence is enough to convict.

While the details of the following story may or may not have anything to do with the Saudi-American relations during the lead-up to 9-11, it is a story that needs to be told. On November 1. 2001, there appeared a news story in the *New York Times* that made headline shaking allegations. The story was written by Joseph Fitchett with the *International Herald Tribune* under the banner heading: "Dubai Clinic Denies Report Bin Laden Met with CIA." The gist of the story alleged that Osama bin Laden had been under hospital care in a Dubai clinic for kidney care for 10 days in July and met there with a U.S. intelligence operative— just weeks before the 9-11 attacks. The source of the story was the French newspaper *Le Figaro* that was based in Paris. The paper had no independent confirmation of the story, which was based on a leak from "someone associated with the management

org, Feb. 6, 2015.

team" at the American hospital in Dubai, where bin Laden was supposedly being treated. Bernard Koval, the head of the hospital said regarding the story, "Osama bin Laden has never been here." (What else would he have said?). According the *Times'* story, a highly placed Arab diplomat in Paris said, "Would Mr. bin Laden have run the risks of prolonged medical treatment in Dubai, a free-wheeling Gulf city-state with an underworld of smugglers and mercenaries easily recruitable to assassinate the man listed as U.S. public enemy No. 1? If he needed treatment, he would have chosen a place where he could count on draconian security like Baghdad or Damascus."

According to the *Le Figaro* story, the head of the CIA station "was seen going into Mr. bin Laden's room. But the 100-bed clinic's boss, Mr. Koval, told reporters in Dubai that this is too small a hospital for someone to be snuck through the backdoor—a phrase apparently applying both to Mr. bin Laden and the local CIA station chief." For its part, the Dubai clinic had plenty of reasons not to go along with the news story, as if it were true, it would have ruined the reputation of the clinic, not to mention cause a worldwide outcry. A doctor who worked in the clinic named Terry Callaway, a Canadian, was said to have treated bin Laden, but he said regarding that allegation, "He's never been a patient here; he's never been treated here."

The story said that the allegation may have been part of a disinformation campaign to begin with, which was a comment made by one unnamed French intelligence official. If disinformation was really behind the *Le Figaro* story then the reasoning probably goes like this. The French had no real reason to back the United States when it invaded Afghanistan and later Iraq, and may have been spewing out disinformation in order to embarrass Washington. There were many on the left in France who believed for years, rightly or wrongly, that bin Laden had been a creation of the CIA, due to the fact that his participation in the financing of the rebels fighting the Soviet forces in Afghanistan was furthering the U.S. side. The story might have been a way of getting back at the United States for whatever views they held.

We now turn our attention to the covert role played in the world of intelligence on the part of various Saudi officials, including Prince

Turki al-Faisal, then head of the Saudi intelligence service (beginning in 1979). This is a strange story indeed, with many permutations and a lot of speculation. In 1976, while in the United States for a speech, Prince al-Faisal made the following remarks. "In 1976, after the Watergate matters took place here, your intelligence community was literally tied up by Congress. It could not do anything. It could not send spies, it could not write reports, and it could not pay money. In order to compensate for that, a group of countries got together in the hope of fighting Communism and established what was called the Safari Club. The Safari Club included France, Egypt, Saudi Arabia, Morocco, and Iran."

The Safari Club is said to have been established on September 1, 1976 by the famous French spy chief (SDECE) Alexandre de Marenches. Millions of dollars were put into the Safari Club and its members met in several places like France and Egypt. According to the organization called History Commons, "The group played a secret role in political intrigues in many countries, mostly in Africa and the Middle East. For instance, a rebellion in Zaire was put down by Moroccan and Egyptian troops, using French air support. It also played a role in the US-Egyptian-Israeli peace treaty of 1979." Joseph Trento, a well-known author in the intelligence field "alleged that the Safari Club and especially the Saudi intelligence agency led by Kamal Adam and his nephew Prince Turki from 1979 onwards, fund off-the-books covert operations for the CIA."

One of its members was Theodore Shackley, a former CIA officer who took part in many agency operations over the years, including the CIA's secret war against Cuba's Fidel Castro, the war in Vietnam, the Iran-Contra scandal during the last years of the Reagan administration.

The CIA as an organization did not have operations control of the Safari Club but its members worked in its shadows, taking on whatever job was handed to them.

The Safari Club was supposed to have shut down operations at some point and its existence was made public not long after the Shah of Iran was deposed in 1979, thus, setting up the role of the mullahs who still run Iran to this day. Coincidence or not, the Safari Club was supposed to have closed up shop at the same time as Alexandre de Marenches retired in 1982. [39]

39 History Commons: September 1, 1976-Early 1980s-Secret Intelligence

However, the story of the Safari Club does not end there. In order to finance its global operations, and to hide its assets, Saudi intelligence minister Kamal Adham was given orders to establish such a link. "With the official blessing of George H.W. Bush, as the head of the CIA, Adham transformed a small Pakistani merchant bank, the Bank of Commerce and Credit International (BCCI), into a worldwide money-laundering machine, buying banks around the world to create the biggest clandestine money network in history. One of the organizations who used the services of BCCI was Osama bin Laden whose al Qaeda used the secret bank to raise and funnel money to its people throughout the Middle East."

BCCI was founded in 1972 by a Pakistani national named Agha Hasan Abedi. BCCI's rationale for being knew no bounds and it took on clients—wherever and whoever would pay—including terrorist groups of all stripes. A CIA officer named Raymond Close who worked with Adham and BCCI, "tapped into the CIA's stockpile of misfits and malcontents to help man a 1,500 strong group of assassins and enforcers." *Time* magazine called BCCI, "a global intelligence operation and a Mafia-like enforcement squad. Operating primarily out of the bank's offices in Karachi, Pakistan, the 1,500 employee black network had used sophisticated spy equipment and techniques, along with bribery, extortion, kidnapping, and even by some accounts, murder. The black network—so named by its own members—stopped at almost nothing to further the bank's aims the world over."[40]

With the connections between BCCI and the CIA as strong as possible, we have to consider the role that CIA Director George H.W. Bush played regarding the Saudis. Adham had been the head of Saudi intelligence at the same time that George Bush was director of the CIA. During this time period, the CIA was working directly to brush up the Saudi intelligence service and Bush and Adham were on good terms. The intelligence leaders in the Middle East had a nickname for Bush and called him "the Saudi vice president."

The United States was not the only country that had ties with

---

Cabal works with Rogue CIA elements to influence Middle East and Africa.

40 History Commons: Shortly After September 1, 1976—CIA and other intelligence agencies use BCCI to control and manipulate Criminals and Terrorists Worldwide.

BCCI, Pakistan being another. "The Pakistani ISI had major connections to the bank. However, as later State Department reports indicated, Pakistan remained a major drug trafficking and money-laundering center despite the bank's closing. The CIA used BCCI to funnel millions of dollars to the fighters battling the Soviet occupation of Afghanistan, according to reports from the *Washington Post.* A French intelligence report in 2001, suggested that the BCCI network has been largely built by bin Laden. The ruling family of Abu Dhabi, the dominant emirate in the United Arab Emirates, owned 77% of the bank."[41]

The connections between bin Laden's al Qaeda are plentiful and wide-ranging, more than was known at the time. This link came from a 70-page French intelligence report which said in part,

> The financial network of bin Laden, as well as his network of investments, is similar to the network put in place in the 1980s by BCCI for its fraudulent operations, often with the same people. The dominant trait of ben Laden's operations is that of a terrorist network backed up by a financial structure. A senior U.S. investigator later said that U.S. agencies were looking into the ties outlined by the French because they just make so much sense, and so few people from BCCI ever went to jail. BCCI was the mother and father of terrorist financing operations. The report identifies dozens of companies and individuals who were involved with BCCI and were found to be dealing with bin Laden after the bank collapsed. Many went on to work in banks and charities identified by the U.S. and others supporting al Qaeda. The role of Saudi billionaire Khalid bin Mahfouz in supporting bin Laden is emphasized in the report. In 1995, bin Mahfouz paid a $225 million fine in a settlement with U.S. prosecutors for his role in the BCCI scandal. Representatives of bin Mahfouz later argued that this report was in fact prepared by Jean-Charles Brisard and not the French intelligence service.[42]

The twisted tentacles of US-Saudi relations came back on full

41 Thompson, Paul, *The Terror Timeline*, Page 242.

42 Ibid. Page 259-60.

view when on October 2, 2018 the brutal murder of *Washington Post* reporter and U.S. resident Jamal Khashoggi took place in Istanbul, Turkey as he entered the Saudi consular complex. Jamal Khashoggi was a Saudi citizen and frequent critic of the regime whose stories in the American press infuriated the royal Saudi family. Under circumstances that are still under investigation, Mr. Khashoggi was killed (and his body was dismembered) by agents of the Saudi government in their consulate. After the killing of Mr. Khashoggi, the government of Saudi Arabia had a number of excuses for his death, even going so far as to say it was a botched rendition effort to take him out of the country. The death of Jamal Khashoggi got the attention of the world and it was speculated in the press that Crown Prince Mohammed bin Salman of Saudi Arabia personally ordered the assassination of Mr. Khashoggi.

Soon after the murder of Mr. Khashoogi, the world's press began writing detailed stories about what happened and the more they wrote about it, the more complex it became. Since Khashoggi was a resident of the United States, but not a citizen, President Donald Trump was asked on many different occasions by reporters to comment on the journalist's death. At first, the president said he had no idea what happened to Mr. Khashoggi and later said he believed it was a rogue operation carried out by certain persons. Latter, the president would change his mind and back the story put out by the Saudi government that it had nothing to do with his death. Like the U.S.-Saudi relationship back in the 1970s and beyond, the United States still looked at the Saudi regime as an ally in the Middle East and as a buffer in its efforts to stop Iran from fomenting more terrorism in the region. It didn't matter that the Saudis had a horrible human rights record, treated women like second class citizens, and ruled the nation with an iron fist. As long as we needed Saudi Arabia for its oil, then its abuses could go unnoticed.

The Trump administration had a good relationship with the current Saudi leader, Prince Mohammed bin Salman and as with the previous rulers whom the United Stated dealt with at the time of the Soviet-Afghan war and the rise of bin Laden, it was business as usual. As the Khashoggi mater broke into an international scandal, with writers and others pointing the finger for the crime at the door of Prince bin Salman, the White House doubled down on saying that they backed bin Salman in its response to the death of Khashoggi. Trump said that we needed the Saudis for investment purposes, including arms sales, and it was too bad if one permanent U.S. resident was killed. Business corrupted all else. Over time, the various U.S. intelligence agencies would conclude that the Saudi regime was responsible for Mr. Khashoggi's death and pinned the deed squarely on Prince bin Salman.

As the story of his death unfolded, the Saudi regime went into overdrove to make up a cover story as to what happened. However, since the crime took place on Turkish soil, the government in Ankara began to look closer at what happened.

The Saudi story changed like the wind and on November 11, 2018, the Saudi deputy public prosecutor Shalaan Shalaan said that the murder was ordered by the head of a "negotiations team" sent to Istanbul by the Saudi deputy intelligence chief to bring Khashoggi back to the kingdom "by means of persuasion or, if that failed, by force."

Investigators concluded that Khashoggi was restrained by his interrogators, and after a struggle ensued, he was injected with a drug, which resulted in an overdose that led to his death. His body was then dismembered inside the consulate. After his body was cut into pieces, it was handed over to a "collaborator" who disposed of the remains. Prosecutor Shalaan further said that five people had confessed to the crime and said, "the crown prince did not have any knowledge about it."

With the world's press coming down hard on the backs of the Saudis, they made a cursory investigation of Mr. Khashoggi's murder. On October 25, Saudi officials said that 18 people had been arrested and five senior government officials were fired. Among the people brought to justice were the deputy intelligence chief Ahmad Asiri and Saud al-Qahtani, who was a well-placed aid to Prince Mohammed bin Salman.

On January 3, 2019, 11 people were put on trial in a courtroom in Riyadh for the killing, and the death penalty was asked for those involved (the names of those accused were never made public).

The United Nations also got involved in the death of Mr. Khashoggi and after its investigation was concluded, it said that he was "the victim of a deliberate, premeditated execution, an extrajudicial killing for which the state of Saudi Arabia is responsible." And who was running that state of Saudi Arabia? None other than Prince Mohammed bin Salman. The woman who lead the U.N team said that there "was credible evidence" that Saudi Crown Prince Mohammed bin Salman and other high-level officials were individually liable."

Jamal Khashoggi was a 59-year-old journalist who worked for the *Washington Post* and had covered the Middle East, the invasion of Afghanistan and bin Laden. He was also close to the Saudi government and was well known throughout the kingdom by its highest officials. After a while he had a falling out with the government and moved to the United States where he continued to write anti-government articles. In his articles, he wrote that he felt threatened by the regime and feared for his life.

But what were the exact circumstances of the events surrounding his death? The reason for his visit to the consulate on 9-28 was to get a Saudi document saying that he was divorced, and that he wanted to marry his Turkish fiancée, Hatice Cengiz (she waited outside the consulate while he was inside). The last time that anyone saw Mr. Khashoggi was an on CCTV camera at 13:14 local time. The poor woman waited up to ten hours for Jamal to come out and returned the next day. A new story was concocted by the Saudi government that said Mr. Khashoggi left the consulate a few minutes or a few hours later. The official story then changed again when it was announced that he had died during a "fight" after resisting attempts to force him to return home.

But what happened next was the most horrible part of the story. The killing team cut his body up into pieces inside the consulate and put it in plastic bags which they had taken in with them. The fact that they had with them plastic bags shows that Saudi officials inside the consulate were going to kill him from the start, no matter anything said to contrary.

It seems that certain conversations inside the consulate were recorded and they tell a vivid tale of deception and murder. Khashoggi was told at one point, "We will have to take you back. There is an order from Interpol. Interpol requested you be sent back. We are coming to get you." Khashoggi replied, "There isn't a case against me. I notified some people outside: they are waiting for me, a driver is waiting for me." It was then that the murder took place. Most likely, Mr. Khashoggi was drugged and suffocated as events unfolded.

Since the tragedy took place on Turkish soil, the government in Ankara took a more than cursory interest in the matter. The leader of Turkey, President Erdogan said that he knew who was responsible for the killing and that it, "came from the highest levels of the Saud government," but he wasn't ready to blame King Salman for the event.

As mentioned before, the United Nations took an active role in following up on the killing of Jamal Khashoggi and they appointed a woman named Agnes Callamard to investigate the case. The U.N. was supposed to be impartial when it came to investigating such high-profile international cases and they undertook this one with eyes wide open. The U.N. report concluded that Khashoggi's death, "constituted an extralegal killing for which the state of the Kingdom of Saudi Arabia is responsible." She also said in her findings, that there was "credible evidence to warrant an investigation into Prince Mohammed and other high-level Saudi officials. She recommended that sanctions be put on certain people in retaliation for the Khashoggi killing. Ms. Callamard said that the probes into the murder by both Saudi Arabia and Turkey "failed to meet international standards."

She also had harsh words for how the judicial process surrounding the murder played out in the kingdom. "The trial is held behind closed doors, the identity of those charged has not been released nor is the identity of those facing the death penalty. At the time of writing, at least one of those identified as responsible for the planning and organizing of the execution of Mr. Khashoggi has not been charged."

Of course, the Saudi government hotly denied the U.N. findings and sent out its Minister for Foreign Affairs, Adel-al-Jubeir to refute the charges. He said that "there was nothing new and it contained clear contradictions and baseless allegations which challenge its credibility."

In the U.N. probe, Agnes Callamard referred to sound recordings that she obtained from various sources in the killing of Mr. Khashoggi. It seems that the Turkish government had shared the recordings with such nations as Saudi Arabia, the U.S., the UK, Germany, and France. Turkey was not one of the nations to divulge the recordings to her. "But in one recording, her report says, two Saudi officials are apparently heard discussing how to cut up and transport Khashoggi's body just minutes before the journalist entered the consulate."

Turkish president Recep Erdogan wrote a column in the *Washington Post* in which he said that it had been established that Khashoggi "was killed in cold blood by a death squad, and that it was premeditated." His article went on to say, "Yet there are other, no less significant questions whose answers will contribute to our understanding of this deplorable act. Where is Khashoggi's body? Who is the local collaborator to whom Saudi officials claimed to have handed over Khashoggi's body?"

Turkish officials were frustrated and embarrassed that such a horrible act could have taken place on their soil. They were in a hard place politically, as Turkey was a member of the NATO alliance yet is a Muslim country whose rule by President Erdogen was tight-fisted. Turkey has to straddle two worlds, one being an ally of the United States (to a certain extent) and another wishing for better relations with Russia. President Trump praised President Edrogan on many occasions on his dictatorial rule and got heated criticism from many in the world community for those words.

Turkish officials said that 15 Saudi agents arrived in Istanbul in the days and weeks before the death of Jamal Khashoggi. They had to stay somewhere, had to have local help and given logistical aid before the attack. Who aided them is still a question to be answered and no further news on that subject is out in the open. The Turks said that these agents disabled the cameras and surveillance footage from the consulate before Khashoggi's arrival. How they did this without being seen is another question to be answered.

The Turkish prosecutor named Irfan Fidan, said that Mr. Khashoggi was suffocated right as he entered the consulate, and that his body was taken apart and destroyed. What we have here seems to be a premeditated murder by the 15 Saudi nationals in the killing of Mr. Khashoggi. But the million dollar question remains: who ordered the killing to take place in the first place? Was it King Salman, a friend of the United States, or was it someone else in the Saudi government or intelligence service? It should be noted that the first foreign trip that President Trump made was to Saudi Arabia instead of countries like Mexico or Canada, like other presidents have made in the past. Was the president's conclusion that Saudi Arabia had no part in the killing of Jamal Khashoggi a part of a quid pro quo from the Saudi Prince for continued U.S. military aid?[43]

As the scandal surrounding the murder of Mr. Khashoggi went on, the Saudi government decided to make one highly-placed official responsible for his death. That person was Major General Ahmed al-Assari who was a longstanding confidant of the crown prince. One reason for the regiMEs trying to blame Mr. Al-Assari would be to deflect any more criticism from the crown prince onto someone else's shoulders.

General Assari was once the government's spokesman for the Saudi led military attack in Yemen, which took thousands of lives. The scenario regarding General Assari was that he was given oral instructions from Crown Prince Mohammed to capture Mr. Khashoggi for an interrogation back in Saudi Arabia. The story goes that the general somehow misunderstood his orders and, under circumstances that are still to be determined, things went horribly wrong and Mr. Khashoggi was killed in the process.

The Turkish government said that four of the suspects in the killing worked in some capacity for the security detail of Prince Mohammed, and that one of them, a man named Maher Abdulaziz Mutreb, was spotted and/or photographed near the prince during the prince's foreign travels. A Turkish newspaper published a photo of Mr. Mutreb entering the Saudi consulate in Istanbul hours after Mr. Khashoggi went into the building. In other photos taken during this time, it shows him outside the Saudi consulate general's home, leaving a Turkish hotel carrying a large suitcase, as well as leaving Turkey from the airport in Ankara, all in the same day. No one is really certain if General Assari was a fallguy in the operation or whether he was taking orders from someone else in the government pecking order, possibly the crown prince himself.[44]

---

43 No author: Jamal Khashoggi: All you need to know about Saudi journalist's death, June 19, 2019.

44 Kirkpatrick, David and Ben Hubbard, "Saudis Weigh Blaming Ally Of the Prince," *New York Times*, October 18, 2019.

The various U.S. intelligence agencies all made their own investigations into the Khashoggi murder but they all came up with different conclusions. For example, the CIA said that it was sure that Prince Mohammed bin Salman was culpable for Mr. Khashoggi's death. The NSA, the National Security Agency, however stopped short of that conclusion and "collected communications intercepts of Saudi officials discussing a plan to lure Mr. Khashoggi back to Saudi Arabia from his home in Virginia, and then detain him. But the intercepts do not reveal whether Prince Mohammed directly ordered the killing of Mr. Khashoggi."

There is an interesting comparisson to be made between the 15 Saudi agents and the men who came to America prior to 9-11. The 15 Saudis who took part in Khashoggi's murder came to Turkey in various groups, had someone in the city who took responsibility for them prior to the killing, gave them maps of the city, and took care of their daily needs. This called for a close-knit operation, one that was thought out months or weeks in advance. An undercover network had to be in place and these co-conspirators fit the bill (the identities of these men are still not known).

The circumstances surrounding the arrival in the United States of the 9-11 hijackers has similar parallels to the 15 men involved in the Jamal Khashoggi murder. For example, Nawaf al-Hazmi, and Khalid al-Midhar arrived in the United States by commercial carrier and were not placed on any watchlist until the year 2000. The CIA knew of their arrival in the country since 1990 but because they committed no crime, they were not arrested. Both men attended the al Qaeda summit meeting in Malaysia in January 2000 where the plans for 9-11 were devised. Many of the world's intelligence services knew about this meeting and were monitoring its progress. More about the Malaysia summit in a further chapter. The Saudi frontman, Omar al-Bayoumi arrived in the U.S. and lived in San Diego starting in April 1999. From there he met with other like-minded Saudis, including two of the 9-11 hijackers. Also in that early group to enter the U.S. were the following: Nawaf al-Hazmi, Salem al-Hazmi and Khalid al-Midhar all of originally received their U.S. visas from the American consulate in Jeddah, Saudi Arabia. The reason they received their visas without any trouble was that they were then not under a watchlist which prevented them from entering the United States. If they were on the so-called watchlist at the time, the men would probably not have been able to enter the country.

While the circumstances surrounding the Saudis in the Khashoggi case and the hijackers who came to the United States prior to 9-11 are not exactly alike, they do present a pattern where co-conspirators aided and abetted these people from the very start.

The Saudi-U.S. connection has grown stronger over the years, despite the ever-changing international political situation due to the U.S.'s neverending need for Saudi oil to run our economy. In the aftermath of the 9-11 attacks, that relationship took a turn for the worse, but with the advent of the Trump administration, that relationship is back to normal. "Normal" meaning it is more important to have the Kingdom of Saudi Arabia as an ally in the Middle East as a foil against Iran, than to stand up for human rights in that country, be it in the way they treat their women citizens, or for backing Prince Mohammed bin Salman in the death of an American resident who dared to challenge the Saudi regime, in more ways than one.

Jamal Khashoggi in 2018.

Chapter 5:

Pakistan's ISI

Over its long history, the CIA has had to make alliances of convenience with disreputable people and organizations in order to further its own ends. During the decades of the 1970s and 1980s, the CIA worked closely with Pakistan's main intelligence agency, a group not noted for its democratic tendencies, a group that was linked to the heroin trade in Central Asia, called the Inter-Service Intelligence, or ISI. The ISI, the CIA, and Saudi intelligence worked in conjunction against the Soviet Union. Information following the 9-11 attacks against the United States revealed a possible sinister connection between the head of the ISI and one of the prime movers in the assaults against America.

As we have discussed previously, the foundation of the ISI goes back to 1948 when it was created by a British army officer, Major General R. Cawhome, who was the deputy chief of staff in the Pakistani army. After the partition of India and Pakistan into two different nations, the President of Pakistan, Ayub Kahan, expanded the role of the ISI to cover internal espionage, and the monitoring of Kahn's internal enemies. The duties of the ISI subsequently expanded into both foreign and internal collection activities, the coordination of intelligence gathering among the various military departments, and the use of its agents to keep the prevailing military government of the time in power. Critics of the ISI have called it "a state within a state," or the invisible government. Since its inception, the ISI has been linked to drug smuggling and the assassination of political opponents of the ruling regime; it was instrumental in the founding of the Taliban in Afghanistan.

Using the decades-long engagements between India and Pakistan over the sovereignty of Kashmir (which is currently recognized as being part of India), the ISI provided insurgents battling the Indian army with training and equipment. It has been estimated by Indian government officials that by 1995, the ISI had trained more than 5,000 men to battle its forces in Kashmir.

Over the years, the ISI took as much power and influence as the various prime ministers would allow. As has been noted, the most influential director, as far as this narrative is concerned, was Lt. General Hamad Gul who worked closely with Western intelligence agencies in ousting the Russians from Afghanistan. During the height of the Soviet-Afghan war, Gul worked not only with the CIA but also the Saudi Arabian intelligence, the GID. Gul answered to Pakistan's President, Mohammed Zia-al Haq, who took control of Pakistan's government in July 1977 when he deposed the regime of Zulfikar Ali-Butto, the father of a latter day Prime Minister, Benazir Butto. President Zia ordered the execution of the elder Bhutto, against the wishes of the United States and other Western nations.

In time, Zia canceled national elections, and was instrumental in the development of the radical political movement called Jamaaet-e-Islamia, which shunned modern dress and politics, and called for an absolute Islamic government in Pakistan.

Despite his pro-Islamic penchant, the new Reagan administration saw President Zia as an ally in Central Asia after the 1979 Russian invasion of Afghanistan. Without Zia's permission, the United States would not be able to funnel military aid to the Afghan rebels via the CIA. In the end, the Reagan administration made a deal with the devil whereby Zia was fundamentally in charge of all covert U.S./CIA military aid to the rebels. Zia forbade the CIA to meet on a regular basis with its Afghan rebel allies, but the agency did so anyway.

The CIA agent who had the most contact with the ISI Chief, Akhtar Abdul Rahman, was Howard Hart. The ISI chief told Hart in no uncertain terms that no CIA officer would be allowed to enter Afghanistan to set up shop or to meet with any potential assets. All weapons shipments would pass through ISI hands, the CIA would be forbidden to directly train the Mujahideen, and all training would he held in Pakistani camps.

While the Reagan administration knew all about the illegal

activities of the ISI, they turned a blind eye toward these transgressions. CIA Director William Casey made a number of clandestine trips to Pakistan where he assessed the military situation, and met with Athkar and planned strategy. Casey said " Akhtar is completely involved in this war and certainly knows better than anyone else about his requirements. We have to support him."

As the war progressed, the CIA under Casey let the ISI arm and train its Afghan clients, who were known to have engaged in such activities as drug smuggling, murder and torture, and who were known to have made any number of anti-American, anti-Western statements.

ISI agents took the war to the streets of Kabul in 1983, killing nine Soviets by detonating a briefcase bomb near Kabul University. Russian soldiers felt the wrath of the CIA/ISI connection, and many were killed by car bombs and other means of assassination.

A rift soon opened up between the CIA and the ISI over the agency's relationship with Ahmed Shah Massoud, whose name has been mentioned in previous chapters in this book. The rift was still in the open when he was tragically assassinated a few days before the 9-11 attacks, and his death turned out to be a prelude to the attacks on Washington and New York.

By 1992, the Afghan rebels had managed to do the impossible—outlast the mighty Soviet army and force them to leave Afghanistan in full retreat. For the United States, the main objective had been accomplished, and by 1992 the CIA had largely left shop in Pakistan.

But changes also took place in Pakistan, when in October 1999, General Pervez Musharraf took power in a coup. The Clinton and Bush administrations decided to overlook Musharrraf's power seizure and threw in their lots with him. From 1999 through September 11, 2001, Musharraf claimed to be reining in the power of the ISI, but they still had considerable influence in his government.

After 9-11, President Bush gave Musharraf an ultimatum: work with the United States in the war against bin Laden or face the consequences. Musharraf decided to cooperate with Washington and opened up his borders to the largest CIA base since the beginning of the Afghan war.

Despite Musharraf's pledge to aid the United States, the fundamental fact was that for years, the ISI had been openly siding with the Taliban in Afghanistan providing intelligence and military equipment during the Afghan-Soviet war. Once the Taliban was safely in power in Afghanistan, elements of the ISI did all they could to beef up the radical, Islamic government, despite the pressure put on them by Musharraf to end their ties.

In 1999, when the Clinton administration was gearing up for a snatch operation in Afghanistan to capture bin Laden, the Pakistani government ordered the ISI to aid the CIA in the planning of the operation, but in reality, the ISI did nothing significant to push the raid along.

The ISI had a checkered past to say the least, and that included murder when necessary. It may have been involved in the abduction and murder of *Wall Street Journal* reporter Daniel Pearl. Pearl and his French-born wife, Marianne, arrived in the Pakistani city of Karachi to do a story on Islamic militants and their relationship with the ISI. Pearl also decided to do a story on Richard Reid, the shoe bomber who was caught when he tried to blow up a jet using an explosive device hidden in his shoe. Pearl's stories were not welcomed by the government in Pakistan and he was watched very closely while he was in the country. It is not out of the question to say that the reporting he was doing, especially on the wrongdoings of the ISI, probably led to his death. For example, on December 24, 2001, he wrote about a connection between the ISI and a Pakistani organization called Umnah Taneer-el Nau, that was working on giving bin Laden nuclear secrets before 9-11.

Daniel Pearl's contact in Karachi was an English speaking man who said his name was Chaudhry Basheer. Basheer was actually Omar Saeed Sheikh, a British-born citizen with ties to the ISI. Days before the Pearl kidnapping, Sheik had met Pearl in Karachi, befriended him, and said that he could deliver the reporter to his contacts who would be able to help him with his expose. That Sheik did deliver Pearl to his contacts is without question. What happened next was simple murder. Pearl was kidnapped by unnamed people, who made a video of his last moments before killing him in a brutal execution. In the investigation that followed the death of Daniel Pearl, detectives unraveled the role played by Sheik, and his ties to the ISI.

Shiekh grew up in London, and attended the London School of Economics. He stayed one year before dropping out. He then traveled to Bosnia in conjunction with an Islamic charity. He then joined other radical Islamic fighters in Pakistan where he took all sorts of military training. He was arrested for plotting the kidnapping of three Westerners, and spent five years in jail. The ISI is reported to have supplied him a lawyer, something that would not have been done if he were not someone high up in the food chain. After serving time in jail, he was released on New Year's Eve, 1999, in return for the release of 154 passengers of a hijacked Indian Airlines plane. After his release from jail, Sheik was in the hands of the ISI, traveling to various camps in Afghanistan, and possibly carrying out operations in India.

Sheikh was complicit in the Pearl kidnapping case and soon Pakistani authorities, under intense pressure from Washington, pulled out all the stops in the effort to find him. He was traced to Karachi where he was finally taken into custody, not by the police, but by members of the ISI. One week after his arrest, he was finally handed over to the police. Sheik admitted that he was a participant in the Pearl abduction, and then confirmed that the reporter was already dead.

As the hunt for Saeed Sheikh was going on half a world away, Sheikh was indicted by a grand jury in the United States which was revealed to the public in February 2002. One of the many U.S. officials who took a backchannel part in trying to pressure Pakistan into releasing Sheikh was the U.S. Ambassador to Pakistan, Wendy Chamberlain. According to the *Los Angeles Times,* Sheikh was traveling freely in Pakistan during his time on the lam without being taken into custody by Pakistani authorities.

Further investigation into the background of Sheikh showed that he was in constant contact with General Mohammed Aziz Kahn, who once served as the deputy director of the ISI, whose responsibility was training for covert operations in Afghanistan and India. His involvement in the death of Danny Pearl puts to rest the fallacy that there was no connection between the reporter's death and the ISI.

A more troubling circumstance that has yet to be fully

documented is a report linking ISI chief Lt. General Mahmud Ahmed to the ringleader of the 9-11 attacks, Mohamed Atta. The backstory to this event is the kidnapping of a wealthy Indian shoe manufacturer who was taken in Calcutta, India. Ransom money from the kidnapping was paid for by an Indian gangster named Aftab Ansari. Ansari lived at the time in Dubai, the UAE and also had ties to the ISI, as well as to Saeed Sheikh. The total amount of the ransom was $830,000 and in a twist that makes one just look up and wonder, Saeed sent about $100,000 to none other than Mohamed Atta, who was one of the hijackers on 9-11 and who had also spent a number of weeks in Florida in plain sight. This begs a few questions. Why did Saeed Sheikh give Mohamed Atta the money, who was the source of the money, and what was their covert relationship? None of these questions have been satisfactually answered and the situation needs more investigation. In a later development to the story, the *Times of India* wrote that Lt. General Mahmud Ahmed, the director of the ISI, instructed Saeed to transfer the $100,000 into Atta's account. This money was supposed to have been passed through a number of cutouts, including a charity called Al Rashid Trust, also through the Taliban, as well as some Pakistani entities.

The money was supposed to have been transferred to Atta's personal bank account in Florida, and the Al Rashid Trust was frozen by the U.S. government after 9-11.[45]

One week before the 9-11 attacks, Lt. General Mahmud Ahmed, the ISI Director, paid an official visit to Washington where he met with high-ranking Bush administration officials in the State Department and with Deputy Secretary of State Richard Armitage. He also met with individuals from both the Pentagon and the CIA, and members of the U.S. Senate (including then Senator Joe Biden). The reason for his visit to Washington was given as "routine consultations between the Pakistani armed forces and the United States."

Lt. General Ahmed remained in Washington on 9-11 due to the grounding of all commercial aircraft after the attacks. No one knows what business was conducted between Ahmed and American authorities, but right after the blasts in Washington and

45 History Commons: Early August 2001-Saeed Sheikh Receives Ransom Money; Sends $100,000 to Hijacker Atta.

New York, the government of Pakistan pledged to cooperate fully in the capture of bin Laden. In a further curious development, Lt. General Ahmed was in Washington when Ahmed Shah Massoud, the leader of the Northern Alliance mentioned above, was killed in his home by two assassins, who were possibly linked to both bin Laden and the ISI.

In the wake of 9-11, the Bush administration decided it had to work closely with Pakistan and the ISI to rout out the terrorists in Afghanistan, despite the well-known fact that the ISI (with the CIA) helped to create the Taliban in the first place, and did all they could during the Afghan war to help their ally with military supplies and intelligence. In the end, the Pentagon and the State Department decided to pay the devil they knew to aid their own ends.

The first signs of the new cooperation between Washington and Karachi came on September 13, 2001, when President Perez Musharraf sent Lt. General Ahmed to meet with the Taliban government in Afghanistan to seek the extradition of bin Laden to the United States. Lt. General Ahmed met in the Afghan city of Kandahar with the Taliban leader Mohammad Omar. The ISI chief passed on his instructions but his mission was a failure. With the task a nonstarter, the United States could now pursue its planned attack on Afghanistan in retaliation for 9-11.

In an about face that caught many observers by surprise, President Musharraf fired Ahmed as ISI chief just as the United States began its counteroffensive in Afghanistan. But the real reason for the dismissal of General Ahmed might not be as cut-and-dried as it may seem.

This revolves around the above-mentioned report of money being given to Mohamed Atta while he was in the United States preparing for 9-11. Citing Indian intelligence reports that were transmitted to the United States, the article said, "The evidence we [the government of India] have supplied to the U.S. is of a much wider range and depth than just one piece of paper linking a rogue general to some misplaced act of terrorism."

It is worth noting a part of the *Times of India* piece in order to fully convey the possible ramifications of the charges in the wake of 9-11.

> While the Pakistani Inter Services Public Relations claimed that former ISI director-general Lt. General Mahmoud Ahmed sough retirement after being suspended on Monday 8 October, the day the U.S. started bombing Afghanistan, the truth is more shocking. Top sources reported here on Tuesday (October 9), that the general lost his job because of the "evidence" India produced to show his links to one of the suicide bombers that wrecked the World Trade Center. The U.S. authorities sought his removal after confirming the fact that $100,000 was wired to WTC hijacker Mohammed Atta by Ahmad Umar Sheikh at the instistence of General Mahmoud. Senior government officials have confirmed that India contributed significantly to establishing the link between the money transfer and the role played by the dismissed ISI chief. While they did not provide details, they said that Indian inputs, including Sheikh's mobile phone number, helped the FBI in tracing and establishing the link.

The reference to Ahmad Umar Sheikh (really Omar Saeed Sheikh) is to the same person who was held on charges of abducting Danny Pearl.

In a subsequent article by Manoj Joshi published in the *Times of India* on August 1, 2003 under the title "9-11 funds came from Pakistan says FBI," we learn that John Pistole, the deputy assistant director of the FBI's counterterrorism division, had "traced the origins of the funding of 9-11 back to financial accounts in Pakistan." The original *Times of India* article linking General Ahmed to Mohamed Atta said that $100k was sent by Omar Saeed Sheikh to Atta in the weeks before 9-11. The FBI has estimated that the cost of the 9-11 attacks was about $175,000 to $250,000, and that the money came from unknown accounts and individuals in both Germany and the United Arab Emirates.

However, the FBI told the 9-11 Commission that when John Pistole used the word "accounts" he did not mean actual accounts with a bank, merely that 9-11 hijacker Khalid Sheik Mohammed who was based in Pakistan, handled the money.

If any segment of the *Times of India* story is correct, the smoking gun linking the head of the Pakistani ISI and the leader of the 9-11 attacks, Mohamed Atta, may have huge consequences on how we look at the events of that tragic day.

Osama bin Laden himself had ties to a number of Middle Eastern intelligence services beginning in the late 1980s, including the Pakistani ISI as well as the Saudi GIP. Bin Laden's construction company helped build the Khost tunnel complex in Afghanistan which was bombed when the Americans attacked after 9-11. There were reports that the ISI helped bin Laden in building the Khost tunnels for their mutual benefit.

Dating back to the early 1990s, the Pakistani government had an interest in the growing Taliban movement led by Mullah Omar, and watched as it morphed into a large-scale military/political movement. Author Steve Coll wrote about the connection saying, "There was a meeting at ISI headquarters with some of the early leaders of the Taliban—not Mullah Omar, but some of his aides—and the ISI chef in the late autumn of 1994." The ISI then began to find willing recruits from religious schools in Pakistan and they soon joined the Taliban. Coll would also write that the Taliban would, in time, become an "asset" of the ISI.

Other authorities in the United States and elsewhere also made the connection between the ISI and the Taliban. For example, in 1996, CNN wrote, "The Taliban are widely alleged to be the creation of Pakistan's military intelligence [the ISI], which, according to experts, explains the Taliban's swift military success."

Counterterrorism czar Richard Clarke said that not only did the ISI create the Taliban, but they also facilitated connections between the Taliban and al Qaeda to help the Taliban achieve victory.

The *Wall Street Journal* said in November 2001, "Despite their clean chins and pressed uniforms, the ISI men are as deeply fundamentalist as any bearded fanatic; the ISI created the Taliban as their own instrument and still support it."

President Benazir Bhutto of Pakistan had her own, strong feelings regarding the Taliban. "I became slowly, slowly sucked into it. Once I gave the go-ahead that they should get money, I don't know how much money they were ultimately given, I know it was a lot. It was just carte blanche."

By the early 1990s (1994 to be exact), the CIA also began to aid the Taliban, not knowing then what it would soon become by the end of the decade. British author Simon Reeves was told by a source in Pakistani intelligence that the CIA provided Pakistan satellite information giving the secret locations of scores of Soviet trucks that contained vast amounts of arms and ammunition. The trucks were hidden in caves at the end of the Afghan war. Pakistan then gave these weapons to the Taliban which they used to take over Afghanistan.[46]

There were many covert ties between the CIA and the ISI during the war in Afghanistan, most of them related to military activities. But there was one cockamamie adventure that has to be seen to be believed. The gist of the story was to turn Soviet soldiers fighting in Afghanistan into drug addicts. The genesis of the story was during the early days of the Reagan administration in which the famous French intelligence officer, Alexandre de Marenches, arrived in Washington to meet with the president. The Frenchman devised a crazy plot in which the U.S., the French, and the Pakistani ISI intelligence services would mount an operation against Soviet troops called Operation Mosquito.

Part of the plan called for the printing of false stories in Russian newspapers designed to demoralize Russian troops then fighting in Afghanistan. "He also suggested that the U.S. take drugs that were seized by the American DEA that would normally have been destroyed and secretly give them to Soviet soldiers. As the story goes, it was decided not to go ahead with it because of the many press leaks that followed its inception. However, a large amount of heroin and other drugs were indeed supplied to the Soviets in Afghanistan which was a contribution to their eventual withdrawal from that nation. We don't know for sure what role the CIA played in the introduction of opium and other drugs to the Soviet troops or the names of these people, as such information would be a closely guarded secret."[47]

---

46 History Commons: October 1994-CIA and ISI Allegedly give help and secret Cache of Weapons to Taliban.

47 History Commons: February 1981 and After: U.S. Allegedly helps turn Soviet Soldiers Fighting in Afghanistan into Drug addicts.

Chapter 6

The FBI's Long Road to 9-11

Since the days of J. Edgar Hoover, the prime focus of the FBI was to investigate crimes after they had been committed, not preventing them before they took place. As the lead investigative agency after the attacks on 9-11, the FBI was put into crisis mode trying to identify the men who carried out the worst terrorist attack on American soil. Within days of the attacks, the bureau was able to identify the nineteen hijackers who crashed into the WTC and the Pentagon, and their pictures were printed in all the newspapers around the globe. The FBI was also in limbo on the day of 9-11. The new FBI Director Robert Mueller had only taken over his post the week before, and it is not known just how thoroughly he was informed of the fact that a number of Saudi citizens were in the United Sates and that some of them had taken flying lessons at different airports throughout the country. Director Mueller, like the rest of the intelligence community, had to scramble in order to connect the dots of what just happened, and it turned out to be a painstaking job to say the least.

As one looks back at the reams of circumstantial evidence that the FBI mishandled or failed to recognize in the years leading up to 9-11, it is obvious that if they had made a major effort to "connect the dots" beginning in 1989, circumstances might have been dramatically different.

As international terrorism began to affect American citizens around the world, the FBI's New York office was designated the originator for all Islamic terror cases. In order to facilitate better cooperation between local and federal law enforcement authorities, the FBI and the NYPF began an intelligence sharing arrangement called the Joint Terrorism Task Force or JTTF. Its goal was to share pertinent information between the two agencies that would better enable them to do their job more effectively. More often than not, cooperation lasted until the front door, with bitter rivalries and deep distrust between the two groups the norm, rather than the exception. This lack of cooperation set the pattern in the decade of the 1990s that resulted in a number of missed opportunities to blunt terrorist attacks in New York.

The FBI's Special Operations Group (SOG) had the job of watching a number of Middle Eastern men, called MEs, who attended the Alkifah Center at the Al Farooq mosque in Brooklyn. The mosque was a hotbed of anti-American, pro-Islamic activity and was the place where the radical blind Sheik Omar Abdul Rahman held forth. Not known to the FBI in 1989 was that Shiek Rahman was being bankrolled by a little known Saudi millionaire named Osama bin Laden.

In July 1989, the SOG team watched as a number of MEs left Brooklyn in a car and traveled along the Long Island Expressway to a shooting range in Calverton, Long Island. Parking near the shooting range, the bureau agents saw the men practice with AK-47 rifles at stationary targets. They followed the men on four different occasions during July and took numerous pictures. While it was no crime to fire an AK-47 at a public rifle range, it did pique the bureau's interest. Unfortunately, no law had been broken and the SOG team had no probable cause to arrest them. If they had been a little more diligent in their active investigation of the MEs at Calverton, they would have been shocked at what would have transpire.

The Calverton shooters had direct links to the blind Sheik and were all identified as being cell members in the 1993 WTC bombing, the assassination of the radical Rabbi Meyer Kahane, and the so-called "Day of Terror " plots to destroy tunnels and landmarks in New York City.

The men whom the SOG team followed were:

•Mahmud Abouhalima, an Egyptian who was a known associate of the WTC planner, Ramzi Yousef, and a New York cabby.

•El Sayyid Nosair, another Egyptian who worked in the Manhattan Civil Courts building as a maintenance man. Nosair would later kill Rabbi Meyer Kahane.

•Mohammed Salameh, born in Jordan, who was a member of Ramzi Yousef's team that struck the WTC in February 1993.

•Nidal Ayyad, a Kuwaiti who attended Rutgers University in New Jersey. He would buy the chemicals that were used by Yousef in the 1993 WTC attack.

•Clement Rodney Hampton-El, an American citizen, Black Muslim, who was later to be convicted in the plots to blow up NYC landmarks.

•Ali Mohammed, a man with a military and terrorist background whose presence among the other MEs should have made the FBI look a lot deeper. Ali Mohammed was an Egyptian army officer and a member of the Egyptian Islamic Jihad group. He was linked to the assassination of President Anwar Sadat of Egypt but was not prosecuted because he was in the United States the time of the 1981 assassination, attending the Army's Special Warfare Operations School at Fort Bragg, North Carolina. In the aftermath of the WTC bombing in 1993, police found a large amount of classified material in the New Jersey home of one of Yousef's accomplices. The top secret material belonged to Ali Mohammed.

In time, Mohammed would become a "contact" agent for the CIA. As the feds began an investigation of him they found out that he was linked to the Middle Eastern terror organization called Hezbollah, and was placed on a State Department watchlist of people who were to be denied entry into the United States. Like the 9-11 hijackers, Ali Mohammed would evade U.S. airport screeners and slip back into the country. Despite his rather sordid background, he was allowed into the U.S. Army and was given a Secret security clearance. Also not known to the FBI (or the CIA) was the fact that he doubled as a bodyguard to Osama bin Laden in Afghanistan. He also took part in a reconnaissance mission to lay the groundwork for the 1998 East African Embassy bombings which were linked to bin Laden.

If the FBI had decided to put forth a full court press and bring in for questioning the men who made up the Calverton shooting cell, who knows how far they would have gone in possibly cracking the 1993WTC bombing before it took place?

In a sidebar to the Calverton cell, the FBI was keeping a close watch on two MEs who were associated with Sheik Rahman, Mahmud Abouhalima and Siddig Ali from Sudan.

In 1993, Siddig Ali and the brother of Abouhalima traveled to Harrisburg, PA where they learned the art of assassination techniques. It was reported that on one of these occasions, the men tested bombmaking materials that were supplied to them by Ramzi Yousef. The two men were watched by the FBI but it was decided not to expend any more manpower and this tentative lead was dropped.

Another potential lead that was not investigated by the FBI and the JTTF revolved around information provided by a man named Garret Wilson, a one-time Army Ranger and a military police officer at a nearby Philadelphia naval facility. In the early 1990s, Garrett Wilson ran a security business to gain extra income and he came in contact with a rather strange and violent clientele. In the 1980s, he met a number of Black Muslims who lived in New York, among them Edwin Ransom and Richard Smith, both associated with the At-Taqwa Mosque in Brooklyn. Wilson sold them arms and taught them defensive techniques when a number of drug dealers tried to destroy their neighborhood.

During the early part of the 1990s however, Wilson was getting some rather interesting requests from these same people. They wanted him` to provide them with military-style rappelling equipment used by the army and special police units. This query piqued his interest and he contacted a fiend in the Naval Investigative Service, John McGuire. The NIS officer sent messages to his colleagues in the intelligence community asking if they had heard of any such requests from their snitches. Months went by before the query came across the desk of John Ligouri at JTTF headquarters.

Nothing panned out until Wilson got an unexpected phone call on October 3, 1992. The call was from Abdul Wali Zindani, who ran the Al Kifah Refugee Center. The Al Kifah Center was at that time the location for the Services Office network, also called

MAK. Unknown to the feds was the fact that Al Kifah was the central conduit for the millions of dollars that were being used to finance the Afghan rebels who were fighting the Soviets since their invasion of Afghanistan in 1979. The primary financier of the MAK at the time was Osama bin Laden. In time, MAK would morph into al Qaeda or "the base."

Another front man behind the MAK was the blind Sheik, Omar Abdul Rahman. After the unexplained death in November 1989 of Abdullah Azzam, who once ran the MAK offices, Shiek Rahman effectively took over the MAK organization and more importantly, the millions of dollars that were flowing in. It is believed that bin Laden was behind the killing of Azzam and his sons.

It is important in this story to recognize just how important these "refugee" centers were in bringing the jihad to America. The original center was set up in Peshawar, Pakistan in the beginning of the 1980s. Led by Azzam, the centers were set up in countries such as France, Great Britain, Germany, and other Middle Eastern nations. MAK stood for Services Office for the Mujahideen. MAK's most influential office in the United States was the Al Farooq mosque in Brooklyn. Other offices were set up in cities like Atlanta and Boston, a total of 30 in all. Another vital link to the story of 9-11 is the center located in Tucson, Arizona where a number of Arab men were taking flying lessons.

Azzam was friendly with bin Laden whose large construction company was hard at work building roads and tunnel complexes for the Mujahideen fighters who were battling the Soviets in Afghanistan. In time, Azzam would bring bin Laden and Sheik Omar Rahman together in a deadly plot to bring the Islamic Jihad to America. Since the Brooklyn mosque was a religious center, the FBI was unable to study the underhanded maneuvering that was going on there.

Abdul Zindani asked Wilson if he could provide "commando-style" training and equipment for an elite unit of about ten men. Wilson talked with Zindani's chief of security to map out the details. The chief of security, one Yaya abu Ubaidah, said that his group was especially interested in learning the intricacies of hostage rescue work.

Wilson contacted his friends in the JTTF and promised to

keep in touch. They did not have to wait long. In November 1992, Wilson got a call from a member of Zindani's group, a man who called himself "Dr. Rashid." This man turned out to be none other than Clement Hampton-El, a member of the Calverton shooting club, and a follower of Sheik Rahman.

Right before Christmas, Wilson and Hampton-El met to discuss their mutual business in Jersey City, New Jersey. Hampton-El told Wilson that he needed his expertise in training eight to ten men in irregular warfare techniques. Hampton-El said that he would arrange for the purchase of a number of AK-47 assault rifles but that he also needed a number of remote-detonator caps, and untraceable weapons. The men would eventually be sent to Bosnia.

Wilson referred this news back to the JTTF and told his colleagues that in his estimation, "It sounds to me like they either want to kidnap or kill someone."

Due to lack of manpower in the NYPD and the JTTF, it was decided not to pursue Wilson's leads, no matter how promising they might have been.

The information provided by Wilson came at the same time when Ramzi Yousef and his cell were making their final preparations, building the bombs that went off on February 26, 1993 at the WTC. It is not too long of a shot to believe that the remote detonating caps requested by Hampton-El, were for that specific purpose.

We now turn to a major part of the pre-9-11 story that would prove to be a major black mark on the ability of the FBI to get inside the radicals surrounding the blind Sheik, and possibly stop the first WTC bombing in its tracks. It is a story steeped in petty jealousies, turf battles, and most of all, ego on the parts of certain high level FBI agents.

The narrative revolves around two individuals, Nancy Floyd, a Texas born FBI agent and her informer in the camp of Shiek Rahman, an ex-Egyptian army officer and Floyd's friend and confidant.

Nancy Floyd came from a military family. Her father served as a major in the Air Force. Nancy attended the University of Texas at Arlington where she got her B.S. in criminal justice in 1982. After graduation she applied for a job with the FBI and was accepted into the program. She passed the rigorous qualifying course at the FBI Academy at Quantico with flying colors. Her first assignment was in Savannah, GA before coming to work at the New York office. She got a choice assignment, working at 26 Federal Plaza in downtown New York, a short distance from the WTC. She worked in Branch A of the FBI's Foreign Counterntelligence Division. Her unit was tasked with the job of following the members of GRU-Soviet military intelligence who mostly worked undercover as members of the Soviet delegation to the United Nations.

Soon Nancy was learning how to keep tabs on possible Russian targets from Len Predtechenskis, a twenty-seven year veteran of the bureau. He would soon take on the job as the FBI's top counterintelligence agent in New York, and would befriend Nancy Floyd in her days of trial that lay ahead.

Predtechenskis assigned Nancy to restart an operation that had been in limbo for many years, the so-called Hotel Asset Program. It was her job to visit the hundreds of hotels in Manhattan, some luxurious, some not, speak to the various hotel managers, and discretely ask them to keep an eye out for any wavering Soviet diplomats who might run afoul of the law. It was during this seemingly routine assignment that Nancy Floyd would meet Emad Salem, an encounter that would profoundly change her life.

Nancy Floyd and Emad Salem first met in 1991 when she was carrying out her job at the Manhattan hotels. Salem came from Egypt, was a naturalized American citizen, and was eager to help his adoptive nation any way he could. He worked at an undisclosed hotel as a guard and she and the Egyptian soon hit it off. Over time, Salem did surveillance work for Floyd, turning in a number of illegal aliens, and building up his bona fides with her. Salem began telling Floyd about the different people he'd come across in the city, one of whom was the blind Sheik Omar Abdul Rahman and his anti-American exhortations at the Jersey City mosque he preached in. Floyd was intrigued with Salem and his wide connections and she persuaded her bosses at the bureau to bring Salem in an as "asset." He was paid five hundred dollars a week and went to work infiltrating the Sheik's cell.

If the FBI agents had been doing their job properly, they would have realized via the men associated with the Calverton shooting range incident, as well as the information provided to them via Garrett Wilson regarding the detonating caps required by Hampton-El, that all of these men were associated at one time or another with the blind Sheik. Emad Salem would join the Sheik's inner circle, and provide an abundance of real time intelligence on the illegal activities going on in Brooklyn and Jersey City.

Two other FBI agents, John Anticev and his associate Detective Lou Napoli, also began tracking the whereabouts and activities of a number of men associated with the Calverton shooters. They began putting the pieces together regarding the shooting of Rabbi Kahane, as well as the activities of his killer, El Sayyid Nosair. They also ran down leads associating Mohammed Abouhalima with the killing of Mustafa Shalabi, the man who once ran the Alkhafh Center in Brooklyn, a hotbed of Islamic agitation in New York. In time, the investigations of Floyd, Napoli and Anticev would intertwine.

Emad Salem had been in the United States for five years before meeting Nancy Floyd. He was raised in Cairo, and attended a technical school. He also served in the Egyptian army and held the rank of major. He told Agent Floyd that he was trained in intelligence work while he was in the army. He also told her that his unit had been responsible for the protection of Egyptian President Anwar Sadat.

In his conversations with Floyd and Len Predchenskis, Salem brought them up to date on who Sheik Rahman really was—that he was the leader of the radical al-Gama'a al-Islamiyya, an Egyptian terror group with a long history of violence in that country. Question: If Len Predchenskis was the bureau's top counterintelligence agent in New York City, why didn't he know about Sheik Rahman before being told about him by Salem? Was it because the bureau was still keeping track of Russian spies even though the Cold War was over, and not concentrating on possible troublemakers from the Middle East?

For days on end, Salem drilled Nancy Floyd with the history of the Middle East and the various radical groups that plied their deadly trade.

Salem's first job as an "asset" was to identify an Egyptian U.N. officer whom the FBI believed might be acting undercover.

Not only did Salem name him, he shocked them by reporting that the same person was working for the CIA.

After passing the test, Floyd introduced Salem to Anticev and Napoli. Salem told them that he knew Abouhalima, whom they were trying to locate. Salem also told them that the redheaded Abouhalima was currently the driver for Sheik Rahman. Salem was now ready to become the FBI's first informant inside the cell run by Sheik Rahman, whose office also proved to be the home to many of the men who would try to blow up the WTC in 1993, and was being secretly funded by Osama bin Laden.

Salem was ready to go undercover for the feds, but under one condition. He did not want this identity to be revealed. He said that his wife and children were still living in Egypt and that he wanted them safe from any reprisals. He also said that he would agree to be wired but that he needed a promise from the FBI that he would not have to testify about his activities in court. They agreed to his demands but said that they could not swear that other people who might come into the case down the line would agree to the stipulation. Now, Salem would become an "intelligence asset."

Before Salem went undercover, his status with the bureau had to be formally approved. Salem would work for the Foreign Counterntelligence Branch. Nancy Floyd would be his contact officer, while Napoli and Anticev would serve as agents who would evaluate the information he provided. He would not have to be wired in the presence of the Shiek nor any other members of his group.

Salem's first assignment was to linger outside the courtroom where the killer of Rabbi Kahane, El Sayyid Nosair was being held. As a fellow Egyptian, Salem had no trouble mixing with Nosair's friends and accomplices. Salem befriended Nosair's cousin, Ibrahmin El-Gabrowny. In a moment that could have led to disaster even before his undercover duties began, Agents Anticev and Napoli, who did not know that Salem was entrenched with the Sheik, noticed him talking with El-Gabrowny, and later, Abouhalima, the man they were pursuing. The redheaded Abouhalima warned Salem that the two agents would try to get him to snitch on them but Salem said he'd never rat on his Egyptian brothers.

Soon, El-Gabrowny introduced Salem to Shiek Rahman and he quickly became a familiar presence at the Brooklyn mosque, a spy in the lion's den.

As the FBI watched the nightly television news they could not have been happier with what they saw. Standing arm in arm with the blind Sheik as he made his way across New York was Emad Salem. As Salem became more ingrained with Shiek Rahman he was given a most important assignment to perform. Shiek Rahman asked Salem to issue a *fatwa,* or religious decree, putting in motion an assassination plot on the life of President Hosni Mubarak. Most of the men involved in the Sheik's entourage came from Egypt though they viewed President Mubarak as more Western leaning in nature and did not like his pro-American stance.

After the conviction of El Sayyid Nosair in the Kahane murder, Nosair was sent to the maximum security prison in Attica, New York. Oftentimes, Salem, along with a number of Nosair's pals from the mosques in New York came up to visit. It was during one of these visits that Nosair asked Salem to put out a hit on the judge who sentenced him to jail, as well as a contract on the life of a New York politician from Brooklyn. More disturbing, Nosair wanted Salem to form a plot to destroy twelve "Jewish locations" centered around the diamond district in Manhattan. All this information was passed along to Nancy Floyd and her FBI bosses. No follow up was ever done regarding the possible plot to bomb the "Jewish locations."

Salem was now the official driver of Sheik Rahman and soon he, along with the Sheik and a few of his followers, took off on a car trip to Detroit, where an Islamic conference was taking place. It was during this trip that Salem was given the *fatwa* to kill President Mubarak.

During his nightly sessions with the men from the Brooklyn and New Jersey mosques, talk of bringing the jihad to the United States was the paramount topic of conversation. Soon, two other men would join the group, men who would later play a small role in the WTC bombing conspiracy: Ahmed Sattar, a U.S. postal worker, and an Egyptian named Ahmed Amin Refai, an accountant who was employed by the New York Fire Department. Oftentimes, Refai was seen on television with Shiek Rahman but neither the

NYPD nor the JTTF sought to open a file on them until much later.

After another trip to Attica to see Nosair, Salem returned to New York shaken. During one of his visits with Nosair, the prisoner told Salem that he wanted him to build bombs which were to be activated by a beeper attached to a phone. Why Nosair wanted Salem to build the bombs wasn't revealed but Nosair was exhorting the members of the Al Kifah mosque in Brooklyn to see if anything could be done to free him from jail.

Events were moving fast now, and Salem was informed by members of the Sheik's cell that a plot to blow up "Jewish locations" around NYC was in the works. Salem was asked by El-Gabrowny if he would be able to locate detonators for the bombs. Salem tried to stall him, saying that it would take time to obtain such materials. "Dr. Rashid," aka Clement Rodney Hampton-El, told Salem that he would be able to provide the cell with automatic weapons. As Salem listened, he realized that the Brooklyn cell headed by Sheik Rahman was planning a major terrorist attack against Jewish locations in the city, as well as the planning the assassinations of a number of public figures. All of this information was passed on to Floyd, Napoli, and Anticev, as well as their superiors at the FBI. Despite the explicit warnings by Salem that something big was about to take place in New York, nothing was done to interrupt the Sheik's plans.

While Salem was reporting on the activities of the Sheik's cell, Nancy Floyd was doing her day job while at the same time taking in all that her prize informant brought in. She would meet Salem at night, after work, oftentimes returning to her home after midnight. If her bosses at the FBI did not realize just how important Salem was, Nancy did everything in her power to keep him happy. Unfortunately, internal politics and jealousies inside the bureau would make life miserable for both Nancy and Salem.

At the time that Salem went undercover, a new management supervisor directing the Floyd-Salem mission took over. The new head of the New York office was Carson Dunbar. Dunbar had previously been a New Jersey State Trooper with limited field experience. Working with Dunbar was Special Agent John Crouthamel, the new branch supervisor responsible for terrorism activities.

Without bringing Nancy Floyd into the picture, Crouthamel met with Salem, Anticev, and Napoli. The gist of the conversation was to have Salem work with the two agents, leaving Nancy out of the picture entirely. The best reporting on the Salem-Floyd story was written by Peter Lance in his groundbreaking book called *100 Years for Revenge: International Terrorism and the FBI: The Untold Story.* Lance says that Len Predtechenskis, Floyd's friend, said that Crouthamel told Salem, "We're gonna get that bitch (Nancy Floyd) off this case." From that point on, the top brass at the New York FBI terrorism unit did all they could to drive Nancy Floyd from her job, and in the process, remove the only lead they had into the growing terror cell in New York led by Osama bin Laden and Sheik Rahman.

Salem's undoing came after he was given a polygraph test that Nancy Floyd did not know about. The test was less than perfect, as far as the FBI was concerned. On July 6, 1992, Carson Dunbar met with Salem without Nancy's presence. Dunbar gave Salem an ultimatum, "Either you wear a wire and agree to testify or I don't want to see you anymore." It was obvious that Dunbar did not like Salem one iota and he wanted to control the "informant" as he called him at all costs. Lance writes that despite the fact that Salem was providing extraordinary information about possible terror attacks against potential targets in NYC, Dunbar said of Salem, "We didn't even know if Salem had the ability to infiltrate the group. If we couldn't trust him, we didn't know if they would trust him. He was not believable to us." With that mindset in place it is no wonder that the FBI failed to connect the dots linking (1)a number of men working out of the blind Sheik's mosque with (2) the February 1993 WTC bombing with (3) the information being provided to them by Emad Salem.

Believing that he was being double-crossed, Salem refused to go along with Dunbar's demand and quit his job. Left out in the cold, Salem, scared and fearing for his life, told the men in the mosque a story that he was being followed by the FBI and would have to divest himself of any more association with them. It wouldn't be until the bombing of the WTC in 1993 by Ramzi Yousef that the feds would regret their decision to terminate Salem and bring him back into the fold.

During the early 1990s, Emad Salem wasn't the only person interested in cracking the den of thieves headed by Sheik Rahman. A lone, New York City firefighter, Ronnie Bucca, would mount a one-man crusade to stem the tide of Islamic jihad that he saw as a threat to New York City. Like Salem, the FBI would not invite Bucca to the dance, leaving him a lone wolf, operating outside the system.

Besides being a member of the NYFD, Ronnie Bucca was a member of the U.S. Army's 242nd Military Intelligence Battalion, with the rank of sergeant. He later transferred to the 3413th MI (Military Intelligence) Department of the 800th MP's. His reserve unit was associated with the secret Defense Intelligence Analysis section located at Bolling AFB in Washington. This unit was part of the super-secret Defense Intelligence agency. Bucca read all the classified materials that he could get his hands on regarding international terrorism, especially as it related to the Middle Eastern conflict. The more he read, the more convinced he became that the United States would become a target of radical Islamic terror groups. What he didn't know, but would soon learn, was that the group he feared the most was only a few miles away.

Ronnie Bucca worked in the elite unit of the NYFD called Rescue One which was responsible for calls in the borough of Manhattan. He broke his back in a fall in 1986 but made a remarkable recovery. After a lengthy recovery process, Bucca was able to rejoin his unit and was called the "Flying Firefighter" by his colleagues.

In July 1992, Bucca put in for a position as a fire marshal with the FDNY's bureau of Fire Investigation. While attending his meetings with the intelligence division he learned that the feds had put an informer inside the blind Sheik's inner circled (Salem), and that he was subsequently let go. As with Emad Salem, it would take the actions of Ramzi Yousef to bring Bucca back to the trail of the "Mozart of terror."

After the WTC bombing of 1993, one of Bucca's best friends, Kevin Shea, was seriously injured when he fell into a four-story pit left after the explosion. During the initial investigation after the bombing, the FBI did not allow members of the fire marshals division of which Bucca was a member to take part in the probe.

As he dug deeper into the intelligence gleaned from his top secret clearance, as well as reading all the open source material available, Bucca was able to lay out the evidence against Yousef and the blind Sheik. The information he collected led him to believe that the followers of Yousef would try again to topple the twin towers. Among the material he found was a statement written by Yousef and published in the *New York Times.* The letter stated that they had placed the bomb in the wrong spot and had planned to topple Tower 1 into Tower 2.

Bucca decided to apply for a position with the JTTF but there were no positions at the time. Undeterred, he set out on a one-man crusade to follow the connecting dots. Using information he collected from his sources at the DEA, Bucca made a chart which connected the men involved in the Day of Terror Plots, as well as those associated with Sheik Rahman: Abouhalima, Salem, Ayyad, and Ajaj. Added to this collection were Ramzi Yousef, and the men the FBI followed to the Calverton shooting range.

By 1999, almost by chance, Bucca would come across a man who worked in the NYFD for twenty-five years who raised his suspicions. The man in question was a U.S. citizen from Egypt named Ahmed Refai, an accountant. Ronnie Bucca learned through his sources that Refai had lost his FDNY ID and was applying for a replacement. Using surveillance films, Bucca knew that Refai had lied when he said he lost his ID. Ronnie talked with Refai's superior Kay Woods, who gave him the most astounding information. It seems that Refai, an insignificant accountant, asked for and was given the blueprints for the World Trade Center.

Digging deeper, Ronnie found out via newsreel film that Refai had been seen walking with Sheik Rahman at various times. Refai later said the he was the Sheik's translator at an immigration hearing and that he also attended the Al-Salam mosque in Jersey City frequented by the Sheik. Ronnie gave his information on Refai to the FBI but they refused to follow up because Refai had committed no crime.

On 9-11, Ronnie Bucca responded to the inferno that was the twin towers. His body was later found amid the rubble.

The seminal event in the lives of Ronnie Bucca, Nancy Floyd, and Emad Salem took place on February 26, 1993, when Ramzi

Yousef and the Calverton shooting range confederates set off a bomb that was secreted inside a Ryder van near Room 107 on the B-2 level of the WTC. The blast created a four-story crater, killed six and wounded over a thousand. Accounts of Ramzi Yousef's flight have been described in previous sections of this work. Suffice it to say that with the attack on the WTC, all bets were off as far as the FBI was concerned. If they didn't have proof positive that Emad Salem was telling the truth about the men associated with Sheik Rahman before, they did now.

In a hastily called meeting, the FBI reinstated Salem as their prime source inside the cell and agreed to pay him not the five hundred a month that he previously received, but a total of $1.5 million.

Salem returned to the field, convinced the mosque members that he was free of bureau surveillance, and burrowed back deep inside the cell. In a matter of luck and sheer perseverance, Salem was able to interrupt a wave of terror attacks dubbed the Day of Terror plot in which Sheik Rahman and a number of his followers were arrested. Their deadly scheme included the bombings of the Lincoln and Holland Tunnels, the U.N. building, and the George Washington Bridge.

Salem was able to locate the whereabouts of the "redhead," Mahmud Abouhalima who was arrested in Egypt. Salem also informed the FBI that a friend of WTC conspirator Mohammed Salameh (who would be arrested after the WTC blast), an Iraqi named Abdel Yasin, was also involved. Following the WTC attack, bureau agents found Yasin in the Jersey City apartment that belonged to Salameh, the driver of the Ryder van. Yasin pleaded ignorance of any knowledge of the events in New York and took the FBI to the location where Yousef mixed the chemicals used in the bomb. Yasin was let go and subsequently fled to Iraq.

The events after the WTC bombing were bittersweet for both Salem and Floyd. Salem lambasted the bureau for not believing him in the first place regarding the goings on at the Brooklyn mosque, saying that if the feds had put their trust in him from the beginning, the WTC attack may have been prevented. Salem was subsequently put into the Witness Protection Service and probably is still there today. But the story did not end there

Salem had in his possession, a number of "bad guy tapes" of conversations that he recorded regarding the FBI foul up, as well as discussions with Nancy Floyd who had harsh words for her superiors. Carson Dunbar ordered Nancy to retrieve the tapes from Salem's home which she did. The tapes did nothing to enhance Nancy Floyd's relationship with her bosses whom she called "gutless" and "chickenshits." In retaliation, the bureau opened up an OPR, or internal affairs investigation of her that would last five years and effectively end her career. In an article in the *New York Post* of March 11, 1994, it was alleged that Nancy was having an affair with Salem, a charge which was false. In the end, Nancy Floyd was found innocent of all the charges.

On 9-11-2001, Nancy Floyd was driving into New York when she saw the billowing flames shoot up from the WTC. All of her years of work with Emad Salem had come full circle.

On October 1, 1996, a jury in the Day of Terror case convicted Sheik Rahman and nine other defendants on forty-eight of fifty counts and he was given a life sentence. As a bonus they also convicted El Sayyid Nosair for killing Rabbi Kahane. It was an ironic twist that the information provided by Salem and Nancy Floyd, which were ignored by the FBI, were instrumental in the convictions of the Shiek and his followers.

In February 1995, Ramzi Yousef was arrested in Pakistan and returned to the United Sates. On January 8, 1998, Yousef was sentenced to 240 years in prison for the bombing of the WTC. After the verdict, the Justice Department unsealed a secret indictment of Khalid Sheikh Mohammed, the uncle of Ramzi Yousef which had originally been closed in 1996. It would later be learned that KSM—Kalid Sheikh Mohammed—slipped through the Philippines police dragnet after the raid of his nephew's bombmaking home in Manila. Why did the FBI seal the indictment of KSM and not open it until two years later? In 1993, did the FBI know of the relationship between KSM and Ramzi Yousef? These questions need answers.

While Ramzi Yousef was languishing in the Metropolitan Correctional Center in New York, a series of most improbable events took place which gave the FBI immense insight into the thinking, and further destructive plans, of Yousef.

Near Yousef's cell was Gregory Scarpa Jr, the son of a well-known member of the Colombo crime family, Gergory Scarpa Sr. The younger Scarpa was in jail on conspiracy and bookmaking charges. In time, these two different men would form a bond which would be monitored by the FBI.

As the two men became better acquainted, Scarpa informed the FBI of his discreet contacts with Ramzi Yosef and the feds made him an undercover informant.

In an intricate arrangement, the FBI allowed Yousef to make his phone calls to a dummy company called the "Roma Corporation." Scarpa convinced Yousef that his mob ties were running Roma and that they would relay any messages Yousef wanted to get delivered.

While in jail, Yousef and Scarpa communicated via what Yousef called his "kites," messages that he would write on any scrap of paper available. It was soon learned that Yousef had put out hits on Mike Garcia, one of the Assistant U.S. Attorneys, and an unnamed federal judge.

Through the investigative work of author Peter Lance, the public record is replete with the FBI's "302" records of the Scarpa/ Yousef correspondence. What it reveals is chilling indeed, and also a blueprint to Yousef's connection to Osama bin Laden.

In a March 5, 1996 "302" read by the FBI, "Yousef told Scarpa I'll teach you how to blow up airlines and how to make bombs and then you can get the information to your people. Yousef told Scarpa I can show you how to get a bomb on an airplane through a metal detector. Yousef told Scarpa he would teach him how to make timing devices."

According to Scarpa, "Yousef wants to hurt the United States government and wants to teach Scarpa how. Scarpa advised Yousef has not asked for any specific help. Scarpa advised "that Yousef wants to blow things up, but he does not say why."

Yousef told Scarpa that during the trial they had a plan to blow up a plane that they are serious and then make their demands, or kidnap and hurt a judge or an attorney so a mistrial will be declared. Scarpa advised that blowing up an airplane during the trial seems easy to Yousef. Yousef never mentioned a specific airline as a target.

Further evidence that Yousef was planning something horrific during his trial came to light on March 11, 1996, a 302 which included talks between Yousef and Eyad Ismoil, who was also being held in connection with the WTC bombing. The relevant portion of the 302 reads as follows:

"Scarpa advised that in the past he has had numerous conversations with both Ismoil and Yousef and that these conversations are continuing. As a result of a conversation with Ismoil which took place sometime during mid to late March of 1996, Scarpa stated that Ismiol had stated that Yousef has something in mind regarding a plan to seriously disrupt the upcoming trial."

On July 17, 1996, TWA Flight 800, a plane from New York to Paris carrying 230 people exploded in a fireball off Long Island. Author Lance believes that the reference made by Yousef referring to "blowing up an airplane during the trial" was a direct reference to the downing of the plane, and a possible connection to it by Yousef or his confederates. Following the TWA 800 incident the judge in the Yousef case polled the jury about the possibility of a mistrial but the jurors decided to go ahead.

A most intriguing 302 record, dated September 9, 1996, gives an alluring clue to the possible relationship between bin Laden and Yousef at the time the latter was serving time in the Metropolitan Correctional Center.

In this memo, Yousef points to a figure whom he calls "Bojinga." After studying the contents of this letter, it is very possible that the person referred to as "Bojinga" is Osama bin Laden.

> Yousef told Scarpa that BOJINGA contacted him during his trial and said that his people (al Qaeda) are going to prepare to hijack an airplane and kidnap a United States Ambassador at the same time if he is convicted. Bojinga told Yousef that the plan would be carried out within one year of Yousef's conviction. Yousef advised that Bojinga said that after they hijack the plane and kidnap the Ambassador that Bojinga will ask for the release of Yousef and all of the defendants in the World Trade Center and the defendants in the Sheik's case..Yousef stated that the hijacking could include more than one airplane. Yousef said that the airplane

> would be hijacked and forced to land in either Afghanistan, Sudan, or Yemen. Bojinga asked if Yousef can arrange through his contacts here in the United States for two to four passports. Yousef said that he has contacted Bojinga to let him know if he can help. Yousef asked Scarpa if Scarpa can get him passports. If so, Bojinga will get an address in Iran or Libya where he can send the passports. Yousef would like Scarpa to provide an address so that Bojinga can send photographs for the passports.

First to the possible identity of "Bojinga." When Yousef was planning his series of airline bombings in the Philippines, the code name he used was "Bojinka," one letter different from the man called "Boginga."

By 1996, the FBI should have known who Osama bin Laden was if they had connected the dots between the WTC conspirators and those connected to the blind Sheik. They should have been able to ascertain that the Egyptian soldier, Ali Mohammed, al Qaeda's double agent in the United States, was also bin Laden's bodyguard. Also, the reference to landing the hijacked plane in Afghanistan or Sudan, two places where bin Laden called home, should have raised alarm. Granted, if the bureau did not have the resources or the knowledge to decipher the true identity of "Bojinga," they could have called the CIA which had a much a larger file on bin Laden and might have been able to provide relevant information.

And in 1996, which Islamic leader could have had the operational know-how, as well as the means to carry out such an elaborate hijacking scheme? Osama bin Laden.

In a March 5, 1996 302, Scarpa tells of the prescence in the United States of a number of cohorts associated with Yousef. "Yousef has indicated that he has four people here. Scarpa described these four people as terrorists already in the United States. Scarpa advised Yousef has not indicated who these four people are or if he is in contact with these four people or how he contacts them. Scarpa does not know if Yousef receives or sends any messages overseas."

What happened to the information provided by Scarpa to the FBI via its intricate sting operation? With the reams of pertinent intelligence provided via the 302s, it should have been obvious to the feds that Yousef was planning something big while in jail. Soon, TWA 800 fell out of the sky while Yousef talked about it beforehand. And what of the mysterious Bojinga? And what about the four terrorists described by Yousef already in the United States? It seems that the FBI decided not to follow through with these promising leads.

After the release of the 9-11 report, information came to light that during this time frame, highly placed members of the Clinton administration were aware that bin Laden was planning the same type of operation talked about by Yousef to Scarpa.

This information was contained in a December 4, 1998 Presidential Daily Brief (PDB) entitled, "Subject: Bin Laden Preparing to Hijack U.S. Aircraft and Other Attacks."

> Reporting suggests bin Laden and his allies are preparing for attacks in the U.S., including an aircraft hijacking to obtain the release of Sheik Umar Abd-al-Rahman, Ramzi Yousef, and Mohammad Sadiq Awad. One source quoted a senior member of the Gama'a At Islamiyya (IG) saying that, as of late October the IG had completed planning for an operation in the U.S. on behalf of bin Laden, but that the operation was on hold. A senior bin Laden operative from Saudi Arabia was to visit IG counterparts in the U.S. soon thereafter to discuss options—perhaps including an aircraft hijacking.
>
> *IG leader Islambuli in late September was planning to hijack a U.S. airliner during the "next couple of weeks" to free Rahman and other prisoners, according to what may be a different source.
>
> *The same source late last month said that bin Laden might implement the plans to hijack U.S. aircraft before the beginning of Ramadan on 20 December and that two members of the operational team had evaded security checks during a recent trial run at an unidentified NY airport.
>
> [Redacted] indicate that bin Laden's organization or its allies are moving closer to implementing anti-U.S. attacks

> at unspecified locations, but we do not know whether they are related to attacks on aircraft.

This shocking PDB not only supported the Yousef-Scarpa conversations but also verified his contention that four men were somewhere in the United States, unnoticed by U.S. intelligence.

However, there is more to the story regarding Greg Scarpa Jr. than his information regarding his activities with Ramzi Yousef while they were both in jail. The story concerns the aftermath of the Oklahoma City bombing in the years after the event took place.

By 2005, Scarpa was incarcerated in the Supermax Federal Prison, aka "The Alcatraz of the Rockies," located in Florence, Colorado. This was one of the most highly guarded prisons in the entire country and housed the worst of the worst when it came to who its inhabitants were. Along with Scarpa at that time were Ted Kazcinski aka the "Unabomber," and Olympic bomber Eric Rudolph, along with his al Qaeda pals, Ramzi Yousef, Abdul Hakim Murad, Eyad Ismoil, and Nidal Ayyad.

During his time in the Supermax, Scarpa was in solitary confinement much of the day, only being allowed to leave his cell for exercise a few hours a day. But in 2005, he was somehow able to find out very important information regarding a cache of explosives that homegrown terrorists might use in another Oklahoma City attack.

The tip that Scarpa got came from Terry Nichols who was the co-conspirator with Timothy McVeigh, who was executed for his part in the Oklahoma City bombing that destroyed the Murrah Federal Building in 1995. It seems that at some point during their stay in the Supermax, Terry Nichols met with Scarpa and told him that a cache of nitro methane buried at Terry Nichols's old home in Herrington, Kansas, might be retrieved and used to mark the tenth anniversary of the Oklahoma City bombing in 2005. Nichols said that the explosives were hidden under a crawl space underneath the house where the FBI had once looked when they went to his house ten years before.

Seeing a chance for a possible lessening of his sentence, Scarpa contacted Angela Clemente, a forensic investigator who had been working to get him a lawyer for many years. Angela

Clemente contacted a friend and colleague, a man named Stephen Dresch, who was a Yale educated Ph.D., and together they contacted members of the staff of two members of Congress to tell them what they knew. The two members of Congress were William Delahunt, a Democrat from Massachusetts, and Dana Rohrabacher, a Republican from California.

According to Ms. Clemente, Scarpa said that Nichols said that there were "others unknown" who were involved in the Oklahoma City bombing case. This ran counter to what Timothy McVeigh told authorities—that he and Nichols were the only ones responsible for the Murrah Building attack.

Scarpa also said that Nichols told him that a man named Roger Moore, who lived in Arkansas and was an arms dealer, had a girlfriend who may have been an FBI informant (Moore testified against both Nichols and McVeigh at trial). It was Moore who supposedly supplied the tubes of the high explosives that were buried in the crawl space.

Angela Clemente said of this episode, "Terry was anxious to have somebody test the boxes the explosives had come in for fingerprints, and that's why he let word of the explosives slip to Greg."

In order to test Scarpa's veracity, the FBI sent in a polygraph expert in March 2005 to conduct a reading on him regarding his allegations. The examiner later said that Scarpa had lied. Ms. Clemente disagreed and said, "First of all, the polygraph specialist sent from D.C. was belligerent to Greg Jr. which violates the protocol. Second of all, he asked about four questions, then abruptly left the test. He went into another room and returned, but he didn't re-inflate the cuff used to measure the subject's responses. Finally, this man abruptly ended the test, and told Greg Jr. he wasn't credible."[48]

Both congressmen pressured the FBI to look further into Scarpa's allegations and in March they returned to the home of Mr. Nichols. They made an investigation of the property and found material in the crawl space that Scarpa had talked about. The seizure of these materials was a black mark on the reputation of the FBI who probably did not find them when they first searched

48 Peterlance.com, Ex-Mafia capo Greg Scarpa Jr. alerts FBI to Terry Nichols's hidden cache of explosives.

Terry Nichols' home ten years before.

The two tips that Scarpa Jr. gave to the feds, the one where he told them about his long talks with Ramzi Yousef in his prison cell and his tip, ten years later, regarding missing evidence at the home of Terry Nichols, were something that the FBI probably didn't want to believe or hear, as it gave credence to Greg Scarpa whom they probably just wanted to be rid of in the first place.

In one final blow to Scarpa's hopes for a lesser sentence after his Nichols revelation, a federal appeals court restored his 40-year prison sentence, leaving him a bitter man. The 2nd U.S. Circuit Court of Appeals in Manhattan refused to give him any time off because of his prior criminal record. The decision was 3-0 and reversed a January 2016 ruling by U.S. District Judge Edward Korman in Brooklyn, New York. That judge said that the government had a "compelling interest in finding bombs hidden by domestic terrorists on American soil" and no interest in arbitrarily failing to credit Scarpa's tip. Circuit Judge Amalya Kearse agreed that Scarpa provided "substantial assistance" in locating the explosives. "But she said Korman went too far by cutting Scarpa's term after prosecutors refused to recommend a reduction, which it often does after receiving help from defendants. Fraudulent cries of Wolf not only cause the misallocation of government resources, but they also make less likely an appropriate government response if the man who cried Wolf subsequently sounds an alarm that is genuine."

As the years before 9-11 passed, the FBI would have more people knocking at their doors with vital information regarding bin Laden and al Qaeda.

In 2001, the U.S. Justice Department decided that they had enough evidence to prosecute Osama bin Laden in absentia for his participation in the East Africa embassy bombings and his relationship to the blind Sheik and Ramzi Yousef. One of bin Laden's most trusted aides would approach the FBI (and later the CIA) giving the United States vital information on how bin Laden's al Qaeda worked.

The man in question was a Sudanese named Jamal al Fadl. Al Fadl was an associate of Mustafa Shalabi, the sheik who was murdered (most likely by Mahmud Abouhalima) and who was seen often at the Al Kifah Refugee Center in Brooklyn. In 1988, he left the U.S. and traveled to Afghanistan to help bin Laden set up al Qaeda, the base.

Bin Laden took an immediate liking to al Fadl and the young man would soon become a courier for al Qaeda and the Sudanese government who were allies Al Fadl was with bin Laden in Afghanistan when al Qaeda was formed and he had a deep knowledge of how the new organization worked. When bin Laden was ejected from Saudi Arabia al Fadl went with him to Sudan to regroup. By 1996, however, Jamal al Fadl had gotten greedy and he began raking off large sums of money from al Qaeda. He stole $110,000 from bin Laden's organization and in the summer of 1996, set about to inform the United States what he knew regarding bin Laden.

At the 2001 trial of the men associated with the East Africa embassy bombings, K.K. Mohammed, 27, from Tanzania, Mohamed al Owhali, a 24-year old Saudi, Mohamed Odeh, 35, from Jordan, and Wadih el Hage, a Lebanese American, al Fadl testified that in the summer of 1996 he advised the U.S. government that al Qaeda was planning to bomb unidentified U.S. embassies around the word. In August 1998, the U.S. embassies in Kenya and Tanzania were attacked. Al Fadl said that Wadih el Hage was bin Laden's personal secretary in the Sudan, and that he was also a pal of El Sayyid Nosair.

For his cooperation in the embassy bombing case, al Fadl was put in the Witness Protection Program and became a confidential informant for the feds. The information provided by al Fadl to the FBI in 1996 gave them one more important link in bin Laden's American connection.

Another possible clue confirming bin Laden's intention to attack the United States came to the attention of the FBI in 2002. A 30-year-old British citizen of Pakistani origin by the name of Niaz Khan contacted the FBI in England with an amazing story. Niaz Khan was a waiter in a restaurant in London and was consumed by gambling debts. In a bizarre set of circumstances, Khan said that he was approached by two men in Manchester, England whom he had never met before, but who apparently knew all about him. The men gave him 5,000 British pounds, said that they could help him, and offered to give him instruction in militant Islamic jihad. Khan decided to join the men, as he had nothing to lose.

Khan said he went to a base in Lahore, Pakistan that was run by bin Laden's al Qaeda fighters. He said that he was given instructions using a Boeing aircraft on hijacking techniques, how to smuggle guns on board planes, and how to gain entry to the plane's cockpit.

After his training, Khan said that he left Pakistan and traveled through the Middle East, then to Switzerland and London, ending up in New York. His orders were to observe in-flight procedures for later use in hijacking attempts. Once in New York, Khan was supposed to meet with his contact at Kennedy Airport. Instead, Khan decided to end his brief relationship with al Qaeda, and took a bus to Atlantic City where he gambled away his money.

While in New Jersey, he contacted the Newark FBI office and told them his story. For almost a month, FBI agents in Newark debriefed Khan about his supposed al Qaeda connection but found his story implausible. When asked what he was supposed to do in the United States, Khan told the FBI that he was not given precise instructions.

FBI agent Joseph Billy Jr., who knew of the Khan interrogations, later said, "An investigation was done on this matter when he came to us. Nothing was discounted. We spent several weeks with him around the clock trying to verify the information." Eventually, the FBI let Khan go because he could not back up his story. He was returned to Britain where he was briefly questioned by Scotland Yard. There is no evidence whatsoever that Niaz Khan was part of, or knew about, the 9-11 plot. Khan's story did not surface until the summer of 2004 and the evidence is not there to either verify or refute his story. This incident was just one more pre-9-11 contact that the CIA was not aware of.

One of the most important clues to unraveling the 9-11 plot took place in the Philippines after the abortive conspiracy by Ramzi Yousef to blow up American airliners crossing the Pacific Ocean. After his plot literally went up in smoke while Yousef, his uncle Khalid Sheikh Mohammed, and their partner, Abdul Hakim Murad, were mixing chemicals needed for the bombs. Yousef and KSM fled and evaded capture. Their fellow conspirator, Abdul

Hakim Murad was not so lucky. He was arrested by Philippine police and underwent intensive interrogation at Camp Crane, the location of the PNP's Intelligence Group. What the PNP learned from Murad was that a third wave of attacks (separate from Bojinka) were being planned by Yousef and his crew, the same type that would be used on 9-11.

The Philippine police officer who had the responsibility of interrogating Murad was Col. Rodolfo Mendoza, an expert in terrorist groups. Contrary to what the FBI would later say regarding the Murad case, Mendoza said that he shared all his information with the bureau.

The FBI missed a wonderful chance to capture KSM right after his nephew escaped from their safe house in Manila. Not realizing how important KSM was to Ramzi Yousef's Bojinka Plot, the FBI allowed him to slip the net in the Philippines and even give an interview to *Time* magazine, telling what he knew about the goings on in the Su Casa guesthouse where they were making the bombs. In fact, an FBI agent named Brad Garrett was in the vicinity of the Su Casa house where Yousef, KSM, and Murad were staying, working with the PNP. Another clue that the FBI was kept in the dark regarding KSM was the fact that he was under a sealed indictment for over a year, just at the time that he was right under their noses. KSM's real identity would not be published until 1998. For over two years the FBI had put a $2 million price on his head but no one in the other law enforcement agencies knew anything about this. The question of why the Justice Department officials kept their mouths closed tightly in the two years of KSM's secret indictment begs for answers.

KSM fled Manila and wound up in Doha, Qatar where the Qatari authorities told the FBI of his whereabouts. While in Qatar, KSM was given protection by the country's leader, Abdullah bin Khalid al-Thani, who served as the interior minister. What happened next is comic opera. According to well-placed sources, an elite FBI hostage team was sent to Qatar to take down KSM. The U.S. was then double-crossed by people in the government who gave KSM warning that the Americans were planning his capture. KSM slipped out of the country and fled to the Czech Republic.

With Murad in jail, Col. Mendoza was able to prod him into revealing the most astonishing information. Murad acknowledged his participation in the 1993 WTC bombing and gave up the name of Ramzi Yousef as its ringleader. In an interrogation session on January 19, 1995, Murad told Col. Mendoza that his cell was planning an attack on CIA headquarters. The plan was to crash a commercial airline into the CIA building. The planning was a cooperative venture between himself and Yousef. While they had this plan as an option, no particular date for such an operation was made.

Murad made another vital statement to Col. Mendoza: "He discussed with me, even without me mentioning that there is really formal training going on of suicide bombers. He said that there were other Middle Eastern pilots training and he discussed with me the names and flight training schools they went to. This was in February of 1995."

In his book *Cover Up,* Peter Lance says that in an interview he did with Col. Mendoza, Murad told him that, "the plan was to hijack airliners." Their targets were CIA headquarters, the Pentagon, and a number of U.S. nuclear plants. Philippine police also said that in their conversations with Murad he expanded their target list by including the WTC, the Sears Tower in Chicago, and the Trans-America Tower in San Francisco. Murad also told Col. Mendoza that he had taken pilot training in the United States and the United Arab Emirates. In 1992, Murad went to New York where he took photographs of the WTC. He later told interrogators that Yousef was determined to do the job right this time, using planes as a weapon of mass destruction.

The crux of the plot was this: Yousef and Murad were planning a split operation not part of the original Bojinka plot. The second plan offered by Murad to Mendoza was the exact one carried out on 9-11.

During Yousef's trial in New York for the Bojinka plot, a number of PNP officers were called to testify. In an amazing development, Col. Mendoza, the man who knew more about the testimony of Murad than anyone else, was not invited to testify. Mendoza's assistant, Major Alberto Ferro could not recall who questioned Murad at Camp Crane, despite the fact that a number of FBI agents were present. In his January 17, 1995 testimony, FBI agent Frank Pellegrinio stated that while he was at Camp Crane he did not know who was questioning Murad. Agent Pellegrino told the court that he was also not aware that Murad was at Camp Crane at the same time he was there.

Murad stood trial with Yousef and Wali Khan Amin Shah in 1996 for their participation in the February 1993 WTC bombing.

The facts presented here detail a huge opportunity that was missed by the FBI in Manila in 1995 regarding KSM and Murad. Why the feds didn't demand that Col. Mendoza appear at Yousef's trial and present his knowledge of the separate plot to fly planes into high profile buildings is a mystery. In April 1995, the PNP handed control of Murad over to the FBI along with Mendoza's detailed notes of his interrogation sessions. Among the information revealed to the FBI by Murad was the fact that ten unidentified Arab men were in the United States taking pilot training —1995— six years before 9-11. After 9-11, Col. Mendoza was amazed that the FBI did not follow up on these leads.

The hot desert of Arizona was not only the home of thousands of retired snow-belt refugees seeking to avoid the cold eastern winters, but the location of a growing Muslim community in the United States. In the events leading up to 9-11, the Phoenix connection would become a huge intelligence blunder for the FBI when it was learned that a number of 9-11 hijackers were taking flying lessons in Arizona flight schools. As early as 1996, the FBI came across a source in Tucson who had a pipeline not only to militant groups in the Middle East but also to Arab men they suspected of taking flying lessons in the area who might be up to no good.

The FBI's informant was an American convert to Islam, Harry Josef Ellen. Ellen lived in Phoenix in 1994 when he first came in contact with the FBI. Ellen also went by the name of Abu Yusef, and in time he set up a benevolent foundation called Al-Sadaqa that aided the poor Palestinians living under Israeli rule. During the 1990s, Harry Ellen went to the West Bank four times, bringing doctors to aid the sick, and even arranged a truce between a number of the various Palestinian groups who were vying for control over anti-Israeli policies. Over time, Ellen made contact with representatives of Yasser Arafat and his PLO.

Back in the United States, the FBI was well aware of Harry Ellen and they decided to make him an asset. They even went so far as to funnel thousands of dollars to Ellen's charity that would then be passed on to the radical terrorist group Hamas which would be used for their anti-Israeli operations. Ellen gave permission to the FBI to bug his home, car, and even his foundation in order to gain intelligence on these radical groups. The FBI agent who ran Ellen during this period was Ken Williams who would later become part of the pre-9-11 story. In the summer of 2001, Agent Williams wrote a memo to FBI headquarters warning them that Arab men were taking flying lessons in U.S. schools.

Giving testimony before a court in 2001, Ellen said, "Williams wanted the transfer of American funds to some of the terrorist groups for violent purposes at a time when the U.S. intelligence community had few assets on the ground who were able to infiltrate Arafat's PLO." Agent Williams decided to remove Ellen from further duty. The reason for agent Williams' decision to pull Ellen out of his orbit was that Ellen was having an affair with a Chinese woman named Joanna Xie whom the bureau believed to be a spy. Whatever grounds Williams had for removing Harry Ellen as a bureau asset, the move also took out a perfect mole who could report on the goings on of Hamas and other radical Middle Eastern terrorist groups. However, the story dies not end there.

In 1996, while in Phoenix, Arizona Harry Ellen came across an Algerian man who told him that he had been training in a local flight school. Ellen described this incident to Agent Williams and further said that he believed this man was up to no good, and should be watched. Ellen told Williams that this Algerian pilot was also in contact with Abu Sief, a member of Sheik Rahman's mosque in Jersey City. Sief, it seems, was also associated with Ramzi Yousef. The identity of the Algerian pilot was Lotfi Raissi. Raissi was taken into custody in Great Britain, but after being questioned by British authorities, was let go. Ellen said that he was asked by Agent Williams to keep an eye out for any strange Arab men taking flying lessons and he complied with that request.

In time, Agent Williams told Harry Ellen to stop his inquiries regarding the Algerian pilot. That the FBI id not follow up on identities of these mysterious Middle Eastern men who were believed to be taking flying lessons in Arizona five years before 9-11 is a troubling fact indeed. What *is* known is that Hani Hanjour, the suicide hijacker who flew his plane into the Pentagon on 9-11 attended a flight school in Phoenix between January and March 2001. The warning given by Harry Ellen to the FBI five years before 9-11 was yet another missed opportunity on the long road to disaster.

The removal of Harry Ellen by Agent Williams parallels the situation between Emad Salem and Nancy Floyd concerning the goings on in New York involving the blind Shiek and his cohorts. Remember that the higher ups in the NY FBI office wanted nothing to do with Emad Salem (and Nancy Floyd) and did all they could to ruin their relationship, even going so far as to remove Salem from the case. In the situation of both Salem and Harry Ellen, the FBI decided it was better not to run these assets in the war against bin Laden and his men, rather than to do the right thing when it came to intelligence monitoring of these radical groups in New York and Arizona. If they had done the right thing at the right time, who knows how the story would have changed,

One of the hijackers on 9-11, Hani Hanjour (who has been mentioned earlier in this work), moved to Arizona in the early 1990s and spent much of the decade in the state. The FBI had no idea that he was in Arizona since he had committed no crime and al Qaeda was not on their radar at that time. It is reported, however, that one FBI informant said of Hanjor, "they knew everything about the guy." The first time that the FBI received hard evidence that some radical Muslims were living in Arizona it came from one of its agents, James Hauswirth, who told his bosses that a group of "heavy duty associates" of al Qaeda leader Sheik Omar Abdul Rahman had arrived in the state after the 1993 WTC attack. These unidentified men were in Arizona to train someone as a suicide bomber. This person was an FBI informant. The bureau found out about this and ordered the above-mentioned agent Ken Williams, who would later write the famous "Phoenix Memo" to higher ups in the FBI, telling them of the many Muslim men who were taking flying lessons in the area, to monitor the goings on. The bureau watched as the informant was taken to a deserted area where he was taught how to use explosives. During this test run, a device was planted under a test car but it failed to explode. After this incident, the FBI basically decided not to take any more action regarding these radical Muslims because they viewed them as a low priority. Agent Hauswirth would later explain the reasoning saying, "the drug war was the big thing back then, and terrorism was on the back burner."

The Phoenix area rivaled New York as the new hotbed of Islamic militancy in the late 1990s. From the Harry Ellen interaction, the FBI learned that a number of unidentified Arab men were hanging around flight schools in the area. By 1991, new information came to the attention of the bureau concerning another group of possible terrorists who were planning to come to the United States for possible flying lessons. While the FBI did not know the identities of these people, it was felt that it had enough information to warrant an investigation. The FBI's Counterterrorism Unit in Washington ordered 24 field officers to look into the matter.

In Phoenix, Agent Williams was put on alert. Despite these warnings it seems that no organized effort to look for these potential terrorists took place, and in November 2000, FBI headquarters sent a memo to its field offices saying that they had uncovered no leads regarding the recruitment of men taking flying lessons.

In September 1999, FBI agents from the Oklahoma City office arrived at the Airman Flight School in Norman, Oklahoma looking into the backgrounds of Ihab Ali Nawawi, who once worked as bin Laden's personal pilot. Ali took lessons at the Airman School in 1993 and was later identified as a conspirator in the embassy bombing in Kenya in 1998. FBI agents arrested Ali in Florida in May 1999. It would later be determined that two of the 9-11 hijackers, Mohamed Atta and Marwan al Shehhi traveled to the Airman School but decided not to enroll (they would instead take lessons in Florida).

Mohamed Atta was involved in another bizarre interaction around the time period late April to mid-May 2000. It did not involve the use of flying schools in the United States for training per se. It did however, have to do with crop dusting as a means of inflicting casualties in the United States.

During that time period, Mohamed Atta had a meeting with

a woman named Johnelle Bryant who worked for the U.S. Department of Agriculture (this meeting took place one month before the U.S. government officially said that he had arrived in the United States). By Bryant's telling, Atta told her in their meeting that "he initially refused to speak with one who is but a female." He asked her for a loan of $650,000 to buy and modify a cropdusting plane, and he said that he wanted to "build a chemical tank that would fit inside a plane and take up every available square inch of the aircraft except for where the pilot would be sitting." He told Johnelle Bryant a lot of personal information about himself including his real name, that he had arrived from Afghanistan, that he traveled around Spain and Germany, and that he wanted to make a trip to New York. He asked her about security at the WTC and other major U.S. landmarks. They also talked about the need for more al Qaeda recruits inside the United States, and, Atta asked her, "How would America like it if another country destroyed Washington and some of the monuments in it like the cities in (my) country had been."

Atta got very distracted when Miss Bryant refused to give him the $650,000 loan he asked her for, and later tried to get it from her wearing a disguise. To her discredit, Miss Bryant did not inform the FBI about her meeting with Atta unit after 9-11. After the incident, Miss Bryant undertook a lie detector test and passed. It is believed that after Miss Bryant refused to give Atta the money for a crop dusting plane to be used in a hypothetical attack, the terrorists linked to bin Laden and al Qaeda decided to go one step further and concentrate on using jumbo jets as their means of mass destruction. The 9-11 Commission failed to mention any of the facts regarding Atta's meeting with Miss Bryant in any of their writings.

Another thing that one should ask about this most interesting encounter is how did Mohamed Atta, a man who was not known in the United States at that time, and who had limited contacts, pick out Johnelle Bryant in the first place. How did he find her and who, if anyone, made the introduction to Atta? This is not a major event in the timeline of 9-11 but one more curious story that has few answers.[49]

49 History Commons: Late April-Mid-May 2000: 9-11 hijacker Atta leaves numerous clues while seeking Crop-Dusting Airplane loan.

By the summer of 2000, the threat level coming from bin Laden's al Qaeda had reached a fever pitch. Communications intercepts from the NSA, National Security agency, whose job it was to monitor global communications, began picking up large scale "chatter" suggesting an attack would take place outside the borders of the United States, although a strike against the U.S. was not discounted.

In Phoenix, Agent Ken Williams was becoming extremely worried regarding the activities of certain Middle Eastern men in his area who he suspected had terrorist ties. He did not know the identities of these men but he soon learned that a number of them were taking classes in airport management. He also noticed a contingent of men with possible terrorist ties attending the Embry-Riddle Aeronautical University in Prescott, Arizona. He believed that these men could possibly be terrorists-in-waiting for some unknown group. Believing he had something of importance, he wrote up his concerns and sent what is now known as the "Phoenix Memo" to his bosses in Washington.

Ken Williams' Phoenix Memo was sent yo the FBI's Radical Fundamentalist Unit in Washington, D.C. which was the repository of all information regarding bin Laden and al Qaeda. The gist of the memo was his fear that radical Islamic men were taking flight lessons in various schools across the United States for possible use in terrorist attacks. Williams asked the FBI to mount a nationwide review of Arab American students going to flight schools in the United States. Nothing of the sort took place because there were too few FBI agents to visit and survey all flight schools in the country.

Agent Williams's heavily redacted July 10, 2001 memo contains the following information:

> Synopsis: UBL [bin Laden] supporters attending civil aviation universities/colleges in the state of Arizona.
>
> Title: Zakaria Mustapha Soubra: IT ORHER (Islamic Army of the Caucasus, Soubra was a Lebanese attending flight training in Prescott, Arizona who served in Chechnya, and was associated with al Qaeda.
>
> Details: The purpose of this communication is to

> advise the bureau and New York of the possibility of a coordinated effort by Usama bin Laden to send students to the United States to attend civil aviation universities and colleges. Phoenix had observed an inordinate number of individuals of investigative nature who are attending or who have attended civil aviation universities and colleges in the state of Arizona.
>
> Phoenix believes that the FBI should accumulate a listing of civil aviation universities/colleges around the country. FBI field offices with these types of schools in their area should establish appropriate liaison: FBHQ should discuss this matter with other elements of the U.S. intelligence community and task the community for any information that supports Phoenix's suspicions. FBIHQ should consider seeking the necessary authority to obtain visa information from the USDOS on individuals obtaining visas to attend these types of schools and notify the appropriate FBI filed office when these individuals are scheduled to arrive in their area of responsibility."
>
> Phoenix has drawn the above conclusion from several Phoenix investigations to include captioned investigation and the following investigations. (Redacted) a, Saudi Arabian national and two Algerian Islamic extremists.

Despite the specificity of these warnings, the bureau gave his memo the classification of "routine" not "urgent." After 9-11, when Williams's Phoenix Memo hit the fan, the top leaders of the FBI said that Williams's warnings were only speculative and said that he had no concrete data that would have prevented the attacks.

Testifying before the Congressional Committee investigating the 9-11 attacks, Ken Williams talked about these events prior to 9-11:

> I cannot sit here and testify today that al Qaeda established a network there. However, looking at things historically in Arizona we have seen persons go to school at the University of Arizona at Tucson who subsequently went on to become rather important figures on the al Qaeda

> organization. Prior to al Qaeda even coming into existence these people were living and going to school in Arizona. As al Qaeda formed and took off and became operational, we've seen these people travel back to the State of Arizona. We've seen Osama bin Laden send people to Tucson to purchase an airplane for him and it's my opinion that's not a coincidence. These people don't continue to come back to Arizona because they like the sunshine or they like the state. I believe that something was established there and I think it's been there for a long time. We're working very hard to identify that structure. So I cannot say with a degree of certainty that one is in place there. But that's my investigative theory.

Another FBI informant who provided information on certain Islamic men in Arizona was an American White Muslim named Aukal Collins who informed to the FBI on 9-11 hijacker Hani Hanjour. The FBI paid Collins to monitor the Islamic and Arab communities in Phoenix between 1996 and 1999. He told the bureau that he was a "casual acquaintance" of Hanjour while the latter was taking flying lessons. He told the FBI that he was concerned about Hanjour because he was associated with a large number of other Arab men taking flying lessons. The FBI later denied that they got useful information from Collins. Collins was sure that the CIA knew about what these Arab men were doing in Arizona and said regarding the events prior to 9-11, "Just think about it—how could a group of people plan such a big operation full of so many logistics and probably countless e-mails, encrypted or not, and phone calls and messages? And you're telling me that, through all of that, that the CIA never caught wind of it?"

The FBI did however ask the CIA to do a name search on a number of those pointed out by Williams but did not give a copy of the memo to agency personnel for their perusal. The CIA's response did not match any known person on the list with names in their database.

In a statement on September 14, 2001, three days after the attacks, FBI Director Robert Mueller, who had only been in office for a month, made a most startling observation, despite what

Williams had previously written. "The tragedies quite clearly astonish and shock me and the country. The fact that there were a number of individuals that happened to have received training in flight schools here is news, quite obviously. If we had understood that to be the case, we would have perhaps—one could have averted this. But beyond that, I and I think everyone else is just astonished at the extent of the tragedy." Three days later, Director Mueller made another extraordinary comment. "There were no warning signs that I'm aware of that would indicate this type of operation in the country."

Perhaps Director Mueller would not have made that comment if he had been informed of the boast by Abdul Hakim Murad about using hijacked airliners to fly into the CIA HQ, and other high-profile buildings in the U.S.

As reported in earlier chapters in this book, BCCI—the rogue bank that was associated with a number of worldwide terrorist groups, including al Qaeda—was investigated by the United States government, including the Justice Department. Senator John Kerry (later to be the Democratic nominee for president in 2004 and Secretary of State under President Obama) opened up a congressional investigation of BCCI, along with the New York District Attorney's office led by Robert Morgenthau (now deceased). Their efforts were thwarted at almost every turn leading Kerry to say, "With the key exception of the Federal Reserve, there was almost no information or cooperation provided by other government agencies." It was reported that Kerry later said that the "Justice Department in particular went to great lengths to block his and Morgenthau's investigations, through a variety of mechanisms, ranging from not making witnesses available, to not returning phone calls, to claiming that every aspect of the case was under investigation in a period when little, if anything was being done."

After the Bank of England finally shut down BCCI in July 1991, Robert Mueller, who at that time was a high-ranking member of the Department of Justice, took over the DOJ's probe of BCCI and in turn, hired a new team of attorneys to work the case. However, according to Sen. Kerry, Robert Mueller's team did not do enough in his opinion to do a proper investigation. Kerry said that the indictments that the DOJ brought forth against BCCI were "less detailed than those of Morgenthau's, and often seemed to be in response to what Morgenthau was doing." President Bush appointed Mueller to become FBI Director shortly before the 9-11 attacks. He would become a household name when he began a probe of Russian influence in the election of Donald Trump in 2016, which was much maligned by Trump's associates, but which detailed numerous aspects of conspiracy and collusion between the Trump campaign and certain Russians, even if no defining criminal activity could be proved.

Unknown to Director Mueller and almost everyone else in the U.S. intelligence community was that one of the 9-11 hijackers, Hani Hanjour, took flying lessons in 1997 in Arizona and got his pilot's license. In April 1999, he was able to get his commercial pilot's certification and then promptly returned to Saudi Arabia.

On August 6, 2001, one month before Ken Williams' memo was sent to FBI HQ, President George W. Bush received the now famous Presidential Daily Brief (PDB) warning of possible al Qaeda attacks on the United States. A part of the PDB which was titled, "Bin Laden Determined to strike in U.S." refers to unusual activities in the United States on the part of al Qaeda. The important portion of the August 6, 2001 PDB that backs up Williams' memo is as follows:

> We have not been able to corroborate some of the more sensational threat reporting, such as that from a [deleted] service in 1998 saying that bin Laden wanted to hijack a U.S. aircraft to gain the release of Blind Sheik Umar Abd-al-Rahman and other U.S. held extremists. Nevertheless, FBI information since that time indicates patterns of suspicious activity in this country consistent with preparations for hijacking or other types of attacks, including recent surveillance of federal buildings in New York. The FBI is conducting approximately 70 full field investigations throughout the U.S. that it considers bin Laden related. CIA and the FBI are investigating a call from our Embassy in UAE in May saying a group of bin Laden supporters in the U.S. planning attacks with explosives.

Speaking of Ken Williams, his fellow FBI colleague Ronald Myers had nothing but praise for his friend: "He is one of the sharpest agents I've ever met. Anyone in FBI management who wouldn't take what Ken Williams said seriously is a fool. It's been my past experience that the smallest bit of information that comes in could turn out to be the most important piece of the investigation." It's too bad that the top officials at FBI HQ did not learn of Williams' memo while there was still time to act on it.

Another missed opportunity by the Justice Department in possibly unraveling the 9-11 plot came with the arrest of the brother-in-law of Osama bin Laden, Jamal Khalifa, in 1994. The case against Khalifa reached the highest levels of the Clinton administration and involved a member of the 9-11 Commission, Jamie Gorelick, who was a top-level member of the Justice Department.

Jamal Khalifa was married to a sister of bin Laden and his expertise of the al Qaeda terror group made him the unofficial "money man" He was also in close contact both with Ramzi Yousef and Ahmed Ajaj in the months before the WTC attack in 1993. When Ajaj was arrested at Kennedy Airport, federal authorities found in his possession the alias used by Khalifa, "Abu Barra." At that point the name "Aby Barra" did not register and no action was taken.

Jamal Khalifa founded the Benevolence International Corporation in the Philippines in 1988 and was a prime recruiter for Arabs wanting to fight the Soviet Union after its invasion of Afghanistan. The organization closed up shop in 1992, and was renamed the Benevolence International Foundation. By whatever name it went, it was a recruitment and money-laundering apparatus led by Osama bin Laden and al Qaeda with his brother-in-law as its prime supporter.

Large sums of money were given by Khalifa's organization to Ramzi Yousef in his abortive Bojinka plot, as well as funds for Yousef's attack on the WTC. Another business run by Khalifa was called Khalifa Trading Industries, an al Qaeda front company. He was also deeply involved with the Philippine terrorist group called Abu Sayyaf. While in the Philippines, Khalifa started a small furniture making company while at the same time, recruitedthousands of Muslim men for the anti-Soviet flight in Afghanistan. Khalifa traveled to the many isolated Philippine villages in the province of Basilan, successfully sending able-bodied men to training camps in Afghanistan.

Khalifa soon came to the United States and he was arrested in San Francisco in December 1994. The Department of Justice got into the act and began deportation proceedings against him. It seems that Khalifa was wanted in Jordan for his part in a terrorist plot to attack movie houses (he was convicted in absentia on these charges).

Another man arrested with Khalifa was Mohamed Loay Bayzid who conspired to buy uranium for bin Laden. The public record is mute as to the whereabouts of Bayzid.

Khalifa was held at a prison in Santa Rita, California on orders from the Immigration and Naturalization Service.

When the feds went through Khalifa's personal belongings, they found numerous items linking him to Ramzi Yousef and the WTC plot. Found were phone numbers used at the Manila apartment where he planned the Bojinka plot, a phone number for Yousef's co-conspirator, Wali Khan Amin Shah, and books on how to train terrorists.

When the Jordanian authorities in the United States learned that Khalifa was in custody they demanded his extradition. On January 5, 1995, Secretary of State Warren Christopher contacted U.S. Attorney General Janet Reno asking that Khalifa be deported. Jamie Gorelick sent a letter to the office of the immigration judge asking that these action be taken.

While these judicial proceedings were going on, both Yousef and Murad were captured but American authorities were still not able to piece together the interrelationships between Khalifa, Yousef, and Murad, despite the drops of evidence they had in their possession.

A long and tedious legal process began with Khalifa's agreement to be sent to Jordan in exchange for the U.S. cleansing his American record of any terrorist charges. Why? It seems that Khalifa may have stayed inside the United States longer than the official record says, and that he may have been questioned during this time period by other U.S. intelligence agencies. If so, who were they, and what did he have to say?

The question regarding the case of Osama bin Laden's brother-in-law begs answers. Why didn't the DOJ connect the dots regarding Khalifa's relationships with bin Laden, Yousef, Murad, and Whali Khan Amin Shah? Surely the feds knew who bin Laden was at the time of Khalifa's arrest yet, no legal proceedings were held against him. And more importantly, why was he allowed to leave the United States in the first place?

Once back in Jordan, Khalifa was cleared of the previous charges leveled against him. He subsequently moved to Saudi Arabia and operated a restaurant.

With the Phoenix Memo case now history, the FBI, in the summer of 2001, would turn its attention to a mysterious French-Moroccan named Zacarias Moussaoui.

Zacarias Moussaoui was a soldier for al Qaeda, took training in bin Laden's Afghan camps, and had direct ties to some of the 9-11 hijackers. His profile fit directly with Ken William's warning about Middle Eastern men taking flying lessons in U.S. schools. In the summer of 2001, Moussaoui was taking flight training at the Pan Am International Flight School in Minneapolis. He paid cash—almost $6,500 for his training, and despite his limited English, told his instructors that he wanted to learn how to steer a 747, and was not really interested in any other type of flight training. One of his instructors at the school grew concerned about Moussaoui and called the local FBI office. On August 16, 2001, when FBI agents arrived at the school, they saw that his visa papers had expired and Moussaoui was arrested.

As the FBI agents began their background check on Moussaoui they learned that he was not your ordinary flight student. He was living in London but was wanted by the French police for recruiting willing followers to the jihad against the West. In previous years, he had traveled between Europe and the Middle East and was a middleman in recruiting men for the war in Chechnya. The French also revealed that Moussaoui had been in Pakistan and Afghanistan.

He arrived in the United States on February 23, 2001, and enrolled in the Airman Flight School near Oklahoma City. In August he transferred to Minneapolis to finish his training. With all this information in hand, the Minneapolis office of the FBI believed that Moussaoui was engaged in possible airline hijacking. The bureau then notified the CIA who aided them in their investigation of the Frenchman. CIA Director George Tenet was briefed on the case as well as members of the CIA's Counterterrorist Center. The agency sent notices to their Paris and London stations describing Moussaoui as a possible "suicide hijacker," as well as an August 24 cable regarding "subjects involved in suspicious 747 flight training." Notes taken by the Minneapolis field office regarding Moussaoui said that he was "an Islamic extremist preparing for some future act of radical fundamentalist goals."

The British intelligence service was asked to supply whatever they knew about him in August, but they weren't able to provide adequate information until after 9-11. On September 13, the British learned that Moussaoui had spent some time in an al Qaeda training camp in Afghanistan.

After his arrest, members of the Minneapolis field office asked for a Foreign Intelligence Service Act warrant to gain access to his laptop computer that they believed might be helpful in their case. In order for a FISA warrant to be granted it would have to be proved that the person under scrutiny had been associated with a foreign power or was a member of a terrorist group. Despite his background, higher ups at FBI HQ refused to allow a FISA warrant to be issued.

One of the members of the Minneapolis office was FBI agent Coleen Rowley, who believed there was more to the Moussaoui story. Rowley entered the FBI in 1980, and was a lawyer for the bureau working on applications for wiretaps and handling organized crime cases out of the New York office. In 1995, she was reassigned to Minneapolis where she was the chief counsel.

Rowley and other members of the staff took matters into their own hands after being shafted by their D.C. bosses. It seems that Rowley and her colleagues called the CIA for information on the suspect without permission. When her superiors found out, she was given a reprimand. Rowley also asked permission to question Moussaoui but was turned down. To make matters worse, Rowley was not informed about Ken Williams's Phoenix Memo. On her own, she sent a letter to the Secret Service informing them of her concerns that Moussaoui was possibly linked with other men who were planning to hijack planes. Again, nothing was done.

Getting ever more frustrated at the lack of cooperation that she was getting from FBI HQ, Rowley, after much soul searching, decided to take matters into her own hands to get her point across. In a gutsy move on her part, she sat down and wrote a 13-page memo directly to FBI Director Robert Mueller, telling him of her concerns about how the Moussaoui case was mishandled.

Her report, which she penned on May 21, 2002, was nothing but a stinging indictment of how the FBI handled the Moussaoui case. It accused the top leaders of the bureau of a lack of cooperation and stonewalling the Minneapolis office investigation.

Rowley wrote that she asked for a FISA warrant to look into Moussaoui's computer instead of going to the U.S. Attorney's office in Minneapolis seeking a criminal search warrant, one that might have been turned down.

After she delivered her memo to Director Mueller, news organizations got a copy of the letter, and soon *Time* printed an exclusive transcript. Whatever chances that the FBI may have had of keeping Rowley's charges secret, they were now out of the box.

It is instructive for the reader to examine closely what she included in her letter as it goes right to the heart of the differences in mindset between those at FBI HQ and the street agents who put their lives on the line each day.

> May 21, 2002
>
> Dear Director Mueller:
>
> I feel at this point that I have to put my concerns in writing concerning the important topic of the FBI's response to evidence of terrorist activity in the United States prior to September 11. The issues are fundamentally ones of INTEGRITY and go to the heart of the FBI's law enforcement mission and mandate.
>
> To get to the point, I have deep concerns that a delicate and subtle shading/skewing of the facts by you and others at the highest levels of the FBI management has occurred and is occurring. The term "cover up" would be too

> strong a characterization which is why I am attempting to carefully choose my words here. I base my concerns on my relatively small, peripheral but unique role in the Moussaoui investigation in the Minneapolis Division prior to, and during, and after September 11.
>
> It is obvious, from my firsthand knowledge of the events and the detailed documentation that exists, that the agents in Minneapolis who were closest to the action and in the best position to gauge the situation locally, did fully appreciate the terrorist risk/danger posed by Moussaoui and his possible co-conspirators even prior to September 11. Even without knowledge of the Phoenix communication, the Minneapolis agents appreciated the risk. So I think it's very hard for the FBI to offer "20-20 hindsight" justification for its failure to act.

The fact is that key FBI HQ personnel whose job it was to assist and coordinate with field division agents on terrorism investigations and the obtaining and use of FISA searches, continued to, almost inexplicably, throw up roadblocks and undermine Minneapolis's by-now desperate efforts to obtain a FISA search warrant, long after the French intelligence service provided its information and probable cause became clear.

Although the last thing the FBI or the country needs now is a witch hunt, I do find it odd that no inquiry was launched of the relevant FBI HQ personnel's actions a long time ago.

Rowley chastised Director Mueller in no uncertain terms regarding his lopsided comments on the possibility that 9-11 could have been prevented:

> Everything I have seen and heard about the FBI's official stance and the FBI's internal preparation in anticipation of further congressional inquiry, had, unfortunately, confirmed my worst suspicion in this regard. After the details began to emerge concerning the recent release of the information about the Phoenix EC, your statement has changed. The official statement is now to the effect that even if the FBI had followed up on the Phoenix lead

> to conduct checks of flight schools and the Minneapolis request to search Moussaoui's personal effects and laptop, nothing would have changed and such actions certainly could not have prevented the terrorist attacks and resulting loss of life. With all due respect, this statement is as bad as the first.

Agent Rowley ended her narrative with these honest and straightforward words:

> Mr. Director, I hope my observations can be taken in a constructive vein. They are from the heart and intended to be completely apolitical. You do have some good ideas for change in the FBI but I think you also not have been completely honest about some of the true reasons for the FBI's pre-September 11 failures. Until we come clean and deal with the root causes, the Department of Justice will continue to experience problems fighting terrorism and fighting crime in general.

The FBI mindset among its agents had come a long way since the time of J. Edgar Hoover. No one could have possibly imagined an agent writing such an explosive and heartfelt letter criticizing their own bureau with Hoover's iron fist looming near. If Hoover had read Rowley's memo, the ground under his grave would surely have moved.

On September 4, 2001, the FBI sent a notice about Moussaoui's arrest to the FAA (Federal Aviation Administration) and said that the suspect might have been planning to hijack aircraft. The FAA did not deem it necessary to warn the major airline carriers about this news.

Had the FBI agreed to the FISA request by the Minneapolis agents regarding the material on Moussaoui's computer they would have been electrified by what they found. Money for his training in the United States was supplied through KSM and another major al Qaeda figure, Ramzi Binalshibh. Binalshibh tried four times to get a visa to enter the United States pre-9-11 but was refused. He was able to wire $14,000 to Moussaoui in Oklahoma around

August 1, 2001 from Germany. After KSM's capture, he told his questioners that while he did not personally know Moussaoui, the Frenchman was slated to take part in a second wave of attacks on the U.S. It seems that Moussaoui was picked by bin Laden personally to partake in the attacks on the U.S.

After 9-11, Ahmed Ressam, the man who plotted to blow up LAX, told interviewers that he recognized Moussaoui from his time in the Afghan camps.

Other information found on his computer were instructions on crop dusting and schematics of large commercial airliners. Also on the hard drive was the phone number of lead hijacker Mohamed Atta, and videos of the flight decks of jumbo jets.

Since his arrest, investigators have debated whether or not Moussaoui was the 20th hijacker.

The Moussaoui case and other things such as Emad Salem, Ken William's Phoenix Memo, the material provided by Harry Ellen, the links to al Qaeda given by Jamal Khalifa, and Col. Mendoza's intelligence concerning Murad and his plans to use planes as weapons of mass destruction, if examined with more interest, would have provided the FBI with a better feel for the events that were unfolding in the summer of 2001.

Information released by the joint House-Senate committee looking into the 9-11 attacks provided the public with the best chance that the FBI had in possibly unraveling the plot. As has been related above, the story revolved around two of the 9-11 hijackers, Khalid al-Midhar and Nawaf al-Hamzi who arrived in the United States in January 2000. Both men settled in San Diego and in April 2000, al-Hamzi took flying lessons at the National Air College in San Diego. In May 2000, both men enrolled in flight training in San Diego.

At the time that al-Hamzi and al-Midhar lived in San Diego, they were in constant contact with an unnamed FBI informant who provided the bureau with information on them. This unnamed informer only knew the first names of the men and relayed that information to his FBI controller. The informant told his bureau handler that they were "good Muslim Saudi youths" who were in America to attend flight school.

In an intelligence blunder on the parts of both the FBI and

the CIA, the CIA did not inform the FBI that the two men had previously attended an al Qaeda summit in Malaysia in which planning for the 9-11 plot was hatched.

The FBI report said they had problems with the informant's bona fides and tried to block his appearance as a witness to give his testimony to the House-Senate Committee. The FBI objected when the committee tried to interview the person and he never did attend any of the committee's sessions.

After 9-11, FBI agents had numerous interrogations sessions with the unnamed source and he repeatedly told them that he was kept in the dark about 9-11 and did not know the real reason why the two men were in the United States.

In his congressional testimony the FBI handler said that the informant did not mention that al Hamzi was taking flying lessons until after the attacks. The FBI, according to the Joint Congressional Account, did not believe the informant when he said he did not recognize the other 9-11 hijacker, Hani Hanjour, when he visited al-Hazmi in San Diego.

The failure of the CIA to inform the FBI that it was aware that al-Midhar had obtained a U.S. visa and was seen in California in March 2000 was an intelligence offense of the first order. If both agencies had been able to track al-Midhar and al-Hazmi in August 2000, they might have been able to break up the 9-11 plot.

The main cause of the FBI's intelligence failure leading up to 9-11 was its inability or unwillingness to work with the CIA, as well as a feeling of hubris about itself. The mindset that had been at work since the days of the J. Edger Hoover/William Stephenson (the head of the British intelligence organization located in the United Sates before World War II) feuds of the 1940s never ended, and that distrust of the other U.S. intelligence agencies only magnified the problem as time went on. The breakdown at the FBI let 9-11 happen. The failure to "connect the dots" was a path that had an inevitable, tragic ending.

One more facet of the FBI's investigation into the first WTC bombing in 1993 which has to be mentioned is the possibility of state-sponsored involvement in the attack. It was blamed on a handful of Muslim men from the New York-New Jersey area who were immediately apprehended, but from the moment that Ramzi

Yousef and his gang planted the bombs at the WTC, some federal officials began talking among themselves that another country may have been behind the attack. The immediate culprit, some said, was Saddam Hussein's Iraq.

One person who discussed that possibility was none other than the FBI's informant in Sheik Rahman's inner circle, Emad Salem. He spoke to another FBI agent and asked, "Is there a lot of suspicion about Iraqi intelligence being involved?" The agent responded by saying, "Yeah."

Reporter Laurie Mylroie, who would later begin an investigative study of the so-called Iraq connection to the 1993 attack, said that in June 1993, Salem met with Barbara Jones, the number two person at the New York district attorney's office. She also said that there were suspicions that Iraq was behind the bomb. Mylroie said that during her work she found out that a number of FBI officials believed there was an Iraqi connection and that the men who were arrested after the fact were just pawns in a higher conspiracy. [50]

One of the FBI agents who had doubts about the determination that Ramzi Yousef et al were responsible for the 1993 WTC bombing was John Anticev, the same man who played a role in the Emad Salem-Nancy Floyd story. At one point after the bombing, Anticev remarked to Salem, "Do you ever think that Iraqi intelligence might have known of these people who were willing to do something crazy, and that Iraqi intelligence found them out and encouraged them to do this as a retaliation for the bombing of Iraq? So the people who are left holding the bag here in America are Egyptian, or Palestinians? But the other people we are looking for, Abdul Rahman, he is gone. I hate to think what's going to happen if this guy turns out to be, if this turns out to be an Iraqi intelligence operation, and these people were used. If he's out of the country, then that is a very big indication that he is directly involved in this, and he, and he split."[51]

As far as FBI HQ were concerned, the case ended with the arrest of those accused, with the exception of Ramzi Yousef

---

50 Mylroie, Laurie, *Study in Revenge: The First World Trade Center Attack and Saddam Hussein's War against America,* American Enterprise Institute, Washington, D.C., 2001, Page 107.

51 Ibid. Page 106.

who fled right after the bombing took place. In Washington, it seemed there was no reason to look into why a nation-state would take part in such a horrific event. And if they had done such an investigation, who would have been the logical suspects? Iran or Iraq? As far as the men responsible for the attack, not all of them were prosecuted. For example, two of the men who were arrested, Ibrahim Elgabrowny and Bilal al-Qaysi, never faced a jury, and two others, Abdul Rahman Yasin and Ahmad Ajaj would only later be indicted for their participation in the WTC attack.

Then there is the mystery of Ramzi Yousef whose life prior to his arrival in the United States is shrouded in deceit and subterfuge. He came to the United States carrying an Iraqi passport even though he was not an Iraqi citizen. The question is, who gave him the passport? Was it someone in the Iraqi government of Saddam Hussein? While Ramzi Yousef was in New York, he was known by his fellows as "Rashid, the Iraqi."

An interesting quote from a man named Abdul Haggag, an Egyptian who was arrested in the second New York City bombing case, and cooperated with the government. Haggag said this about Yousef. "Ramzi Yousef showed up on the scene and brought a number of individuals together and escalated the initial plot. Mahmud stated that Ramzi Yousef used himself and others as pawns and then immediately after the blast left the country. Mahmud advised that the initial plan was not as large as what happened and that Ramzi Yousef was responsible for bringing the individuals responsible together and making it happen." Mahmud also made a reference that law enforcement authorities would not be able to catch Yousef. Haggag questioned why, and Mahmud responded, "Don't ask."[52]

There were other extenuating circumstances swirling around Washington at that time. The bombing took place shortly after Bill Clinton took office and terrorism was not on peoples' minds. The FBI Director at that time, William Sessions, was not long for his job and he would soon be replaced by Louis Freeh.

If the higher ups in the Justice Department did not take to the theory of another country taking part in the 1993 WTC attack, there were others in the intelligence community who had a different perspective. One of them was Vincent Cannistaro

52 Ibid. Page 108.

who held various high-level positions in Washington, including Director of Intelligence Programs at the National Security Council (1984-87), and Special Assistant for Intelligence at the Department of Defense (1987-88). He was also responsible for the intelligence investigation of the Pan Am 103 bombing over Lockerbie, Scotland.

In reviewoing Mylroie's work on the WTC investigation, he wrote a letter dated November 1, 1994 regarding the possible links between Iraq and the WTC attack. "Laurie Mylroie's manuscript on the World Trade Center bombing is one of the most brilliant pieces of research and scholarship in this area that I have ever read. She has not only carefully gathered and set forth the facts of the bombing itself, but has provided original analysis that uncovers linkages that I believe the U.S. government investigators have failed to notice. As only one example, I cite the linkage she has made between the Khansi murders outside CIA Headquarters and the World Trade Center bombing the following month. The alarms she raises about Saddam Hussein's intentions to generate terrorism in the United States are as well founded as they are alarming. A fine piece of work."

Another former FBI agent who was deeply involved in the bureau's investigation of the 1993 WTC bombing was James Fox who also wrote a letter regarding the facets of Ms. Mylroie's book.

Fox was the retired Director of the New York Office of the FBI and was a 31-year veteran of the bureau. Most of his responsibility was in the areas of counterterrorism and counterespionage. He had overall responsibility for the direction of the investigation of the bombing of the WTC in 1993.

This is part of his letter dated October 24, 1994, "I have read the manuscript regarding the bombing authored by Laurie Mylroie. In my view, this work is the most comprehensive and best researched review of the bombing investigation. Admittedly, I have a very keen interest in the bombing, but I found Mylroie's work particularly interesting, and I read it in its entirety in a very short period of time. I found it to be extremely accurate, and although we are unable to say with certainty the Iraqis were behind the bombing, that is certainly the theory accepted by most of the veteran investigators."

So, what we have here are two highly respected U.S. national security professionals who have given their opinion that Iraq was possibly involved in the 1993 WTC bombing. That is not to say that others in the U.S. intelligence community, and elsewhere, had the same opinion. It just shows the divergence of the beliefs of two men who looked at the evidence differently than people at FBI HQ.

Zacarias Moussaoui, prison photo.

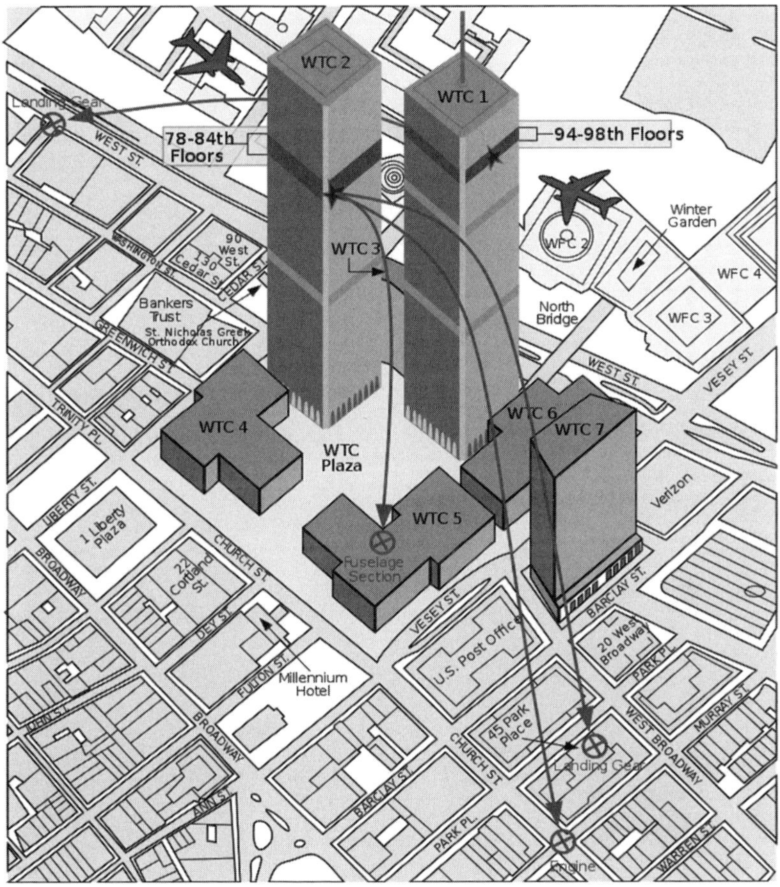

The World Trade Center, September 11, 2001, debris impact areas.

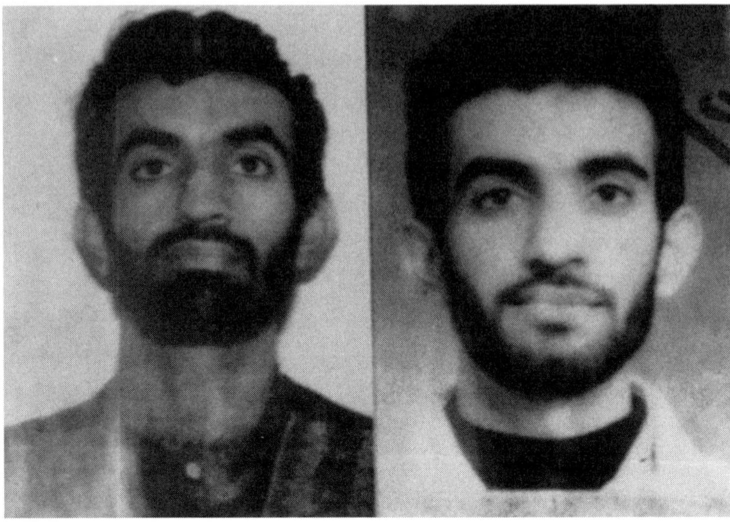

Two photos of Ramzi Yousef from the FBI.

Mohammed Jamal Khalifa was a Saudi businessman from Jeddah who married one of Osama bin Laden's sisters. He has been accused of funding terror plots and groups in the Philippines in the 1990s while head of the International Islamic Relief Organization branch there. He was murdered in Madagascar in 2007.

Chapter 7

The Iraq Connection?

In the immediate aftermath of the 1993 WTC attack, various rumors began swirling around the idea that maybe the bombing was not the work of the radical Muslim men who were arrested by the authorities, but possibly the work of a nation-state that used the arrested men as pawns in a much wider conspiracy. As mentioned in the last chapter, the FBI did not find this option a viable one, despite the fact that some members of the bureau as well as other people in the U.S. intelligence community thought differently.

Throughout history, nations have been the sponsor of state-directed terrorism against other nations for their own ends. This is especially true in wartime. If we go back in history, we can see that Hitler's invasion of Poland was the start of World War II even if the world did not know it at the time. Germany then went on to conquer most of Europe, leaving Britain alone to stop their juggernaut. It was only the Japanese attack on Pearl Harbor in December 1941 that launched the United States into the war which resulted in the defeat of Hitler's empire four years later.

In the months before the start of World War I, Archduke Franz Ferdinand was killed by a group called the Black Hand in the Serbian capital of Sarajevo headed by Colonel Dragutin Dimitrijevic, who was the chief of intelligence for the Serbian General Staff. The assassination took place on June 28, 1914. One month later, on July 28, 1914, Austria-Hungary declared war on Serbia. Over time, Germany allied itself with Austria-Hungary against England and France. This act of terrorism set off the bloodiest war in human history up to that time with millions dead before it was over.

The events of February 26, 1993 in which a group of men living in the New York Metropolitan area carried out the most deadly attack on U.S soil (with the exception of Pearl Harbor) did not require a military response because no nation or state took responsibility for the attack.

As FBI agents began investigating the attack, they might have turned their attention to Iraq if they chose to. Iraq was the logical culprit, as the regime of Saddam Hussein was no friend of the United States, dating back to the time of the Reagan administration when the United States took military action against Iraq for its state sponsored attacks against American targets in Europe which resulted in the death of many Americans.

The reason why the attack on the WTC in 1993 should interest those looking into the 9-11 attack is its mastermind, Ramzi Yousef whose uncle Khalid Sheikh Mohammed was the man behind the 9-ll plot. While Ramzi Yousef was in jail at the time of 9-11, his uncle was leading the plot (along with bin Laden) to bring down the twin towers.

A number of the men connected to the 1993 WTC attack had tenuous ties to Iraq. For example a man named Abdul Rahman Yasin, came from Baghdad, Iraq before the bombing and returned to Iraq shortly afterwards, stopping in the Iraqi embassy in Jordan on his return. Yasin was the sole indicted fugitive from that attack and remained in Iraq until at least 2002, when he was interviewed by the TV show *60 Minutes*.

Another one of the plotters who was arrested after the attack, Mohammed Salameh, had many communications with Iraq in the early stages of the WTC planning. Between June 10 and July 9, 1992, when his phone service was cut off for non-payment, he made 46 calls to Iraq. Just who he was calling is still a mystery and it would be nice to know who he was in contact with in that nation before the attack.

The United States intelligence community in the late 1990s, leading up to the millennium, was getting all sorts of intelligence from its various sources on Iraq covering many subjects, some bogus some legitimate. In February 1992, U.S. sources received information that Iraq had formed a suicide pilot program that it planned to use against British and American forces in the Persian Gulf. When the CIA found[1] out about this plan, they did some digging and found it was not credible.

In a possible action that may have been related to the 9-11 attacks,

1 Paul Thompson, *The Terror Timeline.* Page 24.

in late August 2001, less than one month before the Twin Towers went crashing down, President Hussein put his troops on high alert not seen since the Gulf War. This information was referenced by the newspaper the *Daily Telegraph* which wrote that Hussein apparently made a number of other moves suggesting foreknowledge, and the article strongly suggests Iraqi complicity in the 9-11 attacks.

In April 2001, five months before 9-11, the Bush administration had one of its first high-level meetings on terrorism vis a vi the United States. At that meeting, Richard Clarke advocated that the U.S. needed to support the Northern Alliance led by Ahmad Shah Massoud. However, in the meeting, Deputy Defense Secretary Paul Wolfowitz said that we should not be focusing on the Northern Alliance and bin Laden. He remarked, "I just don't understand why we are beginning by talking about this one man bin Laden, and who cares about a little terrorist in Afghanistan." Secretary Wolfowitz said the U.S. should focus its attention on Iraq and its state sponsored international terrorism. He claimed that in his opinion, the 1993 WTC bombing was done with Iraq's help and rejected the CIA's opinion that Iraq had no part in the bombing plot. Right after 9-11, there was a disagreement among the Bush administration's top national security officials on whom to blame. Wolfowitz wanted to invade Iraq in response to the attack, while Deputy Secretary of State Richard Armitage agreed with Clarke that bin Laden was the culprit.

Paul Wolfowitz, however, was not finished in his quest to link Saddam to the 1993 WTC bombing, even after 9-11. Around June 200l, months before 9-11, Secretary Wolfowitz asked the CIA to look into the contents of Laurie Mylroie's book *A Study in Revenge,* to see if there was anything to her thesis. While Wolfowitz asked the agency to make such a study, there is no concrete evidence to say, one way or another, if his request was approved. He later asked another top-level official in the U.S. government, Thomas Wilson, the director of the Defense Intelligence Agency to do the same. The DIA did not find anything to back up that theory.

One more warning regarding Iraq was made by Richard Perle, then the head of the Defense Policy Board, and a foreign policy advisor to President Bush. On August 6, 2001, Perle wrote a memo on the challenges the U.S. would face in the post-Cold War era. He wrote, "We're concerned about Saddam Hussein, we're concerned about the North Koreans, about some future Iranian government that may have the weapon they're now trying so hard to acquire." One should not be surprised that Iraq was part of the three nations that President Bush mentioned in his January 2002 speech as the "axis of evil."

The United States had, over the years, a longstanding relationship with Iraq. Saddam Hussein was used by the United States and the CIA as a bulwark against the Soviet domination of the Middle East. In its long history, the CIA made relationships of convenience with various military strongmen in the world, mainly in the Cold War era. For example, we supported Batista in Cuba, Diem in South Vietnam, the Shah of Iran, Trujillo in the Dominican Republic, and Noriega in Panama. All these men were ruthless dictators who were eventually overthrown or killed. Saddam Hussein, too, was used by the United States, although he began his life as nothing more than a rabble-rouser and an ineffective assassin.

The United States first began its ties with a very young Saddam Hussein when he took part in a CIA attempt to kill Prime Minister Adb al-Karim Qassim. On July 14, 1958, Qassim and his followers overthrew the Iraqi monarchy of King Fisal II. Iraq, in the 1950s, was seen by the United States as a bulwark against Soviet communism, especially in the Middle East. Iraq's strategic position was heightened by the fact that the country was rich in oil. Iraq also joined the anti-communist Baghdad Pact that included such nations as the United States, Turkey, Britain, Iran, and Pakistan.

According to various intelligence reports of the day, Saddam Hussein was under the control of both the CIA and Egyptian intelligence. One report had him in Beirut, Lebanon where he took training under the aegis of the CIA. CIA officers who knew Hussein in those days said he "was known as having no class. He was a thug—a cutthroat." In Cairo, Saddam often dined at the Andiana café and rarely paid his bills.

The regime of Adb al-Qassim ran out on February 8, 1963 when Baath Party supporters staged a coup that resulted in his ouster from power. Qassim had made the Kennedy administration angry when he took Iraq out of the Baghdad Pact, threatening to allow the Soviets into Iraq. In 1961, he also threatened to invade Kuwait and nationalized a part of the Iraq Petroleum Company.

In the end, Qassim was killed and the Baath Party indulged in an orgy of violence and killing.

Throughout much of the 1960s and 1970s, the United States was beset with problems at home and abroad, fighting a non-winnable war in Vietnam, and supplying military equipment to the rebels fighting the Russians in Afghanistan. In Iraq, Saddam Hussein had taken power and ran that country like his own personal fiefdom. However, the United States once again turned its attention to Iraq when Iran and Iraq began a years-long, bloody war that would leave thousands dead on both sides.

In 1984, the United States and Iraq repaired their mutual diplomatic relations and the first Bush administration looked to Iraq to contain Iran in the Persian Gulf. The United States knew full well who Saddam Hussein was, a ruthless dictator who had no compunction when it came to killing his own people. However, realpolitik dominated Washington and the Bush administration decided it was better to keep Saddam Hussein in power, where we could at least try to control him, than take the chance that an Iranian victory would carve up large chunks of Iraq, thus, allowing the Soviet Union an entryway into the region.

The U.S. even went one step further when it lifted Iraq from the list of nations who harbored international terrorists, even though Abu Nidal was then living in Baghdad.

In Washington, President Bush gave CIA Director William Casey *carte blanche* to aid Iraq, with whatever military/intelligence it needed. Once the decision was made to aid Iraq, Casey contacted Jordan's King Hussein and asked if he could take on the role of middleman in supplying American arms to Iraq. The King was glad to comply, and Casey even met with King Hussein on his visits to Jordan. The CIA station chief in Amman, Jordan oversaw the transfer of war materiel, much of which traveled from Jordan's port of Aqaba to Iraq. At one point in the war, when Iraq faced defeat, King Hussein personally went to Baghdad to present Saddam with U.S. satellite photos.

In 1989, the long and bitter war between Iran and Iraq ended, along with the CIA-U.S. presence in Iraq. No longer wanted or needed. The U.S. would let Iraq face its own miserable problems. The two nations would meet next, barely two years later, when

Saddam took over Kuwait and began the first Persian Gulf War.

After the war, the prevailing attitude in Washington was that somehow Saddam would be toppled either by his own military or by a revolt inside his country. Nothing of the sort happened and the United States had to find another way to topple Hussein. President George H.W. Bush made a speech in which he encouraged Iraqi dissidents to mount an insurrection against Saddam, but did nothing militarily to back his call to arms.

With no sign that Saddam's hold on power was stopping, President Bush signed a finding that allowed the CIA to step in and see if they could provoke any kind of covert mischief against Saddam. The person at Langley headquarters ordered to "create the conditions for the removal of Saddam Hussein from power" was Frank Anderson, chief of the Near East Division of the agency's Directorate of Operations. Anderson had a most difficult task ahead of him; if a coalition of over a half million troops from many nations could not topple Hussein from power, what was Anderson supposed to do with a limited budget and a few resources on the ground? Most of his work entailed the spreading of propaganda that would wind up in the hands of Saddam and his loyalists, describing the horrible fate that awaited them if they continued in office.

Iraq was what was called a "denied area," no CIA agent could enter the country to meet with any dissidents. Saddam had such a tight rein on the opposition that no Iraqi military official was allowed to travel outside of Iraq, thus causing major headaches for any agency personnel willing or able to meet with the resistance.

From the mid-1990s, under the Clinton administration, right up to the 2003 war against Iraq, the CIA mounted a number of clandestine operations inside Iraq. One such CIA effort was described in a book by ex-CIA officer Robert Baer called *See No Evil: The True Story of a Ground Soldier in the CIA's War on Terrorism* (Crown, 2002).

As Baer describes his covert actions inside Iraq, he and his small team entered the country in January 1995 in order to meet with General Wafiq al-Samarrai in the town of Zakhu. The general had defected from Saddam's army in November 1994 to plot against him. Al-Samarrai told Baer that he represented a number of disaffected Iraq generals who wanted to oust Saddam. In their discussions, the general asked Baer if the U.S. government would grant diplomatic recognition to the new leader if the coup succeeded.

As the United States geared up for war against Iraq in 2003, the CIA was given its marching orders by President Bush to shake Saddam's tree and finally right the wrong that had been left over from the 1991 Persian Gulf War.

After 9-11, President George W. Bush declared a war on international terrorism, singling out Iraq, which he believed was one of the prime movers on the world stage. If Richard Clarke is to be believed, days after the World Trade Center bombing in 2001, the President asked Clarke to find out if Saddam Hussein had anything to do with the attacks on New York and Washington. Clarke told the president that all the evidence pointed to al Qaeda and Osama bin Laden. Unmoved, the president unleashed the CIA and the entire military establishment on Iraq.

At CIA headquarters, DCI George Tenet appointed "Saul" (his read identity is still a mystery), as Chief, Iraq Operations Group—bluntly called by its detractors, "The House of Broken Toys," for its lack of success in toppling Saddam—to oversee agency operations inside Iraq. "Saul" was born in Cuba and worked for years in the Directorate of Operations; he had also served as the executive assistant to Tenet's number two, John McLaughlin.

After 9-11, Saul met with President Bush and Vice President Dick Cheney and told them that covert action would not overthrow Saddam. The only thing that would work was a military invasion.

Saul's proposal was approved and on February 20, 2002, a CIA study team arrived in Kurdish-held northern Iraq to pave the way for the later arrival of CIA paramilitary teams. The name given to the group was NILE, "Northern Iraq Liaison Elements." Over time, the CIA would infiltrate two paramilitary teams inside Iraq, with Saul in charge back at headquarters. They began recruiting teams who were supplying them with good intelligence on Saddam's army.

On March 15, 2003, Saul's men went into action, destroying trucks along the Mosul-Baghdad rail line. The rail line was destroyed and a troop train was demolished. Unknown to the American public, the destruction of the rail line set off a number of insurgent attacks on separate military and civilian targets inside Iraq. The CIA had finally been unleashed.

In the end, it was not the CIA who captured Saddam: a tip from someone on the ground led U.S. forces to Saddam's rat hole in Dawr, a town near Tikrit, Saddam's ancestral home.

So, we have two different attacks on the WTC that took place within an eight-year span (1993-2001) that might have been sponsored by Iraq but which was not investigated by the American government. While the evidence shows that Iraq had nothing to do with the September 11, 2001 attacks, which led to a devastating war in the Middle East which cost the United States thousands of lives, that cannot be said concretely when it came to the 1993 WTC bombing. There was a marked difference in the players involved and the scope of the attacks. After the 1993 attack, the FBI did nothing to look into the possible Iraq connection, while after 9-11, the Bush administration looked for some evidence to connect Saddam to the attack, thus, creating an excuse to go to war to avenge the 3,000 Americans killed that day.

Mohammed Salameh, the man who was arrested after he returned the Ryder van to a New Jersey dealership and who was arrested by the FBI, had tenuous links to Iraq in the form of his uncle named Kadri Abu Bakr (on his mother's side). Mr. Kadri Abu Bakr was the number two man in the PLO's "Western Sector" which was a terrorist unit within the PLO. The Western Sector was established in the late 1960s, when the PLO was located in Jordan. At that time, it seems that the Western Sector was heavily influenced by Iraq and the government in Baghdad surely knew all of its members, including Bakr. Abu Bakr was arrested by Israel in 1968 and was sentenced to twenty years but was released in 1986, after serving eighteen years of his term, and deported from the West Bank, and returned to Iraq. As mentioned before, Salameh made 46 calls to Iraq and it is not out of the ordinary to consider that he might have been calling Uncle Bakr to tell him what he and his co-conspirators were planning in New York.

In her book called *Study of Revenge,* Laurie Mylroie wrote that she believed that the Iraqi government had received information via Salameh's calls to his terrorist-linked uncle that something was up in New York, even perhaps the whole plot to bring down the Twin Towers. She speculates that the Iraqi government had Mr. Bakr's phone tapped and would have heard all of his conversations with his nephew. She writes,

> The Iraq regime would have suspected Abu Bakr to tell it about something as important as a bombing conspiracy in New York. Indeed, had Abu Bakr not reported the news to Iraqi authorities, he might have raised suspicions about himself. That in turn, would have made him liable to arrest, interrogation, and torture by Iraqi security forces. Thus, even if Abu Bakr had not been spontaneously inclined to report the actions of his nephew in New York to Iraqi intelligence, a prudent man might well have felt obliged to do so. Perhaps, even, Abu Bakr approved of his nephew's plans.

Enter the picture an American citizen named Abdul Rahman Yasin, then thirty-two years old, who traveled from Iraq to Jordan. He applied for and received an American passport from the U.S. Embassy in Amman, Jordan. Prior to his arrival in Jordan, Yasin had been living in Baghdad and thus had no trouble getting the proper papers to enter the United States. One week after the WTC bombing, Yasin was questioned by the FBI for his possible participation in the bombing plot but they found no sufficient evidence to hold him in custody and he was allowed to leave the country. It seems that while Yasin was living in the United States, Ramzi Yousef and Mohammed Salameh were living in the apartment directly above Yasin's. It is more than likely that the three men were acquainted with each other, due to their origins and religious beliefs. Days after the bombing, FBI agents searched Yasin's apartment where they found traces of bomb explosives on a scale, a tool box, and a shirt. They also found in the garbage jeans with an acid hole burned in them, and torn pieces of a map showing the route to Yousef's other apartment. Yasin was taken into custody where he was questioned by the FBI including agent Neil Herman, the head of the FBI's WTC bombing investigation. During their conversation, Yasin gave them information on both Salameh and Ramzi Yousef, and other members of the bomb plot. A day later, Yasin took the FBI to the apartment where the bomb was made. That same day, he abruptly left the United States and went back to Iraq. Later, Agent Neil Herman said, "There was not enough information to hold him and detain him. And the decision was made, and he was allowed to leave."

After the 1993 WTC bombing, the government of Iraq, if it had some part in the affair, went into damage control. If Ramzi Yousef was one of their own, they would want to distance themselves from his operation as soon as possible. As the smoke from 9-11 cleared, in 2002, the government sent out Deputy Prime Minister Tariq Aziz to make a statement to the press. He said, "I have to tell you that we feared that sending Yasin back to Iraq [in 1993] was a sting operation [enabling the U.S. to] tell people later on, look, this man who participated in that event now is in Iraq, etc. and use it as they are doing now, using many false pretexts, you see, to hurt Iraq in their own way."

Yasin was indicted for his participation in the WTC attack in August 1993 and a $25 million bounty was placed on him. In October 2001, Yasin was interviewed by CBS news in Iraq and he told his questioners that he was part of the bombing plot but said that he was NOT an Iraqi government agent. For their part, the Iraqi's said that Yasin was put in prison without any charges being brought against him. If he was indeed an Iraqi agent, the best place for him to be would be in a closed prison where he would have no access to any journalist with whom he might talk.

Besides certain members of the FBI like James Fox and Vincent Cannistraro, there were other high-level American officials who took an interest in the so-called Iraq connection to the 1993 WTC bombing case. One of these people was former CIA Director James Woolsey who served in that position from Feb. 5, 1993 to Jan. 10, 1995. James Wolsey went to England to investigate any possible Iraq links to Ramzi Yousef's plan. His intention on the trip was to somehow show that Ramzi Yousef and a man named Abdul Basit, a Pakistani student, were one and the same. While in Europe, he paid a visit to the Swansea Institute where Basit once studied. Basit completed his studies at Swansea in June 1989 and upon graduation, returned to Pakistan where he got a job at the National Computer Center in Kuwait's Planning Ministry. One of Woolsey's reasons for going to Swansea was to find out if Basit's fingerprints were on file, and if they matched Yousef's. The newspaper chain Knight Ridder wrote, "Several of those with knowledge of the trips said they failed to produce any new evidence that Iraq was behind the attacks." Another American publication, *Newsweek,* also reported in 2004 that, "the results of the Woolsey mission were exactly what the FBI had predicted; that the fingerprints were in fact identical."

Woolsey's trip to England piqued the curiosity of certain British officials who wanted to know what the ex-CIA chief was up to. It seems that the local police in Swansea were more than curious about Woolsey's presence and they in turn, called the U.S. embassy in London to make inquiries. They wanted to know if Woolsey was there on behalf of the United States government. In time, both the State Department and the CIA found out about Woolsey's trip and they too wanted to know what was going on. One person in the intelligence loop said of the Woolsey trip, "It was a stupid, stupid and just plain wrong thing to do." The Woolsey trip caught the attention of two of the most important Bush administration figures, CIA Director George Tenet and Secretary of State Colin Powell. We don't know what their official reaction was but one can assume that it wasn't positive.

Paul Wolfowitz now resumed his Iraq connection thesis when he asked President Bush to declare Ramzi Yousef an "enemy combatant" while he was then languishing in a Supermax prison. Wolfowitz wanted Ramzi Yousef to be given harsh interrogations by jailers to find out what he knew regarding any further information on terrorist activities, including any more information regarding any Iraq connection to the 1993 attack. The FBI opposed giving Yousef any harsh interrogations and furthermore, debunked any Iraqi connection to Yousef. "At one point, the high-level discussions apparently prompted a top Bureau of Prisons official to make an unauthorized entry to Yousef's cell to sound out his willingness to talk—a move that prompted strong protests to the Justice Department from the bomber's lawyer. The issue was debated at the highest levels of the Bush administration until the start of the U.S. invasion of Iraq after 9-11. One lawyer who was involved in the discussions said of the entire affair said, 'We talked it to death.'[2]

However, it seems that United States government agents took enough notice regarding Secretary Wolfowitz's request for information regarding Yousef that by late July or early August 2001, they changed their minds and opened up a quiet investigation to see where it led. They wanted to know, one way or another, if Ramzi

2 History Commons: 2002-Early 2003-Wolfowitz Still Pushing Unlikely Theory linking WTC bombing to Iraqi Government.

Yousef was really Abdul Basit. Laurie Mylroie wrote that Basit was living with his parents in Kuwait in 1990 when Saddam's troops invaded that country. "During the occupation, Iraqis presumably murdered him and his family and then altered the police file so Iraqi intelligence could use his identity." It is posited by Mylroie and others that Yousef stole the identity of Basit and was then studying in Wales. Woolsey wrote a piece in the *New Republic* which said regarding this theory, "then it was Iraq that went after the World Trade Center last time. Which makes it much more plausible that Iraq has done so again." Woolsey wrote after the 9-11 attacks that, "Intelligence and law enforcement officials investigating the case would do well to at least consider another possibility: that the attacks—whether perpetrated by bin Laden and his associates or by others—were sponsored, supported, and perhaps even ordered by Saddam Hussein. As yet, there is no evidence of explicit state sponsorship of the September 11 attacks. But absence of evidence is not evidence of absence."

Director James Woolsey expanded on his thinking about the 1993 WTC bombing in a far-reaching interview he did with the PBS show *Frontline*. In the interview, he expressed his feelings about the people and events surrounding the bomb plot. He said he first began looking deeply into the event in January 1995 shortly before the capture of Ramzi Yousef and his reading of Ms. Mylroie's book. Woolsey was particularly interested in the activities of Yasin, who was an Iraq-American who fled to Iraq after the bombing. Woolsey brought up the fact that the U.S. government never asked for his extradition from Iraq (and if they did, the Iraqis probably wouldn't have released him anyway).

Woolsey said that most of the people who were arrested following the attack were of limited intelligence, except for Yasin and Ramzi Yousef. He was interested in the fact that after the attack, Ramzi Yousef fled the U.S. carrying a Pakistani passport under the name of Abdul Basit. The question now is who gave Ramzi Yousef the passport under the Basit name and did he have any state sponsored help in doing so? When asked by the Frontline interviewer about Ramzi Yousef, Woolsey said the following: "Don't know. He may be Ramzi Yousef. He may be Abdul Basit, a Pakistani. One thing does seem reasonably clear to me, which is that he's a sophisticated man.

He's a subtle man, and he's the sort of man who might well have a tie to an intelligence organization. I don't think he is some member of a pick-up basketball team who just sort of decided to put some chemicals together and blow something up. I think he's someone's agent and my best guess would be Iraq. But I can't prove it."

When asked if Ramzi Yousef was part of bin Laden's organization he said it was possible, but that he also might have been working for some other intelligence agency as well. "One of the things that makes me the most tired about this public discussion of this issue is that people assume that if someone might have been working with bin Laden, that means he's not also working with an intelligence service. It's entirely possible for Yousef to have been involved with an intelligence service as well, maybe, with bin Laden's organization."

The former DCI criticized the Clinton administration for the way they handled the Yousef case. "I think one of the big mistakes here was that the Clinton administration really turned most of these terrorist investigations over completely to law enforcement and kept it focused on the problem of prosecuting and convicting people, as distinct from looking under the rocks carefully, of possible state sponsorship."

Relating to a possible link to Iraqi state sponsorship, he talked about the fact that Saddam Hussein tried to assassinate the late President George H.W. Bush. He said of Saddam Hussein, "Saddam is a very cynical man and he sees that some of the religious extremists are able to hurt the United States. He likes to see the United States hurt, so he'll make common cause with whoever he needs to."

Unlike many other people in the U.S. government who said that Iraq had no part in the 1993 WTC bombing case, Mr. Woolsey said it had. He was just as convinced of his views as the others were of theirs. When asked to give some evidence for his views on Iraq he said in the *Frontline* interview,

> If the U.S. government would now go back and look at all of these previous terrorists incidents—the bombing in East Africa, the Cole, all the others—and look beyond bin Laden, beyond the terrorists, and see if there is anything anywhere that points toward foreign government involvement—and

> by the way, some of these may be Iran and not Iraq; it's not only a possibility of Iraq—I think they might turn some things up.[3]

He continued on the same path, finishing his theme on Saddam by saying,

> I don't know how many pieces of evidence one needs in the case of someone like Saddam Hussein. We are not, after all, trying to convict him in a court of law beyond a reasonable doubt. We're trying to make a judgment about American foreign policy and national security policy and whether that set of circumstances creates enough material for us to make a judgment that he has been actively involved in terrorist incidents against the United States.

Mr. Woolsey also took on a question about allegations that Saddam's ambassador to Turkey was an intelligence agent and that he possibly went to see bin Laden in Afghanistan. He said he'd heard those rumors that, "[If] Mr. Hijazi went to see bin Laden or anybody in the leadership of al Qaeda in Afghanistan—I think that was 1998—that to me, would be yet another substantial piece of information suggesting that Saddam Hussein and not only al Qaeda has been behind some of these terrorist incidents against us and indeed, that Saddam and al Qaeda could quite well be working together."

His interviewer then asked him a question regarding a possible trip by Mohamed Atta to Prague, Czechoslovakia where he was supposed to have met with some sort of intelligence agent. "There have been reports that on at least one and perhaps more than one occasion, Mr. Atta, who was probably the central figure in the events of September 11—at least of the 19 in this country—when he was living in Hamburg before he came to the United States, visited Prague, met with an Iraqi intelligence officer-someone who was declared persona non grata last spring by the Czech government. That would be yet another one or more indicators of cooperation between terrorists attacking the United States and the government of Iraq."

3 Interviews-R. James Woolsey/Gunrunning for Saddam/*Frontline*/PBS.

Mr. Woolsey's characterization of Iraq as a state sponsor of international terrorism only goes so far. He is right to say that Saddam Hussein was no friend of the United States, and never was, until his death. Also, if one looks at the facts surrounding Ramzi Yousef and Abdul Basit, there are striking similarities. It is entirely possible that Ramzi Yousef took on the Basit persona in some sort of high-leverage international plot to destroy the WTC in 1993 and that the man now serving a life sentence in the Supermax is Abdul Basit, not Ramzi Yousef. It is a lot to think about.

As part of its investigation into the September 11, 2001 attacks, the National Commission on Terrorist Attacks Upon the United States (the 9-11 Commission) made a study of the idea of state sponsored attacks in recent times, including the 1993 WTC bombing and the Abdul Basit-Ramzi Yousef case. On July 9, 2003, they called in Laurie Mylroie whose book had gotten the attention of the Commission to testify before its members. Her appearance was the third public hearing of the 9-11 Commission and the following details were what she told the Commission members that day.

The Commission opened its report by writing, "Prior to the February 26, 1993 bombing of the World Trade Center, it was assumed that major terrorist attacks against the U.S. were state-sponsored. But that bombing is said to mark the start of a new kind of terrorism that does not involve states. That notion is dubious. Rather, the claim that a new, stateless terrorism emerged with the 1993 Trade Center bombing was a convenient explanation in that it required no military response. Once promulgated, it was hastily accepted—even before much progress had been made in the investigation of that attack itself.

"The key point I want to stress is the identity of the terrorist masterminds, individuals like Ramzi Yousef and Khalid Sheikh Mohammed. Their identities rest on documents in Kuwait that predate Kuwait's liberation in 1991, and those documents are unreliable, because of the Iraq occupation."

The first area of interest for the Commission was the 1993 WTC bombing and the fact that certain individuals in FBI's New York office suspected Iraq of complicity, including Jim Fox whose name has been mentioned in a previous chapter. They wrote, "Fox's background was counter-intelligence. He believed the inexperienced individuals he was arresting immediately after the bombing—Mohammed Salameh, the 26-year old Palestinian, detained as he returned to the Ryder rental agency for his deposit on the van that carried the bombing were incapable of carrying out such an attack themselves. The arrests were too easy and their ease suggested to Fox a conspiracy masterminded by others, with Salameh et. al, left behind to take the blame."

Point two was a description of those people who may have been linked to Iraq such as Abdul Rahman Yasin. Point three was the fact that the bombing took place two years after the Gulf War and that Iraq remained America's greatest enemy in the Middle East. Point three detailed Mohammed Salameh's numerous calls to Iraq, some 46 in total before his service was cut off.

Mylroie's main thesis that day was the role played by Ramzi Yousef and his links to Iraq. The points she made were the following: He (Ramzi Yousef) entered the U.S. on an Iraqi passport as Ramzi Yousef and left the U.S. the night of the WTC bombing in the name of Abdul Basit Karim. In December 1992, Yousef went to the Pakistani consulate in New York with Xerox copies of pages from Karim's 1984 and 1988 passports. Yousef claimed to be Karim and said he had lost his passport and needed a new one to return home. The consulate did not like the documentation, because there were no original documents, but still gave Yousef a temporary passport, which he used to flee the U.S.

She then went on to describe the story of Basit Karim and how it related to Ramzi Yousef. Among the highlights were the following.

Abdul Basit Karim was a real person, born in Kuwait where he graduated from high school at age 18. He then studied in Britain for three years and got a degree in 1989 before returning home. The signature in the 1984 passport was different from the signature in the 1988 passport. In the paperwork for the 1984 passport, his permanent address was in Karachi, Pakistan, while the 1988 passport gives a permanent address in Baluchistan. The copies of these two passports have different signatures and different permanent addresses. It looks like at least one page went through a scanner and was changed. A similar problem exists with Abdul Basit Karim's file in Kuwait. As a routine matter, the Kuwait Interior Ministry maintained a resident alien file on Karim. That file was tampered with. Information was taken out. The file should have included copies of the front pages of Karim's passport with the picture, signature, etc. That is missing, and the Kuwaitis attributed it to Iraq's occupation. But the Kuwaitis did not recognize that the whole file had been corrupted.

Ms. Mylroie focused her attention on one main point: was Ramzi Yousef really Karim or were the fingerprint cards switched and the file otherwise tampered with to create a false identity for him? She pointed out the fact that James Fox of the FBI, as well as Judge Kevin Duffy who presided over the Yousef trials, believed that Yousef was not Karim. At the end of the trial, Judge Duffy told Yousef in court, "We don't even know what your real name is. That is correct. Ramzi Yousef is an alias and so is Abdul Basit Karim."

Laurie Mylroie met with a few of Karim's teachers at the Swansea school and they gave her a glowing report on their former student. The said he would never be capable of doing what he was charged with and said that he went to the mosque every Friday for prayers. They also discussed the height of Karim/Yousef. When he was sentenced to jail in the U.S., Yousef was 6 feet tall, while Basit Karim was shorter. His teachers said that Karim was approximately 5'6" or 5'8," and said he was never 6' feet, as was Yousef. Ms. Mylroie wrote of this discrepancy, "If that is right and Yousef is not Karim, that means the fingerprint card in Karim's file was switched, and the file otherwise tampered with. The evident purpose would have been to create a false identity for Yousef. Indeed, this is a standard practice of Soviet-style intelligence agencies. As is well known, intelligence agents not posted to an embassy (and not enjoying diplomatic immunity), are 'illegals.' They are routinely given false identities, or 'legends' to prevent their actions from being traced back to the country they work for. If Karim's file in Kuwait was tampered with to create a legend for Yousef, there is only one party that reasonably could have done so: Iraq while it occupied Kuwait."

Her next point of contention in front of the Commission that day was the 1995 plane bombing plot involving three Baluch men: Yousef, Murad and Mohammed. She began her testimony recalling that after the 1993 WTC bombing, Yousef fled the U.S and wound up in the Philippines where he and his associates were planning to blow up numerous U.S. carriers over the Pacific Ocean. While Yousef fled his hideaway, his co-conspirator, Abdul Hakim Murad, was captured by Philippine police. Also, KSM—Yousef's uncle, was involved in the plane plot and he too fled the Philippines and was subsequently indicted.

In her testimony, Ms. Mylroie concentrated on the roles played by Khalid Sheikh Mohammed. She was told by a U.S. intelligence official, "It wasn't until recently that any of us even realized he was part of al Qaeda. The big problem nailing him down is that the informants we relied on, especially before 9-11, were mujahideen. They'd been in Afghanistan, in Sudan, back in Afghanistan. Khalid was never part of any of that." She also pointed out that two of Yousef's brothers, Abdul Karim and Abdul Monim, were members of al Qaeda and were possibly in line to have played a large part in al Qaeda's operations.

She then wrote, "Also, all of these masterminds are Baluch. And with the possible exception of the cousin (Abdul Aziz) all are supposed to have been born and raised in Kuwait—and their identities are based on documents in Kuwait that predate Kuwait's liberation."

The Baluch are a Sunni Muslim group who lived on both sides of the Iranian-Pakistani border and have sought to have their own country for years. Up until 1993, the State Department had no Baluchi on their terrorist radar and they never threatened U.S. interests.

According to her testimony, Iraq intelligence had a deep relationship with the Baluch and used them against Iran. She said that General Wafiq Samarrai, who headed Iraqi Military Intelligence until 1991, said the Iraqi military ran the Baluch as spies during the Iran-Iraq war out of the Gulf kingdom of Dubai. She postulates, "The only apparent motive of these Baluch individuals for involvement in assaulting the U.S. would appear to be the ties that the Baluch have with Iraqi intelligence. That is particularly so as Yousef, Murad, and Mohammed do not really appear to be Islamic militants, judging from their behavior in the Philippines."

Mylroie speculates that when Iraq took over Kuwait prior to the first Gulf War, someone in its intelligence service faked documents to create legends for the three men.

Another person who believed in the Baluch theory regarding the three men was author James Hoagland. Hoagland wanted to know how al Qaeda grew from virtually nothing on the world stage to being able to down the WTC almost at will, passing by the huge U.S. intelligence network. Mr. Hoagland then hinted at an answer, "Could al Qaeda have been the target of a takeover operation by an intelligence service with good legend-manufacturing skills and a great, burning desire for revenge on the United States?"

Mylroie ended her discussion by making these points. She said that, in her opinion, after al Qaeda came to Afghanistan, Iraqi intelligence made a deal with bin Laden. While bin Laden provided the foot soldiers to attack America, Iraq would provide the necessary training, direction, and the intelligence needed for al Qaeda to succeed in its war against America. While al Qaeda took responsibility for the attacks against American targets, their benefactor, Iraq, was hidden behind various layers and never seen as their masterminds.[4]

In order to further promulgate her Saddam/Iraq connection, Mylroie faced author Peter Bergen on a Canadian news broadcast in February 2003, in the lead up to the Iraq war. Bergen had a less than stellar regard for Mylroie and he called her a "crackpot." Bergen said that Ms. Mylroie opened up the conversation by "lecturing in a hectoring tone: Listen, we're going to war because President Bush believes Saddam Hussein was involved in 9/11. Al Qaeda is a front for Iraqi intelligence and that the U.S. bureaucracy made a tremendous blunder that refused to acknowledge these links. The people responsible for gathering this information, say in the CIA, are also the same people who contributed to the blunder on 9/11 and the deaths of 3,000 Americans, and so whenever this information emerges, they move to discredit it."

Bergen said that her theories defy all "intelligence and common sense, as they imply a conspiracy by literally thousands of American officials to suppress the truth of the links between Iraq and 9-11." Needless to say, they both came away from the

4 National Commission on Terrorist Attacks Upon the United States, Statement of Lauri Mylroie, July 9, 2003.

interview no nearer to an agreement than when they started.

Peter Bergen summed up his thinking about Laurie Mylroie and her conspiracy theories regarding Iraq and 9-11. "Mylroie became enamored of her theory that Saddam was the mastermind of a vast anti-US terrorist conspiracy in the face of virtually all evidence and expert opinion to the contrary. In what amounts to the discovery of a unified theory of terrorism, Mylroie believes that Saddam was not only behind the '93 Trade Center attack, but also every anti-American terrorist incident in the past decade. By the mid-90s, the Joint Terrorism Task Force in New York, the FBI, the U.S. Attorney's Office had all found no evidence implicating the Iraqi government in the first Trade Center attack."

One of the most important events that took place prior to 9-11 was the covert summit meeting of a dozen of bin Laden's al Qaeda members which took place in Kuala Lumpur, Malaysia from January 5 to 8, 2001, nine months before the attacks, including some of the hijackers (more about this meeting in the next chapter). During the meeting, there were discussions regarding the attack on the USS Cole and 9-11. Some of those who attended the meeting were KSM, the hijackers Nawaf al Hazmi and Khalid al-Midhar. Another person who was supposed to have been at the conference, but which was never confirmed, was a man named Ahmad Hikmat Shakir, an al Qaeda agent of Iraqi nationality. If he was indeed in that meeting, there is yet another Iraqi connection, not to the 1993 WTC attack but to 9-11 itself.

Another possible Iraqi link to terrorist activities in the United States came in a report which was dated August 1, 2001 in which it was alleged by the owner of a hotel in Oklahoma City that Zacharias Moussaoui, and the 9-11 hijackers Mohamed Atta and Marwan al-Shehhi all stayed at the hotel the same day. This possible lead was investigated by the FBI but they never took it seriously."The *LA Weekly* speculated that the FBI may have wanted to ignore this lead because it could force the FBI to reopen its investigation of Middle Eastern connections to the 1995 Oklahoma City blast. Convicted bombers Timothy McVeigh and Terry Nichols reportedly stayed at the same motel, interacting with a group of Iraqis during the weeks before the bombing.

In 1994, Mohammed al-Khilewi, the First Secretary at the

Saudi Mission to the United Nations defected and sought political asylum in the United States. He met with a number of FBI agents and offered to give them reams of documents on the Saudi royal family's internal corruption but the FBI refused to look at them. What was so important about this event was the fact that the documents included "details of the $7 billion the Saudis gave to Iraq (Saddam Hussein) for his nuclear program-the first attempt to build an Islamic Bomb. However, the FBI agents were ordered not to accept evidence of Saudi criminal activity, even on U.S. soil."[5]

Earlier in this work, the author told the story of how the George W. Bush administration sought to link Saddam Hussein to the 9-11 attack. In the years since, a number of former Bush administration officials have spoken out regarding what they saw and heard in the days following 9-11. One of these men was Paul O'Neill who served as the Treasury Secretary under President Bush. In his 2004 memoir, Paul O'Neill wrote the following, "From the very beginning there was a conviction that Saddam Hussein was a bad person and that he had to go. There was no dissent amongst top officials to this idea. It was all about finding a way to do it. That was the tone of it. The president saying, "Go find me a way to do this. For men, the notion of pre-emption, that the U.S. has the unilateral right to do whatever we decide to do, is really a huge leap. In the 23 months I was Treasury Secretary, I never saw anything that I would characterize as evidence of weapons of mass destruction."

On February 1, 2001, the Bush administration chaired its second National Security Council Meeting which Paul O'Neill attended. He said that Defense Secretary Donald Rumsfeld argued for the removal of Saddam Hussein, and they talked about a post-Saddam Iraq. Rumsfeld was quoted as saying, that the removal of Hussein would "demonstrate what U.S. policy is all about."

One of the reasons for us going to war against Iraq after 9-11 was the security of Iraq's vast oil reserves. A report was commissioned in April 2001 that was headed by former U.S. Secretary of State James Baker and the Council on Foreign Relations. The report was given to Vice President Dick Cheney who was a longstanding hawk when it came to Iraq. The report said that the United States needed a long-term, cheap supply of oil and that if it ran out, the

5 *The Terror Timeline*, Page 277.

government should do all it could to make sure the spigot never stopped. The report warned "that the United States is running out of oil, with a painful end to cheap fuel already in sight." It argued that "the United States remains a prisoner of its energy dilemma, and that one of the consequences of this is a need for military intervention to secure its oil supply." The report further said that Iraq had to be overthrown in order for us to continue having ready oil supplies in the United States.

Immediately after 9-11, Donald Rumsfeld received information relating to a possible Iraq connection. In notes that were taken in a meeting which were released a year later, the Defense Secretary was told that three of the hijackers were related to al Qaeda. The note stated, "Rumsfeld wanted the best info fast. Judge whether good enough to hit S.H. [Saddam Hussein] at same time. Not only UBL [bin Laden]. Go massive. Sweep it up. Things related, and not." *Time* magazine wrote in May 2002 that Rumsfeld, "has been so determined to find a rationale for an attack that on ten separate occasions he asked the CIA to find evidence linking Iraq to the terror attacks of September 11. The intelligence agencies repeatedly came back empty-handed." Rumsfeld also said that there were better military targets in Iraq than Afghanistan and that is where the focus should be directed.

Another former top-ranking U.S. military officer, retired General Wesley Clark, added his voice to the Bush administration's rush to war against Saddam Hussein. Clark said, "immediately after 9-11 there was a concerted effort to pin 9/11 and the terrorism problem on Saddam Hussein and use the attacks as an excuse to go after the Iraqi dictator." When asked by a reporter where this information came from he said, "Well, it came from the White House, it came from people around the White House, it came from all over." Clark also said that around this time he got a call from an overseas source of his urging him to put forward an Iraqi connection whenever he was on television.

Another possible connection to Iraq which will be given more room later in this book is a suspected trip made by the hijacker Mohamed Atta to Prague, Czech Republic where he allegedly met with an unidentified agent of Iraq. This information was relayed by a single person who lived in the Arab community in that city who said he knew about the meeting. The Czech officials had heard about the meeting but gave it no credence. Yet, the story was just one of the more controversial events surrounding the 9-11 story.

In January 2002, at his State of the Union address, President Bush addressed the Congress and called our enemies "the axis of evil" including Iraq. At that time, Joint Chiefs of Staff Chairman Richard Meyers said, "the goal has never been to get bin Laden." On September 17, President Bush signed a top secret memo directing the military to draw up plans to attack Afghanistan. Also included in that order was an order to the Pentagon to draw up plans to invade Iraq. It seems that Bush had two culprits in mind; bin Laden for 9-11 and Saddam Hussein for whatever reason he could come up with at the time. If the U.S. wasn't willing or interested in taking on Saddam after the 1993 WTC attack, maybe now would be a better time due to the horror of the 9-11 attacks.

Within weeks of the 9-11 attacks, calls from the right wing of the Republican Party as well as a number of right-wing think tanks in Washington began calling for a war against Iraq. One of these was the New American Century (PNAC) which sent a letter to President Bush suggesting an invasion of Iraq. However, there was not total unanimity within the White House as Secretary of State Colin Powell urged that we take on al Qaeda, not Iraq.

Among top-level officials in the Bush administration at that time was Douglas Feith, the Undersecretary of Defense for Policy, who called for an attack on Iraq. Feith created the Counterterrorism Evaluation Group whose goals were to link state actors to various terrorist groups around the world, including the regime of Saddam Hussein. Speaking of the group, the *New York Times* said, "Some intelligence experts charge that the unit had a secret agenda to justify a war with Iraq and was staffed with people who were handpicked by conservative Pentagon policy makers to arrive at preordained conclusions about Iraq and al Qaeda."

The case against Iraq now went to court, when on September 4, 2002, 1,400 relatives of the victims of 9-11 sued Iraq for more than $1 trillion dollars, claiming that they had evidence that Iraq had conspired with al Qaeda on the 9-11 attacks. The group cited an article in an Iraqi newspaper written by Naeem Abd Muhalhal on July 21, 2001. He wrote that bin Laden was thinking "seriously, with the seriousness of the Bedouin of the desert, about the way he will try to bomb the Pentagon after he destroys the White House." He added that bin Laden "is insisting very convincingly that he will strike America on the arm that is already hurting." That phrase seemingly related to the 1993 WTC attack. The lawsuit was based largely on the idea that Iraqi officials were aware of plans to attack American landmarks, yet did not warn their archenemy, the U.S. Former CIA agent Robert Bear was hired by the legal team of the claimants to find evidence of a meeting between Mohamed Atta and Iraqi agents on April 8, 2001, but despite the help of the CIA, he was unable to find proof of any such meeting.[6]

If the Bush administration was trying to link Saddam to 9-11, they were not getting much help from our allies, namely France and England. Both countries' intelligence agencies denied any Iraq-al Qaeda connection, including a meeting between Atta and an Iraq agent in Prague. Vincent Cannistraro, the CIA's former head of counterintelligence said in this regard, "Basically, cooked information is working its way into high-level pronouncements and there's a lot of unhappiness about it in intelligence, especially among analysts at the CIA."

On March 20, 2003, allied forces invaded Iraq, launching an almost twenty year war which, at this writing, is still going on, changing the entire culture of the Middle East for years to come. One of the reasons for the attack on Iraq was the view that Saddam Hussein had weapons of mass destruction which were never found—none had existed.

Two of the top al Qaeda prisoners, KSM—Khalid Sheikh Mohammed—and Abu Zabaida told their interrogators in June of 2003 that bin Laden vetoed a longstanding relationship with Saddam Hussein because he didn't want to be in Saddam's debt.

Vice President Dick Cheney, a neo-conservative when it came to American intervention in the Middle East, said at that time, "I think it's not surprising that people make the connection between Iraq and 9-11. If we are successful in Iraq, then we will have struck a major blow right at the heart of the base, if you will, the geographic base of the terrorists who had us under assault now for many years, but most especially on 9-11."

It seems that VP Cheney was not yet finished with his assertions

6 *The Terror Timeline*. Page 325.

regarding an Iraqi connection to 9-11. In June 2004, he repeated his claim that "Hussein had long-established ties with al Qaeda." This was at odds with the statement by the 9-11 Commission that found no link between Iraq and 9-11. It was reported that Cheney, not yet willing to let go of the Iraq connection said in response to the 9-11 Commission, "that we don't know if Iraq was involved in 9-11, says no one has been able to confirm, or knock down the claims regarding Atta's alleged meeting in Prague. He also said that he probably knows information the commission does not." VP Cheney and the 9-11 Commission agreed to disagree when it came to any ties between Iraq and al Qaeda. One of them is wrong. But who?

Vice President Dick Cheney now made comments regarding the circumstances of none other than Abdul Yasin, a possible Iraq agent and his role in the 1993 WTC events. In an interview he gave on *Meet the Press* in September 2003, he told the following regarding Yasin and Iraq. "We know, that one of the bombers was Iraqi, and returned to Iraq after the attack of '93. And we've learned subsequent to that, since we went into Baghdad and got into intelligence files from the Iraqi government that this individual probably also received financing from the Iraqi government as well as safe haven."

Dick Cheney was one of the point men for the early Bush administration's decision to go to war with Iraq and his views made the president take notice. While the Bush administration was taking flack in the press and from the Democrats for its allegations regarding Saddam's possible acquisition of weapons of mass destruction, Cheney came to the president's defense. Speaking to the conservative group the American Enterprise Institute in Washington, he defended the president's actions. He told the assembled group, "The flaws in intelligence are plain in hindsight, but any suggestion that the prewar information was distorted, hyped, fabricated by the leader of the nation is utterly false."

Cheney was also a supporter of Ahmed Chalabi, who was an anti-Saddam activist in Iraq who had founded the Iraqi National Congress whose ultimate goal was the removal of Saddam from power. Chalabi had friends among the neo-conservative elite in the United States, including Dick Cheney, and Chalabi roamed the halls of Washington seeking support for his efforts. As many friends as Chalabi made in Washington, he made many enemies as well, including many people in the U.S. intelligence community. Former *New York Times* reporter Chris Hedges said succinctly of Chalabi, "I thought he was unreliable and corrupt. But just because someone is a sleazebag doesn't mean he might not know something or that everything he is saying is wrong." Beginning in 1992, the Iraqi National Congress received over $100 million dollars from the United States, much of it being funneled from the CIA and the State Department. Of this sum, almost $33 million came from the Bush administration between 2001 and May 2004, when Chalabi's finding was abruptly cut off by Washington. Chalabi pressed his new conservative friends in Washington to concentrate on the removal of Saddam and forget about Afghanistan.

In an interview he gave to Jane Mayer of the *New Yorker,* Chalabi said the following, "Look, our focus was on Saddam's crimes, moral crimes, genocide. We were not focused on WMD. The U.S. asked us, we didn't bring these people up; they asked us. They requested help from us."

Cheney was also visible in front of the cameras any chance he could get and in the run-up to the attack on Iraq, he accused Saddam of having weapons of mass destruction and said the Iraqi ruler would use them if necessary. All this talk of Saddam's having WMD resulted in the controversy in which it was alleged by Bush that Iraq was in the process of getting enriched uranium from the Congo (Niger) and Somalia. All this led up to the scandal that involved two of Bush's top officials in the White House (Lewis "Scooter" Libby who was Cheney's Chief of Staff and Karl Rove who was a top advisor to President Bush) and veteran CIA officer Valerie Plame Wilson and her husband, former ambassador Joseph Wilson. Wilson would not corroborate the story that Niger was supplying yellowcake uranium to Iraq, so the White House outed his wife's CIA identity. After the Niger-yellowcake-WMD scandal erupted, both Scooter Libby and Karl Rove left the administration under a cloud of corruption.

VP Cheney and Lewis Libby were constant visitors to CIA headquarters while George Tenet was director. They met with CIA officers who were working on Iraqi issues and asked them constant and detailed questions regarding the possibility that Saddam had

WMDs. Cheney was an outspoken critic of the CIA regarding Iraq and said they had made grave errors because they discounted the fact that Saddam might have had such weapons.

Cheney told his CIA briefers that there was a connection between Saddam Hussein and al Qaeda, despite the agency's refusal to agree with him. "It was like they were hoping we'd find something buried in the files or come back with a different answer," Michael Sulick, deputy chief of the CIA's Directorate of Operations, later said. There was no obvious pressure by Cheney and Libby to change the answers. But the questions and the frequent visits by the vice president had created an environment that was subtly, but unmistakably, influencing the agency's work. The CIA's analysts, Sulick believed, had become :overly eager to please."[7]

Lewis Libby too was not a fan of the CIA when it came to Iraq, and badgered the agency to supply them raw data from the intelligence files that came flooding in each day. "Libby sent requests to the CIA that generated between three hundred and five hundred documents, including e-mails, internal memos, and reports. The agency estimated that finding and retrieving from its files all the queries it had received from Libby—and all the responses it had sent back, would take nearly a year."

When the money flow from the U.S. to Chalabi's INC went dry, VP Cheney came to its defense in a public and private way. He lobbied the various departments to have the money restored but to no avail. Cheney supported Chalabi's internal intelligence network inside of Iraq and distrusted the information coming out of Langley headquarters regarding Saddam and his possible WMDs. In one meeting regarding Chalabi and his INC, Cheney said, "We're getting ready to go to war, and we're nickel and diming the INC at a time when they're providing us with unique intelligence on Iraqi WMD."

Cheney was also at loggerheads with Dr. David Kay whose job it was to locate Saddam's WMD. At one point Kay had a meeting in Washington with top members of the Bush team to discuss his hunt for the missing WMDs. At the meeting were Dick Cheney, Donald Rumsfeld, and Paul Wolfowitz. He told them that his search for Saddam's supposed WMDs had come up empty, that

7 Isikoff, Michael and David Corn, *Hubris,* Crown Publishers, New York, 2006, Page 4-5.

there was no smoking gun, so to speak, something they didn't want to hear. He also told them that his team found no evidence of the possibility that the trailer-mounted labs that Saddam was supposed to have were designed for producing biological weapons. After that particular meeting Dr. Kay gave his reflection about what he heard that day. "I came out of the Oval Office uncertain as to how to read the President. Here was an individual who was oblivious to the problems created by the failure to find the WMDs. Or was this an individual who was completely at peace with himself on the decision to go to war, who didn't question that, and who was totally focused on the here and now and what was to come."

Cheney quizzed Dr. Kay about where he was getting his intelligence regarding the WMD program and he assured him that his people were receiving the most detailed information from various sources in the region and that they knew what they were doing. Dr. Kay said that the VP knew what he was talking about in his questions to him and said in that regard, "This was a Vice President who was well read in the intelligence and knew the details of the WMD issue."

The belief that Saddam Hussein had a stockpile of WMDs at that time was highly debatable at best and it not only divided the country, but the Bush administration as well. In October 2002, President Bush said that Iraq had a "massive stockpile" of biological weapons. But CIA Director George Tenet said in early 2004 that the CIA had informed Bush administration officials that it had "no specific information on the types or quantities of weapons or stockpiles at Baghdad's disposal." In December 2002, Bush said, "We do not know whether or not Iraq has a nuclear weapon." Once again George Tenet said the opposite by recalling, "We said that Saddam did not have a nuclear weapon and probably would have been unable to make one until 2007 to 2009."

On the al Qaeda/Iraq front, there was conflicting information as well. On September 18, 2001, Condi Rice received a memo summarizing intelligence on the relationship, which concluded that there was little evidence of links. Nonetheless, Bush continued to claim that Hussein was "a threat because he's dealing with al Qaeda more than a year later."

In August 2002, Cheney said, "Simply stated, there's no doubt that Saddam Hussein now has weapons of mass destruction." It would later be pointed out by *Mother Jones* reporter and author David Corn, that there was "no confirmed intelligence at this point establishing that Saddam had revived his major WMD operation." General Anthony Zini later said of Cheney's remarks, "It was a total shock. I couldn't believe the vice president was saying this, you know. In doing work with the CIA on Iraq WMD, through all the briefings I heard at Langley, I never saw one piece of credible evidence that there was an ongoing program."[8]

Even after leaving public office, the former vice president continued to talk about the Iraq WMD programs, and a lot more. In May of 2018, he appeared on Fox Business for an interview and gave the following comments. He said that the Unites States should continue to station troops in the Middle East for the foreseeable future and warned that other nations in the region may try to acquire WMDs. He said that the United States should reinstate its outdated enhanced interrogation techniques that never worked in the first place. He said of the enhanced interrogation program, "I'd have them active and ready to go, and I'd go back and study them and learn." He still supported the harsh interrogation techniques and said, "People want to go back and try to rewrite history, but if it were my call, I'd do it again."

Dick Cheney was not a novice when it came to his role in national politics. He had a long track record that dated back to the 1970s. In 1969, he ran the Office of Economic Opportunity for his old friend, Donald Rumsfeld who would later serve as Defense Secretary under George W. Bush. He later served as chief of staff for President Gerald Ford who had succeeded Richard Nixon after his resignation after Watergate. After Ford was defeated by Jimmy Carter in 1976 and became President, Cheney returned to Wyoming and successfully ran for congress. In 1988, he was chosen to run the Pentagon by the first President Bush. At the Pentagon, he worked closely with General Colin Powell in the run-up to the first Gulf War and he was now a household name in the country. After Bill Clinton defeated Bush, Cheney returned once again to private life and ran the huge energy firm called Halliburton located in Houston, Texas. It was reported that he earned a whopping $40 million during his five-year term. Cheney was always interested in global affairs,

8 Matthews, Dylan, "No Really, George W. Bush lied about WMDs," *Vox*

especially when it came to the Middle East and its vast oil reserves. In 1993, while he was still serving as Defense Secretary, he released a document called the "Defense Strategy for the 1990s" in which he reasserted his belief that the United States should make plans for future global domination which was outlined in the Defense Policy Guide which was leaked to the press in March 1992. Many people believed that the reason for the attack on Iraq after 9-11 was to get access to Iraq's plentiful oil supplies, rightly or wrongly. Cheney was in lockstep with this line of thinking, dating back to his days at Halliburton. In 2000, Texas Governor George W. Bush chose Cheney to become his vice presidential running mate and they both took office in January 2001, after the disputed election was settled by the Supreme Court.

In April 2001, a report was commissioned by U.S. Secretary of State James Baker and the Council on Foreign Relations called "Strategic Energy Policy Challenges for the 21st Century" which was then given to Cheney while he was vice president. The report says the "central dilemma for the U.S. administration is that the American people continue to demand plentiful and cheap energy without sacrifice or inconvenience." The report argued that, "the United States remains a prisoner of its energy dilemma, and that one of the consequences of this is a need for military intervention." Part of the report said that Iraq had to be overthrown in order for the United States to have access to these oil supplies.

With the collapse of the Soviet Union in 1991, the global power shifted and all eyes looked toward Central Asia and its vast oil supplies. Many of top U.S. oil companies including Exxon-Mobile, Texaco, Unocal, BP Amoco, Shell, and Enron (before its collapse) began pouring billions of dollars into Central Asia to garner the profits that lay waiting at their feet. In the time period of September-October 1995, Unocal signed a $5 billion deal with Turkmenistan to construct two pipelines, one for oil, the other for gas, as part of a larger plan for two pipelines intended to transport oil and gas from Turkmenistan through Afghanistan and into Pakistan. The CIA began to monitor the pipeline dealings when it set up a task force beginning in August 1997. They sent covert experts to such areas as southern Russia, Azerbaijan, Kazakhstan, and Turkmenistan to look for further oil reserves.

In October 1997, Cheney's Halliburton announced a deal to provide technical services and drilling equipment for Turkmenistan. The press report on this deal said, "Halliburton has been providing a variety of services in Turkmenistan for the past five years."

On June 23, 1998, Cheney talked more about the oil in the Caspian area in a talk at the "Collateral Damage Conference" hosted by the Cato Institute. Cheney told the audience, "We oftentimes find ourselves operating in some very difficult places. The good Lord didn't see fit to put oil and gas only where there are democratically elected regimes friendly to the United States. Occasionally, we have to operate in places where, all things considered, one would not normally chose to go. But we go where the business is." He also remarked on the strategic value of the Caspian Basin. "I can't think of a time when we've had a region emerge with the opportunities to become as strategically significant as the Caspian. "

One year later in the fall of 1999, he gave a speech at the London Institute of Petroleum while he was still the head of Halliburton. He said, "By 2010 we will need on the order of an additional fifty million barrels a day. So where is the oil going to come from? While many regions of the world offer great oil opportunities, the Middle East with two thirds of the world's oil and the lowest cost, is still where the prize ultimately lies."

Cheney's Haliburton had its hands in other areas besides the oil business in a rather lucrative way. In December 2001, two months after 9-11, a Halliburton subsidiary was awarded a no-bid contract to provide support for Iraq. Kellogg Brown & Root won a 10-year contract to provide the Pentagon in Iraq to supply U.S. personnel for everything from fighting oil-well fires to building military bases to feeding and housing soldiers. Cheney was a big advocate of using the private sector to do government work that had previously been done for years by the military.

In an astounding bit of nerve, which most people don't know about, on December 4, 1997, representatives of the Taliban arrived in the United States and went to the Texas headquarters of Unocal to negotiate their support for a proposed pipeline. George Bush was then governor of Texas. The Taliban appeared to have agreed on a $2 billion pipeline deal, but wanted only to do the deal if Washington agreed to recognize the Taliban regime. According to the *Daily Telegraph,* "the U.S. government, which in the past had branded the Taliban's policies against women and children despicable, appears anxious to please the fundamentalists to clinch the lucrative pipeline contract." A BBC regional correspondent said "the proposal to build a pipeline across Afghanistan is part of an international scramble to profit from developing the rich energy resources of the Caspian Sea."[9]

From his participation in the Bush White House right up to the prelude to 9-11, his belief that Iraq had a connection to al Qaeda for years, his distrust of the CIA when it came to pre-war intelligence, his advocacy of a preemptive war against Iraq, and his ties to the oil and gas industry via his chairmanship of Halliburton, put Cheney right in the middle of some of the most high-profile and controversial events of the day. He is still a polarizing figure and despite his being out of the limelight, he continues to talk about the things that mattered most to him, even if many of his views have been debunked or put to bed.

One other possible link between Iraq and other terrorist groups which was investigated by skeptical U.S. officials was a supposed training base in Iraq called Salman Pak, a town south of Baghdad. The location Salman Pak was given to a reporter named James Hoagland by a man named Sabah Khalifa Khodada al-Lami, who was a former Iraqi military officer. Al-Lami told the story of a covert deal between Saddam Hussein and certain Arab terrorist groups where training was allowed to take place at the base. It seems that Mr. al-Lami had moved to the United States in 2000 and settled in Fort Worth, Texas under the auspices of the Iraq National Council. In his interview with Hoagland, al-Lami, "gradually outlined to me here Wednesday details of the training given for airliner hijacking and assassinations in the Salman Pak area of Baghdad while he was there." Another of Hoagland's sources was "an Iraq ex-intelligence officer who reportedly told the Iraq National Council about sightings of Islamists training on a Boeing 707 parked in Salman Pak as recently as September 2000. The unidentified former Iraqi intelligence officer, Hoagland reported, told INC agents that he, too, had met with agents of the CIA in Ankara, Turkey, just that week and was treated dismissively. He was later identified as Abu

9 *The Terror Timeline*, Page 130.

Zeinab al-QuRairy."[10]

The Salman Pak story took on a life of its own and many newspapers around the nation took up the beat. The CIA looked into the report but came up with no definite conclusions. One of these stories appeared in a November 8, 2001 edition of the *New York Times,* written by Chris Hedges who worked in the *Times* Paris bureau. The story revolved around two Iraqi military defectors, one of which was a Lt. General in Saddam's spy service. He said, "These Islamic radicals were from countries including Saudi Arabia, Yemen, Algeria, and Morocco. We were training these people to attack installations important to the United States. The Gulf War never ended for Saddam Hussein. He is at war with the United States." The second Iraqi was identified as a former sergeant in the intelligence service who had spent years at the camp.

The Defense Intelligence Agency wrote a report downgrading the information provided by al-Lami and said, "he was intentionally misleading the debriefers and might have fabricated the claims to avoid harsh treatment in prison." In January 2004, al-Lami recanted his story after he was confronted with information from two other al Qaeda captives, KSM and Abu Zubaydah, that the terrorist organization had no substantial relations with Baghdad. Al-Lami said he told the story to avoid being tortured by his Egyptian interrogators. The CIA reported al-Lami's reversal to senior U.S. officials in a January 2004 intelligence document.[11]

The release of the final report of the 9-11 Commission that was supposed to have been made public in January 2003 was delayed for over six months due to haggling among certain members of the Bush White House about what and how much to release, including information on Iraq. One person who had knowledge of these goings-on was former Senator Max Cleland who was a member of the Commission. The former senator had a lot to say regarding the findings of the Commission:

> The administration said the connection [between Iraq and al Qaeda] to scare the pants off the American public and justify the war. There's no connection, and that's been confirmed by some of bin Laden's followers. What you've

10 Hoyle, Russ. *Going to War.* Thomas Dunne Books, New York, 2008, Page 89.
11 Ibid. Page 91-92.

> seen here is the manipulation of intelligence for political ends. The reason the report was delayed for so long—deliberately opposed at first, then slow-walked after it was created-is that the administration wanted to get the war in Iraq in and over, before it came out. Had this report come out in January [2003], like it should have done, we would have known these things before the war in Iraq, which would not have suited the administration.

This chapter has presented the story of Laurie Mylroie and the other neo-conservatives at the time who posit another theory regarding what happened in both the 1993 and 2001 World Trade Center attacks, along with the Ramzi Yousef-Abdul Yasin connection. If one believes in the notion of a conspiracy in all cases, then one has a point to make regarding the true role played by the Muslim men who were arrested after the '93 WTC attack. Could this motley crew of miscreants who had no intelligence or military training almost topple the WTC without any outside help? And who was Ramzi Yousef? Was he just a high-minded terrorist who was able to enter the U.S. undetected and hire a crew to attack the WTC, all on his own? And how outlandish would it be to look deeper into the role, if any, that Iraq played in both attacks? While Saddam Hussein was no friend of the United States, could he have masterminded both the '93 and 2001 attacks on his own? Even though Mylroie's thesis regarding Iraq and the WTC attacks have been debunked, it is worthwhile listening to and studying her opinions, even if they aren't in the mainstream regarding the two events. There is always something one can glean from another person's theories without losing sight of the big picture.

While the FBI bungled the ball regarding the terrorist presence in the United States in the months and sometime years leading up to 9-11, across the world there were signs of a new and horrific series of events that were coming to our shores, in ways that we could never have imagined possible.

Chapter 8

Warning Signs and Secret Meetings

20-20 hindsight is a wonderful thing to have. It gives the viewer an opening into events that have already taken place, and makes us aware of how things might have been different if we only knew what was coming.

In the aftermath of 9-11, we now know that the American government, in the months leading up to that terrible day, were given credible evidence from various sources that some type of attack was in the works against the mainland of the United States. The warning signs were so numerous during 2001 that it would have taken an incredible genius to sort out all the warnings and make some sense out of them. As it were, all the signals were not analyzed properly and no credible actions were taken by the Bush administration to counteract them.

In May 2005, previously unknown information from Ahmed Ressam, who was charged with plotting the so-called Millennium attacks against Los Angeles airport and other U.S. targets was brought to light. Court documents released in the Ressam case revealed that in the spring of 2001, Ressam told FBI interrogators that 9-11 plotter Abu Zubaydah told him that al Qaeda was planning to smuggle into the United States terrorist operatives, carrying explosives in order to carry out a terrorist attack in the U.S.

After his arrest, Ressam helped the government break up a number of terror cells in Canada and the U.S. After months in jail, it seems that Ressam had a change of heart and decided not to continue his cooperation with the FBI. However, that did not stop the bureau from gleaning as much information from him as possible.

Ressam's warnings about a possible al Qaeda attack on the U.S. was part of the now famous PDB—Presidential Daily Brief—that was issued for President Bush called "Bin Laden Determined to Strike in U.S." Critics of President Bush cite the PDB as information about a likely al Qaeda attack on the U.S. that was ignored by the Bush administration.

Ressam's new information came in a series of FBI interviews with him in the summer of 2001. He said that he took training at an al Qaeda camp in Afghanistan from 1998-1999, and had met Abu Zubaydah, a top bin Laden aide. According to court documents, "Abu Zubaydah asked Mr. Ressam to send him original Canadian passports so Abu Zubaydah could get people to America." Abu Zubaydah wanted an operation in the U.S. Abu Zubaydah also talked to Mr. Ressam about the need to get explosives into U.S. for operations, but this wasn't re: Mr. Ressam's operation." According to the court documents, "Mr. Ressam does not know if any explosives made it to the U.S. Once possible operation initiated, operators would not talk about it to anyone, including Abu Zubaydah."

Despite these warnings, it seems that Ressam was not privy to the particulars of the 9-11 attack. Ressam is quoted as telling the FBI, "Abu Zubaydah talked generally of big operations in the U.S. with big impact, needing great preparations, great perseverance, and willingness to die. Mr. Ressam had told gov. [sic] of plans to get people hired at airports, of blowing up airports, and airplanes."

At trial, Ressam was found guilty of trying to blow up LAX and was given a 130-year jail term. But as time went on, he decided not to cooperate anymore with the government and as of May 2005 his sentencing for his actions was postponed. According to prosecutors in the Ressam case, Ressam said, "that he had been asked so many questions and in such a manner that he could not say whether the statements being attributed to him were true."

In light of Ressam's warnings of Abu Zubaydah's plan to bring explosive laden terrorists into the United States in order to blow up airports and planes, why wasn't that information immediately handed over to domestic security—FAA-INS\CIA—and given the intense scrutiny it deserved?

Intelligence concerning a possible terrorist attack on the

United States in 2000 also came from foreign intelligence sources, including many of this country's allies in Europe and the Middle East.

One such intercept came on August 12, 2000 when Italian intelligence agents were able to intercept calls coming and going from a suspected terrorist cell belonging to al Qaeda in Milan, Italy. From 1999 until the summer of 2000, intelligence listeners were able to monitor communications from a Yemeni national buy the name of Abdulsalam Ali Abdulrahman to an Egyptian named Es Sayed regarding a large terrorist strike that would make worldwide headlines. Es Sayed was told the attack "will be written about in all the newspapers of the world. This will be one of those strikes that will never be forgotten. This is a terrifying thing. This is a thing that will spread from south to north, from east to west. The person who came up with this program is a madman from a madhouse, a madman but a genius."

Another part of the message to Es Sayed says, "I'm studying planes. I hope, God willing, that I can bring you a window or a piece of an airplane the next time we see each other."

This information was given to the FBI and the CIA and both groups tried to solve the riddle but were not able to, due to lack of sufficient data.

Another cryptic conversation that was picked up by Italian intelligence took place on January 24, 2001. The conversation this time was between Es Sayed and another man named Ben Soltane Adel, who both belonged to an al Qaeda cell in Milan. Their talk centered on the illegal use of passports by other al Qaeda members. "Will these work for the brothers who are going to the United States?" asked Adel. Sayed reproached him by saying, "Don't ever say those words again, not even joking. If it's necessary whatever place we may be, come up and talk me in my ear, because these are very important things. You must know that this plan is very, very secret, as if you were protecting the security of the state."

What the two men were referring to were the generating of illegal passports and documents that were to be handed over to the 9-11 hijackers.

This information was given to U.S. authorities in March 2001. Once again, the FBI did not know exactly what the conversation meant and were unable to act on it.

Es Sayed was killed by a U.S. drone strike in Pakistan in either May or June of 2012, according to government officials. He was once described as bin Laden's ambassador to Italy and at the time of his death was central to al Qaeda's operations in Afghanistan and Pakistan. His death was part of America's controversial drone program in which targets were pinpointed by American military leaders inside the United States. The military then sent unmanned drones to take out their targets. At the time of his death, his name appeared on U.S. and U.N. terror blacklists and he was convicted in absentia for the massacre in Luxor, Egypt in which 62 people, mostly tourists, were killed by gunmen. He was sent to Italy to oversee al Qaeda's Milan cell in 1998, where he was monitored by local intelligence agents.

One warning came from an unlikely source, Russian President Vladimir Putin. In 2001, the relations between the United States and Russia were not as bad as they are now. The countries were on a semi-friendly basis, and it would be another 15 years before the Russians would meddle in our presidential election on behalf of Donald Trump. In an interview given on MSNBC Vladimir Putin "indicated that he had warned the USA in the strongest possible terms for several weeks prior to the attacks. These warnings were specific enough to note that approximately 25 hijackers would be involved in flying civilian airliners on suicide missions against prominent American targets. One can only assume that the Russian warnings were based on a similar mixture of intelligence coming from signals surveillance and human intelligence sources."[12]

It seems though that there is more to the story about Putin and his 9-11 warnings than meets the eye. This information is provided in the book *Hidden Finance, Rogue Networks and Secret Sorcery* by Joseph Farrell. He wrote the following on this new, Russian angle,

> September 12, 2001. Yesterday at the headquarters of Central Intelligence in Langley a confidential meeting between one of the Deputy Directors of CIA and a special messenger of Russian intelligence service took place. According to *NewsRa* sources he delivered to his American

12 Farrell, Joseph, *Hidden Finance, Rogue Networks and Secret Sorcery.* Adventures Unlimited Press, 2016, Page 111.

> colleague some documents, including audiotapes and with telephone conversations relating to terrorist attacks on Washington and New York last Tuesday. According to these sources, Russian intelligence agents know the organizers and executors of these terrorist attacks. More than that, Moscow warned Washington about preparations for these actions a couple of weeks before they happened.
>
> Russian intelligence service states that behind the terrorist attacks on Washington and New York stands the organization of Osama bin Laden, Islamic movement of Uzbekistan and Taliban government. According to our intelligence agents among terrorist there are at least two Uzbeks, natives of Fergana who arrived in the USA on forged documents about two months ago. A terrorist group which realized actions against the USA consisted of at least 25 people. All of them had a special training on the territories of Afghanistan and Pakistan including piloting of aircraft.[13]

A more startling interpretation of what happened on 9-11 came from a Russian woman named Dr. Tatyana Koryagina, of the Russian Institute of Macroeconomic Research that was under the Russian Ministry of Economic Development. She said the following regarding 9-11, "The 9-11 attacks were not the work of nineteen terrorists but of a group of extremely powerful private persons seeking to reshape the world. This group, she added, has assets of $300 trillion, which it will use to legitimize its power and create a new world government."[14] This article appeared in the Russian newspaper *Pravda* on July 12, 2001.

Another warning came from two FBI translators, Sibel Edmonds and Behrooz Sarshar. Both Edmonds and Sarshar told higher ups in the bureau that one of their informants, who had been working for them for over ten years, received information from sources in the Middle East that members of al Qaeda were planning massive strikes against the U.S. and locations in Europe using planes as weapons of mass destruction. The source told them that al Qaeda already had sleeper cells inside the United States and

13 *Hidden Finance*, Page 118-119.
14 Ibid. Page 119-120.

were just waiting for the go-ahead signal.

Behrooz Sarshar said that his sources came from various places around the globe including Iran, Afghanistan, and Hamburg, Germany. Part of the 9-11 plot was hatched in Hamburg, Germany. Among the 9-11 hijackers who stayed in Hamburg were Mohamed Atta, Said Bahaji, and Ramzi bin al-Shib. The three men moved into an apartment located at 54 Marienstrasse, and resided there until February 2001. Over a two-year period, almost thirty Middle Eastern men resided at 54 Marienstrasse, which was constantly monitored by German police.

The FBI, under heavy criticism after 9-11, said that the information provided to them by the two translators was not specific enough for them to take serious action.

Sibel Edmonds however, sharply disagreed with the FBI's interpretation of the facts that were given to them by her partner. Ms. Edmonds said, "There was general information about the time frame, about the methods to be used but not specifically about how they would be used and about people being in place and who was ordering these sorts of terror attacks."

In May 2001, reports arrived in Washington via Canadian intelligence sources that warned of an impending al Qaeda attack by unknown men who had entered the United States via Canada. The report said that the attack would be carried out with explosives but it did not know where the attacks might be. This message was shared with the various U.S. intelligence agencies.

In an eerie coincidence, the Department of Defense ran a drill with its medical team at the Pentagon in May 2001 simulating a crash of a hijacked 757 airliner into the building.

During 1998 and 1999, MI6, the British intelligence service, contacted the American government in relation to information it obtained about possible al Qaeda attacks against U.S. interests.

In a report by MI6 to the American embassy in London, British agents told of obtaining information that a plot was afoot to hijack aircraft and fly them into unnamed buildings. These findings concerned Osama bin Laden, and said the attacks were to be used in "unconventional ways." Once again, no specific targets were mentioned, and U.S. intelligence had no way of confirming or denying the reports. These same MI6 reports said that an attack could be mounted in Europe, and a possible target was the U.S. embassy in Paris.

An unusual source that supposedly knew about a terrorist attack on the United States came forward on September 16, 2001, five days after 9-11. A priest named Father Jean-Marie Benjamin, 55, of France, told the ZENIT News Agency that before the attacks, he had been contacted by certain Muslim men who told him that a terrorist attack by commandos was in the planning stage. The targets were supposed to be in both the U.S. and England, but the attack on England was called off at the last minute.

Father Benjamin was an expert on the Muslim world and its culture. He worked at the United Nations from 1983 to 1988 and then turned to the priesthood, and was ordained as a minister in 1997.

After the attacks on 9-11, Father Benjamin had a closed-door meeting with Italian Foreign Minister Renato Ruggiero and told him what he knew.

Father Benjamin was not sure why he was picked out by these men but he surmised that he was chosen because of his work in the Middle East over the years. He refused to name the people who gave him this information, citing privacy issues.

"Although I am friendly with many Muslims," said Father Benjamin after 9-11, "I wondered why they were telling me, specifically. I felt it my duty to inform the Italian government."

Father Benjamin might have been an unusual person to be told such vital information. But as the summer of 2001 went on, other, more verifiable sources came forward warning the U.S. that something terrible was in the works.

The intelligence service of Jordan, GID, related to the CIA in the months leading up to 9-11 news of an impending attack by al Qaeda that was to be carried out inside the U.S., using aircraft as weapons. Once again, no particular target was mentioned.

Over the years, the CIA and the GID had an ongoing cooperative relationship when it came to sharing of intelligence. Jordan was a strong ally of the United States despite their differences over the issue of Israel and the Palestinians. In 1999, the GID, with U.S. help, thwarted an attack on tourist sites in Jordan during the 1999 New Year's Eve celebrations.

Another unconfirmed report came via a Moroccan agent by the name of Hassan Dabou. News of Mr. Dabou's revelations came via newspapers in France and Morocco. It seems that Dabou had infiltrated al Qaeda and retuned to tell the Moroccan intelligence service that bin Laden was preparing "large scale operations in New York in the summer or autumn of 2001."

This news was supposed to have been relayed to the CIA, although no official confirmation by the agency was ever forthcoming regarding the bona fides of Hassan Dabou.

Another ally of the United States, France, was also instrumental in giving us warnings about an impending attack. Their crack intelligence service, the DST, issued a warning that there would be worldwide attacks against American targets and that the order to attack was to come from Afghanistan. Also, the government of Egypt in the person of its president, Hosni Murbarak, warned the U.S. of an impending attack. If this was true, then the United States surely double-crossed Egypt in later years. When the so-called "Arab Spring" came into existence throughout the Arab world, the government of Hosni Mubarak in Egypt was one of the first to feel the sway of democracy. When riots broke out all across Egypt, the United States did nothing to stop the people's revolt and the government of Mubarak was overthrown.

From 1999 to 2000, leads were analyzed at home by the NSA—the National Security Agency—that led U.S. intelligence to the fact that a suspected Middle Eastern terrorist network was in place. The NSA is responsible for the interception and analysis of signal communications across the globe (SIGNIT). Its headquarters is at Fort Meade, Maryland, and its budget, as well as its manpower is one of the most highly guarded secrets in the U.S. intelligence community. Huge satellite dishes located in the United States and elsewhere around the world (Australia is one listening post) pick out selected words that are intercepted via phone, fax, and computers. These words are then analyzed by NSA skilled technicians and worked up into real-time information that aids in the tracking of terrorists around the globe.

In 1999, NSA communications picked up a suspected terrorist web that was located somewhere in the Middle East. Two of the men whose communications were picked up were to Nawaf al-

Hazmi and a man named Khaled. The Khaled mentioned in the NSA sweeps might have been either Khalid al-Midhar or Khalid bin-Attash.

The information obtained on the men by the NSA interpreters was not sold enough to link them to bin Laden or any other known terrorist group but they were now persons of interest to U.S. intelligence.

In 2000, the NSA acquired information relevant to al-Midhar and reported this information to the CIA, and the FBI. What these agencies did, if anything, with this information, is not known.

The CIA then asked permission from the NSA to transmit this intelligence (concerning al-Midhar) to other U.S. intelligence agencies. This was granted, and for the first time the CIA had a possible link centering al-Midhar with bin Laden, and some sort of nefarious terrorist service in the Middle East.

Another incident of suspicious activity took place in May 2001 in New York City. This event revolved around the activities of three men from Yemen who were taken into custody when they were caught taking pictures of federal buildings in lower Manhattan including 26 Federal Plaza which housed several federal agencies. Their photos included FBI headquarters, police stations, and other highly sensitive areas. After being interrogated by the FBI the men were released. However, they said they were taking pictures on behalf of another man who lived in Indiana. When FBI agents got around to seeking the identity of this other man, he was gone.

The activities of these Yemeni men was part of the PDB—Presidential Daily Brief—that was given to President Bush on August 6, 2000. Part of the PDB as it refers to these men is as follows: "suspicious activity in this country consistent with the preparations for hijackings or other types of attacks, including recent surveillance of federal buildings in New York."

In the spring of 2001, Egyptian President Hosni Mubarak passed along information gleaned from its own agents who had penetrated al Qaeda. This information, which was passed along to the CIA, said that bin Laden was preparing to assassinate President Bush when he attended the G-8 summit meeting in Italy on June 13, 2001. Extreme security measures were taken to guard the summit leaders and no incidents were reported.

From late 2000 right up to the summer of 2001, reports from the Israeli intelligence service, Mossad, were being passed along to the CIA concerning alleged al Qaeda terrorists inside the United States. In August 2001, one month before 9-11, the Mossad passed along a list of 19 terrorists who were living in this country to the American government. It is interesting to note that there were 19 hijackers who flew the planes into the WTC and the Pentagon on 9-11, the same number that was given to the CIA by the Israelis. Another interesting connection is the fact that Israelis identified four of the men who took part on 9-11 and gave that information to the U.S. Those men were Nawaf al-Hazmi, Khalid al-Midhar, Marwan al-Shehhi, and Mohamed Atta.

The FBI was not made aware of this information but both al-Hazmi and al-Midhar were put on the U.S. government's terror watchlist that same day. Why weren't the other men, if their identities were also provided to the U.S., also put on the terror watchlist?

The reports coming from the Mossad were part of an alleged Israeli spy ring composed of so-called "art students" that had been operating inside the United States during 2001. The fact that Israel was spying inside the United States is not as sinister as it seems. There is an unwritten rule by allied intelligence services that as long as agents from one country do nothing illegal inside the territory of the home country where they are working, their actions will not be interfered with.

The first hint by the U.S. that centered on an Israeli spy ring was reported by the DEA—Drug Enforcement Agency—in January 2000. This was the beginning of what would be called the "art student spy ring." Over the next year, these "art students" (if that is what they really were) were in the United States monitoring the activities of suspected Arab men in Florida, the same place where Mohamed Atta and other 9-11 hijackers were living and taking flying lessons.

During this time, American newspapers wrote that some Israelis were inside the United States distributing the drug Ecstasy. These persons were being observed by the DEA.

After 9-11, the complete story of the alleged "art student spy ring" was published by German as well as American newspapers, the accounts of which were hotly denied by the CIA.

It is argued that these people were targeting American military bases inside the country including Tinker Air Force Base in Oklahoma City. On April 30, 2001, U.S. military authorities sent out a warning about "possible intelligence collection being conducted by Israeli art students." Just why "art students" were sneaking up on an American air base is not known, possibly to draw airplanes? Shortly after these warnings were issued, about 120 of these Israeli nationals were expelled from the United States.

In March 2002, reports about the art student spy ring were published in the French daily newspaper *Le Monde.* The paper replayed the DEA story but added more material to it. The paper said, "a vast Israeli espionage network operating on American territory has been broken up."

The United States and Israel were at each other's throats in 1986 when another spy incident reared its ugly head, and threatened to disrupt the usually good relations between the nations. This incident involved the activities of Jonathan Jay Pollard, a Jewish American who worked for the Navy. Pollard, along with his wife, gave top secret material to Israel and forced a scandal that affected both nations' security.

The *Le Monde* narrative said that the Israeli operation was a very detailed plan that had many facets to it. The report regarding the supposed activities of the Israeli spies took an interesting turn when it said that over a third of the Israelis were living in Florida in the summer of 2001 and were keeping a close watch on the activities of Muslim men who were living in the Hollywood, Florida area. Mohamed Atta, the so-called ringleader of the 9-11 plot was living in Florida in the summer of 2001, taking flying lessons. According to the *Le Monde* narrative, "this coincidence could be the source of the American view that one of the missions of the Israeli students could have been to track al Qaeda terrorists on U.S. territory without informing federal authorities."

U.S. intelligence, as well as the Air Force, were aware of the Israeli incursion into the U.S. and kept a watch on the goings-on. U.S. authorities first began their investigation of the art students in February 2001.

Just why the Israelis were operating inside the United States in the months leading up to 9-11 is a mystery. The U.S. government hotly denied that any hanky-panky was being conducted by the "art students" despite the fact that they were deported back to Israel once their mission had ended.

On the other side of the coin, if Israel had any information on the Muslim men they were following in Florida in the summer of 2001, did they, or did they not inform the FBI of their suspicions? Just what made the Mossad send a team of agents thousands of miles from home just to keep watch on a band of nondescript Muslim men in another country? Did they know something we didn't know at the time?

To further add fuel to the already hot Israeli 9-11 story, five Israelis were arrested in New Jersey right after 9-11 and were held in detention in the U.S. for a period of two months. The men who were taken into custody were working for a company called Urban Moving Systems located in Weehawken, New Jersey. Urban Moving was supposed to be a cover for the Mossad. The FBI knew all about the activities of Urban Moving and subjected the detainees to a thorough investigation session before evicting them from the United States. One FBI official said, "the assessment was that Urban Moving Systems was a front for the Mossad and operatives employed by it. The conclusion of the FBI was that they were spying on local Arabs but that they could leave because they did not know anything about 9-11."

The five men who were arrested in New Jersey were Sivan and Paul Kurzberg, Oded Ellner, Omer Marmari and Yaron Shmuel. Upon their arrest, police found $4,000 and a box cutter inside their van. The men were turned over to the INS, and then to the FBI who took over the job of interrogating them. They were then transferred to the Metropolitan Detention Center in Brooklyn. By October 2001, the five men were deported back to Israel.

While the men were under U.S. control, it was learned from intelligence sources that two of the five men were employed by a foreign intelligence agency (possibly Mossad), and the FBI began a Foreign Counterintelligence investigation. Once back in Israel, the men involved in the case refused to talk to reporters.

In March 2002, highly placed U.S. government officials denied any plot by Israel to spy inside the United States. A Justice

Department spokesman said, “This seems to be an urban myth that has been circulating for months. The department has no information at this time to substantiate these widespread reports about Israeli art students involved in espionage.”

Just what the Israeli “art students” were doing in Florida at the time that Atta and others were living there, begs for a more thorough investigation.

The plot against America that would culminate on 9-11 was hatched in Afghanistan by bin Laden and his top leaders. However, one of the most important al Qaeda operations took place in Germany in the months and years prior to 9-11. Four of the lead hijackers on 9-11, as well as other like-minded men, met and lived in Hamburg, Germany where both the CIA and the German intelligence service, BfV, or the Office for the Protection of the Constitution, Germany’s FBI, kept a close watch on their activities. After 9-11, we would learn that the CIA did not share all the information that they had on the so-called Hamburg cell with their German counterparts. In hindsight, one wonders if all the intelligence obtained by the CIA and the Germans were available to each party, might the plot have been unrolled before it began?

From 1993 to 2000, four of the main participants in the Hamburg cell, Mohamed Atta, Ramzi bin al-Shib, Marwan al-Shehhi, and Ziad Jarrah, made their way to Germany for study and other nefarious activities. In Hamburg, they met like-minded Muslims who shared their religious and political views, attended mosques, and planned the deadliest strike against the United States.

Mohamed Atta, an attorney’s son from Egypt, obtained a degree in architectural engineering in 1990 from Cairo University. In 1992, he left for Hamburg, Germany where he stayed with a family whom he had previously met while in Cairo. They allowed Atta to live with them while he attended classed at the University of Hamburg. He learned German and could speak it well. He later transferred to the Technical University of Hamburg-Harburg, where he took up classes in city engineering and planning. He took classes until 1999 and received his degree.

While in Germany, Atta went to the Quds mosque in Hamburg and became enamored of Muslim religious teachings. The Atta that practiced religious Muslim views was not the same man, persons who knew him said, when he later moved to Florida in preparation for 9-11. In the Sunshine State, Mohamed Atta found an American girlfriend, drank liquor, attended strip clubs, and took drugs—not your typical religious zealot. While he was living in Florida, Atta found time to attend a Mosque run by a man named Gulshair el-Shurkrijumah, a cleric who had previously worked with the blind Sheik in Brooklyn, Rahman. Another of the 9-11 hijackers who attended the mosque was al-Shehhi. While in Florida a rather interesting figure named Adnan, who was the son of el-Shurkrijumah and who was known as a senior figure in al Qaeda, was seen with Atta in Miami on May 2, 2001. What the men were doing in Miami is not known but one can assume that it had to do with the upcoming attacks that took place five months later. When the 9-11 Commission wrote its report, they wrote little about the connection between Atta and Adnan el-Shurkrijumah and it was just a footnote in "a subsidiary document, its Terrorist Travel staff report which was published in August." This information on the Atta/el-Shurkrijumah connection was gleaned from the secret Able Danger program that will be written about in the next chapter.

Another interesting thing was the fact that the FBI had them both under surveillance as they attended various mosques in the United States. Also, Gulshair el-Shurkrijumah, the father of Adnan, "was in receipt of monies from the Saudi embassy in Washington, and it is also possible there was some involvement with a terrorist finance investigation that may have been ongoing."[15]

Atta hated Jews, Americans, even the regime of Iraq's strongman, Saddam Hussein, whom he saw as an American lackey in the heart of the Middle East.

Ramzi bin al-Shib was born in Yemen in 1972. From 1987 to 1995, he worked as a clerk at the International Bank of Yemen, not a particularly radical profession. In 1995 he tried to get a U.S. visa but was turned down. Instead, he departed for Germany under the alias Ramzi Omar, saying he was a Sudanese who wanted political asylum. He stayed in Hamburg until his asylum petition was rejected in 1997 and went back to Yemen. (He would later

---

15 Fenton, Kevin, *Disconnecting the Dots: How the CIA and FBI Officials Helped Enable 9-11 and Evaded Government Investigations,* Trine Day, Walterville, Oregon, 2011, Page 172-173.

come back to Germany using his real name.) Like Atta, he went to college in Germany but was expelled in September 1998 for poor performance.

In 1998, both bin al-Shib and Atta lived together in a small apartment in Hamburg. They were soon joined by another man from the United Arab Emirates, Marwan al-Shehhi.

Marwan al-Shehhi was born in 1978 in the UAE. As a young man he joined the military and would soon be given a scholarship that sent him to Germany. He arrived in Germany in April 1996, and lived for a time with a German family.

He went to the University of Bonn and strangely left the school after his request for a leave was denied. In 1998 he returned to Germany and was reunited with his pals, Atta and bin al-Shib. Together, the three men formed what was to be the basis of the Hamburg cell that was aligned with Osama bin Laden's al Qaeda.

Once in Hamburg, the religious conversion of Atta and al-Shehii was completed. They were now both radicalized into anti-Western, anti-Jewish views, spurning Western ways and dress and taking up the Palestinian cause.

The fourth man to enter the Hamburg cell was Ziad Jarrah, an unlikely candidate to become a 9-11 participant. He was born in 1975 in Lebanon, came from a wealthy family, and went to private schools. In April 1996, he left for Germany with a cousin and enrolled in a junior college in Greifswald. It was at the college that he met, and had a relationship with, a Turkish woman named Aysel Senguen. In time, Jarrah spent most of his time with Aysel and they even talked of marriage. Like Atta, and al-Shehhi, he soon turned away from the Western ways he seemed to enjoy and returned to his severe Muslim roots.

In September 1997, he took up aircraft engineering at the Technical University of Hamburg-Harburg and was soon associated with Atta, bin al-Shib, and al-Shehhi. In time, Jarrah told Aysel that he was planning to join a jihad against the West, and they had numerous fallings-out regarding his Muslim associates. One can only sympathize with young Aysel who thought she had a well put together young man, someone who shared her dreams and plans. It must have been devastating for her to have been told that Jarrah was now leaving her for a jihad, something she probably had no knowledge of.

It was at the Quds mosque in Hamburg that Jarrah and bin al-Shib would meet and discuss the Koran, and their hatred of the Jews and the West.

One of the featured speakers at the mosque was a fiery Syrian orator named Mohammad Haydar Zammar. Zammar's name was known by both the CIA and the German police and his movements were monitored carefully. Zammar fought in Afghanistan against the Russians beginning in 1991, traveling to Pakistan under a German passport. He later proved to be a moving force in the transformation of bin al-Shib and his Hamburg circle.

For a number of years, Zammar lived in Saudi Arabia and worked as a translator for a German-Saudi company. He also spent time traveling to such high-risk places as Bosnia where he took up arms with other like-minded Muslims. By 1996, he was in Afghanistan where he pledged allegiance to al Qaeda. Upon his return to Germany, he was put under surveillance by the police.

By 1999, under Zammar's wing, Atta, Jarrah, al-Shehhi, and bin al-Shib were to undergo another religious transformation, from students living in the West to ardent jihadists, ready to take up bin Laden's call. In 1999, as they prepared to leave Germany, they unknowingly were to become the newest front line soldiers in Osama bin Laden's declared war on the United States.

Zammar's activities were well known to the German police who had kept a file on him for at least ten years. Along with Zammar, German intelligence also kept a close watch on another of his associates, Mounir el-Motassadeq, also part of the Hamburg cell. Police would see both Motassadeq and Zammar in association with Said Bahaji, a roommate of Mohamed Atta.

Zammar traveled to Afghanistan in late 1999 and his trip overlapped that of Mohamed Atta. He later said that he had no knowledge of the 9-11 attacks and told a reporter, "God knows, and in all honesty, I did not know anything about the 9-11 strike. They did not tell me anything."

The German government looked into the goings-on of Zammar while he was in country and they wrote up a report on his activities. The German official who did the report was Guido Steinberg who investigated Zammar's involvement in the 9-11 attacks on behalf of the German government. "The German investigation found that the members of the Hamburg cell had been suspicious of Zammar, in part because he was 'very chatty.'"

In December 2001, he was arrested in Morocco and was then transferred to Syria, apparently as part of the CIA's "extraordinary rendition" program. While he was in Syrian custody, Zammar was said to have been tortured by his captors and was given questions to answer by both the United States and Germany. He was held in the Sednaya prison near Damascus. In 2007, a Syrian court sentenced him to 12 years in prison for four offences, including membership in the outlawed Syrian Muslim Brotherhood organization. Six years later, as Syria was entangled in a horrible civil war that left thousands dead and the country in ruins, he was released as part of a prisoner exchange between the Syrian government and the hardline Islamist rebel group called Ahrar al-Sham. It is not really know for sure what happened to Zammar next, but in early 2014 he was pictured attending a meeting between IS militants and Syrian tribal leaders. It was also rumored that in 2014 he was sent to Egypt by IS leader Abu Bakr al-Baghdadi to persuade a jihadist group operating in the Sinai Peninsula to swear allegiance to al-Baghdadi.

In 2018 it was reported that Zammar was detained in Syria by Kurdish fighters. He was captured by U.S.-backed forces of the Syrian Democratic Forces alliance and it was not known if he was fighting for the Islamic State.

The Hamburg cell was located at 54 Marienstrasse, a nice, four-bedroom apartment. They would stay in the house until February 2001. During that time period, six men would be in and out of the Marienstrasse apartment at different times.

German police would oftentimes tap el-Motassadeq's phone calls, as well as those of Said Bahaji whom they would listen in on during 1998.

Also coming to the 54 Marienstrasse address was Khalid Sheik Mohammed, the mastermind of 9-11. KSM was a wanted man by the United States and it is almost inconceivable that the German police did not recognize who he was (but maybe they didn't know). The CIA at this time was also keeping track of Mohamed Atta but they did not reveal that information to their German counterparts.

Having a different viewpoint than that of the 9-11 Commission, German authorities believed that by 1999, the members of the Hamburg cell had all but decided to mount an attack against the United States using aircraft as weapons of mass destruction. According to Kay Nehm who was the lead prosecutor in Germany, "At the latest in October 1999, [the Hamburg group's radicalization] led to the idea of attacking the United States using airplanes, a concept possibly inspired by ideas from other representatives of the international network. The group members then traveled to Afghanistan in order to discuss details with members of the international network and to obtain financial and logistical support."

By late 1999, it was time for the Hamburg cell members to make their way to Afghanistan for the next part in the 9-11 preparations. Jarrah left Germany on November 25, 1999, flying to Karachi, Pakistan on a Turkish Airlines flight. The next to leave was Atta who took the same airline to Pakistan. Next to depart were al-Shehhi and bin al-Shib. The other members of the cell, Bahaji, Essabar, and Motassadeq would not arrive in Afghanistan until 2000.

Upon arriving in Afghanistan, they went to a safe house in Kandahar called the Al-Ghumad House, where they were interviewed by three unknown Saudis. Once in Kandahar, the Hamburg cell members were to meet up with two other men who would take part in the 9-11 attacks, Nawaf al-Hazmi and Khalid al-Midhar. These two men would crash American Airlines Flight 77 into the Pentagon.

While these men were to be the pilots of the hijacked airlines on 9-11, other men, the so-called "muscle," a total of 13 in all, were also recruited in Afghanistan during this time. It is widely believed that the muscle men did not fully know their role in the 9-11 hijackings (they probably did not know they were slated to die that day).

The plotters gave code names to their targets during the planning stage in Afghanistan. The WTC was called "the Faculty of Town Planning," the Pentagon was "the Faculty of Fine Arts," and the Capitol was the "Faculty of Law." This was one of the original targets but the plane was diverted by the heroic actions of the passengers and crashed into a fie;d in Shanksville, Pennsylvania.

All these plans went unnoticed by the CIA who had no agents able to infiltrate al Qaeda during this critical period. This was not entirely the CIA's fault. There were very few agents of the clandestine service who were fluent in the Afghan language who could conceivably have been infiltrated into al Qaeda's midst. It would have taken years to implant a "sleeper" into bin Laden's inner circle, and if they had succeeded in planting an agent close to bin Laden, there was no certainty that this person could have known enough to foil the plot.

But what is known is that both the CIA and German intelligence were effectively monitoring the Hamburg cell for a long time and had enough clues as to who these men were, even if they did not know exactly what they were up to. Like the strained relationship between the CIA and the FBI, the CIA and the German intelligence service did not always share their intelligence concerning the goings-on in Hamburg.

For example, Mamdouh Salim, a known al Qaeda member from the UAE, was arrested in Munich, Germany on September 20, 1998. Salim took part in the 1998 African embassy bombings and was known to the CIA. In an unusual move, the FBI did not provide their German counterparts with their knowledge of who Salim was, and his possible connection to al Qaeda. While in Germany, Salim opened up a bank account along with another known al Qaeda terrorist named Mamoun Darkazanli. Darkazanli cropped up on the CIA's radarscope as early as 1993 and was regarded as a top level money launderer. It is not clear at this point whether an investigation by either the U.S. or Germany was opened on Darkazanli's activities.

On January 31, 1999, a German intercept of Mohammed Zammar reveals that a certain "Marwan" called the Zammar residence. This "Marwan" it turns out, was really Marwan al-Shehhi, a member of the Hamburg cell. Marwan was calling from the UAE and they gave this information to the CIA. It is not clear what the agency did with this information after they received it from the Germans.

In December 1999, the CIA tried to recruit Mamoun Darkazanli whom they had been following for months. His al Qaeda ties were well known to both the U.S. and Germany and the Americans thought he would be a perfect infiltrator inside al Qaeda. After almost a year of surveillance of Darkazanli, and with no tangible results, a CIA operative named Thomas Volz met with members of the German intelligence service, LfV. The CIA man informed his German colleagues that the U.S. believed that Darkazanli had information about a possible al Qaeda attack, and despite U.S. efforts to "turn" him, nothing came of these efforts.

The lack of success in turning Darkazanli would later come to haunt Western intelligence. After Darkazanli turned down a request to be an informer on al Qaeda, he went to Spain in January 2000 where he met with Barakat Yarkas in Madrid. Darkazanli and Yarkas, who was also the leader of al Qaeda in Spain, held extensive meetings that were observed by Spanish police. It is still unclear if at that time the agency knew about the Darkazanli-Yarkas meeting and if anything of substance was done about it.

Another person the CIA had been watching closely while he was in Germany was Mohamed Atta. For the first six months of 2000, Atta was followed by the CIA but they failed to inform the LfV of all they had on him. On May 18, 2000, Atta left Germany carrying a valid visa and traveled to the United States.

Another lead the CIA failed to follow up on Atta concerned his e-mail messages to various U.S. flight schools. He wrote to one school saying, "We are a small group (2-3) of young men from different Arab countries. Now we are living in Germany since a while for study purposes. We would like to start training for the career of airline professional pilots. In this field we haven't yet any knowledge, but we are ready to undergo an intensive training program."

Why the CIA, who had numerous reports of Arab men wanting to take flying lessons (Moussaoui, the Phoenix memo incident, the Bojinka plot in Manila, Wali Khan Amin Shah and his revelations about using planes to attack U.S. buildings) did not or could not link Atta, a known al Qaeda terrorist who was interested in taking flying lessons, is one of the biggest mysteries surrounding the pre 9-11 planning.

On September 13, 2001, German police arrived at Darkazanli's residence but he had since fled.

By 2000, the members of the Hamburg cell had lived in Germany anywhere from five to eight years, and had assimilated themselves into Western dress and culture while still adhering to their traditional Muslim ways. While in Germany they traveled secretly to Afghanistan where they took part in guerilla warfare excersizes supported and financed by Osama bin Laden. The members of the cell met with bin Laden and his chief lieutenants and were chosen by the top leaders of al Qaeda to participate in what would be called the "planes operation" that would take place on 9-11. With their education complete, Mohamed Atta and his cellmates prepared to leave Germany for the United States for the final leg of their dangerous journey.

The first member of the Hamburg cell to arrive in the United States was Marwan al-Shehhi who arrived on May 29, 2000, landing at Newark airport from Brussels. He used a new passport that hid the fact that he had been in Afghanistan, a fact that would have prevented him from entering the country. The next to leave for America was Mohamed Atta who arrived in the Czech Republic on June 2 by an overland route. He then took a flight from Prague to Newark where he met up with al-Shehhi.

A brewing controversy regarding Atta's trip to Prague and his actions in that city is still being debated, long after the event, despite the conclusion of the 9-11 Commission that nothing nefarious took place. The debate surrounds a report that while in Prague, Atta met with a top Iraqi intelligence agent named Ahmed Khalil Ibrahim Samir al Ani at the Iraqi Embassy on April 9, 2001. At the time of this alleged meeting, the CIA was alerted and the FBI legal attaché in Prague met with his Czech counterparts to discuss the matter. The FBI attaché was informed that a Czech source was the initiator of the information and that the Czechs believed the account of the Atta/al Ani meeting to be true. Also confirming the meeting was the Czech Interior Minister.

Records concerning Atta were used to discredit this Czech report by U.S. officials. The FBI said that Atta was in Florida on April 6, 9, and 10, and that his cell phone was used during this time period. This is not to say that someone else could not have been using his cell phone and that Atta may have been somewhere else (possibly Prague) at this time. The Czech government did a check of its records dealing with Atta's supposed trip to their country and said that he was not there during this time. The Czech government said that Atta's supposed clandestine meeting with al Ani never took place, and that the Iraqi was actually about 70 miles away from Prague on April 8-9.

Months later, al Ani was questioned about his alleged meeting with Atta and he said that no such meeting ever took place. Also, KSM, said that he knew of no meeting between Atta and al Ani.

The Bush administration, especially, Vice President Dick Cheney, made much of this possible bin Laden/Iraqi connection in the aftermath of 9-11. Such a meeting, if it was to be proven, according to Bush administration officials, would have placed the blame for 9-11 squarely on Iraq's shoulders. As of now, no solid proof that any meeting between the two men took place. However, the 9-11 Commission wrote of the incident, "These findings cannot absolutely rule out the possibility that Atta was in Prague on April 9, 2001. He could have used an alias to travel and a passport under that alias, but this would be an exception to his practice of using his real name while traveling (as he did in January and would in July when he took his next overseas trip). The FBI and CIA have uncovered no evidence that Atta had any fraudulent passports."

The story of a possible Atta/al Ani meeting was not new inside the Washington Beltway. The story was reported by *New York Times* reporter William Safire, who wrote that the meeting was "an undisputed fact." As mentioned in a previous chapter, the story was picked up and disseminated by Laurie Mylroie and James Woolsey. Bush administration officials passed the story around that Atta had visited Iraqi intelligence at least twice—in June 2000 and again in 2001, and on April 8-9. The top men in the Bush administration passed on information to the vice president and others interested in the story that Atta had also met with the Iraq charge d'affaires in Prague and that al Ani had ordered Iraq intelligence to give Atta a certain amount of money. Another White House report said that several workers in the Prague airport had identified Atta after September 11, 2001 and "remember him traveling with his brother Farhan Atta."

In the hectic days after 9-11, the CIA asked its partners to find out anything they could on Atta and his possible Prague meeting. Czech intelligence had received an interesting report from one of its informants who had connections inside the Middle Eastern community that he had seen Atta's pictures in the paper and thought he had spotted the same man five months earlier with al Ani outside the Iraqi Embassy. The Czechs then sent a picture taken outside of the Iraqi Embassy that day that showed an unidentified Middle Eastern-looking man, who they suggested, might have been the 9-11 hijacker.

"We knew right away that's not Atta," said one U.S. counterterrorism official who examined the photo when it arrived at Langley. "The guy in the photo was bigger, a broad shouldered guy in a leather jacket. He looked sort of like an Albanian thug. Atta was a little scrawny guy. There's no way it was Atta." The picture was analyzed by both the FBI and CIA labs and they could make no final determination as to who was in the photo. They did say however, the man in the picture was *probably* not the 9-11 hijacker.[16]

"We looked at this real hard because, obviously, if it were true, it would be huge," one senior U.S. law enforcement official told *Newsweek* at the end of April 2002. "But nothing has matched up."[17]

Officials at both the CIA and the FBI were at odds with the White House contention of a possible Atta/al Ani meeting and said so in private so as not to have the wrath of the Bush administration come crashing down on them. According to David Corn and Michael Isikoff in *Hubris,* "None though, would challenge the policy makers. 'Who is going to question the vice president when he keeps espousing this shit?' asked the U.S. counterterrorism official who investigated the Atta issue. 'Nobody at the FBI or CIA is going to speak up and say, stop the bullshit.'"

In a sidebar to this convoluted story, the White House, under the guise of the vice president's office, asked Secretary of State Colin Powell to mention the Atta-Prague connection when he was scheduled to address the United Nations in his slideshow of evidence about Saddam Hussein's supposed WMD in the lead-up to the Iraq war. This was not done.

16 Isikoff and Corn, *Hubris,* Page 103-104.

17 Ibid. Page 104.

Here is what we know about the possible Atta/al Ani meeting from the available record.

Ahmad al Ani served as the consul at the Iraqi embassy in Prague, the Czech Republic from March 1999 to April 21, 2001 and was involved in agent recruitment at that time. Mohamed Atta applied for a Czech visa on May 26, 2000 in Bonn, Germany identifying himself as a "Hamburg student." Just prior to his leaving for the U.S., Atta made two trips to the Czech Republic in 2000. The first was on May 30, when he went without a visa to the transit lounge of Prague airport; the second was by bus to Prague on June 2 with a visa.

On April 4, 2001, Atta checked out of the Diplomat Inn in Virginia Beach and cashed a check for $8,000 from a SunTrust bank. He was not seen again in the U.S. by anyone before April 11, 2001.

Al Ani was seen meeting with a young Arab-speaking man on the outskirts of Prague about 11 am on April 9 by a watcher from Czech intelligence. Al Ani was expelled from Prague less than two weeks after that meeting. Al Ani always denied that he had ever met with or seen Atta when he was taken into custody by American authorities in July 2003, however, after seeing Atta's picture the Czech watcher identified the Arab-speaking man meeting al Ani as Mohamed Atta.

George Tenet, the CIA Director at that time testified before a Joint Committee of Congress on June 18, 2000 and made the following comments. "Atta allegedly traveled outside the U.S. in early April 2001 to meet with an Iraqi intelligence officer in Prague; we are still working to confirm or deny this allegation. It is possible that Atta traveled under an unknown alias since we have been unable to establish that Atta left the U.S. or entered Europe in April 2001 under his true name or any known aliases." Furthermore, Spanish authorities found evidence that two Algerians by the names of Khaled Madami and Moussa Laouar provided false passports to Mohamed Atta and his associate Ramzi bin al-Shib.[18]

This story gets more complicated with the arrest of two Iraqi intelligence agents in Germany at the end of February 2001, an event that was not mentioned in the 9-11 Commission Report or

18 www.edwardjepstein.com/PragueApril 2004.

by many mainstream news outlets at the time.

One of those that did mention the incident was an Arab newspaper based in Paris by the name off *Al-Watan al-Arabi*, and what they wrote was rather interesting to the story:

> *Al-Watan al-Arabi* (Paris) reports that two Iraqis were arrested in Germany, charged with spying for Baghdad. The arrests came in the wake of reports that Iraq was reorganizing the external branches of its intelligence service and that it had drawn up a plan to strike at U.S. interests around the world through a network of alliances with extremist fundamentalist parties. The most serious report contained information that Iraq and Osama bin Laden were working together. German authorities were surprised by the arrest of the two Iraqi agents and the discovery of Iraqi intelligence activities in several German cities. German authorities, acting on CIA recommendations, had been focused on monitoring the activities of Islamic groups linked to bin Laden. They discovered the two Iraqi agents by chance and uncovered what they considered to be serious indications of cooperation between Iraq and bin Laden. The matter was considered so important that a special team of CIA and FBI agents was sent to Germany to interrogate the two Iraqi spies.[19]

What we do know is that Czech intelligence had a close watch on al Ani and had more than an interest when he told British intelligence in 1998 about a plot to blow up the Radio Free Europe station in Prague in retaliation for its broadcasts into Iraq. The Czechs subsequently expelled al Ani from the country. He then fled back to Iraq.

For all the contradictory evidence surrounding this matter, the Czechs stuck to their story regarding Atta having met with al Ani. "Part of the reason for this insistence is not just a belief in their source, but also a corroborating entry in al Ani's datebook, which the Czechs apparently discovered during a surreptitious search of the Iraqi embassy after Saddam's fall in April 2003. The datebook

19 Morrissey, Edward, "Rethinking Prague," The Weekly Examiner.com, August 23, 2005.

contained an entry for an April 2001 meeting with a "Hamburg student," the same description used by Atta himself when applying for his visa."

However, the 9/11 Commission disregarded the Czech intelligence report and said instead that Atta had never gone to Prague in April 2001. Their reasoning went as follows: Atta's cell phone was used in the U.S. on April 6, 9, 10, and 11. There are no U.S. records of Atta's traveling under his own name. No pictures of anyone who looked like Atta in the Czech Republic on those dates. Testimony from two al Qaeda sources—Khalid Sheikh Mohammed and Ramzi bin al-Shib.

So, this is where the Atta/Prague/al Ani story rests as of today. One never knows if further information will become available, but that doesn't seem probable.

We now return to the activities of the Hamburg cell and their arrival in America. Ziad Jarrah arrived in the United States on June 27, 2000, landing in Atlanta. He "lost" his Lebanese passport and was using another passport, as well as having a five-year, B1/B2 multiple entry visa. Once in the country, he went to Venice, Florida where he enrolled at the Florida Flight Training Center. Jarrah got his private pilot's certificate in August 2001 and was able to travel unnoticed by U.S. authorities back to Germany where he was reunited with his girlfriend, Aysel Senguen. They made a trip to Paris and shortly thereafter, he came back to the United States using his false passport.

Atta, who was supposed to have been a very busy man, having time to travel to Prague to meet with al Ani, traveled to the Airman Flight School in Norman, Oklahoma with his pal, al-Shehhi. However, they then went to Florida and enrolled in the Huffman Aviation School in Venice, where they took classes in the Accelerated Pilot Program. By the summer of 2000, both Atta and al-Shehhi had received their pilot's license. One of the mysteries of the entire 9-11 saga would revolve around the activities of some of the hijackers in Florida which will be written about later in this book.

In the fall of 2000, both Atta and al-Shehhi applied to the INS to change their immigration status from tourist to student, citing their flight school training. In September 2001, they transferred to another flight school, Jones Aviation in Sarasota. The men had many run-ins with their instructors at Jones and they were not liked at all by those they encountered at the school. They also failed their Stage 1 flight test in October of that year. They left in a huff and returned to Huffman in Venice.

Ramzi bin al-Shib tried to come to the U.S. but was denied a visa. He returned to Yemen and was still refused a visa. Undaunted by bin al-Shib's inability to enter the U.S., bin Laden gave bin al-Shib the job of acting as the money facilitator between their student pilots in the United States. Working along with KSM, bin al-Shib sent the Florida pilots $10,000 in wire transfers during the summer of 2000.

In their final report, the 9-11 Commission made a detailed investigation of how the hijackers were financed as they came to the United States and it is an interesting tale to tell. Bin Laden's al Qaeda absorbed most of the costs before the hijackers arrived in the United States. According to Khalid Sheikh Mohammed, the Hamburg cell members, including Atta, al-Shehhi, Ziad Jarrah, and Ramzi bin al-Shib each received $5,000 to pay for their return from Afghanistan to Germany in late 1999 or early 2000, after they had been selected to join the plot, and the three Hamburg pilots also received more money for travel expenses from Germany to the United States. Once the non-pilot muscle hijackers received their training, each received $2,000 to travel to Saudi Arabia to obtain new passports and visas, and ultimately $10,000 to facilitate travel to the United States, according to KSM.

The 9-11 Commission report said:

> We have found no evidence that the Hamburg cell members received funds from al Qaeda earlier than late 1999. Before then, they appear to have supported themselves. For example, Shehhi was being paid by the UAE military, which was sponsoring his studies in Germany. He continued to receive a salary through December 23, 2000. The funds were deposited in a bank account in the UAE and then wired by his brother, who held power of attorney over the account, at Dresdner Bank in Germany. bin al-Shib was employed intermittently in

> Germany until November 1999. Jarrah apparently relied on his family for support. Indeed, bin al-Shib said that Jarrah always seemed to have plenty of money in Germany because his parents gave it to him.

There is one last story that should be told regarding the members of the Hamburg cell and the people who were involved in it. There has been speculation that KSM was seen in Hamburg and had some interactions with the other members who were there at that time. It has been reported that a senior intelligence official said, "Several different sources had placed Mohammad at the Hamburg apartment that was used for meetings by three of the Arabs who are believed to have piloted the hijacked planes, as well by several others implicated in planning and funding the operation."

This new information relating to KSM and the Hamburg cell was gleaned from interrogations of captured al Qaeda members in Afghanistan and other places around the world, as well as "tracing documents" and other raw intelligence collected in recent months, indicating that Mohammed was one of the few people with direct knowledge of the recruiting, training, funding, and other operational details behind the attacks. The number of people central to this plan was very small, said one official, who spoke on the condition of anonymity. "He was one of them. He is the Forest Gump of al Qaeda," a Bush administration official said. "He has more of a presence in some of their plots than we had previously known."

KSM, as we now know, was the mastermind of 9-11, as well as being the uncle of Ramzi Yousef. But in the years before 9-11 and his subsequent arrest years later, the U.S. intelligence community had little to go on him as far as his terrorist links were concerned. "Khalid Sheik Mohammad had been quiet and had stayed out of the airways," one official said. "In hindsight, I don't think people appreciated how important a player he had become in the al Qaeda hierarchy. We are learning all that now."

According to the new information on KSM, his whereabouts at that time were not known but it was believed that at least one unsuccessful covert operation was launched to capture him in the late 1990s in the Middle East.

As it relates to KSM, it is still unclear when he visited Hamburg, Germany and whether he did indeed meet up with his fellow conspirators, Mohamed Atta, Marwan al-Shehhi, and Ziad Jarrah. This is one more piece in the continuing saga of the events prior to 9-11 revolving around the Hamburg cell and its activities.[20]

The 9-11 Commission looked into the possibility that the Spanish al Qaeda cell which was led by Barkat Yarkas, provided any funding to support the 9-11 attack:

> Al Qaeda also paid for the training camps at which the 9/11 hijackers were selected and trained. We have not considered this expense as part of the pilot costs, because the camps existed independently of the plot. The marginal cost of training the hijackers is a plot cost, but any estimate of it would be little more than a guess.
>
> The best evidence indicates that approximately $300,000 was deposited in the hijackers' bank accounts in the United States by a variety of means. Just prior to the flights, the hijackers returned about $26,000 to one of their al Qaeda facilitators and attempted to return another $10,000, which was intercepted by the FBI after 9-11. The FBI, therefore, believes it has identified all sources of funding. Our investigation had revealed nothing to suggest the contrary, although it is possible that the $300,000 estimate omits some cash that the hijackers brought into the United States and spent without depositing into a bank account or otherwise creating a record.
>
> Al Qaeda funded the hijackers in the United State by three primary and unexceptional means: (1) wire or bank-to-bank transfers from overseas to the United States, (2) the physical transportation of cash or traveler's checks into the United States, and (3) the use of debit or credit cards to access funds held in foreign institutions. Once here, all the hijackers used the U.S. banking system to store their funds and facilitate their transactions.
>
> Upon their arrival in the United States, the hijackers

20 Drogin, Bob and Josh Meyer, "Alleged 9/11 Mastermind linked to Hamburg Cell," *Los Angeles Times*, June 6, 2002.

> received a total of approximately $130,000 from overseas facilitators via wire or bank-to-bank transfers. Most of the transfers originated from the Persian Gulf center of Dubai, UAE, and were sent by plot financer Ali. Ali is the nephew of KSM, the plot's leader, and his sister is married to convicted terrorist Ramzi Yousef. KSM provided the bulk of the money later in 2000 via a courier. Although Ali had two bank accounts in the UAE, he kept most of the funds for the hijackers in a laundry bag at home.
>
> Ali transferred a total of $119,500 to the hijackers in the United States in six transactions between April 16, 2000 and September 17, 2000. Nawaf al Hazmi and Khalid al Midhar, received the first wire transfer." The money was transferred through a variety of banks including the Wall Street Exchange Center in Dubai to an account at the Union Bank of California. The money then flowed through a correspondent account at the Royal Bank of Canada. Ali brought the $5,000 to the Exchange Center in cash. The Wall Street Exchange Center required identification, and it made a copy of Ali's work ID, along with his cell phone number and work address—all of which helped the FBI identify him and his subsequent aliases after 9-11. Ali wired the money to the account of a San Diego resident whom Hazmi met at a mosque and had solicited to receive the transaction on his behalf. [21]

These wire transfers to the hijackers showed a large-scale knowledge of finance and money laundering on a level that the 19 hijackers were incapable of doing themselves. The moneymen of al Qaeda were the brains behind the financial transactions and had to have learned this behind-the-scenes maneuvering from others who had knowledge of such operations.

Another of bin al-Shib's tasks was to help Zacharias Moussaoui, another potential hijacker, enter into the United States. During a trip to London, Moussaoui and bin al-Shib met and planned strategy. Moussaoui was able to enter the United States and took up flight training at the Airman Flight School in Norman,

21 Appendix A: The Financing of the 9/11 Plot: Terrorist Financing, Staff Monograph.

Oklahoma. Moussaoui would later become involved in the FBI's Phoenix memo episode wherein FBI agents in Oklahoma drafted a report to Washington telling them that certain Arab men were taking flying lessons, and that an investigation should be mounted.

With the use of false passports, the Hamburg cell members were able to come and go to the United States and back without being stopped. Neither the FBI nor the CIA knew they were here, despite their being observed in Germany for a long period of time.

The Southeast Asian country of Malaysia would be another clandestine way station on the long road to 9-11. It would also be the site of another intelligence failure providing information that the FBI and CIA did not take advantage of, again, mostly due to intra-service squabbles and hubris.

In early 2000, a number of men who would eventually take part in the 9-11 attacks, as well as other al Qaeda operatives, including the leading al Qaeda representative in Southeast Asia, met in the Muslim-dominated nation of Malaysia to plan strategy on the planes operation.

In January 2000, three Saudi citizens, Khalid al-Midhar, Nawaf al-Hazmi and Nawaf's brother, Salim al-Hazmi, arrived in Kuala Lumpur for strategy sessions. Another hijacker, Ziad Jarrah, was stopped in the U.A.E. because of irregularities in his passport that same month.

Khalid al-Midhar, Nawaf al-Hazmi, and a man named Khalid bin-Attash, one of bin Laden's top operatives, attended a meeting in a home that belonged to Yazid Sufast, a Cal State graduate from Malaysia who would later be arrested and tell U.S. authorities about his al Qaeda connections, from January 5 to 8, 2000. The CIA alerted Malaysian intelligence regarding the meeting and they monitored the progress of the three men. It is not known exactly what transpired at the closed-door meeting but all the available information gleaned since that time points to the events of 9-11. On January 5, 2000, CIA headquarters notified friendly intelligence services around the world "that we need to continue the effort to determine if there is any true threat posed." The CIA then informed the FBI regarding the Malaysia meeting but it seems that the bureau did not follow up.

Of all the men who attended the conclave, the CIA had a lot of information regarding Khalid al-Midhar. They had his first name, his passport number, and birth information. We also learned that he had a multiple-entry visa that had been issued to him in Jeddah, Saudi Arabia on April 7, 1999, which would expire on April 6, 2000.

Upon his arrival in Kuala Lumpur, the CIA began writing cables that were sent to Langley headquarters regarding the activities of al-Midhar. He arrived on January 5 and met with other Arab men who were not identified. This cable, referred to as the "first Malaysia cable," did not contain any information regarding passports or visas.

It appears that this first Malaysia meeting cable was given to the FBI and was sent up the chain of command at Washington headquarters. A threat update was issued regarding al-Midhar but it was edited in the FBI's SIOC. The 9-11 Commission would write of this event saying, "However, we were not able to determine who in the FBI received this information from the CIA or who edited the January 5 threat update. No one we interviewed at the FBI said they recalled handling the information related to Midhar or the January 5 threat update. The threat update contained no reference to Midhar's passport information or his U.S. multiple-entry visitor's visa. The January 5 threat update was the only official document from this period located by the FBI that referenced the Malaysia meetings that were discussed in the first CIA Malaysia meeting cable."

An unidentified CIA operative who was cooperating with the FBI regarding the Malaysia meeting and al-Midhar in particular said, "This continues to be an intelligence operation. Thus far, a lot of suspicious activity has been observed but nothing that would indicate evidence of an impending attack or criminal enterprise."

On January 6, 2000, while the meeting was still in progress, two of the participants left for Thailand and Singapore and returned within 24 hours. Those involved in this unexpected travel were later identified as Nawaf al-Hazmi and Khalid bin-Attash.

Within days of the first cable regarding al-Midhar being sent by the U.S. intelligence community a second cable was sent by the CIA, providing new information about the activities of al-Midhar. This cable, "the second Malaysia meeting cable," provided information about al-Midhar's activities once he left the Kuala

Lumpur airport and his meetings with various individuals.

On January 8, the CIA reported in another internal cable that a new individual had joined Midhar and the others, and that additional surveillance photographs were taken. The cable did not state how many pictures were taken or what would be done with the photos.

In another cable sent five hours later, the CIA reported in an internal cable that Midhar and two of the unidentified men—one of whom turned out to be Hazmi—departed Malaysia from Kauala Lumpur airport en route to Bangkok, Thailand.

On January 9, the CIA's bin Laden Unit prepared a cable asking that al-Midhar and his friends be identified while in Thailand. CIA records show that on January 13, the CIA was attempting to locate al-Midhar and his traveling companions. In addition, al-Midhar had been watchlisted at the airport in the event that he attempted to leave Thailand.

Several weeks later, CIA officers in Kuala Lumpur followed up with their Bangkok counterparts for additional information about al-Midhar and his traveling companions. Approximately two weeks later, Bangkok reported that there was a delay in responding due to difficulties in obtaining the necessary information.

In early March 2000, officials in Bangkok reported internally that they had identified one of al-Midhar's traveling companions as Nawaf al-Hazmi. The cable reported that Hazmi had traveled to Bangkok on January 8 and had subsequently traveled on a United Airlines flight to Los Angeles, California on January 15. The cable also stated that al-Midhar arrived in Bangkok on January 8 but that it was unknown if and when he had departed. In addition, the cable identified the third traveler as Salah Saeed Mohammed Bin Yousef. Another person who went to Bangkok was Khalid bin-Attash, who was part of the failed attack on the USS *Sullivans*. Bin-Attash would later have more success, when, on October 12, 2000, a bin Laden attack squad launched a strike on the USS *Cole* in the harbor of Aden, Yemen, in which 17 U.S. sailors were killed.

Bin-Attash was front and center in the intelligence community's investigation of the USS *Cole* attack. From November 22 to December 16, 2000, the government of Yemen provided photos of bin-Attash to the leaders of the *Cole* investigation including

John O'Neill and Ali Soufan. Agent Soufan then sent a picture of bin-Attash to the CIA, as well as to another FBI agent based in Islamabad, Pakistan. The FBI agent was identified as Michael Dorris and the CIA agent was named "Chris." "Chris" then sent the photo to a source, and the source, who was only called "Omar," confirmed that the man in the photo was bin-Attash. with the identity of bin-Attash as part of the *Cole* bombing, the footprint of al Qaeda was now front and center.

Another important person linked to bin-Attash was Fahad al-Quso who was also involved in the *Cole* incident. Al-Quso gave a large sum of money to bin-Attash in early December 2000, and subsequent investigations by the FBI would find phone calls between al-Quso's Bangkok hotel and a phone booth in front of the condominium where the al Qaeda summit was held (Malaysia). "The CIA was aware by June 2001 that al-Midhar is the son-in-law of Ahmed al-Hada, a Yemeni extremist who runs a communication hub for Osama bin Laden, but it is not known whether they obtained this information now or at some other time."

There was even some speculation by the CIA at one point that bin-Attash and Khalid al-Midhar were the same person. The abovementioned source named "Omar" identified a photo of Khalid bin-Attash and the CIA officer named "Chris" was told that bin-Attash and al-Midhar might have been the same person:

> CIA records show that none of the FBI detailees accessed this early March cable. The OIG found no documents or witnesses indicating that the information that Hazmi had traveled to Los Angeles on January 15, 2000, was shared with the FBI at this time. Rather, as we discuss below, this fact was not shared with the FBI until August 2001 (one month before 9-11). Omar said that the photo of al-Hazmi, who the CIA apparently did not recognize at the time, actually shows bin-Attash. As Omar cannot identify al-Midhar, he said he could identify bin-Attash, this indicated that al-Midhar and and bin-Attash were not the same person. The identification caused the CIA to believe that bin-Attash attended al Qaeda's Malaysia summit. Although this belief is based on mistaken identification, it is

> actually correct, as bin-Attash was present at the summit—the CIA has photos of bin-Attash there, but failed to show them to Omar. This identification is important because bin-Attash was a known bin Laden operative connected to the USS *Cole* attack and the East African embassy bombings. The CIA also knows that al-Midhar and al-Hazmi were at the Malaysian summit, so this could connect them to the *Cole* attack.[22]

Cofer Black, whose name has been mentioned earlier in this book, told the 9-11 Commission about the people involved in the Malaysia summit.

> Our records establish that the special agents from the FBI's New York Field Office who were investigating the USS *Cole* attack reviewed the information about the Kuala Lumpur photo in late January 2001. However, there is no documentary record of information about the second identification placing bin-Attash in Kuala Lumpur with the two hijackers being passed to the FBI at this time.
>
> We found no indication that CTC (Counterterrorism Center) personnel took any action with regard to the important information that Hazmi had traveled to the United States. For example, he was not placed on any U.S. watchlists. The day after Bangkok reported about Hazmi's travel to Los Angeles, one office that received the Bangkok cable sent a cable to the CTC stating the Bangkok cable regarding Hazmi's travel had been read "with interest." Yet, despite this effort to flag the significance of this information, the cable was not shared with the FBI and did not result in any specific action by the CIA. It was not until August 20001 that FBI headquarters personnel learned that on January 15, 2000, both al-Midhar and Hazmi had left Thailand and traveled to Los Angeles, California, where they were both admitted into the United States on a non-immigrant visas and authorized to remain until July 14,

22 History Commons: January 4, 2001: Informer sees known Al-Qaeda leader in Malaysia Summit Photos.

> 2000.[23]
>
> On December 31, Khalid al-Midhar flew from Kuala Lumpur to Bangkok; the next day he flew to Hong Kong aboard a U.S. airliner. He flew in first class, which he realized was a mistake because this seating assignment on the flight did not afford him a view of the cockpit. He claims to have done what he could to case the flight, testing security by carrying a box cutter in his toiletries kit onto the flight to Hong Kong. He returned to Bangkok the following day.

At this point, the mysterious Arabs separated and the CIA was unable to monitor their activities. In an egregious blow by U.S. intelligence, two of the men whose names came up in the Malaysia meeting, Nawaf al-Hazmi and Khalid al-Midhar, entered the United States. Al Hazmi came in January 2000, and al-Midhar at the same time (at some point in his stay in the U.S., al-Midhar would leave and return). The remaining hijackers would all enter the U.S. between May 2000 and June 2001.

None of the 9-11 hijackers were ever noticed in the State Department Watch List of potential terrorists as they entered the United States.

It was not until the summer of 2001 that the State Department asked that a visa search be put into effect regarding al-Midhar and al-Hazmi. Their names came up positive, meaning that they were someplace in the United States (they settled in San Diego, California, and used their real names when they rented an apartment). Both men were in the U.S, eighteen months before being placed on the State Department's Watch List, a glaring error that cannot be explained. Even more baffling is the fact that the CIA did not inform the FBI that both men were somewhere inside the United States, making it almost impossible to track them down. By the summer of 2000, the CIA team that had been watching the two men after the Malaysia meeting dropped the matter and went on to other duties.

There was one more step that the CIA would take in order to try to tie up all the loose ends regarding the Malaysia summit. An officer in the CIA hierarchy, Tom Wilshire, recommended to his superiors

23 The Malaysia meetings and surveillance of Midhar.

that an officer be tasked with the job of reviewing the information about al Qaeda's Malaysian summit and any connection between some of the participants and the USS *Cole* attack. The person who was assigned to do the job was Margaret Gillespie, who was an agent on loan from the FBI. In his book called *The Looming Tower,* author Lawrence Wright wrote the following about this incident: "But Wilshire did not reveal that some of the participants might be in the United States. More important, he conveyed none of the urgency reflected in an e-mail he sent to his superiors around this time; he told Gillespie that she should examine the material in her free time. She didn't get around to it until the end of July." This delay on the part of Gillespie resulted in it taking her three months to find out that some of the 9-11 hijackers had already entered the United States. It wasn't until late August 2001, one month before 9-11, that Gillespie alerted one of Wilshire's associates at the FBI to their presence in the country.

In her search for answers, Margaret Gillespie checked a CIA database called Interlink and found out that both Nawaf al-Hazmi and Khalid al-Midhar had been at the Malaysia summit. Interlink only had information that the CIA made available to other intelligence agencies. "However, she did not examine the CIA's Hercules database. It is unclear why she did not do this, whether as an FBI agent, she had access to it. If she did access it, she would have had a complete picture of the CIA's knowledge of al-Midhar and Al-Hazmi and would know al-Midhar had a U.S. visa and Al-Hazmi had traveled to the U.S.—as Gillespie was only working this line of inquiry in her free time, she did not put together the information contained in the Hercules system until late August."[24]

This begs an answer. Why did Margaret Gillespie not devote her full time to tracking down the leads in the Malaysia Summit of a group of well-known al Qaeda members? Maybe at the time, the top men at the FBI did not find it sufficiently interesting to mount a full-time investigation for whatever reasons they had. Is this dereliction of duty or just another slip up in the events that were going on at the time?

Later, after reviewing the Malaysia information as well as the USS *Cole* information, Gillespie said, "It all clicks for me." The

24 History Commons: Mid-May 2001: CIA Assigns Officer to Examine Malaysia Summit in Her free time.

Justice Department's Office of Inspector General would find that Gillespie's actions on receipt of the information clearly indicated that she understood the significance of this information. She took immediate steps to open an intelligence investigation.

Since the release of the 9-11 Commission report we now have a much more detailed account of the people and events related to the Malaysia meeting.

According to the report, Khalid al-Midhar, Nawaf al-Hazmi, and another man named Abu Bara, all spent time in an al Qaeda training camp called Mes Aynak in Afghanistan. This camp was located near an old Russian copper mine that had been turned into a state-of-the-art jihadist training facility. Opened in 1999, the camp gave recruits instructions in commando operations, hand-to-hand combat, motorcycle training, and basic English classes.

After they completed training at Mes Aynak, Hazmi, al-Midhar, and Abu Bara headed for Karachi, Pakistan where they met KSM who gave them further instruction in preparation for 9-11. Among the activities practiced under KSM's tutelage, were learning English phrases, reading all sorts of aviation magazines cover to cover, learning how to use American phone directories, and how to read airline tables, and Internet searches of U.S. flight schools.

"In early December 1999, Khalid and Abu Bara arrived in Karachi. Hazmi joins them there a few days later. On his way to Karachi, Hazmi spent a night in Quetta (Pakistan) at a safe house where, according to KSM, an Egyptian named Mohamed Atta simultaneously stayed on his way to Afghanistan for jihad training."

If seems that for whatever reason, al-Midhar did not go to Karachi with the other men. KSM later said that it was possible that he was briefed by bin Laden or his top aid, Mohammed Atef, at some previous time.

According to KSM, Khalid, Abu Bara, and Hazmi came to Kuala Lumpur from Karachi, while al-Midhar arrived via Yemen. KSM further stated that Hazmi and Midhar arrived in Kuala Lumpur carrying Yemeni documents and then flew on to the United States using their Saudi passports that would hide the fact that they had been in Pakistan. KSM said that he faked Hazmi's

Saudi passport that showed that he arrived in Malaysia via Saudi Arabia by way of Dubai. KSM also revealed that Khalid and Abu Bara's mission in Kuala Lumpur was to analyze airport security in case al Qaeda decided to mount an attack in Southeast Asia at a later date.

Another person who would play a part in the Kuala Lumpur meeting of bin Laden's henchmen was a shadowy player in international terrorism, Riduan Isamuddin, a.k.a, Hambali. Malaysian officials have compared Hambali to certain members of the American mafia. "If Abu Bakar [a radical spiritual leader in Malaysia] is the godfather, Hambali is the consiglieri or chief advisor and operational director."

The 9-11 Commission revealed that when Khalid and Abu Bara arrived in Malaysia, they contacted Hambali to tell him of their presence in their country. On February 7, 2002, Abu Bara was arrested in a raid of an al Qaeda safe house in Karachi, Pakistan. Another 17 men were also taken into custody. After his arrest, Abu Bara was sent to the U.S. Naval base prison at Guantanamo Bay, Cuba were many of the terrorists involved in the 9-11 attacks were placed.

Hambali led an interesting life, traveling from country to country, taking up al Qaeda's bidding. He set up shop in the village of Sungai Manggis, Malaysia, about an hour north of Kuala Lumpur. He had previously fought with bin Laden in Afghanistan in the late 1980s. He also took part in the 1995 Bojinka plot with Ramzi Yousef in the Philippines. Even though the CIA knew of his participation in the Malaysian summit, as well as his links to other international terrorists, the United States government refused to take any action against him or put him on any watchlist for further investigation.

Hambali was an ingenious man and he was part of a front company called Konsonjaya. One of the people he was associated with in the founding of this company was Wali Khan Amin Shah, a member of the Bojinka plot with Ramzi Yousef. *Time* magazine later reported, "In the first clear indication of Hambali's direct links to Osama bin Laden, Philippine police phone taps showed that frequent calls were made from the Konsonjaya office in Malaysia to the Manila office of Khalifa (bin Laden's brother-in-law), who headed a charitable organization which was allegedly a conduit for al Qaeda funds. The Associated Press will also report that the Philippine police investigation of Bojinka uncovered information pointing to Hambali but it seems these links to Hambali and other support cells in Southeast Asia are not acted on by Philippine intelligence. It is unknown how much of this is shared with U.S. intelligence at the time."

The Malaysian contingent also stayed at the home of Yazid Sufaat, a 1987 graduate of Cal State with a degree in biological sciences. He would be arrested on December 9, 2001 and began telling U.S. Intelligence what he knew about al Qaeda and the Malaysia meeting. It has also been alleged that Sufaat played host to Zacarias Moussaoui who was taken into custody by the FBI in the summer of 2001 for passport violations at a flying school he was attending. It has also been alleged that Sufaat gave Moussaoui $35,000 during his stay in Malaysia.

According to published accounts, Hambali ordered Sufaat to arrange for Khalid al-Midhar and Nawaf al-Hazmi, two of the 9-11 hijackers, to stay at his home for a three-day period in January 2000.

The CIA was aware of the Malaysia meeting and asked the Malaysian intelligence service to monitor what was going on. Since the CIA had no real knowledge of what was taking place at the meeting, they did not ask Malaysian authorities to make any arrests.

As mentioned before, the Malaysian security forces had been monitoring the meeting and had passed their information along to the CIA. Also, they had photographs of the men and they also passed along these photos to the CIA. This information was sent to the CIA's Counterterrorism Center and was analyzed by Cofer Black, the unit's head. Black also informed DCI Tenet about the goings-on in Kuala Lumpur. Other members of the Clinton administration who were kept abreast of the Malaysian meeting were FBI Director Louis Freeh, and the president's National Security Advisor, Sandy Berger.

On January 8, 2000, the Malaysian meeting ended and the various participants went their separate ways. However, the agency did not know enough to ask the NSA to place Khalid al-Midhar on its terrorist watchlist. In a stunning omission, al-Midhar and Nawaf al-Hazmi still are not placed on the watchlist. In another move that later caused controversy, the CIA did not inform the FBI that al-Midhar was carrying a U.S. visa, nor did they give the FBI the last name of al-Hazmi. When the CIA went through its huge data base they came up empty on both men. However, they did not check with the NSA who did have information on both men.

When one looks back at the goings-on at the Malaysia summit, the objective viewer is struck by what was taking place. Once again, hindsight is a wonderful thing when seen after the fact. But what the Malaysian authorities saw, and passed on to the CIA, was the fact that a large number of known international terrorists were meeting in one location for over a week. Yes, the ground rules stated that no audio surveillance was to be taken but just the fact that all these men were in one place at one time, ostensibly planning something besides visiting the tourist sites in Malaysia, should have rung alarm bells at both intelligence services. Could a covert entry have been carried out to plant bugs in the rooms when they weren't there have led to a major breakthrough?

When one looks at the failure of the CIA to share the information it had on al-Hazmi and al-Midhar, two possible conspiracy theories come into mind. This is just speculation on the writer's part but it is worthwhile spending a few minutes fleshing out these possible scenarios.

One involves the activities of John O'Neill. O'Neill was one of the most important FBI senior agents at the time and if it weren't for his high lifestyle and the sometimes incompetent way he handled his FBI duties, he might have been on a fast track for a top job at the bureau. He was not liked very much by members of the CIA, especially those members who were tracking bin Laden and his henchmen around the world. The members of the CIA who were on the front lines of this investigation knew that if they shared all their information with O'Neill and his fellow FBI agents, their hold over their top secret information might be compromised. This was especially true of Michael Scheuer who was the man most responsible for the creation of the CIA's Alec Station whose main job was to track bin Laden's activities worldwide. The Alec Station had begun operations with twelve employees in 1996, and would grow to twenty-five by the time of the Malaysian meeting.

By 1993, Alec Station had thirty-five volumes of material on bin

Laden, consisting mostly of transcripts of telephone conversations that had been sucked up by the electronic ears of the National Security Agency. The thirty-five volumes in Alec Station painted a picture of a messianic billionaire from a sprawling, influential family that was closely connected to the rulers of the Kingdom of Saudi Arabia. He had made a name for himself in the jihad in Afghanistan against the Soviet occupation.

The people who worked at Alec Station had less experience than their counterparts and most of them were women. Their primary job was to stop any attack on the United States, a position that would make anyone nervous on a day-to-day basis (these women employees would sometimes be called "The Manson Family").

The members of Alec Station at the time were the following people: Michael Anne Casey, Alfreda Bikowsky, Tom Wilshire, Doug Miller, Richard Blee, Mark Rossini, Charles Frahm, a person only known as "Eric," Michael Scheuer, Margaret Gillespie, and Lynne Matthews. It was up to these dedicated people to take on a huge task that was doomed from the start because of the hubris of both the CIA and the FBI that would hamper the task at hand.

The employees of the Alec Station were livid as some of its members held John O'Neill primarily responsible for the firing of Mike Scheuer. "Only a few months before, the senior FBI agent assigned to Alec had demanded the authority to release CIA information to the bureau, and the quarrel over this matter had gone all the way to Freeh and Tenet, the respective heads of the two institutions. Scheuer was forces to step down, but the FBI agent who did gain that authority developed cancer and had to resign only a few days before the Malaysia meeting." [25]

From the CIA's perspective, it would have been in its best interest not to allow John O'Neill anywhere near its most secret intelligence. Was there a decision made at Langley HQ not to allow O'Neill and his FBI counterparts access to their material, a conscious effort to keep him at bay, no matter the consequences? For John O'Neill was the ultimate bull in a china shop and there was no way to determine just how much damage he could have done.

Alec Station was first set up in what was called a "virtual" station, its employees given one important and all-consuming job.

25 Wright, Lawrence, *The Looming Tower: Al Qaeda and the Road to 9-11,* Alfred Knopf, New York, 2006,. Page 313.

The station was part of the CTC—Counterterrorism Center—whose mandate was to investigate terrorist financial links, but it soon morphed into the unit that was to track Osama bin Laden. As mentioned before, the head of Alec Station was Mike Scheuer who had extensive experience in the CIA; as the investigation of bin Laden went on, would acquire as many adversaries as he had friends.

In 1996, Alec Station obtained information from another intelligence unit (the NSA in particular) about bin Laden's activities in Yemen. They fought tooth and nail to get all the transcripts of the information picked up by the NSA, and in time they were provided. As the investigation of al-Hazmi and al-Midhar went on, there was increasing tension between the FBI and Alec Station as to what type of information was to be shared by the agencies. Shouting matches and threats of people being prosecuted were as common as a cold and tensions were always on the rise when the two agencies attended joint meetings. In regards to both al-Hazmi and al-Midhar, one account of a meeting said, "But the FBI agents suddenly couldn't remember details about who said what, who reported what, to whom, about the presence of two al Qaeda agents in the U.S. prior to the 9-11 attacks."

In 2008, the Congressional Quarterly did a study of what was supposed to have happened in a Justice Department inspector general interview with two men, Doug Miller, an FBI agent at Alec Station and Mark Rossini, an FBI agent also assigned to Alec Station. In an excerpt from the Congressional Quarterly Report, it said,

> But Rossini and Miller did come clean during an internal FBI investigation, which remains under wraps. Sources with direct knowledge of the FBI's internal probe say that the agents provided the bureau with unadulterated versions of their CTC experiences, including orders they were given by the center's then Deputy Director, Tom Wilshire, to withhold intelligence about the movement of al Qaeda operatives into the country from the FBI.
>
> This clearly implies that the FBI, which is part of the Justice Department inspector general's report was based on a raft of falsehoods, and then decided to keep this

> secret while the entire U.S. intelligence community was re-organized and the U.S. made war in Afghanistan and Iraq.[26]

The actions of the FBI were not the only ones to be chastised in regards to the presence of the two hijackers in the country. According to the executive summary of the CIA inspector general's report, there are a number of people who were taken to task regarding terrorists in America prior to 9-11.

•Richard Blee. Some sections of the executive summary appear to refer to him, but are redacted. It seems to criticize him for failing to properly oversee operations related to KSM, failing to ensure the FBI was informed al-Hazmi had entered the U.S., and failing to do anything about a-Hazmi and al-Midhar in 2001.

•Unnamed officer, for failing to ensure the FBI was informed al-Hazmi had entered the U.S., and for failing to do anything about al-Hazmi and al-Midhar in 2001.

•Deputy Chief of Alec Station, Tom Wilshire. Some sections of the executive summary appear to refer to Wilshire, but are redacted. It seems to criticize him for failing to ensure the FBI was informed al-Hazmi had entered the U.S., and for failing to do anything about both men in 2001.

•Director of Central Intelligence George Tenet (July 1997-July 2001), for failing to personally resolve differences between the CIA and NSA that impeded counterterrorism efforts.

•CIA Counterterrorist Chief Jeff O'Connell (1997-1999) for failing to properly manage CIA counterterrorism funds, for staffing Alec Station with officers lacking experience, expertise and training, for failing to ensure units under him coordinated coverage of Khalid Sheikh Mohammed, for poor leadership of the CIA's watchlist program, for poor management of a program under which officers were loaned between CIA and other agencies, and for failing to send officers to the NSA to review its material.

•CIA Counterterrorist Center chief Cofer Black. Black (summer 1999-December 2002) moved to a counterterrorism position at the State Department, then served as vice president of the notorious private security contractor Blackwater USA from 2004-2008, for failing to properly manage CIA counterterrorism funds, for

26 Fenton, Kevin, *Disconnecting the Dots*, Page 65.

staffing Alec Station with officers lacking experience, expertise and training, for failing to ensure units under him coordinated coverage of KSM, for poor leadership of the CIA's watchlist program, possibly for failing to ensure the FBI was informed al-Midhar had entered the U.S., possibly for failing to do anything about al-Hazmi and al-Midhar in 2001, for poor management of a program where officers were loaned between CIA and other agencies, and for failing to send officers to the NSA to review its material.

These were damming indictments to be sure, but in the end, no official in a high-ranking position in any of the intelligence agencies was ever fired in the wake of 9-11.

Another black mark on Alec Station came in a book written by Michael Scheuer in 2008 in which he said, "In early 2004, the 9-11 Commission indicated that they were intending to name a young CIA officer as the only individual to be publicly identified for a pre-9-11 failure. A group of senior CIA officers let it be known that if the officer was named, information about the pre-9-11 negligence of several very senior U.S. officials would find its way into the media. The Commissioners dropped the issue."

In his book called *Disconnecting the Dots,* Kevin Fenton says the unnamed junior officer referred to might have been Tom Wilshire, or possibly a woman whose name was referred to only as "Michelle" who was the senior officer responsible for investigating the Yemen site bin Laden was then making his central hub of operations.

There were many unexplained events that were not put in the official 9-11 Report, and while the following story is not part of the Alec Station investigation, it is well worth describing.

This event centers on an E-4B "Doomsday Plane," which is a command and control aircraft, also known as the "Flying Pentagon," which was seen over Washington D.C. at the time that the Pentagon was hit. This event was mentioned by John Farmer in his book called *The Ground Truth.* Mr. Farmer was a team leader on the 9-11 Commission and his group was aware of the plane's existence but it was never put into the official report. According to Farmer, "The reason for the omission was that the administration deemed any information regarding the plane or its flight path highly confidential. Like other omissions, however, it has led some to believe that the plane played a significant role in the events of that morning. It did not. In that respect, the omission was regrettable."

Other reporting on Farmer and the "Doomsday Plane" was done by Mark Gaffney in his book called *The 9-11 Mystery Plane and the Vanishing of America.* Gaffney's book corroborated the story of Mr. Farmer and as author Fenton points out, if it weren't for the efforts of Mr. Gaffney, it is possible that Mr. Farmer would never have admitted the existence of the plane in the first place.[27]

What is glaring in the whole 9-11 saga and the CIA's failure to locate the hijackers before the day of the attack, is just how extensive was the role of KSM in the plot. There are mountains of evidence linking him to the Bojinka plot and his family relations with Ramzi Yousef, much of which has been previously related in this book. But his tentacles went far beyond the Bojinka plot and the 1993 WTC bombing. For example, the CIA said it never had any evidence linking KSM to al Qaeda until early 2002. But KSM was the fourth target on the agency's hit list in Afghanistan in November 2001, after bin Laden, his deputy Ayman al-Zawahiri and al Qaeda military commander Mohammed Atef.

It seems that the various agencies who did reporting on the 9-11 attack, the 9-11 Commission and the Congressional Inquiry, came up with different versions of just how important, or not, KSM really was. The 9-11 Commission wrote, "Although we readily equate KSM with al Qaeda today, this was not the case before 9-11. KSM, who had been indicted in January 1996 for his role in the Manila air plot, was seen primarily as another freelance terrorist, associated with Ramzi Yousef. Because the links with KSM and bin Laden or al Qaeda were not recognized at the time, responsibility for KSM remained in the small Islamic Extremist Branch of the Counterterrorism Center, not in the bin Laden unit."

Despite this report, the CIA did have knowledge of KSM and his links to al Qaeda, yet they still said he was a minor player. The CIA also knew that he had attended the Malaysia summit with the other hijackers and this should have raised a red flag at Langley headquarters. Their report on him goes on to say, "Moreover, because KSM had already been indicted, he became targeted for

27 Fenton, Kevin, *Disconnecting the Dots*. Page 166-67.

arrest. In 1997, the Counterterrorist Center added a Renditions Branch to help find wanted fugitives. Responsibility for KSM was transferred to this branch, which gave the CIA a man-to-man focus but was not an analytical unit. When subsequent information came, more critical for analysis than for tracking, one unit had the job of following up on what the information might mean."[28]

Another damming indictment of KSM and the CIA was written by the Congressional Inquiry: "CIA disseminated a report that KSM had traveled to the United States as recently as May 2001 and was sending recruits to the United States to meet colleagues already in the country, this did not cause the Intelligence Community to mobilize, even though it contained apparently significant [redacted] information. The report explained that KSM was a relative of convicted World Trade Center bomber Ramzi Yousef, appeared to be one of bin Laden's most trained lieutenants and was active in recruiting people to travel outside of Afghanistan, including the United States to carry out unspecified activities on behalf of bin Laden. The clear implication of his comments, according to the report, was that they would be engaged in planning terrorist related activities."

Another report on KSM came to the CIA in August 2001, when it was reported that KSM's nickname was Mukhtar. The Commission calls this the "final piece of the puzzle" linking KSM to al Qaeda and the 9-11 plot, but goes on to say that its importance was not appreciated.

The 9-11 Commission had its own version of the links between KSM and al Qaeda but these weren't the same sentiments as those of the Congressional Inquiry. In their report, they said that,

> This assessment changed in 1996 when a foreign government shared information that bin Laden and KSM had traveled together to a foreign country (Brazil) the previous year. In August 1998, after the bombing of the U.S. Embassy in Nairobi, another foreign government sent CIA a list of the names of individuals who flew into Nairobi before the attack. Based on information delivered by another liaison service, CIA recognized that one of the passengers' names was an alias of KSM. The liaison report

28 *Disconnecting the Dots*, Page 358.

> also described KSM as close to bin Laden. In an interview, the FBI agent responsible for the KSM case (apparently Frank Pellegrino) could not remember this information, even though it had been disseminated by the CIA. This information, and subsequent reporting led to CIA to see KSM as part of bin Laden's organization. Several CIA cables indicate that following up on information relevant to KSM was essential, given his past activities and his likes to al Qaeda.

If KSM was not seen as a major player in the upcoming plot, why is it that the CIA was intercepting his calls? Reporter Jonathan Landay from the news organization Knight Ridder said that the NSA had been monitoring KSM's phone calls with Mohamed Atta prior to 9-11 but did not share that information with other U.S. agencies. An important phone call was monitored on July 20, 2001 of a conversation between KSM and Ramzi bin al-Shib who attended the Malaysia meeting with the other hijackers.

The U.S. intelligence agencies were also very interested in KSM's use of his alias, Mukhtar. They were eager to find out just who he was and they pulled out all stops to find him. The FBI in particular was interested in finding out who the mysterious Mukhtar was and where he stood in the terrorist world. The FBI would still be trying to find out about him even after 9-11.

It seems that the CIA was already planning a high-stakes scheme of its own to kill not only bin Laden and his number two, al-Zawahiri, but al Qaeda's military commander Mohammed Atef and Khalid Sheikh Mohammed. This raises a number of questions in regard to the U.S. intelligence agency's thoughts on KSM and how high he was in al Qaeda's pecking order. Author Ken Fenton writes about this area of investigation saying, "Nevertheless, his inclusion among the top four targets in Afghanistan is startling if we accept the narrative that the CIA did not know of his role in the 9-11 operation, thinking of him primarily as 'another freelance terrorist.' It suggests that the CIA then understood the information it had on KSM better than the 9/11 Commission later claimed, and that when the FBI told it that KSM was responsible for 9-11, the CIA was not surprised."

Another top al Qaeda leader who identified KSM by his alias was Abu Zubaida who was wounded and captured on March 28, 2002. When Abu Zubaida was transferred to a CIA black site in Thailand he was first interviewed by FBI agent Ali Soufan, who had worked closely with John O'Neill on the investigation of al Qaeda, and especially of the USS *Cole* bombing. At that meeting (and before the CIA interrogation team arrived) Soufan showed a picture of KSM to Abu Zabaida who said in reply, "That's Mukhtar." Once the CIA interrogators arrived to talk with Abu Zubaida, Ali Soufan and his FBI partners were ordered out of the room and they never talked with Zubaida again. In the end, the FBI was not able to find out any more information regarding the detention and interrogation of captured al Qaeda suspects, thus,making the trust between the CIA and the FBI all but nonexistent. This is the famous "wall" separating the CIA and the FBI in the lead up to 9-11 where it was more important to keep secrets from one another than share vital information before it was too late.

As we can see, Alec Station was knee deep in its hunt for al Qaeda, including its two men al-Midhar and al-Hazmi who were ensconced in the U.S. doing who knows what. They never gave this information to the FBI, again, for reasons we don't really know. Maybe Alec Station wanted to use both men for some reason of their own, maybe some sort of clandestine operation inside the U.S. (something that their charter prohibited them from doing). In the world of lights and shadows, some things are explained, while others remain in the dark.

The second conspiracy theory has to do with the government of Saudi Arabia and its connection to al-Midhar and al-Hazmi. Earlier in this book the writer talked about a person named Omar Bayoumi, who befriended both men in San Diego. The FBI believed at the time that he might have been on the payroll of the Saudi government. In his book *The Looming Tower,* Lawrence Wright wrote the following on this matter:

> If Bayoumi was sent to oversee the two men, who sent him? Perhaps he was their al Qaeda contact. They certainly needed a caretaker. The fact that Bayoumi went directly from the Saudi consulate to the restaurant, however,

> suggests to some investigators that the two future hijackers were already under surveillance by Saudi government officials who were aware of their relationship in al Qaeda. The CIA is the only government agency that knew who Hazmi and Midhar were and that they were in America. The CIA tracked Midhar and Hazmi from Kuala Lumpur to Bangkok to Los Angeles. Perhaps the agency decided that Saudi intelligence would have a better chance of recruiting these men than the Americans. That would leave no CIA fingerprints on the operation as well.

Despite these very disturbing leads, it seems that a cover-up of these events went into overdrive. This information was not published in the official 9-11 report but was recorded in the form of a footnote. The man responsible for this lack of oversight was Dieter Snell, who insisted that this material be deleted from the report, as he was not 100% certain of the Saudi links. Snell was backed up by Philip Zelikow who saw the material as not of any merit.

This is a very interesting and disturbing observation. Was the CIA even thinking of recruiting these two men while they were in the country? The agency had no knowledge of what they were doing in the States and what they were up to. And why would the Saudis recruit them? Maybe to put a spy inside the organization that bin Laden ran in order to keep an eye out for what he was doing? After all, the Saudis had expelled bin Laden from his home country and were probably desperate to find out what their old nemesis was up to. These are two interesting scenarios to look into, as they add more mystery to an already complex case.

This so-called Saudi connection with the two hijackers was given more leverage by two espionage writers of some note, Joe and Susan Trento. In an article they wrote regarding any possible links with al-Midhar and al-Hazmi they state, "A former CIA officer who worked in Saudi Arabia described what he says happened. We had been unable to penetrate al Qaeda. The Saudis claimed that they had done it successfully. Both al-Hazmi and al-Midhar were Saudi agents. We thought they had been screened. It turned out that the man responsible for recruiting them had been loyal to Osama bin Laden. The truth is bin Laden himself was a Saudi agent at one time. He successfully penetrated Saudi intelligence and created his own operation inside. It was a huge mistake. The reason the FBI was not given any information about either man is because they were Saudi assets operating with CIA knowledge in the United States."[29]

The Trentos later wrote more about the subject of al-Hazmi and al-Midhar being part of a larger plot hatched by Saudi intelligence. They wrote that the CIA believed that the Saudis has successfully placed moles inside al Qaeda who would report back to them on what they found. They postulate that the moles were never properly vetted to see if their bona fides were correct and that in reality, the men were triple agents in the employ of bin Laden. "Saudi intelligence had sent agents Khalid al-Midhar and Nawaf al-Hazmi to spy on a meeting of top associates of al Qaeda in Kuala Lumpur, Malaysia, January 5-8, 2000. The Saudi/CIA hope was that the Saudis would learn details of bin Laden's future plans. Instead, plans were finalized and the Saudis learned nothing, says a terrorism expert who asks that his identity be withheld."

According to the authors, top members of the CIA had convinced themselves that the Saudis had placed agents of their own service inside al Qaeda, i.e., al-Hazmi and al-Midhar and that the CIA purposely failed to tell the FBI about this rather interesting fact, and that they were inside the United States. "Had the CIA shared what it knew, the FBI might have had a chance at preventing the 9-11 attacks."

There were some members of the Alec Station however, who had a rather dim view of the Saudi intelligence service, and, in a note to DCI George Tenet in 1997, called them a "hostile service" when it came to dealings with al Qaeda. According to certain CIA sources, some of the information given by the U.S. to Saudi intelligence wound up in the hands of al Qaeda. Some of these concerned certain NSA intercepts, "which included conversations among suspected al Qaeda operatives in Saudi Arabia. But after the CIA gave the intercepts to the Saudis, the suspects quickly stopped using the communications that the Americans had been monitoring, making it far more difficult to track the terrorists."

29 Trento, Joe, "The Real Intelligence Cover-up: America's Unholy Alliance," *Stories That Matter* August 6, 2003.

Whatever the truth is regarding the two men being plants of the Saudi government inside al Qaeda, the possibility is still a real stretch of the imagination. Conspiracy theories abound in a case like this and nineteen years after the fact leads the trail cold, if there ever was one to begin with.

The Trentos would write more about the secret relationship between the United States and the government of Saudi Arabia, especially its intelligence service, in their 2005 book called *Prelude to Terror: The Rogue CIA and the Legacy of America's Private Intelligence Network*. It is a story right out of a good spy novel, with individuals involved in illicit dealings, foreign powers vying for influence, and a network of private people whose lust for power and influence spanned many decades and a myriad of scandals.

They trace the relationship between president George H.W. Bush and the Saudi royal family beginning when the Saudis first provided money to the Texas oil industry in the early 1970s. George Bush had a close relationship with a man named Sheikh Kamal Adham, the Director of Saudi intelligence. They were supposed to have first met when Bush was the ambassador to the United Nations. Another prominent Saudi whom Bush was looking into was Kamal Adham's nephew Prince Turki bin Faisal, who would later himself become director of Saudi intelligence. Among the Americans who cultivated Turki at that time were a rogues gallery of former CIA agents who were involved in a multitude of political scandals throughout the years, including Frank Terpil, Edwin Wilson, Theodore Shackley, and Thomas Clines. There is not room enough in this narrative to give the life story of these men, save to say that they were involved in the Iran-Contra scandal, the plots to kill Fidel Castro, and a secret relationship with Libyan strongman Qaddafi, among other nefarious persons.

All this was going on when the Congress of the United States began investigating the CIA after the Watergate scandal and other abuses of the CIA and FBI. The Trentos write that at that time, Prince Turki and Kamal Adham played an intricate role in establishing a secret spy network off the books of the CIA to run covert operations. Adham was approached by Clark Clifford, a power player in Washington for decades. "Clark Clifford approached

Kamal Adham and asked that the Saudis consider setting up an informal intelligence network outside the United States during the investigations." Robert Crowley, who knew about the plan said, "Worldwide covert operations for the agency were funded through a host of Saudi banking and charity enterprises. Several top U.S. military and intelligence officials directed the operation from positions they held overseas, notably former CIA Director Richard Helms, at the time Ambassador to Iran."

Prince Turki was responsible for funding a number of these off the books operations and the CIA was none the wiser. According to Thomas Clines who took part in these activities, "these operations were so sensitive, they could not be revealed." Another participant in these activities, Mike Pilgram said, "It got to the point where we were used to support GID operations when the CIA could not."

This secret network was made public by none other than Prince Turki himself in a speech he gave in February 2002 at Georgetown University. He said that with the CIA then being investigated by Congress, a private security and spy service called the Safari Club was formed to fill the void. The Safari Club included France, Egypt, Saudi Arabia, Morocco, and Iran. The purpose of the Safari Club was to share intelligence in the Cold War against Russia, especially in Africa. With the CIA being helpless, the Safari Club members took over. "And so, the Kingdom, with these countries helped in some way, I believe, to keep the world safe at the time when the United States was not able to do that. That, I think, is a secret that many of you don't know. I am not saying it because I look to tell secrets, but because the time has gone and many of the actors are gone as well."[30]

In order to hide their funds during this time period, the Saudis opened up a bank account at the Riggs bank in Washington. Over time, tens of millions of dollars were transferred between the CIA and accounts that were controlled by the Saudi government. Edwin Wilson, a major intermediary in these plots said of the Riggs/ CIA account, "If I needed money for an operation, Prince Turki made it available."

Adham also worked with the Saudis to open another banking institution in Saudi Arabia to funnel these covert monies for

30 Trento, Joseph, *Prelude to Terror.* Carroll and Graf Books, New York, 2005. Page 101-102.

intelligence purposes. In 1976 an institution called Nugan Hand Bank was opened in Saudi Arabia. The Nugan Hand Bank is a story in itself but suffice it to say that they were the perfect money conduit that the CIA needed. The bank had a notorious reputation for handling all sorts of illegal and illicit transactions dating back to the late 1960s when Nugan Hand handled the profits from the drug smuggling operations then going on in Southeast Asia during the Vietnam War.

Nugan Hand Bank was established in 1973 in Australia to help fund CIA operations worldwide. Frank Hand was a lawyer who had not had a very stellar reputation when it came to doing business. Mike Hand was a soldier who had no experience in banking but as the old saying goes, it is not what you know but *who* you know. The people in the know for both Hand and Nugan were certain high-ranking people at the CIA and their helpers like Ted Shackley and William Colby who would later become director of Central Intelligence. Hand and Nugan hired a number of old boys from the U.S. intelligence community to work for them, many of whom worked in Laos and Vietnam.

So, it came as no surprise that Prince Turki and his family allowed Nugan Hand Bank to set up shop in Saudi Arabia with the help of Adham to do the dirty work of espionage that the CIA was unwilling or unable to do at that time.

In *Prelude to Terror,* Joe Trento wrote that Kamal Adham was so influential in intelligence circles that he was able to have Director of Central Intelligence George Bush to place Egypt's Vice President Anwar Sadat on an intelligence payroll, in effect, making Adham Sadat's controller. "This relationship gave Adham leverage when the time came to persuade Sadat to sign the Camp David accords" which led to a peace treaty between Israel and Egypt that is still in place today.

Adham not only had influence when it came to raising covert money but also had a hand in establishing a covert military network that caused mayhem around the Middle East. They scoured the Middle East for mercenaries and came up with a 1,500 man army, a group of assassins and enforcers to do their dirty deeds. *Time* magazine wrote about Adham's secret army saying it was a "black network. It combined intelligence with an effort to control a large portion of the world's economy."

One more thing on Adham as it relates to this story of intelligence and covert dealings. In 1978, a group of foreign investors attempted to buy First American Bankshares, the largest bank in Washington, D.C. Kamal Adham was the frontman for the investment group which soon got the attention of the Federal Reserve Bank in the United States. The Fed contacted the CIA to find out what information they had on Adham and his ties to First American Bankshares. The Federal Reserve was probably shocked to find out what the CIA told them regarding Adham and it is not certain just how much their brothers at Langley gave them. The sale of American Bankshares was approved in 1982 and it turned out that Adham was fronting for the secret criminal bank called Bank of Credit and Commercial International or BCCI (see Chapter 4 for more information on BCCI). The CIA kept accounts at First American and it was said at the time that "Government investigators now had proof that First American had long been the CIA's principal banker." Some of the more than 50 agency accounts uncovered at the bank dated back to the 1950s. BCCI owned the CIA's bank for a decade. By 1985, the CIA would secretly inform the Treasury Department on the bank's control by BCCI, which was illegal. But no action was taken, then or later, until BCCI was shut down. Senator Kerry's BCCI investigation would later conclude, "Even when the CIA knew that BCCI was as an institution a fundamentally corrupt criminal enterprise, it used both BCCI and First American, BCCI's secretly held U.S. subsidiary, for CIA operations. In the latter case, some First American officials actually knew of this use."[31]

At the end of 1999, Saudi intelligence director Prince Turki al Faisal said that he contacted members of the CIA informing them that the Saudis had put al-Midhar and al-Hazmi's names on their own terror watchlist. According to Director Turki, "What we told the CIA was these people were on our watchlist from previous activities of al Qaeda, in both the embassy bombings and attempts to smuggle arms into the Kingdom in 1997." The CIA later denied that they received any word from Prince Turki regarding these two men.

31 History Commons: 1978-1982-Criminal BCCI Secretly Buys CIA Main U.S. bank, Even as CIA uses bank for covert operations.

On August 31, 2001, barely one month before 9-11, Prince Turki was abruptly replaced as director of Saudi intelligence after 24 years. It was believed by officials at that time that he had gone out of favor with the rulers of the kingdom and was replaced by Nawaf bin Abdul Aziz, his nephew and the king's brother. Abdul Aziz had no intelligence experience to speak of and Turki's release was felt not only in Saudi Arabia but in Washington as well where agents couldn't understand why such a move was taken in the tension-filled months before the Washington and New York attacks.

Prince Turki said that al Qaeda had attempted to smuggle weapons into the Kingdom of Saudi Arabia to mount attacks on certain police stations. However, the plot was uncovered before it took place. While all this was going on, both al-Midhar and al-Hazmi were in Saudi Arabia and moved into and out of the country at will. Also, a man named Abd al-Rahim al Nashiri, who was an associate of al-Midhar, was implicated in a plot to smuggle Russian antitank missiles into Saudi Arabia in the time period of January 5-8, 2000. The Saudis uncovered the plot and told the United States about it.

In the month prior to 9-11, it seems that diplomatic relations between the U.S. and its erstwhile ally Saudi Arabia were in freefall. On August 27, 2001, Crown Prince Abdullah, the leader of the kingdom, had grown so upset with the Bush administration's policy towards Israel that he threatened to cut off diplomatic relations. On that date the Crown Prince wrote to President Bush saying, "This is the most difficult message I have had to convey to you that I have ever conveyed between the two governments since I started working here in Washington in 1982." The message ended by saying, "Therefore, the Crown Prince will not communicate in any form, type or shape to you, and Saudi Arabia will take all its political, economic aid security decisions based on how it sees its own interests in the region without taking into account American strategic decisions regarding Sharon's policy." He was referring to the harsh conditions imposed by Israeli Prime Minister Sharon regarding the Palestinian people and their quest for a separate homeland from Israel.

President Bush responded quickly by telling the Crown Prince, "I want to assure you that the United States did not make any strategic decision." Later, on the same subject, Secretary of State Colin Powell confronted Prince Bandar and chewed him out saying, "What the f—k are you doing? You're putting the fear of God in everybody here. You scared the shit out of everybody." Bandar replied, "I don't give a damn what you feel. We are scared ourselves."[32]

Seeing that a possible break in relations between the two nations was on the brink, President Bush caved to the Saudis and wrote the following note to Crown Prince Abdullah: "Let me make one thing clear up front; nothing should ever break the relationship between us. There has been no change in the strategic equations. I firmly believe the Palestinian people have a right to live peacefully and safely in their own homeland, just as the Israeli's have the right to live peacefully and safely in their own state."

Hindsight is a very productive way of seeing things, and if President Bush had had a look into the future, he probably would not have made such a commitment to the Crown Prince. In that hectic week before 9-11, when the Saudi and U.S. government swere exchanging diplomatic messages, the last stages of the plot to attack America were in process.

In relation to al Hazmi and al Midhar, the New York FBI office asked that a formal investigation be launched to see if the men were in the United States. They wanted a criminal investigation to be set up but were turned down at FBI HQ. Instead, an "intelligence case," not including any intelligence information gathered by the CIA or FBI on the men, proceeded. In a cryptic e-mail written by an FBI agent regarding the search for al-Midhar and al-Hazmi he says, "Whatever has happened to this-someday someone will die— and wall or not [the intelligence wall separating the FBI and CIA] the public will not understand why we were not more effective and throwing every resource we had at certain problems."

On August 29, 2001, one week before 9-11, the FBI checkedthe registers of the Marriott hotels in New York and Los Angeles looking for any record that al-Midhar had checked in. Nothing wasfound.

By 9-11, all was in place. The hijackers and the muscle had purchased their tickets and have arrived at their assigned

32 History Commons: August 27, 2001. Saudis Threaten to End Their Alliance with U.S.

airports. All the years of planning, from the remote mountains of Afghanistan to the hot streets of Malaysia and Spain, to the cold avenues of Hamburg, had been perfected.

In the United States, the FBI and CIA, despite numerous warnings and leads from friendly intelligence services, had not connected the dots. The intelligence wall separating the intelligence services had not worked properly. Disaster lay ahead.

More Warning Signs

In the two years prior to 9-11, there were multiple warnings from various intelligence services that something was about to take shape, warnings that meant nothing at the time, but when looked at in total, meant a whole lot. For example in late 2000, British investigators teamed up with their partners in the Cayman Islands and began a yearlong investigation of three Afghan men who had arrived illegally in the Caymans. In June 2001, the Afghan men were overheard talking about hijacking attacks against targets in New York City, and were taken into custody. The information about the three Afghan men was forwarded to the United States but it is not known what, if anything, was done in this regard. In late August 2001, right before the attacks, an anonymous letter to a Cayman radio station alleged that these same men were al Qaeda agents who were organizing a major terrorist act against the U.S. via an airliner or airliners.

In late July 2001, Afghanistan's Foreign Minister Wakit Ahmed Muttawakil learned that bin Laden was planning a "huge attack" inside the United States. The attack, he said, was in the works and it would kill thousands of people. This information was given to him by the leader of the rebel Islamic Movement of Uzbekistan, which had an alliance with al Qaeda. Muttawakil sent this information via courier to the U.S. authorities where it was looked at, but due to the overwhelming amount of threats, it wasn't handled at the time.

In late July 2001, a warning came from an unusual source, from the Argentine Jewish community in which it was said, "an attack of major proportions was planned against either US, Argentina, or France. The information came from an unidentified intelligence agency."

An undercover agent based in Morocco who had burrowed deep inside al Qaeda, learned that bin Laden was "very disappointed" that the original 1993 bombing of the WTC by Ramzi Yousef and his gang had been unsuccessful. The agent said that bin Laden was planning "large scale" operations in New York in the summer or fall of 2001.

In 1999, two years before 9-11, the British intelligence service contacted the United States government with a warning that al Qaeda was planning to use commercial aircraft in "unconventional ways," possibly as flying bombs. On July 16, 2001, the British passed along a message to the U.S. saying that al Qaeda was in the "final stages" of preparing a terrorist attack in Western countries.

In June 2001, German intelligence warned the U.S., Britain, and Israel that Middle Eastern terrorists were planning to hijack commercial aircraft and use them as weapons to attack "American and Israeli symbols which stand out." This warning came from Echelon, a spy satellite network that was partly based in Germany.

In late July 2001, Egyptian intelligence got a report from one of its undercover agents in Afghanistan that "20 al Qaeda members had gone into the U.S. and that four of them were taking flying lessons on Cessnas." The information was passed on to the CIA but it fell into the cracks of information that was not dealt with at the time.

In late summer of 2001, Jordanian intelligence intercepted a message stating that a major attack was in the works and was being planned inside the U.S. and that aircraft would be used. The code name for the mission was "Big Wedding," which was in fact, the code name for the September 11 operation. The message was indeed given to U.S. intelligence for its review.[33]

In September 1999, a report was made for the U.S. government entitled "Sociology and Psychology of Terrorism." It stated that al Qaeda expected to pursue retaliation for the U.S. cruise missile attacks against bin Laden's camps after the embassy bombings and that it could take different forms including an attack on Washington, D.C., including federal buildings, using suicide bombers. The buildings mentioned in such an attack were the Pentagon, the CIA headquarters, and the White House.

33 History Commons: They tried to warn us; Foreign Intelligence Warnings Before 9-11. Paul Thompson.

In anticipation that a future terrorist attack might take place at the Pentagon, a drill was carried out from October 24 to 26 for such an eventuality. "For years, the staff of the Pentagon joked that they worked at Ground Zero, the spot at which an incoming nuclear missile aimed at America's defenses would explode." On 9-11, it wasn't a Russian nuke that struck the Pentagon, but the hijacked Flight 77 (again, there are numerous theories about the Pentagon crash, but it is not part of the narrative of this book).

In the months leading up to 9-11, especially in the summer of 2001, many of our allies gave us explicit warnings about possible attacks on the U.S. One of these came in July 2001 from the government of India about an impeding attack but the details of the plot were unknown. The report said, "two Islamist radicals with ties to Osama bin Laden were discussing an attack on the White House." This report, inexplicably, was not given to U.S. authorities until two days before 9-11.

A disturbing report came from an unexpected source, actor James Woods. Woods was flying first class on a plane when he noticed four Arabic-looking men who were seated in the first class part of the plane. Woods believed these men were some sort of terrorists and told the flight attendant that he thought the plane was going to be hijacked. The pilot of the plane was told of Woods'worries and he was assured that the cockpit doors were locked and could not be entered. The actor was not questioned until after 9-11, but the men he saw may have been part of bin Laden's 9-11 crew, taking part in pre-hijacking exercises to see how the flight attendants worked and how the plane operated on its daily runs.

On August 16, 2001, the Federal Aviation Administration (FAA) issued a warning to the major airlines that possible hijackers might be able to use leather weapons that were disguised in luggage or other means of accommodation. Later, the airlines said they never received any such warning by the FAA. On 9-11, the hijackers used lethal weapons, box cutters, etc., to storm the planes' cockpits and take over the planes before crashing them into the WTC.

On August 27, 2001, Spanish police were able to tape a number of coded communications from a person located in Great Britain, who mentioned the name "Shakur." The caller was Barakat Yarkas (also called Abu Dahdah), who was the leader of an al Qaeda cell in Spain. In the records of an investigation by a Spanish judge, he said that a call from Shakur proved that a major strike was in the works. "Shakur said he was giving classes and that in our classes we have entered the field of aviation, and we have even cut the bird's throat." Another part of the taped conversation read, "We are going to cut the eagles throat," which most likely referred to the United States as the eagle. The Spanish cell, which was run by Yarkas, was a hub for financing and recruiting for al Qaeda. On November 11, 2001, Yarkas and ten other Spaniards were arrested and charged with al Qaeda terrorist activities.

Days before 9-11, a British source said that shortly before 9-11, bin Laden contacted a person who lived in Pakistan and he told that person that something would take place around the 9-11 time frame and that repercussions would follow from that event. Bin Laden then phoned an associate in Afghanistan and told him the same news. The contents of this intercept were never made public by the British government so we have no concrete idea of what the listeners overheard.

In the days before he was killed, Northern Alliance leader Ahmed Shah Massoud had "gained limited knowledge" regarding an al Qaeda operation against the United States. Massoud was killed on September 9, and if he had prior warnings that something was afoot, he may have been killed before he had time to warn the United States of what he had heard.

After 9-11, British Prime Minister Tony Blair said that shortly before 9-11, bin Laden told his followers to come back to Afghanistan because something was about to happen around that date. It's possible that bin Laden did not want any of his associates to be picked up in any unforeseen circumstances and that they would be better protected in the safe confines of Afghanistan.

In June 2002, President George W. Bush, for the first time, admitted that there was a breakdown in the collecting of intelligence prior to 9-11. He said, "In terms of whether or not the FBI and the CIA were communicating properly, I think it is clear that they weren't." When he addressed nation three days after the attacks, he backtracked a little by saying, "Based on everything I've seen, I do not believe anyone could have prevented the horror of September 11." Later, *Newsweek* wrote that the FBI had prepared a detailed chart showing how agents could have uncovered the terrorist plot if the CIA had told them what it knew about the hijackers Nawaf al-Hazmi and Khalid al-Midhar sooner. One FBI official said in this regard, "There's no question we could have tied all 19 hijackers together."

FBI Director Robert Mueller testified before the Congressional 9-11 Inquiry and in his testimony which was released in September 2002 said, "To this day we have found no one in the United States except the actual hijackers who knew of the plot and we have found nothing they did while in the United States that triggered a specific response about them." The 9-11 Commission would say that the hijackers "were not as isolated during their time in the United States as has been previously suggested." Mueller also said, "There were no slip-ups, discipline never broke down. They gave no hint to those around them what they were about."

In October 2002, NSA Director Michael Hayden testified before a Congressional inquiry and gave his views of the pre-9-11 intelligence failures. He said that the NSA had no indications that al Qaeda was targeting New York and Washington "or even that they were planning an attack on U.S. soil."

There were other warning signs by people not in government in the days before 9-11 that went under the radar or were not mentioned after the fact in the popular press. How these people learned of what was about to take place is not known, but their stories lend credence that that something spectacular was about to take place in the United States in the upcoming months. Here are some of their stories.

On July 16, 2001, a reporter from the *Village Voice* was told by a cab driver that he was leaving the country and going to Egypt in late August or early September because he had gotten e-mails from people who told him that bin Laden was planning a terrorist attack in New York and Washington. The FBI spoke to this man after the fact and released him from custody.

In early September 2001, a security guard who lived in Seattle, Washington, and who was of Middle Eastern heritage, called a pal who lived on the east coast and told him that he heard that terrorists were planning an attack on the U.S. After the attacks, this person called the FBI and told them his story. The man was questioned by the FBI but they decided that he was not part of the plot and let the matter drop.

It seems that a number of people who attended certain mosques in New York were aware that something was afoot. In one of these mosques, worshipers were told not to be in lower Manhattan on 9-11. The FBI's JTTF interviewed some of these people and many backed up the story. However, a number of the leaders of these mosques had no idea what their followers were talking about.

There were reports of unusual trading of certain companies on the New York Stock Exchange in the days before the attack. Whether or not they had any merit is debatable, but they were too numerous to ignore. In early September 2001, there was an increase in short selling of stocks of American and United Airlines on the NYSE. There was a 40% increase in short selling in the previous month for these two airlines, compared to an 11% increase for other airline companies. United stock dropped 43% and American dropped 39% the first day that trading opened after 9-11.

In order to determine if there was any validity to the charge of insider trading, a number of nations, after 9-11, began an internal investigation to look into the matter. The governments of Belgium, Cyprus, France, Germany, Italy, Japan, Luxembourg, Monte Carlo, the Netherlands, Switzerland, and the United States began an intensive review of the trades in the days before the attacks.

As with many other aspects of the official 9-11 Commission's review of the attacks, skeptics faulted them for not really doing a far-reaching investigation of the alleged insider trading activities. "The reasoning goes like this," the Commission wrote in their report, "If we assume that we know who the perpetrators were, (i.e., the popular version of al Qaeda), and those who were involved in the trades did not appear to be connected to those assumed perpetrators, then insider trading did not occur."

The Commission members wrote more on this matter saying, "This Commission concluded that exhaustive investigations by the SEC and the FBI uncovered no evidence that anyone with advance knowledge of the attacks profited through securities transactions." In a footnote, the Commission acknowledged "highly suspicious trading on its face, but said that this trading on United Airlines was traced back to a single U.S. based institutional investor with no conceivable ties to al Qaeda."

A number of experts in the use of insider trading, as well as some university professors knowledgeable in this area, made a number of studies of the alleged trading scheme and came up with what they described as discrepancies in their work. In 2007, the 9-11 Commission addressed some of the criticism and wrote the following in their report. They released a memorandum of the FBI investigations on which its report was based. "A careful review of this memorandum indicates that some of the people who were briefly investigated by the FBI, and then acquitted without due diligence, had links to al Qaeda and to U.S. intelligence agencies. Although the elapsed time between the informed trades and these new confirmations might prevent legal action against the guilty, the facts of the matter can help lead us to the truth about 9-11."[34]

An interesting sidebar to the insider trading story concerns Osama bin Laden's possible links to various worldwide banking systems in the years before 9-11. After the attacks, an Italian newspaper reported that, "Six or seven years ago, probably in 1995, secret services from various European countries investigated the possibility that al Qaeda, Osama bin Laden's organization, was using a Milan stockbroker firm to operate on Europe's money markets." The Italian intelligence agency, as well as other European services, looked into the matter. It was also reported, "We neither know the name of the Milan stockbroker, nor whether the initial suspicions have ever been confirmed." It was also reported shortly after 9-11, that Italian stock authorities were investigating abnormal movements in share prices on the Milan stock exchange prior to the terrorist attacks.[35]

A rather curious event took place on September 6, 2001 when a New York student forecasted upcoming attacks. The teacher, Antoinette Di Lorenzo, was teaching an English class to a group of Pakistani immigrants, when she noticed one of the students looking out of the window. The class was held in lower Manhattan.

34 Evidence for Informed Trading on the Attacks of September 11, World-wide web.

35 History Commons: 1995: Bin Laden investigated for Using European Stock Markets.

When the teacher asked the student what he was looking at, he looked at the WTC and said, "You see those two buildings? They won't be standing there next week." Like other such events, the FBI investigated the case and found it credible, not the urban myth that has come over this event.

Another such event took place on September 10, 2001, when a Dallas fifth grader told his teacher that, "Tomorrow, World War III will begin. It will begin in the United States, and the U.S. will lose." The FBI was informed of this event, but decided not to investigate any further.

On September 10, 2001, three men who were in a Daytona Beach, Florida bar, made a prediction, "Wait until tomorrow. America is going to see bloodshed." Whoever these men were, they had some foreknowledge of what was to come, but were not the hijackers of the planes. It should be noted that prior to 9-11, Mohamed Atta was in Florida doing all sorts of nefarious things and was in contact with a number of Americans of certain ill repute. Was there a connection between Atta and these unidentified persons?

Hours before the attacks, San Francisco Mayor Willie Brown received a warning from his security people while he was at an airport, telling him to be careful about traveling. Brown was scheduled to fly to New York the next day.

On October 16, 2001, the Financial Services Authority, which was Britain's main financial regulator, cleared bin Laden of possible insider trading. There had been suspicion in the banking industry that members of al Qaeda had cashed in on the U.S. attacks, dumping airline, aerospace, and insurance company shares before 9-11. The authority said that after a thorough investigation, it found no hard evidence of any such deals in London. On September 24, Belgium's Financial Minister had claimed there were strong suspicions that British markets may have been used for 9-11 insider trading in early September.

Allen Poteshman, a professor of finance at the University of Illinois, published a paper which demonstrated that the insider trading options on United Airlines and American Airline stocks indicated that someone profited from foreknowledge of 9-11. Professor Poteshman concluded his report by saying, "There is evidence of unusual option market activity in the days leading up to 9-11."[36]

For two years after 9-11, the Securities and Exchange Commission and the Chicago Board of Trade conducted their own investigations regarding the claim of insider trading. In the ensuing months, *Slate* magazine reported that the abovementioned organizations refused to make any comment on what their probes found. "Neither has announced any conclusions. The SEC has not filed any complaint alleging illegal activity, nor has the Justice Department announced any investigation or prosecution. So, unless the SEC decides to file a complaint—unlikely at this late stage—we may never know what they learned about terror trading."

Closing the matter on any possible insider trading in the pre-9-11 attacks, on September 19, 2003, the FBI held a press briefing to clear the air. FBI spokesman Paul Bresson announced that the bureau had come to the conclusion that there was no insider trading in U.S. securities markets by people with advance knowledge of the 9-11 attacks. According to Bresson, "the vast majority of pre-attack surge of trading in options that bet on a drop in the stock of AMR Corp. which owns American Airlines, and UAL Corp., which owns United Airlines, was conducted by investment hedge funds implementing bearish investment strategies or hedging a line position of common stock, and was not linked to terrorists."

The wires were burning red in the late summer of 2001. The Bush administration was warned that bin Laden was preparing to attack the United States. The FBI and the CIA were targeting a group of Arabs who were taking flying lessons in the United States. Our foreign allies were giving us ample warnings that something horrific was about to happen. Complacency was in the air. Nothing could harm us. We had two oceans protecting us from an attack. What could go wrong?

---

36 The information in this section comes from Paul Thompson in the *Terror Timeline.* Pages 61-68.

Chapter 9

Able Danger

In late 1998-1999, while the Clinton administration was using the CIA and the American military in the hunt for Osama in Laden, another secret unit was established to track bin Landen and his al Qaeda network. This unit was kept secret from the public until after the events of 9-11, when all the pertinent information from that event was made public. By the time this program, called Able Danger, was revealed, the story of 9-11 had taken a new and unsettling turn.

In order to get some background on Able Danger, we have to go back to remarks made by the Chairman of the Joint Chiefs of Staff, General Henry Shelton. "Right after I left SOCOM [Special Operations Command], I asked my successor to put together a small team, if he could, to try to use the Internet and start trying to see if there was any way we could track down Osama bin Laden or where he was getting his money from or anything of that nature."

The initial Able Danger team consisted of six people (intelligence officers). The team, however, put their attentions not on the hunt for bin Laden, but instead, on data mining tasks that were related to Bosnia and China for the better part of 1999.

One person who was instrumental in the creation of Able Danger was General Peter Schoomaker, head of SOCOM. SOCOM was based in Tampa, Florida and its duties included the use of America's secret warriors (i.e. commando units).

A noted attorney based in Washington, Mark Zaid, who represented a number of whistleblowers in 2005, wrote succinctly about the purpose of Able Danger. "In the most understandable and simplistic terms, Able Danger involved the searching out and compiling of open source or other publically available information regarding specific targets or tasks that were connected through associational links. No classified information was used. No government databases were used. The search and compilation efforts were primarily handled by defense contractors, who did not necessarily know they were working for Able Danger, and that information was then to be utilized by the military members of Able Danger for whatever appropriated purposes."

Congressman Curt Weldon (R-PA), who had an avid interest in the program, went even further when he talked about Able Danger. He said the purpose of the program was to enable it to "manipulate, degrade, or destroy the global al Qaeda infrastructure." It took the Able Danger team until the end of 1999 to really start its investigation of al Qaeda.

It seems that Rep. Curt Weldon was not only interested in Able Danger, but he had his fingers in other controversies as well. In mid-1999, he began a study that looked into possible Chinese front companies in the U.S. that were seeking to get technology for the Chinese military. The two people who were tasked with making the report were Dr. Eileen Preisser and Michael Maloof. Dr. Preisser ran the Information Dominance Center at the U.S. Army's Land Information Warfare Activity and would later be entangled in the Able Danger program. By the time the study was completed, it would expose a number of high-profile people then in government to high scrutiny. Their report found that Chinese front companies in the U.S. were posing as U.S. corporations that wanted to acquire technology from U.S. defense contractors. In a highly unusual move, and one that had no real motive, when the study was completed in November 1999, the General Counsel's office in the Office of the Defense Secretary ordered the study be destroyed. Rep. Weldon used his considerable influence to have the report saved from destruction, even complaining to Army Chief of Staff Eric Shinseki. Rep. Weldon also wrote a letter to FBI Director Louis Freeh, asking that the bureau begin an espionage investigation of the Chinese behavior (Freeh never responded to Weldon's request).

During this probe, some high-profile people were connected, in one way or another, to the Chinese scandal including Condoleezza Rice, former Defense Secretary William Perry, and others. While these officials did nothing wrong, it put a black mark on their reputations, but was not an impediment to them serving in later administrations.

As it related to this incident, news reports began circulating in the not-so-mainstream press about the abovementioned people and China. These reports came via the WorldNetDaily and NewsMax and they connected both Secretary Perry and Ms. Rice to Hua Di, a Chinese missile scientist and possible spy, and posed questions about their relationship with one another. Di defected to the U.S. in 1989 and later worked at Stanford University's Center for International Security and Arms Control. Di went back to China and was sentenced to ten years in jail for writing articles that were said to reveal Chinese military secrets.[37]

Some of the information gathered by Able Danger was collected on behalf of Major General Geoffrey Lambert, the J3 at the U.S. Special Operations Command. There were eleven people in the unit, of which six persons were with SOCOM'S Able Danger program, while four others, including Dr. Eileen Preisser and Major Eric Kleinsmith, worked with the Army's Land Information Warfare Activity unit. The LIWA had been doing data mining in a number of areas, including international drug cartels, corruption in Russia and Serbia, terrorist links in the Far East, and the spread of military technology to China.

We now add a name to the Able Danger program, a person who would be linked to its work and the controversy around it. The man in question is Lt. Colonel Anthony Shaffer. At that time, Lt. Col. Shaffer was running a military unit called Stratus Ivy that was located in the Department of Defense. According to Shaffer, Stratus Ivy was ordered to "take on out of the box ideas, and develop them into real intelligence operations." One of the areas that they looked into was bin Laden's ever growing al Qaeda. The information that was gleaned from these various secret operations was a large amount of data from open sources, including the Internet, chat rooms, news reports from television and other venues, web sites, etc.

Col. Shaffer was the man for the job to run Able Danger as

37 History Commons: Mid-1999-November 1999: Data Mining Study causes controversy by connecting Prominent U.S. Figures to Chinese Military Weapons Purchases.

far as his experience was concerned. He was commissioned in the Ohio National Guard in 1983, and he later took training at the super-secret CIA training facility called "The Farm" which was located at Camp Peary in Virginia. He also worked in the Pentagon as an intelligence officer at the Pentagon's J2 directorate and also as a clandestine operative with the J3 unit.

The above discussion mentioned Dr. Eileen Preisser who eventually testified before a congressional briefing on the Able Danger program. Her testimony was not released to the public, but in the interim, a congressman who heard her testimony gave some clarification on what she said. Rep. Christopher Shays (R-CT) reported that Dr. Preisser said that by using high-speed computer systems which were able to "digest, you know, literally floors' worth of material, she can take relationships that are seven times removed, seven units removed, and when she does that, she ends up with relationships to the bin Laden group where she sees the purchase of chemicals, the sending of students to universities. You wouldn't see it if you isolated it there, but if that unit is connected that unit, you then see the relationship."

In reference to Dr. Preisser's comment about tracing the use of chemicals, it is worthwhile to note that the CIA was said to have been monitoring Mohamed Atta while he was in Germany in the spring of 2000 and that he was buying a large quantity of chemicals. Atta also sent a number of e-mails to the U.S. in the spring of 2000, inquiring about flight schools for himself and his fellow 9-11 hijackers. It seems that Dr. Preisser's revelations had some resonance, and while she wanted to testify in open session, the powers that be refused to let her talk in an open forum.

While the Able Danger program was getting underway, they began getting brush-back from the CIA, who saw in their work, an undercutting of their own mission. The reader should be reminded of the non-cooperation between the CIA and the FBI in the years before 9-11. This lack of cooperation made it almost impossible for the services to track down the hijackers who were in the United States taking flying lessons and mixing into our daily life.

The CIA saw in Able Danger an impediment to their work, just as they did with the FBI. In October 1999, Captain Scott Phillpott, the head of the Able Danger program, asked Lt. Col. Anthony

Shaffer to talk with a CIA representative who worked for CIA Director George Tenet and try to convince him that the Able Danger program would not make things difficult for the agency. Shaffer later said of this encounter, "I clearly understand the difference. I clearly understand. We're going after the leadership. You guys are going after the body. But, it doesn't matter. The bottom line is, CIA will never give you the best information from 'Alex Base' [Alec Station] or anywhere else. CIA will never provide that to you because if you were successful in your effort to target al Qaeda, you will steal our thunder. Therefore, we will not support this." Shaffer also said, "To my knowledge, and my other colleagues' knowledge, there was no information ever related to us because the CIA chose not to participate in Able Danger."

Rep. Curt Weldon recounted a meeting he had on November 4, 1999 with the deputy directors of the FBI and the CIA relating to the sharing of information. Weldon suggested that the government set up a national network of data sharing that would aid in tracking all sorts of terrorists or domestic hate groups. His suggestion got nowhere, and the CIA representative said in that meeting, "We don't need that. We've put language in three successive defense bills."

By December 1999, Able Danger really got underway, and began looking into all aspects of al Qaeda. As their data mining began to morph into a well-oiled machine, analysts were able to find "a surprising presence in the U.S. and that al Qaeda had a worldwide footprint." They collected so much information that it was beginning to seem that they'd be overwhelmed by what they found. "By the spring of 2000, they were able to isolate 20 people about whom Special Operations wants further analysis. The Able Danger team created massive charts, measuring up to 20 feet in length and covered in small type, to show all the links between suspects that have been discovered."

The Able Danger team now began setting its sights on a number of al Qaeda operatives who were associated with bin Laden. This included the members of the Hamburg, Germany cell which included Mohamed Atta, Said Bahaji, and Ramzi bin al-Shib. The members of the U.S. Army intelligence unit who were asked to look into the operations of al Qaeda made up a flow chart that included the names and pictures of four of the future 9-11 hijackers, who were then based in Brooklyn, New York. The four men in question were Mohamed Atta, Marwan al-Shehhi, Kalid al-Midhar, and Nawaf al Hazmi. The chart was then given to members of the U.S. Special Operations Command in Tampa, Florida. They recommended to the FBI that they mount an operation to stop the al Qaeda cell before they could do any possible damage to the United States. In a stunning move, lawyers who worked for the Southern Command said that anyone who had a green card had to be granted the same rights as U.S. citizens, so the information about the cell could not be shared with the FBI. The legal team directed them to put yellow stickers over the photographs of Atta and his cohorts, to state that they were off limits to further scrutiny.

Lt. Col. Shaffer said of this development that an unnamed two star general who was his boss in the chain of command was "very adamant about not looking into Atta. I was directed several times to ignore Atta, to the point where he had to remind me he was a general and I was not, and I would essentially be fired." Col. Shaffer also said that the decision regarding the cell members was made by General Geoffery Lambert, and that General Peter Schoomaker, the head of SOCOM, was not made aware of what was going on.

As time went on, much of the criticism regarding Able Danger centered on the fact that the U.S. had a chance to stop the attack if they had done a better job in intelligence gathering. As we have seen, the members of the Hamburg cell were under constant surveillance by various Western intelligence agencies, including Germanys. An intelligence failure that could have changed things was the fact that there was a $2 million reward on the head of Khalid Sheikh Mohammed who attended the Hamburg summit, but the U.S. did not inform its German counterparts of this fact.

It was later reported that Mohamed Atta was under surveillance by the CIA while he was living in Germany and was observed buying large amounts of chemicals in Frankfurt for use in the production of explosives for biological warfare operations. The U.S. authorities, who knew about Atta's alleged purchase of these chemicals, failed to tell the Germans about this story. "The disclosure that Atta was trailed by police long before September 11 raises the question why the attacks could not have been prevented with the man's arrest." To muddy the waters a little more regarding Atta during this time, we have a report by a German intelligence official who said, "We can no longer exclude the possibility that the Americans wanted to keep an eye on Atta after his entry into the United States."[38]

This assertion regarding Atta's possible American connection was discounted by the congressional investigation that looked into the allegation. They said, "the intelligence community possessed no intelligence or law enforcement information linking 16 of the 19 hijackers (including Atta), to terrorism or terrorists groups." The *New York Times* wrote about this development, "The account [Able Danger] is the first assertion that Mr. Atta, an Egyptian who became the lead hijacker in the plot, was identified by any American government agency as a potential threat before September 11."

More information on Able Danger and the German cell was given in 2002 by David Edger who had direct knowledge of these events. Between 1997 and 2001, Mr. Edger was the CIA Station Chief in Berlin, Germany, and was the man responsible for monitoring the Hamburg cell. After his retirement from the CIA, he moved back to Oklahoma where he began a teaching career. He gave an interview to the Norman *Transcript* in which he revealed some interesting information. The newspaper reporters wrote the following regarding what Mr. Edger told them. "Up until his appointment with the University of Oklahoma six months ago, Edger's work with the CIA focused on terrorist groups in Germany. One of the three cells he was tracking included some members of the people responsible for the Sept. 11 attacks on the World Trade Center. He said that although officers knew members of the cell and some of what they were doing, they had no idea that they would meet in London and go to different parts of the U.S., where they would learn to fly planes to crash into the World Trade Center. 'In that case, we failed,' Edger said.{ Mr. Edger was never interviewed by the 9-11 Commission, nor did he make any further interviews with any other news outlet except for the Norman *Transcript.*[39]

38 History Commons: January-May 2000: CIA possibly has 9/11 Hijacker Atta under Surveillance in Germany.

39 History Commons: February 12, 2002: Former head of CIA efforts in Germany says CIA tracked some of the people responsible for 9/11 in Germany.

According to the 9-11 Commission, only three of the 9-11 hijackers were known to the U.S. intelligence community before the attacks; Nawak al-Hazmi, Salem al-Hazmi, and Khalid al-Midhar.

The Able Danger team worked out of offices at Fort Belvoir where the reams of data mining was looked at and analyzed. After some time of analysis, they were able to identify the important al Qaeda cell located in Yemen as a key "hotspot" in their operations. This was done within weeks of the USS *Cole* bombing. In the investigation of that incient the FBI, under the leadership of John O'Neill, took a prominent role. In their work, they were able to find out that the al Qaeda cell in Brooklyn which was run by the blind Shiek, Omar Abdul Rahman, and his associate Ali Mohammad was directly tied to bin Laden's network. According to author Peter Lance who did extraordinary work in the investigation of 9-11, "the LIWA/DIA data mines went even further putting Ali Mohammad and bin Laden's brother-in-law, Mohammad Jamal Khalifa in the al Qaeda inner circle."

Peter Lance writes that a chart of the members of bin Laden's group was declassified in March 2000 which showed a picture of Ali Mohammad at Fort Bragg, North Carolina inside a diagram box with the photos of bin Laden, Al-Zawahiri, Mohammad Atef, Wadih el-Hage, and Mohammad Jamal Khalifa. "The box linked the Sheik Rahman-Ramzi Yousef New York cell via the Egyptian Islamic Jihad and the Abu Sayyaf Group in the Philippines which was also linked to the Yousef-KSM-Murad-Wali Khan Manila cell responsible for the 9-11 attacks."

All this information flew in the face of the 9-11 Commission who said that Yousef was not involved and that the plot had its origins in Afghanistan in 1996, four years before 9-11.

For the members of Able Danger, things were now to go from bad to worse. All their hard work in identifying the hijackers before 9-11 and trying to analyze all the information from their various sources and methods, were now to be for naught. In April 2000, high-ranking officials located in the Pentagon ordered that the 2.5 terabytes of al Qaeda information that was data mined by the unit, be destroyed. As author Lance says of this incredible incident, What happened a year and a half before the 9-11 attacks, the dots weren't just disconnected, they were obliterated."

There is more to the story of how the data was destroyed. A man named James Smith was working in March or April 2000 for a private company called Orion Scientific Systems on a contract basis for Able Danger. He said that around that time, armed federal agents came into Orion's offices and confiscated its Able Danger material. Orion's contract was then cancelled and Smith had nothing more to do with the program. Smith, however, had a number of unclassified charts of the work he was doing stashed in his car. One chart showed a picture of Mohamed Atta on it. This chart was eventually discarded in the summer of 2004. Smith summed up his work for Able Danger saying, "All information that we have ever produced, which was all unclassified, was confiscated and to this day we don't know who by."

The American people were not then told of the work of the Able Danger team, and it would take another few years before the story of Able Danger would be brought to light for all the world to see.

By 2003, the 9-11 Commission had begun and a secret meeting was held at Bagram Air Force Base (of all places) with Commission member Philip Zelikow in attendance. At the meeting were three members of the U.S. Defense Department, along with Col. Anthony Shaffer. Col. Shaffer later told the Commission's staff all about what Able Danger was and his role in it. He told them, "We found two of the three cells which conducted 9-11, to include Mohamed Atta." Zelikow then told Col. Shaffer that when they got back to the United States, they wanted more information on his unit. The story of what Able Danger did was not mentioned in the 9-11Commission's final report, a glaring failure to be sure. After reports of Able Danger went public, the members of the Commission went into overdrive to try to cover up certain facts surrounding their work. A spokesperson for the Commission said they had been briefed on the unit, but they were not informed that it had identified Mohamed Atta or any of the other hijackers as potential threats. Two high-ranking members of the Commission, former New Jersey Governor Thomas Kean and Lee Hamilton, said in an official statement that a memo was prepared by the Commission staff and said that, it "does not record any mention of Mohamed Atta or any of the other future hijackers, or any suggestion that their identities were known to anyone at the Defense Department before 9-11.

Another person in the know about Able Danger who had a lot to say was Captain Scott Phillpott. On July 12, 2004, he met with Detrich Snell, a member of the 9-11 Commission staff in Washington, D.C. Scott Phillpott said that he saw a document which was made by Able Danger in 2000 that described Mohamed Atta as part of a Brooklyn, New York al Qaeda cell. He said this information was not included in any report he saw. The Commission tried once again to cover its tracks saying, "the Commission later claimed that Phillpott's information does not mesh with other conclusions they are drawing from our investigation." Consequently, the commission staff concluded, "the officer's account is not sufficiently reliable to warrant revision of the report or further investigation." The reason Able Danger was not mentioned in the 9-11 Commission's final report (get this) was, "because the operation itself did not turn out to be historically significant."

James Smith, the Orion contractor made this comment on the closing down of Able Danger by the inspector general "because of a claim that we were collecting information on U.S. citizens" which was against the law. Another reason for its closure was the possibility that certain, sensitive data might fall into the hands of the Chinese government. Lt. Col. Anthony Shaffer blamed the change in leadership when the Bush administration took over in January 2001. "Once the four star [General Peter Schoomaker] went away, it was pretty much like the world closing around us." Schoomaker retired in November 2000. There was no political will to continue at that point in time. Plus, my direct leadership, Colonel Gerry York and General Bob Harding, had moved on as well. Therefore, I had a new chain of command above me. They were risk adverse. This [Able Danger] operation, as with other operations which were very high risk, high gain, some of which are still ongoing—seemed not to be appreciated by the incoming leadership." Shaffer also said that Colonel Mary Moffitt, who replaced Col. Gerry York, in the spring of 2001, "dismantled the Defense [human intelligence] support to Able Danger just months before the 9-11 attacks, and I became focused on shutting down our support to Able Danger under the guise of 'reorganization,' and in the end, disestablished Stratus Ivy (the unit Shaffer once headed) and its cutting edge focus."

One of the many criticisms of the disbanding of the Able Danger program after it was revealed to the public, was the fact that the unit had identified Mohamed Atta before 9-11. Two of the principle players in the Able Danger drama, Lt. Col. Anthony Shaffer and Scott Phillpott, attested to that fact. Scott Phillpott said in this regard, "My story is consistent. Atta was identified by Abel Danger in January-February of 2000." The abovementioned James Smith also backed up the Atta story and Able Danger. He said, "I am absolutely positive that Atta was on our chart among other pictures and ties that we were doing mainly based upon terror cells in New York City."

The Mohamed Atta/Able Danger story was related once again by Al Felzenberg, the former chief spokesman for the 9-11 Commission. Mr. Felzenberg said that he was informed on the project by two military officers in July 2004 and told what they were doing. He was told by these military officers that the program had identified Mohamed Atta as a member of the Brooklyn al Qaeda cell. As mentioned before, this information was left out of the final 9-11 Commission report (deliberately or not is not known). Able Danger was originally reported to the public by the *New York Times* on August 9, 2005, and Mr. Felzengberg confirmed that in a meeting which took place in October 2003 there was no references to Mohamed Atta or the Brooklyn cell. "But Felzenberg did not tell the newspaper about the July 2004 briefing, which apparently had provided the commission with far more details about the Able Danger program." Two members of the commission, Tim Roemer and John Lehman. said they were never briefed on Able Danger before the Commission's final report was published.

A major question must be asked in relation to the above material. Why was it decided to keep the knowledge of Able Danger from certain members of the 9-11 Commisson in the first place? A second question is why the Able Danger program was left out of the final report? One would think that the members of the 9-11 Commission, men with high integrity and many years of public service, could surely keep a secret about a program that had found out the lead hijacker on 9-11, months before the attack took place. One can make a supposition that the Commissioners did not want to look bad in the eyes of the public who were eager to read their final narrative regarding the failure to inform the public about their knowledge of Atta. If the Commission held back information on Atta, what other bombshell information may they have been hiding? The 9-11 Commission was criticized in the end for many things, but two of their most glaring omissions were the knowledge of Atta—and the failure to include Able Danger in their final report.

Other members of the Commission besides Tim Roemer and John Lehman had things to say regarding Able Danger and the Atta allegations. Commission Chairman Thomas Kean said that there was no evidence that anyone in the government knew about Mohamed Atta before 9-11, and there were no official documents to dispute that claim. How does Chairman Kean's story stand up to scrutiny when most of the documents relating to Able Danger were destroyed? Another member of the Commission, Slade Gorton said, "Bluntly, it just didn't happen and that's the conclusion of all 10 of us." Congressman Curt Weldon said in regard to Slate Gordon's remarks that the Commissioners never met with anyone from Able Danger, "yet they chose to speak with some form of certainty without firsthand knowledge."

With Able Danger now out of the bag, the Congress got involved and beginning in September 2005, a public investigation was mounted. The Senate Judiciary Committee headed by Sen. Arlen Specter (R. Pa.)—the man who coined the phrase "magic bullet" in connection with the Kennedy assassination—led the probe. He and the other members of his committee wanted to know about Able Danger's identification of Mohamed Atta one year before 9-11, as well as why the unit was disbanded. The committee wanted to hear the following witnesses: Col. Shaffer, Scott Phillpott, James Smith, and Dr. Eileen Preisser. In an audacious move by the high-ups in the Pentagon, one day before the hearings were to begin, they ordered the abovementioned witnesses not to show up. Lt. Col. Shaffer remembered that event saying, "I was told by two Defense Department officials today directly that it is their understanding that Defense Secretary Rumsfeld directed that we not testify." The Defense Department said the reason they didn't want these people to talk in open session was because classified material might be leaked to the public.

Senator Specter shot back at this blatant obstruction saying, "That looks to me like it may be obstruction of the committee's activities, something we have to determine."

A second open session on Able Danger was held on February 15, 2006. Deputy Secretary of Defense for intelligence Stephen Cambone was one of the witnesses ordered to testify. He had the audacity to contradict the other people who testified before about the identification of Atta by saying that the unit failed to find any chart with Atta's picture. Rep. Curt Weldon, who wanted to make public all material on the 9-11 attack, including Able Danger, got into a shouting match with Cambone and said during that session, "There's been no investigation! There's been no analysis of Able Danger by the 9-11 Commission or anyone else." At this session, unlike the first one, the following people testified: James Smith, Anthony Shaffer, and Eric Kleinsmith, who was chief ofintelligence for the LIWA unit. Col. Scott Phillpott also testified in a closed session. In another incident that muddied up the waters, the congressional committee asked Commission member Dietrich Snell to testify. However, his boss, then New York State Attorney General Eliot Spitzer, refused to allow Snell to appear.

Dietrich Snell was one of the most influential members of the panel that looked into the 9-11 attacks and in the process, got as much criticism as any other member. He was a former federal prosecutor in the Southern District of New York and helped prosecute the members of the Bojinka plot. In June 2004, in a brazen act, he and fellow Commission member Philip Zelikow deleted certain passages linking two of the hijackers, Khalid al-Midhar and Nawaf al-Hazmi, to suspected Saudi government operatives from the final text of the 9-11 report. These sections were drafted by two of Snell's team members, Mike Jacobson and Raj De, and dealt with Omar al-Bayoumi, a Saudi who helped the two men in San Diego. Snell, it seems, was doubtful about the al-Bayoumi connection and decided not to have that material put in the report. Jacobson was notified of the editing session just before midnight.

He called Raj De and they both went to the Commission's offices to talk about the matter. Snell said that the final report should not contain allegations that could not be verified one hundred percent. However, both Jacobson and De said that demanding this level of proof would exonerate the guilty. While the material linking the two hijackers was omitted, Jacobson and De were allowed to write certain endnotes as they saw fit. Material unfavorable to Pakistan was also omitted from the report.

To add to this story, on February 23, 2004, a Saudi diplomat named Fahad al Thumairy, was interviewed by the 9-11 Commission and made false statements regarding al Hazmi and al-Midhar. The Commission members thought al Thumairy was a middleman of some sort for 9-11 hijackers al Hazmi and al Midhar. It seems the commission had a large file on al Thumairy and used it to their advantage when questioning him. This information was given to them by the FBI.

Philip Shenon, who wrote a book on the 9-11 Commission, said that al Thumairy "had orchestrated help for the hijackers through a network of Saudi and other Arab expatriates living in Southern California and led by al Bayoumi." Al Thumariy was interviewed in Riyadh, Saudi Arabia by Raj De and other staff members, in the presence of certain Saudi individuals. Al Thumairy said, "I do not know this man al-Bayoumi." The commission members told him that they had records of him and al-Bayoumi speaking to each other in the time period from December 1998 to December 2000. He then reluctantly said he knew him "solely on religious matters." Raj De then told al Thumairy that the U.S. had his phone records "which tell a different story."

Snell was also involved in the case of a man named Mounir el-Motassadeq, an alleged member of Mohamed Atta's Hamburg al Qaeda cell and an accessory to the 9-11 plot. On February 18, 2003, el-Motassadeq was convicted by a German court of being an accessory to the plot and was given a fifteen year jail term. Motassadeq said that he knew a number of bin Laden's followers, including Atta, Marwan al-Shehhi, Ramzi bin al-Shib, and Ziar Jarrah, among others. He said that he had been given power of attorney over al-Shehhi's bank account and admitted that he had taken training in a camp in Afghanistan from May to August

2000. However, he said that he had no role in the 9-11 attacks but the jury found otherwise. At court, Mr. Motassadeq's lawyers tried unsuccessfully to have two of his cohorts, bin al-Shib and Mohammed Haydar Zammar, testify on his behalf. This led to an overturning of his conviction and subsequent retrial.

In March 2005, a retrial was held in Germany for el-Motassadeq and one of the witnesses was Dietrich Snell. He told the court that the 9-11 Commission had concluded that the Hamburg cell members which included Atta and the others, did not develop the idea of the 9-11 plot by themselves, but instead, were recruited by bin Laden when they were in Afghanistan in late 1999. Snell said that, "Ultimately, we did not arrive at the conclusion that there was solid evidence of any contact between the Hamburg cell members and al Qaeda leaders about the plot before the Hamburg group's trip to Afghanistan." Throughout his tenure as a member of the Commission, Snell failed on numerous occasions, to explain how the other members of the panel came to that conclusion, "saying the sources remained classified." The judge who supervised Mr. Motassadeq's trial later criticized the United States for not being fully in cooperation with the trial and commented, "How are we supposed to do justice to our task when important documents are withheld from us?" El-Motassadeq said that Mohamed Atta once told him, "We are going to do something big. The Jews will burn; we will dance on their graves."

Years before he was a 9-11 Commission member, Snell was an Assistant U.S. Attorney in New York and, along with fellow lawyer Mike Garcia, was the prosecutor in the case against the Bojinka plot leaders, Ramzi Yousef, Abdul Hakim Murad, and Wali Kahn Amin Shah. The attorneys laid out for the jury over a thousand exhibits over a four-day period. They described Yousef's plot in the Philippines where the Bojinka plot was hatched but, purposefully or not, decided not to call as a witness Rodolfo Mendoza, a lead interrogator in the Philippines and a very import person who knew a lot about what was being hatched in that country.

When it came to prosecuting Yousef and his men during this time period, Snell had his own beliefs as to how big (or small) the terrorist threat to America was at that time. This was years before 9-11 and the world was a different place as far as a-worldwide terrorist conspiracy was concerned. As far as Snell and other lead prosecutors in the Bojinka plot were concerned, the terrorists who threatened New York were "a loose amalgam of Sunni Islamists," and thus were hard to track.

As Peter Lance points out in his book *Triple Cross,* there were almost two dozen terrorists who were known to federal authorities at that time. Among them were the following: the blind Sheik Omar Abdul Rahman, Jamal al-Fadl, Mohammed Atef, Ayman al-Zawahiri, El Sayyid Nosair, Mohammed Salameh, and Osama bin Laden. There were 13 men of Egyptian origin, one Saudi national, one Palestinian, one from Kuwait, one American (Clement Rodney Hampton-El), and one Sudanese, among others.[40]

On March 15, 2004, in an unusual move, Peter Lance was allowed to meet with Commission members to hear what he had to say regarding his investigation of 9-11. He met with Dietrich Snell at the Commission's New York office for a wide-ranging session. It was an adversarial meeting to say the least. There was no note taker, as Snell wrote his notes in a small pad. Peter Lance opened up his testimony by asking the following questions:

1) Why did you limit the Bojinka evidence at trial?

2) Did you know about Colonel Mendoza's revelations?

3) Why did agent Frank Pelligrino testify that he didn't know Yousef's partner Murad was being questioned at Camp Crane in Manila until late March of '95, when he'd been at the base for two months?

"Each time I asked a question, Snell would smile and say, 'that's classified, or I can't discuss this.' He was polite and cordial. At the end of my testimony, he said he would send me a document request asking for additional research material."

Instead of sending the material to Snell, Lance sent the documents to Tom Kean who was the 9-11 Co-chairman. "But when the commission's final report was published, that evidence was represented in a single footnote, which didn't even mention Col. Mendoza by name—even though he was the investigator who had first uncovered Yousef's suicide-by-plane hijack plot."

Dietrich Snell was also involved in the case of mafia wise guy

40 Lance, Peter, *Triple Cross,* Regan Books, New York, 2006. Page 277.

Gregory Scarpa Jr. who was in jail with Ramzi Yousef, and who played a sting operation via the FBI on Yousef to find out what he knew about al Qaeda and bin Laden. Scarpa's story is told in a previous chapter of this book so it is not necessary to go further into that aspect of the case. However, Dietrich Snell, along with his fellow prosecutor from the SDNY, Patrick Fitzgerald, paid a visit to see Sacrpa Jr. on March 7, 1996 at the Metropolitan Correctional facility in New York where he was housed. The reason for the meeting was a proffer session with Scarpa where his testimony would be heard and evaluated as his trial began. Snell, according to Peter Lance, "was a witness to the intelligence the former Colombo wise guy was getting from Ramzi Yousef—the architect of both WTC attacks." Snell gave his testimony to the 9-11 Commission, according to author Lance, "But some Justice Department officials had buried that intel [the information given by Scarpa from his conversations with Yousef regarding active bin Laden cells in NYC] the evidence now suggests, in order to save those sixty remaining Colombo war cases in the EDNY [Eastern District of New York]. Not a word about that ends/means/ decision appeared in Snell's testimony, or in the 9-11 Commission's final report."

Snell's partner in the case was Patrick Fitzgerald, who would, many years later, be involved in the court case against Vice President Dick Cheney's aide, Lewis "Scooter" Libby in the Valerie Plame Wilson spy leak case. Fitzgerald was the special prosecutor in the case which lasted three years (2003-2006), and whose mandate was to determine whether Bush administration officials broke the law in leaking word to various reporters that Valerie Plame Wilson was a CIA employee. Fitzgerald was able to indict Libby on obstruction of justice charges and perjury. President Donald Trump would later pardon Scooter Libby for his involvement in the Plame affair.

At that time, Patrick Fitzgerald was the head of Organized Crime and Terrorism in the SDNY and was in reality running the FBI's Squad I-49, or the bin Laden unit. Fitzgerald said that the first time he heard the name al Qaeda came in 1996, when bin Laden snitch, Jamal al-Fadl, arrived at the U.S. embassy in Eritrea and surrendered.

As the Feds were compiling their case in the so-called "Day of Terror Plots" in New York, two bin Laden offices in New York were organized, the SDNY and the FBI's New York Office. Among those who played a large part in that probe were Patrick Fitzgerald, Andrew McCarthy, Special Agent Jack Cloonan, and Dan Coleman, a Special Agent for the FBI. Both Coleman and Fitzgerald went overseas to interrogate al-Fadl in Germany in the fall of 1996. Dan Coleman represented the FBI at the CIA's Alec Station, and was privy to all that went on there. Other members of the I-49 squad were Louis Napoli, John Anticev, Mike Anticev, Richard Karniewicz, Carl Summerlin, a New York police detective and also a New York State trooper, Kevin Cruise, Mary Deborah Doran and supervisor Tom Lang. The I-49 unit also worked closely with John O'Neill, who ran the New York FBI office. In its initial work, the team ran the investigation of the crash of TWA Flight 800 in July 1996, as it went down off Long Island and was in their jurisdiction. Another reason they worked on the case were that there was initial reports that the plane had been taken down by unidentified Middle Eastern terrorist groups. (Other reports said that a missile that was supposed to have been fired from either land or sea, brought down the plane.) As time went on, however, I-49 would focuses much of its attention on bin Laden, working parallel with the CIA's Alec Station, where animosity flared at certain points between the units.

One of the most important people the I-49 squad and the Alec Station centered on was Jamal al-Fadl, who was an al Qaeda operative who met with the FBI in the time period of the late 1980s until 1995, and gave them a treasure trove of information on the operations of al Qaeda. Dan Coleman, who was part of the I-49 squad said of al-Fadl, "He's been very, very important to us. When it comes to understanding al Qaeda, he's the Rosetta Stone." Mike Anticev said, "He spoke to us in great detail, and everything that he told us panned out." Up to that time, Jamal al-Fadl was the most important al Qaeda member to talk with the FBI, and he gave them invaluable information of the inner workings on the group that the U.S. government badly needed to understand its new enemy. (Al-Fadl had no knowledge of the 9-11 plot.)

Patrick Fitzgerald also had a role to play in the arrest of

Wadih el-Hage, bin Laden's former personal secretary. When el-Hage returned to the United States from overseas on September 23, 1997, he was given a subpoena to testify before a grand jury. Fitzgerald claimed that el-Hage chose to lie repeatedly to the grand jury, but even in his lies he provided some information of potential use to the intelligence community—including potential leads to the location of his confederates and wanted missing files."El-Hage was not immediately arrested and went back to Texas, where he lived in the early 1990s. He subsequently left Texas and was questioned about the embassy bombings in East Africa. He was arrested and found guilty for his role in the embassy attacks.

As time went on, Fitzgerald's star would rise in legal circles and he became the lead prosecutor in the case *United States of America v. bin Laden.* He was the lead prosecutor in the African embassy bombing case in 2001, and won a conviction of bin Laden in absentia. He was then appointed as a U.S. Attorney in Chicago. It was then that he took on the Valerie Plame leak case and became a national figure.

Fitzgerald later expanded on his first knowledge of bin Laden. "I didn't know the word al Qaeda when we were prosecuting people in '93, '94, and '95. And then this elusive figure came to the attention of the American government called Osama bin Laden. And I remember early in 1996 we were all trying to figure out, was Osama bin Laden as bad as people were saying in the national security community? Because he seemed to be coming up everywhere. He was like Elvis. Every time you read about a terrorist group in a different country carrying out violent action, you heard the name of Osama bin Laden and you wondered whether it was just sort of a fictional person in different countries, or did bin Laden know precisely what these people were doing?"[41]

As the New York Office began its investigations into the origins of the Day of Terror Plots and bin Laden, they followed two different tacks: intelligence gathering and the criminal side.

As the date for the trial of the Day of Terror Plots neared, Andrew McCarthy and Patrick Fitzgerald, decided not to include a person who would have been a real asset in the case, Ali Mohammed, and did not even indict him in the case. Ali Mohammed was an Egyptian military officer who became an American citizen and

41 Lance, Peter, *Triple Cross*. Page 220.

who was one time, a personal bodyguard to bin Laden.

Ali Mohammed was one of the most interesting and important characters in the whole bin Laden terrorist world of the 1990s and beyond, yet the Justice Department, Patrick Fitzgerald and Deitrich Snell decided he was too important to press charges against. For example, Fitzgerald knew from the contemporaneous record that Ali Mohammed taught surveillance and countersurveillance techniques, assassination protocols, kidnapping, the use of codes and ciphers and other intelligence methods to al Qaeda personnel in Afghanistan. He made at least 58 trips over the years between Afghanistan and the United States. For a well-healed U.S. prosecutor, Fitzgerald should have been aware of who Ali Mohammed was and his terrorist pedigree. It is inconceivable that he and the other prosecutors in the SDNY office were not informed of the vast file the Feds had on Mohammed as they were preparing their work against bin Laden. Nafil Sharef, a university professor and former Egyptian intelligence officer, said regarding Ali, "For five years he was moving back and forth between the U.S. and Afghanistan. It's impossible the CIA thought he was going there as a tourist. If the CIA hadn't caught on to him, it should be dissolved and its budget used for something worthwhile."

This is the same Ali Mohammed who, in February 1994, went to Sudan and trained bin Laden's bodyguards. While in Sudan, he arranged security for a meeting between bin Laden and Imad Mugniyah, the security chief for the Lebanese militant group Hezbollah. Mugniyah was linked to the 1993 bombing of the U.S. Marine barracks in Beirut, Lebanon. At that meeting, the men discussed forthcoming operations. Mohammed later said that Hezbollah provided explosives training for certain members of al Qaeda and Islamic Jihad.

In February 1995, the U.S. government filed a confidential court document linking bin Laden and other people as possible co-conspirators in the New York City "landmarks plot." The name of Ali Mohammed was on that list. Mohammed was living for a time in California, still acting as a double agent. Patrick Fitzgerald said that when Mohammed's California home was searched in 1998, investigators found a "sensitive sealed document from the trial of the blind Sheik Omar Abdul Rahman with notations indicating that he sent it to the head of the Kenyan al Qaeda cell to be taken to bin Laden. I shudder to think of the people who may read this statement and where it may be found some day." The *Washington Post* wrote that in 1998 after hearing his court testimony, "The FBI began to focus on Mohammed as a potential terrorist suspect," despite the fact that he was a double agent, working for the U.S.

While he was living in California, Fitzgerald, along with FBI agents Jack Cloonan and Harlan Bell, went to visit Ali Mohammed and took him to lunch in a restaurant in Sacramento. The purpose of the meeting was to cultivate Mohammed and gain his cooperation. Their ultimate reason for the meeting was to gain his confidence and try and persuade him to work with the FBI.

When the SDNY was prosecuting those responsible for the East Africa bombings in Kenya and Tanzania, the American public, via the mainstream media, really had no clue as to the extent of what bin Laden and his henchmen were really up to. There was no public record of anything relating to the double agent, Ali Mohammed. Whether this was done deliberately on the part of the prosecutors at the SDNY is an open topic to this day, but when the truth of the plot was revealed in October 2003, the public learned a different story from what had been put out. Two years after the Africa bombing attack the backstory of that event, as far as American law enforcement was concerned, was revealed by Robert Windrem of NBC News who filed a report which said in part, "Newly disclosed documents in the East Africa embassy bombings case show that U.S. intelligence was aware of Osama bin Laden's terrorist cell in Kenya two years before the August 1998 bombings that killed 224 people, including 12 Americans. As early as August 1996, the intelligence community bugged the Nairobi phones of bin Laden's personal secretary Wadih el-Hage, and others in the Kenyan capital, according to court records."

Mary Joe White, who was Patrick Fitzgerald's boss and the U.S. Attorney for the SDNY, was as happy as a clam when the convictions for the embassy bombings came down. She, like the other prosecutors in her office, knew the public hadn't been given the whole story and she made the following statement in the spring of 2001, "These verdicts are a triumph for world justice and for world unity in combating international terrorism."

There is one final story in the saga of Patrick Fitzgerald and the FBI and the terror cases in which they worked for years to uncover, or in some case, not uncover, nefarious plots. It concerned a movie about these events that author Peter Lance was approached to take part in. Lance was approached by Jonathan Towers, the producer of a movie called *Inside 9-11,* which was a four-hour documentary on the 9-11 attacks. Lance was one of many other journalists who were interviewed for the film, and he was more than happy to help out. Lance told Towers that he was working on a book regarding the FBI and Ali Mohammed, and his work was soon optioned (the book in question was *Triple Cross).* Lance went to Washington where he met with executives from the National Geographic Channel who were going to release the film.

Lance then wrote a twelve-page, ten-act treatment outlining the two major parts in the Ali Mohamed story: his dealing with al Qaeda and bin Laden, and how the Feds, notably Patrick Fitzgerald and the FBI's New York office, allowed him to operate in full bloom.

The film went into production in the spring of 2006; Lance was to narrate and was the co-executive producer. Some of the early footage was filmed in New York, the scene of the crime, so to speak. The movie was called, *Triple Cross: Bin Laden's Spy in America,* and it aired on August 28, 2006. It was not what Lance had envisioned it to be. As he wrote in *Triple Cross,* "not a word about FBI-DOJ negligence could be found in the documentary. Except for a brief super at the top of the program, reading, 'Based in part on the book *Triple Cross* by Peter Lance,' there wasn't a frame of my narration or on-camera presence—nor was the book even mentioned, even though the inclusion of the cover was specified in my contract with Towers Productions."

After the film was nationally aired, Lance said what was shown in the movie was "a whitewash of my findings." There was no mention of Able Danger in the film; nothing relating to the jail-house meetings between Ramzi Yousef and Gregory Scarpa Jr,; and nothing about Patrick Fitzgerald's earlier warning about how important Ali Mohamed was to the entire terror plots then being hatched. The Towers Production Company failed to let Peter Lance have the research materials he needed for on-camera interviews that were essential for the movie to be seen as being credible.

Lance was angry and disgruntled at how the movie took shape and he didn't mince words about how he felt, "Most important, as I've discovered after five years of research, the FBI has failed to reform in the wake of 9/11. The Nat Geo Documentary gave lip service to the tragic Ali Mohammed story, but failed to provide a single word of critical analysis to help viewers understand how Fitzgerald and Squad I-49 had failed to protect them against bin Laden's principle spy."[42] (The author has seen the DVD referred to above and Peter Lance was not interviewed on camera for the show.)

The destruction of the Able Danger documentation began roughly from May to June 2000. The man who was ordered to do the destruction was Major Eric Kleinsmith. Major Kleinsmith said that by April of 2000, Able Danger had collected "an immense amount of data for analysis that allowed us to map al Qaeda as a worldwide threat with a surprisingly significant presence in the United States." The order to destroy the documents came from Army intelligence and Security Command General Counsel Tony Gentry, who joked to Major Kleinsmith telling him, "Remember to delete the data—or you'll go to jail." Other materials related to Able Danger were destroyed in March 2001 and in the spring of 2004.

The final indignation in this whole sordid drama came on September 19, 2005, four years after the attacks, when Lt. Col. Anthony Shaffer had his security clearance revoked by the government. There is a question that needs to be asked in this matter. Was Col. Shaffer's security clearance removed because of his public testimony and high profile position in Able Danger and its revelations—a form of retaliation? Was that action taken because he had the gumption to reveal material that some people in the government did not want made public? While Col. Shaffer's revelations about Able Danger may not fit exactly in the category of a so-called whistleblower, his knowledge about the inner working of Able Danger made him a target for those whose agenda may not have been what other public servants may have done if they were in his place.

42 *Triple Cross*. Page 464-468.

Col. Shaffer's attorney, Mark Zaid (who also represented the so-called whistleblower in the 2019 Ukrainian scandal involving the Trump administration), summed up his client's position saying, "I specialize in security clearance cases. Based on years of experience I can say categorically that the basis for the revocation was questionable at best."

A further indignity against Col. Shaffer, one that goes to the very heart of our democracy, took place in 2010 when he published a memoir of his time in the Army called *Operation Dark Heart: Spycraft and Special Ops on the Frontlines of Afghanistan—and the Path to Victory,* which was published by St. Martin's Press. In retaliation for the book's publication, the U.S. Department of Defense oversaw the destruction of 9,500 copies of the book. The Pentagon said this was the first time that it took such action in its history because the book contained classified information—but it may not have been in time to keep the secrets from becoming public.

The Defense Department purchased the entire print run from St. Martin's Press for $47,000, a few weeks before its official publication date. However, the book was not totally banned from publication and it was eventually released when a large portion of the text was excised. A total of 250 sections were blacked out and deleted. Before all the damage was done, St. Martin's sent 200 uncensored review copies to different media outlets across the country.

In 2009, Shaffer sent a copy of the book to the commanders in the Army Reserve, which cleared it for publication. "He submitted the manuscript up the chain of command," said Shaffer's attorney. "As a general rule, that's what you're supposed to do. That's true, except the book deals with information Shaffer encountered while under the jurisdiction of the DIA—which makes the subject matter of interest to the Pentagon."

The *New York Times* got ahold of one of the unredacted copies and said that much of the material in the book was available on Wikipedia. "They wanted Shaffer's code name Chris Stryker taken out of the book, even though that same name had been approved for use in public testimony back in 2006," said his lawyer.

The controversy over the book caught the attention of many in the media who saw the actions taken by the DOD as an infringement of the right of free speech and freedom of the press. One of the outlets that came to Shaffer's aid was the Federation of American Scientists. Steven Aftergood, who worked for the Federation, said in regard to the Shaffer book, "I think the Pentagon made a mistake in judgment." He said he found the government redactions "appalling." To say that Col. Shaffer had gotten the shaft from the American government, the same government to wlhich he devoted his career in the first place, is a shame in the first degree. He and his Able Danger team uncovered certain facts which embarrassed the government after 9-11 and they decided to take retribution on Col. Shaffer in reprisals for their own mistakes. He should have been treated better.[43]

43 Suddath, Claire, "How Not to Censor a Book: Pentagon Makes a Best Seller, " contenttime.com, September 30, 2010.

Amanda Keller in Florida circa 1999.

Rudi Dekkers at his flight school circa 2000.

Chapter 10

Mohamed Atta, the Hijackers, and Florida

The 9-11 Commission Report, in its final version, paid no attention to Mohamed Atta's stay in Florida, nor the people he met in the Sunshine State. According to the report, the hijackers had little or no associations with the people they came in contact with during their stay in the United States. That is especially true as it related to Mohamed Atta and his Florida sojourn, in the months leading up to the attacks. Since the issuance of the 9-11 report, new, detailed information concerning Atta's stay in Florida, and his links with men with criminal backgrounds, have been discovered.

The authors of a groundbreaking book on the role of Atta and his American accomplices have been completely ignored by the mainstream press, as well as the members of the 9-11 Commission. The work in question is called *Welcome to Terrorland: Mohamed Atta & the 9-11 Cover-Up in Florida* by Daniel Hopsicker.

Welcome to Terrorland was never reviewed by the mainstream press who wrote reams of articles and think pieces on the 9-11 tragedy, giving the reader only that information that was put forward by the government and the individual papers' correspondents.

Daniel Hopsicker, the author of the anti-establishment book *Barry & the Boys? The CIA, the Mob and America's Secret History,* has woven together the definitive story of Mohamed Atta and his American connections in Florida prior to 9-11. The book, the contents of which should have been reviewed by the 9-11 Commissioners before publishing their findings, put to rest the fable that Atta was the lone nut pilot who was just following the precepts of Allah and Osama bin Laden. It seems that Atta had a penchant for girlie bars, liked to drink to excess, and had an American girlfriend whom he lived with in Florida. He also had many connections with strange people in the months leading up to 9-11, two men in particular, Dutchmen Rudi Dekkers and Arne Kruithof, both of whom were well known to U.S. law enforcement authorities as being men whose scams crossed two oceans.

While it is well known that Atta and his fellow hijacker, Marwan al-Shehhi attended mosques in other parts of the country, while they were in Florida, they attended at least one mosque that was called the Al Hijrah mosque run by Gulshair Shukrijumah which was located in Miramar, Broward County. Atta and several other of the hijackers lived near the mosque and had easy access to it and the people who attended its services. It was from this mosque that Atta and his fellow hijackers would learn the lay of the land in Florida, make clandestine connections, and begin to take flying lessons which caught the attention of a number of people who began to take a second look at them and what they were up to.

However, as is the case with many other parts of the 9-11 story and its myriad of characters and interlocking parts, there is more to the story of Gulshair Shukrijumah than meets the eye. It seems that the elder Shukrijumah was a close associate with the blind Sheik, Omar Abdul Rahman, and had at one time been an imam at the Al Farooq mosque in Brooklyn where Abdul Rahman preached. He also acted as the blind Sheik's translator and testified for the defense at the WTC bombing trial of Clement Hampton-El.

As mentioned in the last chapter, the Able Danger data mining program identified Atta before the 9-11 attacks, and the ensuing controversy that surrounded that fact. It seems that Able Danger identified Atta, as well as three other hijackers, al-Shehhi, Khalid al-Midhar, and Nawaf al-Hazmi, as members of the cell that they called "Brooklyn." An article addressed some questions realted to Able Danger's indetification of the men:

> However, the FBI informant saw Atta at the mosque in early 2001, whereas Able Danger linked him to the Brooklyn cell in January 2000. It is unclear how Able Danger could have made the link before Atta officially

entered the U.S., although Atta used a bewildering array of aliases—the 19 hijackers together racked up a total of 364 aliases and name variants—and it is impossible to rule him out entering the U.S. under another name."

"One possibility is that there was a prior link between Atta and the Shukrijumahs—how likely is it that Atta and the other hijackers just happened to move in on the doorstep of a known associate of the Blind Sheik and his son, one of al Qaeda's top US-based operatives? There may well have been prior links between Atta and the Shukrijumahs, which able Danger learned of. For example, Atta made two green card lottery applications in late 1999 and it is possible he gave the Shukrijumahs' address in this context."[44]

The story of Mohamed Atta covers the entire state of Florida, from the fishing piers of Key West, the southernmost part of the United States, to the retirement homes of Daytona Beach, Venice, Hollywood, Coral Springs, and Orlando. It is a telling story of flight training, of meetings with mysterious Saudis, and lying lessons given to Atta and his fellow conspirator Marwan al-Shehhi by Rudi Dekker and Arne Kruithof. It is an account that flies right in the face of the "official" FBI report which decided not to run a full court press into the criminal lives of Dekkers and Kruithof, both of whom had firsthand connections with Atta and al-Shehhi. Another person associated with Atta was an American flight school owner named Wally Hillard of Naples, Florida who was responsible for bringing large numbers of Arab flight students to Florida. He was also the man who eventually bought Rudi Dekkers' Huffman Aviation, the same flight school where Atta took flying lessons.

The connection between Dekkers, Kruithof and Hillard are just the tip of the iceberg as far as the Florida story involving the 9-11 hijackers is concerned. What is more interesting is why, of all places, did Mohamed Atta pick Venice, Florida to use as his American base of operations?

Located on Florida's Gulf Coast, Naples is not your ordinary type of town that caters to international terrorists. It is a quiet retirement community whose residents get excited when one of them gets a hole in one on the local golf course. But Venice was

44 Gulshair Shukrijumah: Atta's Able Danger Link?

the home of Mohamed Atta and Marwan al-Shehhi who took flying lessons at the Venice airport. The airport that served as Atta and al-Shehhi's training ground was owned by Rudi Dekkers who, it is alleged, charged the two men double what other flying schools charged. The men paid $28,000 for their lessons. In an interesting note to the Venice story, Ramzi bin al-Shib, one of the members of the Hamburg cell, tried to enter the United States via Venice before he was refused a visa to come into the country.

If bin al-Shib was not allowed to enter the U.S. it seems that his replacement, Zacarias Moussaoui, did indeed travel to Venice to join his co-conspirators. After 9-11, FBI agents questioned Arne Kruithof on his possible connections with Moussaoui.

While residing in Venice, Atta liked to go to Sharky's Billiard Bar where, it is assumed, he practiced pool. In their post 9-11 investigation, the FBI said that Atta had left Florida weeks prior to the attack. However, residents said that they saw Dekkers and Atta at Sharky's in the weeks leading up to 9-11.

In his reporting on the Venice connection to 9-11, Daniel Hopsicker, writing in *Welcome to Terrorland,* says that after the attacks, FBI agents removed all of the local police files on Dekkers, loaded them into a Ryder truck and took them away. Why were Dekkers' files so important that the Feds had to remove them from the local jurisdiction?

The story of Mohamed Atta in Florida would not be complete without mentioning that this so-called devout Muslim, who hated everything American, had an American girlfriend named Amanda Keller.

Amanda Keller worked as a stripper, and for an escort service called Fantasies & Lingerie. Atta and Amanda lived together for two months in Venice. Their relationship, if one could call that, as rough and tumble, not many attachments, and certainly nothing that would last. Both Amanda and Atta frequented many of the bars in the Sarasota area where the drinks were plentiful, and, according to Keller, Atta would meet up with pilots from Germany and Africa. Who these foreign pilots that Atta was supposed to have met is still a mystery, if it in fact was true. Their relationship lasted only two months, at which time Amanda broke off the affair.

It seems that Amada met a handsome man named Garret at a

nightclub and soon Amanda asked Garret to stay at her apartment (along with Atta). In retaliation for Amanda ditching of him, Atta killed Amanda's cats, cutting them up into little pieces.

Amanda Keller lived at the Sandpiper Apartments in Venice, and it was in that same apartment complex that Atta reportedly shared a separate apartment, at one time, with Marwan al-Shehhi, and possibly four other people. A neighbor of Keller's, Stephanie Frederickson, said, "One day in the middle of March, she brought home Atta." She called him "a really nasty guy," and said that he had "no patience, and seemed mad at the world."

Another person who knew of the Atta-Keller relationship was Charles Grapentine, who was the manager of the Sandpiper Apartments. He said he saw Atta in the complex for a period of three weeks in April 2001. Keller's mother, Susan Payne, further said of Atta, "I didn't like him; he just seemed strange." To make this story stranger, a couple named Tony and Vonnie La Conca, who lived in North Port, said that a man named "Mohammad," briefly rented a home from them. When questioned by local authorities after 9-11, the couple said that he was about 25 years old, "very polite, very handsome" with "beautiful, unblemished skin."

In the days after the attacks, both Amanda Keller and Stephanie Frederickson would have important stories to tell regarding Mohamed Atta. Keller said that when she moved out of Venice to a new place of residence, the FBI called her on a regular basis; she said that she was being intimidated by the FBI. "They told me not to talk to anybody, to keep my mouth shut," she said.

Ms. Frederickson said this regarding her interactions with the FBI, "At first, right after the attack, the FBI told me I must have been mistaken in my identification [of Atta]. Or they would insinuate that I was lying. Finally they stopped trying to get me to change my story, and just stopped by once a week to make sure I hadn't been talking to anyone. Who was I to tell? Most everyone around here already knew."

Charles Grapentine, the owner of the Sandpiper complex also had run-ins with the FBI regarding his identification of Atta in Venice. The bureau "called me a liar, and told me to keep my mouth shut."

A former manager at Huffman Aviation in Venice, which Atta attended in late 2000, alleged that the FBI intimidated him and told him to keep quiet. He says that the FBI was "outside my house for hours after the attack." He claimed that his phone was tapped after 9-11 and added, "I thought these guys [Atta and his associates] were double agents. Why is that so incriminating?"[45]

The reference by the former manager at Huffman Aviation to Atta and his associates as "double agents," was mirrored by a British intelligence officer by the name of Colonel John Hughes-Wilson. Writing in 2004, Col. Hughes-Wilson said that at the same time that Atta and Marwan al-Shehhi were taking flying lessons at Huffman Aviation, "A CIA front company called Air Caribe was also operating out of the very same hangar at Venice airport." He said, "this highly curious coincidence must inevitably raise some suspicions of just how much the CIA really did know before 9-11. Was the CIA trying to infiltrate and 'double' the US-based al Qaeda cell, in the hope of using it against Osama bin Laden's organization in the future?"

While we know that Atta and al-Shehhi trained in Florida, there were reports coming out after the attacks that caused a whole lot of controversy, to say the least. Whether they are true or not is to be debated. Here is the story.

Post 9-11, there were media reports that suggested that some of the 9-11 hijackers took training at U.S. military bases, including the Pensacola Naval Air Station, where many foreign nationals were trained. One such person was hijacker Ahmed Alghamdi who lived in Pensacola until about August 2000. One neighbor said that Alghamdi was part of a group of Arab men who oftentimes met at The Fountains apartment complex near the University of West Florida. This person said of these meetings, "People would come and knock on doors. We might see three or four, and they were always men. It was always evening. They would go and knock, and then it would be a little while and someone would look out the window to see who it was, like they were being very cautious. Not your normal coming to the door and opening it."

There was speculation in the local media that some of the abovementioned people might have stolen military identification

45 History Commons: FBI Intimidates Witnesses who saw Atta in Venice; Tells them to keep quiet.

from real military servicemen who were stationed at various military bases around the area. This was just one more "to be determined" story of the 9-11 plot that was never given much credence by the media or the investigating authorities.

One of the many discrepancies concerning Atta in Florida is the timeline of his whereabouts and what he was doing. The official story is that Atta arrived in the U.S. at Newark Airport on June 3, 2000. In July, both he and al-Shehhi were residing in Florida, taking flying lessons from Rudi Dekkers' Huffman Aviation. In December 2000, both men moved to the Miami area where they took lessons in a simulator at the SinCenter in Opa-Locka.

Dekkers told the assembled newsmen at his home after the attacks that Atta and al-Shehhi paid their bills at Huffman and left for good. They supposedly left Florida in December for greener pastures. But if they were not in Florida for the eight months prior to the attacks (which was contradicted by many locals in the Florida area), where did they go?

What we do know is that Atta and al-Shehhi lived in Venice for a week in July 2000 with Charlie Voss who was employed at Huffman Aviation, before he sent them packing. They then lived in the community of Nokomis near Venice from July to December 2000 in an apartment owned by Steve Kona, who was a member of the Venice Fire Department. While in Florida, Atta used the alias "Mohammad Arajaki," which he used when opening up bank accounts.

A person who disputes the official story that Atta left Florida in December 2000 was Paula Grapentine who lived in the Sandpiper Apartments in Venice. She recognized Atta's face after the attack and said that Atta had lived there "earlier this year," meaning 2001. If Grapentine said that Atta was still living there during part of 2001, then either she or the FBI is lying (Charles Grapentine, Paula's husband, said that Atta was probably still in Venice in April 2001).

Another incident that needs to be further explained is the trip that Atta, Amanda, and several of Atta's friends (Peter and Stephan, plus a girl named Linda) made to Key West on February 25, 2001. Peter and Stephan, it seems, were German nationals. How and where Atta met them, and under what conditions, is not known.

In Key West, they took in all the usual sights, rented a room, just ordinary tourists, drinking daiquiris and visiting the various museums that lure thousands of people on a yearly basis. But, according to Amanda, an undisclosed person flew to Key West to meet with Atta. No one knows what transpired between Atta and this, yet to be named person. According to Daniel Hopsicker, a number of Arabs who lived on Big Pine Key suddenly left their homes just hours after the 9-11 attacks, just as FBI agents were ready to spring into action. Was there any connection between Atta, his mysterious fly-in visitor, and the Arabs living in the Keys?

Shortly after the 9-11 attacks, the FBI discovered an important fact that puts into dispute one of the basic tenets of Mohamed Atta's time in the United States: the fact that before coming here to take "flying lessons," he was already a licensed pilot. Atta's some time girlfriend, Amanda Keller, told the bureau that Atta had a number of phony IDs in his flight bag that he always kept shut. She also said that Atta had more than one pilot's license from other countries. If that is so, why did he invent a cover story about learning how to fly airplanes in small, out of the way airports like Huffman Aviation? Is there something to the story of Mohamed Atta in Florida that the FBI is not telling?

Another wrinkle in the story of Atta and al-Shehhi during their Florida sojourn is the possibility that both men attended an as yet unnamed flight school before coming to Rudi Dekkers' Huffman Aviation. Dekkers told the national media that Atta said they had left another flight school near Tampa but refused to name it. Why keep it a secret?

The official story is this: They took flying lessons at Huffman from July to December 2000. They then spent three short weeks at Jones Aviation in Sarasota. In December they arrived at the Professional Aviation School at the Charlotte County Airport. Nowhere in the official government reports is there any mention of their time at the Charlotte County Airport. In the time that Atta was at Charlotte, the school was filled with mostly students from Tunisia. It seems that the Tunisian students had a gripe with the owner of Charlotte Airport, David Beyers. The students said they never received the proper training they paid for, and soon, the airport closed its doors. After Charlotte went belly up. Atta, al-Shehhi, and the other Tunisians headed back to Venice and Huffman Aviation. Was there any connection between Atta and the Tunisian students at Charlotte Airport?

Rudi Dekkers, the Dutch national and flight school instructor, had a more intimate relationship with Mohamed Atta and Marwan al-Shehhi than has previously been reported. As the owner of Huffman Aviation, Dekkers reported that a large number of his students came from the Middle East, including his two most notorious students, Atta and al-Shehhi. Dekkers taught his students how to fly single-engine airplanes, not the large, commercial planes used in the 9-11 attacks. He taught up to 400 students at his two training facilities in Florida, gladly accepting their money and giving them just the kind of instruction they asked for.

Rudi Dekkers had a most unusual attachment to Huffman Aviation to begin with. It seems that Wally Hillard was the main financial person in the Huffman business and Dekkers became its sole stockholder. The *St. Petersburg Times* wrote about Dekkers and said in one of its columns, "He seems to have benefited from the same type of casual scrutiny of visa applicants that let the 9-11 hijackers live and train here [in the US]—Even the Federal Aviation Administration and numerous lawsuits—this is the kind of checkered history, experts say that should have raised questions both before and after the 9-11 attacks about Dekkers' fitness to run a school that trained pilots."

In the Netherlands, Dekkers ran a computer company that went bankrupt and then he moved to, of all places, Naples, Florida in 1992. After running a computer chip exporting company, he started Ambassador Airways. He began having financial troubles, and at one point, the Naples Airport refused to even sell him fuel for his planes, even if he paid in cash. At one point in 1999, the FAA revoked his pilot's license for a 45-day period for a variety of reasons, including "operating an aircraft in a careless or reckless manner." Despite all his troubles, Wally Hillard came to the rescue and loaned him $1.7 million to buy Huffman Aviation. Dekkers then spent some of his newfound money doing advertising overseas, including in Germany and other European nations. Huffman Aviation was just up the road from Florida Flight Training Center, where hijacker Ziad Jarrah, the pilot of Flight 93, took his lessons. Dekkers closed Ambassador Airways in December 2001 due to financial difficulties.

Dekkers was well known to American law enforcement authorities as he set up shop at Huffman Aviation. He was under indictment in Florida, as well as being wanted for crimes in the Netherlands. He owed the government of the Netherlands three million dollars dating back to the early 1990s, due to his stating that he had more assets than he really had. He was also under indictment by Florida officials on criminal fraud charges. Back in Holland, he was persona non grata, and was also being investigated on similar charges. Despite his disreputable persona, he was never deported by the U.S. back to Holland.

Employees at Huffman Aviation said after the attacks that the FBI agents who came to talk with Dekkers seemed to already know him and did not push him too hard in their questioning. Later, Dekkers would tell the FBI that his students only trained on small, single engine planes, not the jumbo 747s that were used in the attacks on the Pentagon and the WTC. If Atta and his fellow terrorists did not learn how to fly large planes under the auspices of Rudi Dekkers, where did they gain this skill?

One of the many controversies surrounding the time that Mohamed Atta spent in Florida, was his association with Rudi Dekkers, and how close or distant it was. This question is partly answered by a number of employees of the Venice Yellow Cab Company who were interviewed by the FBI three days after the attack. "They knew each other well—very well—they were friends," said one Yellow Cab driver named Bob Simpson. "They were going to a nightclub in Sarasota, talking and very sociable with each other. He and Atta were friends, you could tell."

Simpson first took Atta and Dekkers from Huffman Aviation to a restaurant in downtown Venice; it was on a second ride that he picked them up at the Pompano Road residence of former Huffman employee Charlie Voss, and took the two to a Sarasota nightclub Atta is known to have frequented.

"Then a lot of times, with a new flight student, Rudi would take them over to Sharky's for lunch, and I'd get the call to pick them up. Dekkers also regularly used our cars to do things like go to lunch, because he usually flew in by helicopter and didn't have a car at the Venice Airport."

The manager of the Yellow Cab Company later said that all these trips were recorded in the firm's logs and said that the FBI was also interested in any cab rides that Atta took.

All this flies in the face of the assertion by the FBI regarding Atta's movements prior to the attacks, as well as assertionsby Dekkers himself. In his testimony before the House Judiciary Committee in March 2002, Dekkers said that his relationship with Atta had not been close, and had ended the previous December, nine months before the attack.

"On December 24, 2000, Atta and al-Shehhi rented a Warrior from Huffman Aviation for a flight," said Dekkers, telling of his last encounter with Atta.

"Atta and al-Shehhi returned to Huffman Aviation to make final payments on their outstanding bills. Because they were not taking any more flying lessons, they were asked to leave the facility due to their bad attitudes and not being liked by staff and clients alike. Huffman never heard about or from them again until September 11, 2001."

On September 14, 2001, Simpson was contacted by the FBI in regards to what he knew about Atta. The FBI showed him pictures of the hijackers and asked him if he could identify any of them. He picked out Atta and told them that he had driven him around during the month of August.

Simpson also said the following:

> They were especially interested in a rich Saudi guy that I'd been sent back to pick up at the Orlando Executive Airport. They said they already knew that he'd ridden in my cab because they'd gotten my cab number from a surveillance camera there.

The FBI agents asked specific and direct questions focused on several trips to the Orlando Executive Airport beginning in December 2000, said Simpson, who told them he had been asked to drive there by a mysterious Middle Eastern convenience store owner in Venice who was an associate of Atta's, and who left town shortly after the attack.

In another interesting bit of news, Simpson said that he saw Zacarias Moussaoui in Venice.

"In the official chronology of the period, from January to April 2001, FBI investigators state they were not sure where Atta and al-Shehhi were, and that they may have traveled back to Germany, since Atta reportedly received a visitor's visa in Hamburg and reentered the United States during this time." [46]

There were also inconsistencies in the statements that Dekkers made concerning his relationship with Atta and al-Shehhi following 9-11. Many credible witnesses in the Venice area spoke of an on-going connection between the two hijackers and Dekkers, despite the fact that Dekkers had, on numerous occasions, said he only had a business association with the two men.

Rudi Dekkers and his Dutch compatriot Arne Kruithof would come to be known as the "Magic Dutch Boys" by the local media. Both came from Holland, and opened competing flight schools in the Venice, Florida region—Dekker's Huffman Aviation, and Kruithof's Florida Flight Training Center. Yet, the men say they never knew each other prior to coming to Florida!

Arne Kruithof was a partner with a German national named Paul Schreier from Munich. They owned a company called Aviation Aspirations. Aviation Aspirations had a strange scheme called the "Mentor Programme." The Mentor Programme said the following, "The help is both financial and practical. We now provide one-to-one practical assistance from experienced Professional Pilots whom we have established throughout the world."

It is interesting to note that Paul Schreier was responsible for bringing Mohamed Atta and members of his secret Hamburg cell from Germany to Florida where they showed up at Dekkers' Huffman Aviation. Coincidence or not?

In time, 400 foreign nationals would attend both men's schools, including other members of the 9-11 hijack crew. The connection between Paul Schreier, Rudi Dekkers, and Mohamed Atta still has not been explained fully, and is one facet of the investigation that the 9-11 Commission never even looked into.

Writing in *Welcome to Terrorland,* author Hopsicker relates

46 Hopsicker, Daniel, "Mohamed Atta and Rudi Dekkers Seen Together in Venice in weeks before Sept. 11 attack." From the Wilderness Publications.

that a report in the French newspaper *Le Monde* said that Yeslam bin Laden, a brother of Osama bin Laden, provided Dekkers' Huffman Aviation in Venice with a number of students for flight training. It seems that a company owned by Yeslam bin Laden called Avcon Air Center, worked out of the Venice facility and gave instruction to a few of the 9-11 hijackers. For his part, Yeslam bin Laden said that it was only a coincidence that his students took their training at the Venice airport.

Hopsicker also reports that only days before the 9-11 attacks, four unidentified men who were taking flight training at Dekkers establishments quickly left the country (these men were all Saudis—as mentioned before in this narrative, all of Dekkers records were quickly removed by the FBI in the days after 911. Why?).

In 1999, the Venice Flight School was sold by Stanley Huffman from Naples to a financier named Wally Hillard and Rudi Dekkers. The deal went through so fast that the city authorities in Naples did not have time to approve it. In time though, Dekkers' finances went south and he could not even pay his employees. It soon became obvious that Dekkers had little or no experience in operating an airport facility and broke FAA rules left and right. Federal investigators also looked into illegal computer operations begun by Dekkers at the Venice facility. In 1993 or 1994, the DEA and the U.S. Customs Service had ongoing investigations of him and a warrant was issued for his arrest for the illegal sale of computer chips.

If Dekkers was so strapped for cash in the early 1990s, and was being investigated by the feds for various illegal acts, how and where did he get the money to buy Huffman's flight school a few years later?

The other member of the so-called "Magic Dutch Boys" was Arne Kruithof from Rotterdam in the Netherlands. He owned the Florida Flight Training Center just down the road from his fellow countryman in Venice. Ziad Jarrah, a member of Atta's Hamburg cell, took flying lessons under the direction of Kruithof. So, what do we have? A number of the 9-11 hijackers were taking flying lessons just miles apart, from two different Dutch nationals who said they never heard of each other before coming to Florida.

While he was at Kruithof's establishment, he became acquainted with Arne, and said that Jarrah, "told [me] that he knew somebody who was also interested in getting a commercial pilot license. He said his name was Ramzi something. When I found out that [Ramzi's] English was poor, we referred him to a language school through which he tried to obtain a visa. When I asked Ziad why, if he knew, his visa was denied, he said, 'No, I do not know that.' We then made a few phone calls, but nobody could tell us anything."

Kruithof said of his student Ziad Jarrah, "He is not just nice, but he had qualities you look for in a dear friend, someone you can trust." He told the 9-11 Commission members that Jarrah "was polite and easy to deal with, and does not show any hostility to the United States, or the West."

A differing account of Ziad Jarrah came from a fellow flight student named Thorsten Biermann, who roomed with Jarrah for six weeks. He described him as "introverted, a loner, he kept his distance." Biermann once flew with Jarrah on a round-trip to Fort Lauderdale, where, upon their return, Jarrah insisted on both flying and manning the radio, and twice ignored Biermann's pleas to refuel when the weather worsened. Biermann said, "I decided I did not want to fly with him anymore, and everyone I knew who flew with him felt the same way. It was as if he needed control."

Both Dekkers and Kruithof were involved in near fatal airplane/ helicopter crashes in the aftermath of 9-11. The helicopter with Dekkers crashed near Fort Meyers, Florida in January 2003. His flying partner in the chopper, Tony Douangdara, was pulled safely from the chopper. In 2011, Dekkers said that he was convinced that someone tried to kill him, but he didn't mention any potential suspects.

On June 26, 2002, Arne Kruithof and two other men, Glenn Goodman and John Mills, were involved in another crash after leaving Venice Airport for a routine flight. It seems their plane began to bank toward the ground shortly after takeoff. Despite the wreckage of the plane, no one was seriously hurt. Was there more to these two incidents than meets the eye, or were they just random happenings to two men who were deeply involved in the 9-11 story?

What *is* known is this. Mohamed Atta, Marwan al-Shehhi,

and at least six other 9-11 hijackers took flying lessons under the auspices of two Dutch nationals, Rudi Dekkers and Arne Kruithof in Venice, Florida. Both Dekkers and Kruithof were well known to U.S. intelligence and police authorities since arriving in the United States. Both men survived near fatal air crashes. Dekkers was *well* connected with Mohamed Atta, despite his efforts to distance himself from him. Atta and his cohorts were in Florida in August 2001, contrary to the official timeline given to the public by the 9-11 Commission. The FBI, to this day, nineteen years after 9-11, has yet to give the American public a true account of Mohamed Atta's Florida adventure.

Atta and Oswald

When looking at the story of Mohamed Atta in the days and months before 9-11, there are a lot of discrepancies regarding his actions, as well as the people he came in contact with, especially during his short stay in Florida. A number of conspiracy writers have looked into the roles of Mohamed Atta and Lee Harvey Oswald, the alleged assassin of President John F. Kennedy. While their stories are not totally related, there are a number of similarities that have come to the fore. Some have alleged that both Atta and Oswald were somehow placed as fall guys in the history changing events they were involved in. It is worthwhile here to look at both men and see what the similarities are, in order to get a fuller picture of who they were.

Both Atta and Oswald were young men when they took part in their respective tasks. One (Atta) was educated, while the other (Oswald) was not. Both men had traveled a great deal prior to the time their events unfolded, and both men were on the radar of U.S. authorities.

Atta had traveled to such places as The Netherlands, Germany, the Philippines, Czechoslovakia, Afghanistan, Spain, and other parts of the United States. As seen in a previous chapter in this book, there were numerous reports (later not fully confirmed) that Atta was in Prague, Czech Republic, supposedly meeting with an agent of the government of Saddam Hussein.

In Oswald's case, he "defected" to the Soviet Union in September 1959, after getting a hardship discharge from the

Marine Corps on the flimsy assertion that his mother was ill and need his help. Instead of going back to Fort Worth, Texas, he applied for,and received a passport in record time, and headed to the Soviet Union. He was supposed to attend the Albert Schweitzer College in Zurich, Switzerland, he but he never showed up. He made his way to France and then went to the Soviet Union where he promptly went to the American Embassy in Moscow and told them he was renouncing his American citizenship. After the Russians decided not to allow him to stay permanently in their country, Oswald slashed his wrists and after his recovery, was sent to the city of Minsk where he worked in a radio factory. There he lived the high-life, and soon married a young Russian woman named Marina. The Oswalds stayed in Russia for over two years and then abruptly, came back to the United States. Once back home Oswald was never questioned by the CIA and he was not charged with treason by the U.S. government.

He did, however, have run-ins with certain FBI agents in Dallas, namely James Hosty, whom Oswald accused of threatening his wife and making life difficult for both of them. For someone the U.S. government thought of as a "loner," he had a lot of eyes on him.

As seen in this chapter, Mohamed Atta led a double life in Florida, living with a stripper, Amanda Keller, drinking alcohol (which most devout Muslims never do), taking flying lessons at flight schools, and making certain acquaintances with American citizens, including Rudi Dekkers, cab driver Simpson, and a host of others.

One of his most audacious actions, and one that left a trail for further investigations, took place in April 2000, When Atta attempted to get a U.S. government loan to purchase and modify a crop duster plane for use in the chemical trade. The person Atta talked to in order to get this loan was a federal employee named Johnell Bryant. In their conversations, Atta talked about security at the World Trade Center and other buildings in D.C. He also told her that he was a supporter of bin Laden and al Qaeda. By this action, Atta was leaving a trail that any inquisitive investigator would have followed up on, but that was not the case.

Like Atta, Oswald (or someone who was impersonating

him), made his presence known in Dallas in the weeks before the assassination. For example, someone using Oswald's name, went to a car dealership saying they wanted to buy a car. However, the real Oswald did not have a driver's license so he couldn't have legally driven a car to begin with. While at the car lot, the person pretending to be Oswald got into a heated argument with the salesmen whom he told that he had lived in Russia and that he liked their type of government. Being the honest American citizen that he was, the salesmen kicked Oswald out of his place of business. Similarly, a person named Oswald was at a shooting range near Dallas and began shooting at another person's targets. Again, "Oswald" told the person whose targets he was shooting at that his name was "Oswald" and told him to basically screw off. These are actions the real Oswald would probably not have taken. Someone was pretending to be him.

He also left clues out in the open when he made himself conspicuous in New Orleans in the summer of 1963 as a one-man member of the anti-Castro Fair Play for Cuba Committee. He was passing out Pro-Castro leaflets when he was accosted by a man who was anti-Castro in his leanings, and whom Oswald had previously met. They got into an altercation (possibly staged) and Oswald was arrested by local police. Upon his arrest, Oswald asked for, and was granted, an interview with a member of the New Orleans FBI office who came down to headquarters to take his statement. Why Oswald wanted to talk with an FBI agent in that circumstance in not known, but it certainly left a huge open trail for further investigation.

While Mohamed Atta was in Hamburg, Germany attending a pre-9-11 summit (which was being watched by Western intelligence services) and meeting with KSM, his fellow conspirators were seen leaving and arriving in Germany coming from and going to other locations around the globe (Thailand, for example). In 1995, Atta was investigated by German authorities for drug-related crimes but was never charged. His later girlfriend, Amanda Keller, said that Atta had "massive supplies of cocaine" while he was living with her in Florida, and that he was able to refresh these supplies as he needed them.

In another move that could be seen as conspicuously leaving

a trail, Atta abandoned a stalled aircraft on a runway at Miami International Airport in December 2000. The FAA threatened to investigate this serious matter, but again, nothing was done.

In another interesting Atta story, three months before 9-11, in June 2001,a warrant was issued for Atta's arrest in Florida. He was ticketed by the Florida police for not having a driver's license (like Oswald), and the warrant was issued because he never showed up for his court hearing. He was not arrested following this incident. He was pulled over by police in July 2001 for speeding in Delray Beach, Florida. "Instead of being arrested on the outstanding warrant (supposedly still not entered in the computer system more than a month later), Atta was simply given a warning."

As with Oswald, Atta had a relationship with certain members of the CIA, for example, a person named Luai Sakra, who was supposed to have met with Atta sometime before 9-11.

Luai Sakra had a checkered past to say the least. He was an al Qaeda operative who began working as an informant for the CIA, Syrian intelligence, and Turkish intelligence. Sakra was a Syrian who attended the Khaldan training camp in Afghanistan in 1997, and became acquainted with bin Laden's comrade-in-arms, Abu Zubaida. It seems that Abu Zubaida liked Sakra so much that he gave him the job of building an al Qaeda network in Turkey in 1999. The Syrian government began hunting for him for his role in a revolt in a Lebanese refugee camp.

Sakra was captured in 2005, and a Turkish newspaper said of him, "Sakra has been sought by the secret services since 2000." Sakra was interrogated twice by the CIA in the year 2000. Following the interrogations, the CIA offered him employment. He also received a large sum of money from the CIA, but the agency lost track of him. He was briefly arrested by the Turks but was let go for some unknown reason. He then moved to Germany where he was in attendance with some of the 9-11 hijackers. He also claimed that he trained some of the 9-11 hijackers in Turkey starting in late 1999. According to his lawyer, the following hijackers took training with him in Turkey: Majed Moqed and Satam Al Suqami.

Sakra was supposed to have told Syrian intelligence on September 10, 2001, the day before the attacks, about what was to take place the next day. George Tenet, the CIA Director at the time of 9-11, wrote in his book called *At the Center of the Storm,* "that a source we were jointly running with a Middle Eastern country went to see his foreign handler and basically to told him something big was about to go down." This was most likely a reference to Laui Sakra. "Tenet's revelation strongly supports the notion that Sakra in fact accepted the CIA's offers in 2000 and had been working with the CIA and other intelligence agencies at least through 9-11."

In September 1963, two months before the Kennedy assassination, Oswald made a brief trip to Mexico City. While in Mexico City, Oswald visited with both the Cuban and Soviet embassies and met with a high-ranking Soviet intelligence officer named Valarie Kostikov, who was also a member of a Russian assassination squad. Ostensibly, Oswald was in Mexico City to get a visa to travel back to Russia via Cuba. There is also evidence that Oswald was impersonated by someone who was using his name while he was in Mexico City (called the "Unidentified Man" by Kennedy assassination researchers).

The fact that Oswald came back to the United States without any punishment by the U.S. government made some people suspect he was a member of the U.S. intelligence community. While living in Dallas, Texas, Oswald was befriended by a wealthy man of Russian heritage named George De Mohrenschildt, who was investigated by the FBI as possibly being a foreign spy for the Germans in the late 1930s into the 40s. George De Mohrenschildt and his wife took Lee and Marina Oswald under their wings and tried to set them up within the expat Russian community there. It is not known if De Mohrenschildt had any connection with the U.S. intelligence community.

When George first met with Oswald, he didn't quite know what to make of him. He found him most intriguing, yet didn't want to get involved with him right away. He didn't want to get involved with him until he had the chance to have him checked out. Interesting enough, the man George turned to in order to find out who Oswald was, was his friend J. Walton Moore, a CIA agent in the Domestic Contact Division who was stationed in Dallas. Moore reassured him that he was not under any FBI surveillance because of his association with Oswald. De Mohrenschildt asked Moore if Oswald was dangerous in any way. Moore replied that Oswald "was a harmless lunatic," and was of no concern to the CIA, despite the fact that he lived in the Soviet Union for over two years and no one really knew what he was doing there. Thus, with Moore's assurance, De Mohrenschildt began to cultivate Lee Harvey Oswald.

The parallels between Mohamed Atta and Lee Harvey Oswald are intriguing at best, and the question to be answered is were they both part of some covert program of the government who that was using them for some purpose of their own?

While America has been terror free since 9-11, this cannot be said for the rest of the world. In the ensuing twenty years, major terrorist attacks have taken place in Bali, Indonesia, Saudi Arabia, Madrid, Spain, Paris, France, Morocco, Turkey, and London. Will America be next? Surely the remnants of al Qaeda had not forgotten their prime target. The offshoot of al Qaeda is the terrorist group ISIS which raised its ugly head in Syria and other parts of the Middle East. While the leader of ISIS has been killed, that organization learned its lessons from bin Laden's al Qaeda and will do all in its power to continue its war on America and its allies.

The FBI, in order to counter this on-going threat, has made major changes in its ranks. A new intelligence bureau was put into effect to focus directly on foreign intelligence matters. They are now sharing much more information with the CIA and other intelligence components of the government than ever before. But how long will that last if there is another major terrorist attack on U.S. soil? What will the ramifications be for the FBI and CIA if that reality is put to the test? Will we see the same backbiting and name calling that happened after 9-11?

The old adage that if one doesn't learn from history, the same patterns will eventually happen again, is most appropriate to the rivalry between the CIA and the FBI. In this case however, failure is not an option. The stakes are just too high for a breakdown in communication that was the hallmark of the FBI-CIA relationship for fifty years. Who will watch the watchers will determine how successful we are in insuring that another 9-11, or worse, doesn't happen.

After all we have seen in this narrative, as well as the documentary record of the events of 9-11, the following quote is hard to swallow. According to ex-CIA agent Robert Baer, a high-ranking CIA official told him before mid-January 2002, in an off-the-record comment, "When the dust finally clears, Americans will see that September 11 was a triumph for the intelligence community, not a failure." Commenting on what he was told by this unnamed person, Baer said, "I'm scared to death of what lies ahead." Maybe we all should be.

Lee Harvey Oswald in custody moments before his assassination by Jack Ruby—a model for Mohamed Atta?

Appendix 1: The Day of 9-11

There were many different events that were going on the day that 19 hijackers crashed their jets into the twin towers and the Pentagon. Some of these events are still being debated among the 9-11 investigative community for their discrepancies with the facts that became the official story. This chapter will reveal a number of these incidents that took place in order to give a wider context to what we witnessed that day.

As the 19 hijackers were boarding their planes in Boston and other locations around the east coast, there was a scheduled military exercise going on inside the United States. This involved an exercise being conducted by NORAD's Northeast Air Defense Sector (NEADS) in Rome, New York, which was a weeklong event given the code name Vigilant Guardian. The man responsible for this exercise was Lt. Colonel Dwane Deskins who was the regional mission crew chief. Vigilant Guardian was described as "an exercise that would pose an imaginary crisis to North American Air Defense outposts nationwide, as a simulated air war, as well as an air defense exercise simulating an attack on the United States." According to the 9-11 Commission, it "postulated a bomber attack from the former Soviet Union." On 9-11, the program was still in operation and it couldn't have come at a worse time for its participants to work in. NORAD's war room was located deep within Cheyenne Mountain in Colorado which was one of the most heavily fortified command posts in the United States and was built to withstand a nuclear explosion.

Press reports later gave a fuller accounting to the public of what Vigilant Guardian was all about. *Vanity Fair* magazine said it "is designed to run a range of scenarios, including a traditional simulated hijack in which politically motivated perpetrators commandeer an aircraft, land on a Cuba-like island, and seek asylum."

This operation had all facets of NORAD on alert throughout the nation and its members were ready for any scenario that might come up. They had no idea that while their game scenario was going on, a real-world crisis of the same making was taking place right under their noses. Lt. Colonel Dwane Deskins said that NORAD officials were not informed in real time if the actual hijacking then taking place was part of the exercise or not. Colonel Robert Marr, in charge of NEADS, said, "We had the fighters with a little more gas on board. A few more weapons on board."

Under normal conditions, NORAD had fifteen minutes to scramble its jet fighters in case of an emergency. While Vigilant Guardian was underway, the jets were on a 6 to 8 minute readiness warning, and one has to wonder why they were not able to intercept at least one of the hijacked planes in that time frame. In 2000, U.S. jet fighters were scrambled a total of 129 times for various reasons, including pilots who had mistakenly ventured into restricted air space, pilots who did not file proper flight plans, or used the wrong radio frequencies.

On the night before 9-11, President Bush spent the night at the Colony Beach and Tennis Resort in Longboat Key, Florida. He was scheduled to sit in with a group of children at a school the next day, and it would be there that he first heard of the attacks. It was reported that surface to air missiles were placed on the roof of the resort, which is not done under normal circumstances. Early that day, a van, occupied by men of Middle Eastern origin, arrived at the resort and told the secret service that they had a "poolside" interview with the president. Since no such meeting was scheduled, they were turned away.

At 8:21 a.m. on 9-11, Boston flight controllers lost contact with American Airlines Flight 11 and controllers reported that the plane was off course and had turned off its transponder and radio. This should have been a signal that something seriously wrong was going on in the plane.

On that day, many of the top leadership of the country were scattered around the world. President Bush was in Florida; Secretary of State Colin Powell was in Lima, Peru; General Henry Shelton, the Chairman of the Joint Chiefs of Staff was in the air en-route to Europe; Attorney General Ashcroft was flying to Milwaukee, Wisconsin; Vice President Dick Cheney and National Security Advisor Rice were at their offices in Washington; Defense Secretary Donald Rumsfeld was in his Pentagon office; terrorism "czar" Richard Clarke was at a meeting in the Ronald Reagan Building three blocks from the White

House.

In the Atlantic City, New Jersey area, two F-16 fighters were conducting practice-bombing runs in the Pine Barrens. The jets were only 8 minutes from New York but were not alerted of the emergency. Shortly after the second WTC crash at 9:03 a.m., these planes were ordered to land and were refitted with air-to-air missiles, and then sent airborne. They were sent to Washington but did not arrive until 11 a.m.

Around 8:37 a.m., Boston control notified NORAD about the hijackings. The officers who were conducting Vigilant Guardian were unsure if the warnings were part of the exercise or not, but by the time it was all sorted out, it was too late to have taken any concrete actions against the hijacked planes.

At 8:46 a.m., Flight 11 hits the North Tower of the WTC, supposedly carrying 10,000 gallons of fuel, and flying at a speed of 470 mph. The plane hits the 93rd through 98th floors of the 110-story building. At the time of the attacks, there were between 5,000 and 7,000 people at the twin towers, not the total number normally there.

At 8:46 a.m., three F-16s based out of Andrews Air Force Base are flying a practice run off North Carolina and are recalled back to base, but do not start patrolling over D.C. until 10:45.

CIA Director George Tenet is having breakfast with former Senator David Boren when he is first notified of the attack. Boren later said, "I was struck by the fact the messenger used the word 'attacked.'" Tenet then told Boren that it had bin Laden's "fingerprints all over it." Tenet then was supposed to have said, "I wonder if this has something to do with the guy Zacharias Moussaoui who trained for a pilot's license."

8:55 a.m. President Bush arrives at the Booker Elementary School for his photo- p with the teacher and the students. Bush is informed of the event, but there are conflicting accounts as to whether it was an accident or not. Around 9 a.m., the president is informed of the actual events in New York and leaves the school about fifteen minutes later. The president would later say of this hectic time, "I am very aware of the cameras. I'm trying to absorb the knowledge. I have nobody to talk to. I'm sitting in the middle of a classroom with little kids, listening to a children's story and I realize I'm the commander in chief and the country has just come under attack." The president stayed for another ten minutes so as not to upset the children. (The book the president was reading to the children was called *The Pet Goat*.)

At 9 a.m., Operation Northern Vigilance is abruptly canceled due to the real-life hijackings. The *Toronto Star* would later write, "Any simulated information, what's known as an inject, is purged from the radar screens." Therefore, many minutes into the real 9-11 attack, there may have been false radar blimps causing confusion.

9:03 a.m. Flight 175 crashes into the South Tower of the WTC, live on television. The plane hit the 78th to 84th floors. One hundred people are initially killed at that time. A total of 2,810 people were killed when both towers collapsed.

At 9:03 a.m., fighter jets still did not have permission to shoot down any of the hijacked planes. Only the president can give that order, but President Bush did not do so at that time.

9:27 a.m. Vice President Dick Cheney and National Security Advisor Rice are located in the bunker of the White House and are notified that a hijacked plane (Flight 77) is headed for Washington at a range of 50 miles out. They find out that the plane's transponder has been turned off and it disappears from the radar screens.

9:29 a.m. President Bush makes his first statement on the events of the day, "Today we've had a national tragedy. Two airplanes have crashed into the World Trade Center in an apparent terrorist attack on our country."

9:30-9:37 a.m. In an apparent misunderstanding, three jets from Langley Air Force base are scrambled but controllers do not give them destination orders. Accounts have said that the planes were ordered to either Washington, New York, or Baltimore. The planes did not travel at their normal rate of speed, following peacetime regulations as they took off. The *Wall Street Journal* wrote of this incident, "Once they got into the air, the Langley fighters observed peacetime noise restrictions requiring that they fly more slowly than supersonic speed on takeoff over water, pointed away from Washington, according to testimony from the 9-11 Commission."

9:34 a.m. President Bush leaves the Booker Elementary School and heads for the Sarasota airport. A few days later, the local Sarasota paper wrote the following story, "Sarasota barely skirted its own disaster. As it turns out, terrorists targeted the president and Air Force One on Tuesday, maybe while they were even on the ground in Sarasota and certainly not long after. The Secret Service learned of the threat just minutes after Bush left Booker Elementary. Kevin Down, a Sarasota police officer at the scene recalls, "I thought they were actually anticipating a terrorist attack on the President while we were en-route."

Before 9:37 a.m. Defense Secretary Donald Rumsfeld is meeting in the Pentagon with Congressman Christopher Cox and is unaware that Flight 77 is approaching. The topic of conversation is missile defense. As they are watching news from New York City, Rumsfeld told Cox, "Believe me, this isn't over yet. There's going to be another attack, and it could be us." In another version of the conversation, Cox said that Rumsfeld remarked, "If we remain vulnerable to missile attack, a terrorist group or rogue state that demonstrates the capacity to strike the U.S. or its allies from long range could have the power to hold our entire country hostage to nuclear or other blackmail. And let me tell you, I've been around the block a few times. There will be another event."

9:37 a.m. Flight 77 crashes into the Pentagon, killing about 125 people who are on the ground. Flight 77 hits the side of the Pentagon that was recently renovated, and was the only part of the building that had a sprinkler system. Many conspiracy theorists believe that Flight 77 did not hit the Pentagon, that it was a bomb or something else. One person who believed a bomb hit the building was April Gallop who worked in the west side of the building and was taking her son to the day care center before going to work. After she was cared for by rescue workers, she said that she was approached by certain people who told her that a plane hit the building. "But I was there," she said, "and I never saw a plane or even debris from a plane. I figured the plane story is there to brainwash people." [1]

After 9:37 a.m. The FBI confiscates film taken from a nearby gas station located near the Pentagon at the time of the crash. The footage of this film was never made public.

Between 9:45 and 9:55 a.m. Richard Clarke, the terrorism "czar" institutes the Continuity of Government plans. All the important government officials who are in the line of succession were taken to undisclosed locations across the nation. At this time, the order to shoot down any hostile planes is finally given.

9:48 a.m. The United States Capitol is evacuated.

1 Farrell, Joseph, *Hidden Finances,* Page 55-56.

9:56 a.m. Air Force One leaves Sarasota airport without a jet fighter escort. That will not happen until one hour later.

9:59 a.m. The South Tower of the WTC collapses. It was hit by Flight 175 at 9:03, fifty seven minutes earlier.

At the same time, Richard Clarke is told by Dale Watson of the FBI that some of the hijackers have been identified per the plane's manifest to be members of al Qaeda. Clarke replied, "How the (blank) did they get on board then?" He is told, "Hey, don't shoot the messenger, friend. CIA forgot to tell us about them." One of the names on the manifest is Mohamed Atta.

10:03 to 10:10. Flight 93 crashes near Shanksville, Pennsylvania, but there are major discrepancies as to the exact time it went down. Some of the passengers on Flight 93 engaged the hijackers and the plane subsequently crashed. The plane broke up in different pieces before it crashed and parts were found up to 8 miles away. Witnesses reported seeing another, smaller plane circling the area where Flight 93 went down, flying at tree-top level. One eyewitness said the plane was white with no markings on it, but the person said she believed it was from the military. The witness said she was contacted by the FBI and was told that there was no plane around. "They did not want my story—nobody here did," she said.

10:10 a.m. It is at this time that all branches of the U.S. military are put on high alert. They go to DEFCON Three (or DEFCON Delta), which is the highest alert for the U.S. nuclear weapons arsenal in 30 years. There is a difference in opinion as to who made this decision. Defense Secretary Rumsfeld said that he made the recommendation after talking with Joint Chiefs of Staff Chairman Richard Meyers. At 10:15 a.m. the huge, bomb-proof doors at Cheyenne Mountain in Colorado were closed for the first time in response to the day's events.

10:24 a.m. All international flights coming into the United States from overseas are diverted to other destinations by the Federal Aviation Administration, most going to Canada where the thousands of passengers are well taken care of.

10:32 a.m. There is reportedly a threat made to Air Force One that Vice President Dick Cheney conveyed to President Bush. In the call, the president is told that it would take from 40 to 90 minutes for a fighter escort to arrive and guard AF One. There were reportedly many people in government who were skeptical that this threat was real. For example, Congressman Martin Meehan (D) said, "I don't buy the notion that Air Force One was a target. That's just PR, that's just spin." A person who had information regarding this incident said, "It did two things for Cheney. It reinforced his argument that the President should stay out of town, and it gave George W. Bush an excellent reason for doing so."

10:35 a.m. President Bush and Air Force One head to Barksdale AFB in Louisiana instead of heading back to Washington. There is fear among those in the president's party that the threat to Washington is not over and that the White House might have been a target.

11:00 a.m. U.S. Customs says that after reading the hijacked planes manifest, they were able to identify all 19 hijackers, including Khalid al-Midhar and Nawaf al-Hazmi. Two of the hijacker's names were listed on the watchlist of August 2001. A report on this matter would later say, "And by looking at the Arab names and their seat locations, ticket purchases and other passenger information, it didn't take a lot to do a rudimentary link analysis. Customs officers were able to ID 19 probable hijackers within 45 minutes. I saw the sheet by 11a.m. And that analysis did indeed correctly identify the terrorists."

12 Noon. Senator Orin Hatch (R), who is a member of both the Senate Intelligence Committee and the Judiciary Committee, said he was "briefed by the highest levels of the FBI and the intelligence community. He said, they've come to the conclusion that this looks like the signature of Osama bin Laden, and that he may be the one behind this." This statement should not have come as a surprise to anyone in the intelligence community of the United States on September 11, 2001. As noted in this narrative, there were innumerable warnings from both foreign and domestic sources, that bin Laden was a growing threat to the United States and that his al Qaeda was planning something spectacular against the U.S. in the near future. "The system was blinking red," said one report, but the warnings weren't heeded in time.

12:16 p.m. All U.S. airspace has been cleared of all remaining planes in the air, except for military aircraft.

1:30 p.m. President Bush's party leaves Louisiana and now goes to Offutt Air Force Base in Nebraska.

2:40 p.m. Defense Secretary Rumsfeld is given a report from the CIA that three of the hijackers were members of al Qaeda. Notes of the people who were in the room when this took place were released one year later. The notes said, "One guy is an associate of USS *Cole* bombing." (This is reference to al-Midhar and al-Hazmi). Rumsfeld was also given information "an al Qaeda operative had advanced details of the 9-11 attack." According to the aide's notes, "Rumsfeld wants the best info fast. Judge whether good enough to hit S.H. [Saddam Hussein] at same time. Not only UBL [bin Laden]. Go massive. Sweep it all up. Things related or not."

4:33 p.m. Air Force One leaves Nebraska for Washington, despite conflicting reports of still more possible planes unaccounted for.

5:20 p.m. Building 7 of the WTC complex collapses. The building is 47 stories tall and was not hit by any planes. No one is sure as to why the building fell, and there are many scenarios as to why it collapsed. The building contained a 6,000 gallon diesel tank between its first and second floors, as well as another four tanks which held as much as 36,000 gallons, below street level. A 2002 government report on the collapse of building 7 said, "The specifics of the fires in WTC 7 and how they caused the building to collapse remain unknown at this time. Although the total diesel fuel on the premises contained massive potential energy, the best hypothesis has only a low probability of occurrence." CBS News reporter Dan Rather said that the collapse of building 7 is "reminiscent of when a building was deliberately destroyed by well-placed dynamite to knock it down."

6:54 p.m. President Bush arrives back at the White House and sees the destruction at the Pentagon from his helicopter.

8:30 p.m. President Bush addresses the nation on the day's events.

9: p.m. The president meets with his senior national security officials at the White House where the news of the day is discussed. It is decided that al Qaeda and Osama bin Laden are responsible, as well as the Taliban who are harboring bin Laden in Afghanistan. The discussions that were held that night mark the beginning of President Bush's war on terrorism, as well as the justification for going to war with Saddam Hussein in 2003,with all the human suffering and global consequences that arose from it. (Note: The information in this Appendix came from Paul Thompson's book, *The Terror Time Line.*

Appendix 2
The Escape

Shortly after the hijacked planes hit the WTC and the Pentagon, the Federal Aviation Administration (FAA), grounded all commercial flights in the airspace of the United States. The only planes that were allowed to fly were military jets circling over the major cities of the United States, looking for any further threats from the sky. With the collapse of the twin towers, the powers that be could not know if there were any more threats out there that had to be addressed. For a few days, the United States looked like it did at the dawn of the age of flight, with only the birds flying lazily over the farms and cities of the nation. If one closed one's eyes, they might have seen Orville and Wilbur Wright flying their makeshift plane over the dunes of Kitty Hawk, North Carolina, opening the dawn of what would become the conquering of the skies. But what most Americans, who were still reeling from the events of the day, did not know was that there was a secret exodus of certain Arab people, all of them living in the United States, connected to the Saudi royal family, as well as certain relatives of the mastermind of the attacks, Osama bin Laden. All were planning to secretly leave the country, with the aid and assistance of the American government.

The prime movers in this secret drama were President George W. Bush and Prince Bandar bin Sultan bin Abdul Aziz, the Saudi Arabian ambassador to the United States. From his perch in Washington, Prince bin Sultan was making plans to secretly take 140 Saudi nationals who were living and working in the United States back home. Besides the members of the royal family, called the House of Saud, were members of the bin Laden family who were also legally in the country. All this secret maneuvering was done with the approval of President Bush, whose family had a longstanding, and sometimes secret relationship with the Kingdom of Saudi Arabia, going back decades.

Prince Bandar bin Sultan was a prominent figure in the diplomatic world in Washington, being the longtime ambassador to the United States as well as being a close friend of the Bush family, including the current president, George W. Bush. Prince Bandar was reportedly an investor in the Carlyle Group with President Bush senior. He gave $1 million to the George H. W. Bush Presidential Library and a $1 million painting to President George W. Bush.

At age 52, Prince Bandar was a notable figure among the Washington chic set, going to football games, hosting lavish parties where alcohol was poured with gusto (despite the Muslim ban on drinking), and doing America's bidding in the Middle East. He knew all the right members of Congress, Democrats as well as Republicans, and wined and dined them all.

His father was the Defense Minister of Saudi Arabia, Prince Sultan who was second in the line of succession in the Kingdom. He was also the nephew of King Fahd, the old Saudi ruler, and the grandson of the late King Abdul Aziz, the founder of modern Saudi Arabia.

The United States and Saudi Arabia had ties that began in the World War II era when the two nations cemented relationships, with the Saudis providing the United States with much needed oil in return for a pledge to help the Saudis in the future. Through much of the 1970s and 80s, the United States armed Saudi Arabia, supplying them arms and ammunition to fight off any potential enemies. (Note: Israel was not one of these countries, and the nations had a clandestine diplomatic relationship that was hidden from the world.)

Later in the century, Saudi Arabia would become the home of a leading citizen, and later a major embarrassment, Osama bin Laden.

However, on 9-11, that did not matter to most Americans who just saw their nation attacked. It was soon announced that a majority of the hijackers were from Saudi Arabia and that was all that mattered. The Saudis were responsible for 9-11, and there could be no denying that fact.

There were Saudis living in various sections of the United States and it would take all of Prince Bandar's logistical skills to get them out safely. On the night of 9-11, the Prince got a call from CIA Director George Tenet, as per reports of the time, that 15 of the 19 hijackers were from the kingdom. The prince reportedly said upon hearing the news, "I felt as if the Twin Towers had just fallen on my head."

At the time of 9-11, there were a number of the bin Laden family living in the United States, residing in New York, Florida, Boston, and Kentucky, among other places. They were mostly wealthy people, whose spending habits would rival any Hollywood actor or actress. Some were successful lawyers. There were also racehorse owners, one of whom was Saudi Prince Ahmed bin Salman who bought two horses in Lexington, Kentucky for $1.2 million on September 12, one day after the attacks. Ahmed bin Salman went to college at the University of California Irvine and later became chairman of Saudi Arabia's Research and Marketing Group, a publishing company based in Saudi Arabia and England. He was a horse-raising aficionado, and in 1994, he and a college friend began a business called the Thoroughbred Corporation which bought and trained some of the best racehorses in the country. Among the horses they trained were Sharp Cat, Lear Fan, Royal Anthem, and their most prized possession, the 2001 Horse of the Year, Point Given, which won two legs of racing's Triple Crown.

After the attacks, Ahmed bin Salman tried to separate himself from bin Laden and his henchmen. He said, "America is home to me. I am a businessman. I have nothing to do with the other stuff. I feel as badly as any American and I am extremely astonished by the terrorism. We have had terrorism in Saudi Arabia and we know how painful it is."

A brother of Osama (whose name was not mentioned) was so afraid of his personal safety that he called the Saudi embassy in D.C., asking for help. He was put up in the Watergate Hotel in Washington and told not to let anyone in.

In a brazen move, a Saudi prince sent a message to the Tampa, Florida police chief telling him that a number of Saudis who were connected to the royal family were living in the area, and might become potential targets of attack.

Prince Bandar was in constant touch with certain members of the Bush administration, including Secretary of State Colin Powell and National Security Advisor Condoleezza Rice. In order to get his fellow countrymen out of the United States, he needed their help, as well as that of his friend in the Oval Office, George W. Bush.

Prince Bandar opened up a channel from their Washington Embassy to all Saudis who were living in the country to call for further information. The phone lines were busy that day, as frantic

Saudis tried to make plans to leave the country.

Prior to 9-11, a meeting was scheduled in the White House between Prince Bandar and the president, and despite the attacks, the meeting took place on September 13, 2001. But the political landscape had drastically changed in just two days, and the meeting took on a whole new meaning. It is not known if the plans for getting the Saudis out of the country was mentioned, but events that followed made it clear that Washington had the Prince's back.

The story of the escape from the United States by the 140 Saudi nationals living in the U.S. was told by three reporters who worked for the *Tampa Tribune* in October 2001. It was a story that no other paper in the country wanted to write about, and it took a lot of digging by the reporters (Kathy Steele, Brenna Kelly, and Elizabeth Lee Brown) to piece it together.

The man at the center of the story was a forty-nine year old former policeman, now a private investigator, named Dan Grossi who got a call from a person at the Tampa police department who asked him if he was interested in a new job. Grossi had worked for the Tampa PD for over twenty years and he was well known in the department as someone who could be trusted with sensitive matters. Since the attacks, the Tampa police were giving extra security to the many Saudi students and others who lived in the area. Mr. Grossi was asked if he would take on the job of escorting these students from Tampa to Lexington, Kentucky because the police were unable to do the job. He was asked to go to the local airport where a plane would be made available to take these people out of Tampa. Grossi was skeptical, as he knew that all commercial aviation was grounded, but he decided to take on the job anyway. He then asked his friend and former FBI agent named Manuel Perez if he would be interested in helping him. Perez said yes and they began their unexpected journey.

On September 13, two days after 9-11, Dan Grossi got a call and was told that the Saudis in question were to be sent to the Raytheon Airport Services, a private hangar at Tampa International Airport. At this point, private airlines were still not cleared to fly but he was assured that the plane he was going on would take off, nonetheless.

It was at this point that three young Saudis arrived at the airport and were taken aboard the ten-passenger Learjet, their destination Lexington, Kentucky. As Grossi later said, "Flight restrictions had not been lifted yet. I was told it would take White House approval. I thought the flight was not going to happen." Speaking of the passengers, Grossi said, "It happened so fast. I just knew they were Saudis. They were well connected. One of them told me his father or his uncle was good friends with George Bush senior."

But now a curious thing happened. The FAA later said that no approval for the flight was given and the flight "never took place." The White House later said they had no knowledge of the flight.

Nevertheless, the flight took almost two hours and they landed at the Blue Grass Airport in Lexington, where the students deplaned and were taken away by an unnamed American who then facilitated their departure from the U.S. to Saudi Arabia. Grossi said of this incident, "My understanding is that there were other Saudis in Kentucky buying racehorses at that time, and they were going to fly back together."

In other parts of the country, seven planes were made available by the Saudi government to get their countrymen out of the U.S. There were now conflicting statements from the FBI and Prince Bandar as to what role the FBI played in this development. The bureau said they had nothing to do with the departures, while Prince Bandar said the opposite. "I can say unequivocally that the FBI had no role in facilitating these flights one way or another," said Special Agent John Iannarelli." Prince Bandar said, "With coordination with the FBI, we got them all out."

Now, it was time for the members of the bin Laden family to make their escape. Two planes were made available to ferry the bin Ladens away, and they picked up people across the country. In Orlando, Florida, Khalil Bin Laden, a sibling of Osama, was taken aboard. From Orlando, the plane headed for Dulles Airport outside of D.C., and then to Boston's Logan Airport on September 19, where other members of the bin Laden clan were located.

After a long hassle between the FBI and the Saudi embassy in Washington, the bureau was able to check the papers of the people already on the planes and did not take any further investigative actions.

On September 18, at Logan Airport, a Boeing 747 that had about thirty first-class seats had been chartered by the bin Laden family and it took off with only five passengers on the night of September 19. It is interesting to note that two of the planes that hit the twin towers originated at Logan on 9-11, so the allowance of this bin

Laden chartered plane raised a number of eyebrows. (Logan Airport officially opened for business on September 15, three days before the bin Laden flight departed.)

In the days after 9-11, life for Muslim Americans changed completely. Attorney General John Ashcroft had said that the government, "'had a responsibility to use every legal means at our disposal to prevent further terrorist activity by taking people into custody who have violated the law and who may pose a threat to America.' By the weekend after the attacks, Ashcroft, to the dismay of civil libertarians, had already put together a package of proposals broadening the FBI's power to detain foreigners, wiretap them, and trace money laundering to terrorists. Some suspects would be held for as long as ten months at the American naval base in Guantanamo, Cuba."[2]

The story now concerns just what role the American government played in the great escape of the 140 Saudi nationals from the United States. Who was responsible, and what did they do?

One of the participants in the plan to send the Saudis back home is a familiar name in this narrative, that of terrorism czar, Richard Clarke. Clark and other members of the Bush administration were located in the basement of the White House, making instant decisions as the crisis unfolded. Clarke, who had a front row seat in the fight against bin Laden since the Clinton administration, had this to say regarding the Saudis, "Somebody brought to us for the approval of the decision to let an airplane filled with Saudis, including members of the bin Laden family, leave the country. My role was to say that it can't happen until the FBI approves it. And so, the FBI asked us—we had a live connection to the FBI—and we asked the FBI to make sure that they were satisfied that everybody getting on that plane was someone that was O.K. to leave. And they came back and said yes, it was fine with them. So we said, fine, let it happen."

Later on, Clarke said he did not know exactly who requested the Saudis to leave, but it was either the FBI or the State Department. Both the State Department and the FBI said that the request did not come from them.

Clarke said that he assumed that the FBI had vetted those leaving the country and said in this regard, "I have no idea if they did a good

2 Unger, Craig, *House of Bush, House of Saud: The Secret Relationship Between the World's Two Most Powerful Dynasties,* Scribner, New York, 2004. Page 13.

job. I'm not in any position to second-guess the FBI." In a statement, Prince Bandar replied that the FBI played a role in the evacuation.

From the Saudi side, Nail al-Jubeir, who was a spokesman for the Saudi embassy in Washington, said the flights received approval from "the highest level of the U.S. government" (meaning the president).

Author Craig Unger writes in *House of Bush, House of Saud,* that Prince Bandar might have contacted George H.W. Bush or James Baker, both of whom had longstanding ties with the various Saudi rulers, as well as commercial ties.

Over the next several days, as regular commercial planes were given permission to return to the air, all the Saudis had left the United States, many going to Europe, as well as other places around the world, before heading to Saudi Arabia. The great escape had been completed.

However, Saudi cooperation did not last long. When U.S. troops attacked the Taliban in Afghanistan (the Taliban had been hiding bin Laden after 9-11 and refused to give him up), the Saudis refused to allow the U.S. to use Saudi bases to mount military operations (so much for our loyalty in sending their people home).

It seems that money was still more important than the horror that had taken place on 9-11. It seems that the Saudis were in the process of signing a $25 billion gas exploration project in Saudi Arabia which involved eight large oil companies, which were run by Crown Prince Abdullah and the minister for foreign affairs, Prince Saud al-Faisal, James Baker's firm, Baker Botts, was playing a large advisory role."

The Saudis never took public responsibility for the attacks, despite the fact that a majority of the hijackers were of Saudi origin. For example, Prince Nayef Ibn Abd-Al Aziz, the minister of the Interior said that the Zionists were responsible for the attacks and would stand to benefit the most. "It is impossible," he said, "that nineteen youths, including fifteen Saudis, carried out the operation of September 11."

Soon, though, an event took place in faraway Pakistan that would add a new measure of controversy to this highly charged story.

On March 28, 2002, a joint American-Pakistani military raid resulted in the arrest of Abu Zubaydah, the thirty-year old chief of operations for al Qaeda, and a compatriot of bin Laden. He was also the man responsible for the attack on the USS *Cole* in Yemen, and one of the most wanted men in the world at that time.

Abu Zubaydah's interrogation by his American captors was harsh, to say the least, and he was given such drugs as Sodium Pentothal (truth serum). He had two sets of interrogators, one American, the other being Arab Americans who posed as Saudi agents. Once the sessions got under way, Abu Zubaydah dropped a bombshell right into the Americans' laps. He asked his interrogators to call a certain member of the Saudi royal family and gave them the phone number. "He will tell you what to do," he said.

The phone number of the high Saudi he told the Americans about was none other than Prince Ahmed bin Sultan bin Abdul Aziz, the racehorse owner who had been taken out of the United States after 9-11.

The story of Abu Zubaydah was told by author Gerald Posner in his book *Why America Slept,* and it caused quite a stir when it came out. According to Posner's account, the Saudi royal family had made a deal with al Qaeda by which the kingdom would help the Taliban as long as al Qaeda kept its terrorist tactics out of Saudi Arabia. Abu Zubaydah also said that he worked with Prince Ahmed and two other members of the royal family, Prince Sultan bin Faisal bin Turki al-Saud, a nephew of King Fahd, and Prince Fahd bin Turki bin Saud al-Kabir, a twenty-five year old distant relative of the king.

If the naming of these high Saudi leaders was not enough, he dropped another missile right in their collective laps. He said, "Ahmed knew beforehand that an attack was scheduled for American soil that day [9-11]." Posner writes, "They just didn't know what it would be, nor did they want to know more than that. The information was passed to them, said Zubaydah, because bin Laden knew they could not stop it without knowing the specifics, but later they would be hard-pressed to turn on him if he could disclose their foreknowledge."[3]

Abu Zubaydah's allegation posed a huge problem for the Bush administration. Not only had fifteen Saudi men been part of the hijacked planes operation, but now it was alleged that the Saudis knew in advance of the attack itself. Posner writes in his book that the CIA conducted an investigation to see if anything Abu Zubaydah said was true, and the report came back on an inconclusive basis. The agency then contacted Saudi intelligence to ask if they had any information that Prince Ahmed might have been a secret al Qaeda operative. The Saudis said no.

3 Ibid. Page 266.

On May 7, 2002, the horse owned by Prince Ahmed, War Emblem, ridden by jockey Victor Espinoza, won the Kentucky Derby at Churchill Downs. War Emblem started the race as a 20-1 shot.

Two weeks later, War Emblem also won the Preakness Stakes in Baltimore, Maryland, but failed to win the Triple Crown, the highest honor in horse racing.

A series of events would now take place that would spark the interest of any would-be conspiracy theorist. On July 23, 2002, Ahmed's cousin, Prince Sultan bin Faisal was killed in a one-car crash while en route to a funeral. On July 30, 2002 Prince Fahd bin Turki, the other man who was mentioned by Abu Zabaydah, was found in the middle of the desert, apparently dead of thirst.

On September 4, 2003, a spokesman for the Saudi government, Nail al-Jubeir, gave an interview to CNN. He was questioned by CNN newscaster Paula Zahn who asked him the following question: "Could you tell us unequivocally tonight that no one on board [these planes] had anything to do with either the planning or the execution of the September 11 plot?"

His answer was: "There are only two things that I'm aware about. That there is the existence of God and that we will die at the end of the world. Everything else, we don't know."

Bibliography: Books

Bergen, Peter, *Holy War: Inside the Secret World of Osama bin Laden,* The Free Press, New York, 2001.

Coll, Steve, *Ghost Wars: The Secret History of the CIA, Afghanistan, and bin Laden from the Soviet Invasion to 9-11-2001,* Penguin Books, New York, 20004.

Davis, Jana, *The Third Terrorist: The Middle East Connection to the Oklahoma City Bombing,* Thomas Nelson Books, New York, 2004.

Farrah, Douglas, and Stephen Braun, *Merchant of Death: Money, Guns, and the Man Who Makes War Possible,* John Wiley and Sons, New York, 2007.

Farrell, Joseph, *Hidden Finance, Rogue Networks, and Secret Sorcery,* Adventures Unlimited Press, Kempton, Ill., 2016.

Fenton, Kevin, *Disconnecting the Dots,* Trine Day Publishers, Walterville, Oregon, 2011.

Gertz, Bill, *Breakdown: How America's Intelligence Failures led to Sept. 11,* Regnery Books, Washington, D.C. 2002.

Hopsicker, Daniel, *Welcome to Terrorland: Mohamed Atta and the 9-11 Cover-up in Florida,* The Mad Cow Press, Eugene, Oregon.

Hoyle, Russ, *Going to War,* Thomas Dunne Books, New York, 2008.

Isikoff, Michael, and David Corn, *Hubris: The Inside Story of Spin, Scandal, and the Selling of the Iraq War,* Crown Publishers, New York, 2006.

Kross, Peter, *The Secret History of the United States,* Adventures Unlimited Press, Kempton, Ill., 2013.

Ibid, *American Conspiracy Files,* Adventures Unlimited Press, Kempton, IL, 2015.

Ibid, *Tales from Langley: The CIA from Truman to Obama,* Adventures Unlimited Press, Kempton, IL., 2014.

Lance, Peter, *Triple Cross,* Regan Books, New York, 2006.

Ibid, *1000 Years For Revenge: International Terrorism and the FBI—The Untold Story,* Regan Books, New York, 2003.

Ibid, *Cover-up: What the Government Is Still Hiding About the War on Terror,* Regan Books, New York, 2004.

Miller, John, Michael Stone and Chris Mitchell, *The Cell: Inside the 9-11 Plot and Why the FBI and CIA Failed to Stop It,* Hyperion Books, New York, 2002.

Minter, Richard, *Losing Bin Laden,* Regnery Books, Washington D.C. 2002.

Mylroie, Laurie, *Study in Revenge,* The AEI Press, Washington, D.C., 2001.
Posner, Gerald, *Why America Slept: The Failure to Prevent 9-11,* Ballantine Books, New York, 2003.
Reeve, Simon, *The New Jackals: Ramzi Yousef, Osama bin Laden and the Future of Terrorism,* Northeastern Press, 1999.
Strasser, Steven, Editor, *The 9-11 Investigations,* Public Affairs, New York, 2004.
Summers, Anthony, *The Eleventh Day: The Full Story of 9-11,* Ballantine Books, New York, 2012.
The Nine-Eleven Commission Final Report of the National Commission on Terrorist Attacks Upon the United States, W.W. Norton, NY, 2003.
Thompson, Paul, *The Terror Time Line,* Regan Books, New York, 2004.
Unger, Craig, *House of Bush, House of Saud,* Charles Scribner, New York, 2004.
Wright, Lawrence, *The Looming Tower: Al Qaeda and the Road to 9-11,* Alfred Knopf, New York, 2006.

Magazines and Other Resources

Browne, Ryan, and Jim Sciutto, *Congress Releases Secret 28 Pages on Alleged Saudi 9-11 Ties,* July 15, 2016.
Drogin, Bob and John Mayer, *Alleged 9-11 Mastermind Linked to Hamburg Cell,* LA Times, June 6, 2002.
Eggen, Don, and Walter Pinkus, *The Book on Richard Clarke,* Washington Post, March 13, 2004.
Epstein, Edward, *Atta in Prague?,* www.wsj.com/articles.
Fitchett, Joseph, *Dubai Clinic Denies Report bin Laden met with CIA,* New York Times, 11-1-2001.
History Commons on the world wide web—The best site for 9-11 research in this author's opinion.
Hopsicker, Daniel, *Mohamed Atta and Rudi Dekkers Seen Together in Venice in Weeks Before Sept. 11 Attacks,* www.FromtheWilderness .com.
Kiely, Eugene, *Saudi Arabia and the 9-11 Terrorist Attacks,* Factcheck Posts.
Mansheurus, Laura, *Witness in Bombing Trial Says He Withheld Names of Friends,* New York Times, July 7, 2001.
Miller, Greg, *Revolving Door from CIA to Blackwater,* www.latimes.com, August 21, 2009.
Morrissey, Edward, *Rethinking Prague,* www.Washingtonexaminer, August 23, 2005.
No author, *Jamal Kashoggi: All You Need to Know about Saudi Journalist's Death,* June 19, 2019.
Read, Russ, *Mueller report: Eric Prince's Secret Meeting with Russia Fell Apart After its Aircraft Carrier Went to Libya.,* www.Washingtonexaminer.com. April 20. 2019.

Risen, James, and Mazzetti, *Blackwater Guards Tied to Secret CIA Raids,* New York Times, December 10, 2009.
Saahill, Jeremy, *Blackwater's CIA Assassins,* www.TheNation. August 20, 2009.
Stempel, Jonathan, *Mafia Soldier's Prison Term Restored Despite Oklahoma City Bombing Tip,* Reuters, June 22, 2017.
Suddah, Claire, *How Not to censor a Book. Pentagon Makes a Best Seller,* Content, Time.com.
Whipple, Chris, *What the CIA Knew before 9-11: New Details,* Politico, 11/13/15.
Within, Dig, *Oswald & Atta, Erratic, Protected and Seeking Attention.*

BIGFOOT NATION
A History of Sasquatch in North America
By David Hatcher Childress

Childress takes a deep look at Bigfoot Nation—the real world of bigfoot around us in the United States and Canada. Whether real or imagined, that bigfoot has made his way into the American psyche cannot be denied. He appears in television commercials, movies, and on roadside billboards. Bigfoot is everywhere, with actors portraying him in variously believable performances and it has become the popular notion that bigfoot is both dangerous and horny. Indeed, bigfoot is out there stalking lovers' lanes and is even more lonely than those frightened teenagers that he sometimes interrupts. Bigfoot, tall and strong as he is, makes a poor leading man in the movies with his awkward personality and typically anti-social behavior. Includes 16-pages of color photos that document Bigfoot Nation!

320 Pages. 6x9 Paperback. Illustrated. $22.00. Code: BGN

PROJECT MK-ULTRA
AND MIND CONTROL TECHNOLOGY
By Axel Balthazar

This book is a compilation of the government's documentation on MK-Ultra, the CIA's mind control experimentation on unwitting human subjects, as well as over 150 patents pertaining to artificial telepathy (voice-to-skull technology), behavior modification through radio frequencies, directed energy weapons, electronic monitoring, implantable nanotechnology, brain wave manipulation, nervous system manipulation, neuroweapons, psychological warfare, satellite terrorism, subliminal messaging, and more. A must-have reference guide for targeted individuals and anyone interested in the subject of mind control technology.

384 pages. 7x10 Paperback. Illustrated. $19.95. Code: PMK

LIQUID CONSPIRACY 2:
The CIA, MI6 & Big Pharma's War on Psychedelics
By Xaviant Haze

Underground author Xaviant Haze looks into the CIA and its use of LSD as a mind control drug; at one point every CIA officer had to take the drug and endure mind control tests and interrogations to see if the drug worked as a "truth serum." Chapters include: The Pioneers of Psychedelia; The United Kingdom Mellows Out: The MI5, MDMA and LSD; Taking it to the Streets: LSD becomes Acid; Great Works of Art Inspired and Influenced by Acid; Scapolamine: The CIA's Ultimate Truth Serum; Mind Control, the Death of Music and the Meltdown of the Masses; Big Pharma's War on Psychedelics; The Healing Powers of Psychedelic Medicine; tons more.

240 pages. 6x9 Paperback. Illustrated. $19.95. Code: LQC2

JFK: THE FRENCH CONNECTION
By Peter Kross

One day after the assassination of President Kennedy, the FBI deported a known French assassin named Jean Souetre—a member of the militant, anti-Charles de Gaulle organization called the OAS. Chapters include: The First Assassin; The Mafia and Uncle Sam; The Heroin Trail; QJ/WIN and Patrice Lumumba; The US Senate Select Committee on Intelligence "Assassination Reports"—The CIA and Lumumba; Who Was Souetre?; Who Was Mertz?; The Steve Rivele Investigation; The Guns of Dallas; more.

384 Pages. 6x9 Paperback. Illustrated. $18.95. Code: JFKF

ANTARCTICA & THE SECRET SPACE PROGRAM
From WWII to the Current Space Race
By David Hatcher Childress

Childress brings us the incredible tale of Nazi submarines and secret weapons in Antarctica and elsewhere. He then examines Operation High-Jump with Admiral Richard Byrd in 1947 and the battle that he apparently had in Antarctica with flying saucers. Through "Operation Paperclip," the Nazis infiltrated aerospace companies, banking, media, and the US government after WWII. Childress discusses the secret technology involved, anti-gravity propulsion technology, electro-gravity and free-energy, and secret bases on the Moon and Mars. Does the US Navy have a secret space program that includes huge ships and hundreds of astronauts? With a 16-page color section.

392 Pages. 6x9 Paperback. Illustrated. $22.00 Code: ASSP

AMERICAN CONSPIRACY FILES
The Stories We Were Never Told
By Peter Kross

Kross reports on conspiracies in the Revolutionary War, including those surrounding Benedict Arnold and Ben Franklin's son, William. He delves into the large conspiracy to kill President Lincoln and moves into our modern day with chapters on the deaths of JFK, RFK and MLK., the reasons behind the Oklahoma City bombing, the sordid plots of President Lyndon Johnson and more. Chapters on Edward Snowden; The Weather Underground; Patty Hearst; The Death of Mary Meyer; Marilyn Monroe; The Zimmerman Telegram; BCCI; Operation Northwinds; The Search for Nazi Gold; The Death of Frank Olsen; tons more. Over 50 chapters in all.

460 Pages. 6x9 Paperback. Illustrated. $19.95 Code: ACF

THE JFK FILES
What the Government Has Kept Secret for Decades
By Peter Kross

In October 2017, 2,800 files about the 1963 murder were made public for the first time, bringing to the fore revelations that the Soviet spy agency KGB believed then-Vice President Lyndon Johnson may have conspired to assassinate Kennedy. More files were released in April 2018, but many original documents remain sealed. Chapters include: Operation Tumbleweed; Oswald in Mexico City; Soviet Reaction to the Kennedy Death; The Secret Soviet Murder Plan; The Hoover-Ruby memo; RFK & Operation Mongoose; "El Mexicano"; The Tale of Frank Sturgis; The Onassis-Mahue Connection; LBJ & Covert Action; Operation TILT; Project JMMOVE; The Somoza Plan; Howard Hunt's Secret JFK Assassination Probe; more.

426 pages. 6x9 Paperback. Illustrated. . $19.95. Code: JFIL

THE SECRET HISTORY OF THE UNITED STATES
Conspiracies, Cobwebs and Lies
By Peter Kross

This book tells the stories of unexplained events in our history, as well as mysteries that have never been solved. The events covered in the book range from the American Revolution, the Civil War, World War II, the Cold War, the assassinations of the 1960s, the Iraq war and the events leading up to 9-11. Among the subjects covered are the following: the plot to oust FDR; Flight 19; Who killed JFK?; Nixon and the mob, Watergate and the CIA, Iran-Contra, and the intelligence failures that led up to 9-11. These stories are fascinating accounts of the underside of our history that will amaze the reader.

438 Pages. 6x9 Paperback. Illustrated. $19.95. Code: SHUS

ORDER FORM

10% Discount When You Order 3 or More Items!

One Adventure Place
P.O. Box 74
Kempton, Illinois 60946
United States of America
Tel.: 815-253-6390 • Fax: 815-253-6300
Email: auphq@frontiernet.net
http://www.adventuresunlimitedpress.com

ORDERING INSTRUCTIONS

- ✓ Remit by USD$ Check, Money Order or Credit Card
- ✓ Visa, Master Card, Discover & AmEx Accepted
- ✓ Paypal Payments Can Be Made To: info@wexclub.com
- ✓ Prices May Change Without Notice
- ✓ 10% Discount for 3 or More Items

SHIPPING CHARGES

United States

- ✓ Postal Book Rate { $4.50 First Item; 50¢ Each Additional Item
- ✓ POSTAL BOOK RATE Cannot Be Tracked! Not responsible for non-delivery.
- ✓ Priority Mail { $7.00 First Item; $2.00 Each Additional Item
- ✓ UPS { $9.00 First Item (Minimum 5 Books); $1.50 Each Additional Item

NOTE: UPS Delivery Available to Mainland USA Only

Canada

- ✓ Postal Air Mail { $19.00 First Item; $3.00 Each Additional Item
- ✓ Personal Checks or Bank Drafts MUST BE US$ and Drawn on a US Bank
- ✓ Canadian Postal Money Orders OK
- ✓ Payment MUST BE US$

All Other Countries

- ✓ Sorry, No Surface Delivery!
- ✓ Postal Air Mail { $19.00 First Item; $7.00 Each Additional Item
- ✓ Checks and Money Orders MUST BE US$ and Drawn on a US Bank or branch.
- ✓ Paypal Payments Can Be Made in US$ To: info@wexclub.com

SPECIAL NOTES

- ✓ RETAILERS: Standard Discounts Available
- ✓ BACKORDERS: We Backorder all Out-of-Stock Items Unless Otherwise Requested
- ✓ PRO FORMA INVOICES: Available on Request
- ✓ DVD Return Policy: Replace defective DVDs only

ORDER ONLINE AT: www.adventuresunlimitedpress.com

10% Discount When You Order 3 or More Items!

Please check: ✓

☐ This is my first order ☐ I have ordered before

Name

Address

City

State/Province | Postal Code

Country

Phone: Day | Evening

Fax | Email

Item Code	Item Description	Qty	Total

Please check: ✓

Subtotal ▸

Less Discount-10% for 3 or more items ▸

☐ Postal-Surface — Balance ▸

☐ Postal-Air Mail (Priority in USA) — Illinois Residents 6.25% Sales Tax ▸

Previous Credit ▸

☐ UPS (Mainland USA only) — Shipping ▸

Total (check/MO in USD$ only) ▸

☐ Visa/MasterCard/Discover/American Express

Card Number:

Expiration Date: Security Code:

✓ SEND A CATALOG TO A FRIEND: